Too Big to Fail

POLICIES AND PRACTICES IN GOVERNMENT BAILOUTS

Edited by Benton E. Gup

PRAEGER

Westport, Connecticut
London

Library of Congress Cataloging-in-Publication Data

Too big to fail: policies and practices in government bailouts / edited by Benton E. Gup.
   p. cm
  Includes bibliographical references and index.
  ISBN 1–56720–621–2 (alk. paper)
  1. Business failures. 2. Business failures—United States. 3. Bank failures. 4. Bank
failures—United States. 5. Intervention (Federal government). 6. Bankruptcy. 7. Corporate
reorganizations. 8. Corporate turnarounds. I. Gup, Benton E. II. Financial Management
Association International. Meeting (2002 : San Antonio, Tex.)
HG3761.T665 2004
338.7′4—dc21   2003053030

British Library Cataloguing in Publication Data is available.

Library of Congress Catalog Card Number: 2003053030
ISBN: 1–56720–621–2

First published in 2004

Praeger Publishers, 88 Post Road West, Westport, CT 06881
An imprint of Greenwood Publishing Group, Inc.
www.praeger.com

Printed in the United States of America

The paper used in this book complies with the
Permanent Paper Standard issued by the National
Information Standards Organization (Z39.48–1984).

10 9 8 7 6 5 4 3 2 1

Jean, Lincoln, Andrew, Jeremy, and Carol

Contents

Preface

The term *too big to fail* (TBTF) is usually associated with large bank failures. TBTF is one form of government bailouts, and it covers a much wider scope of organizations than banks. Following the September 11, 2001, terrorist attacks, the Federal Aviation Administration shut down all air traffic in the United States for several days. Subsequently, the government provided $5 billion in compensation to air carriers for the ground stop, and up to $10 billion in additional aid to a floundering industry.

Other relatively recent examples that reflect the wide scope of bailouts include Chrysler, the Farm Credit System, Lockheed Aircraft, New York City, and Penn Central Railroad. The bailouts were in the form of loan guarantees, subsidies, warrants, and other means. The U.S. government actually profited from the Chrysler bailout.

Government bailouts are not new, nor are they limited to the United States. In the late 1700s, the British government's financial assistance to the financially distressed East India Company contributed to the Boston Tea Party in America. Within the last decade, government bailouts have occurred in the Australia, the Czech Republic, Hungary, Indonesia, Poland, and elsewhere.

This book presents the views of academics, practitioners, and regulators from around the globe about the financial implications of such bailouts. The views expressed in some of the articles are controversial and are intended to stimulate debate. The book should be of interest to anyone who pays taxes, is concerned about government policies, or works for the select organizations that are TBTF.

The book is divided into three parts. Part 1 gives different historical perspectives and examples of TBTF in the United States. Part 2 provides an international perspective on TBTF, with examples from different countries. Part 3 gives a fresh look at current Government Sponsored Enterprises—Fannie Mae and Freddie Mac—in the context of TBTF. Are they too big to fail? It also examines why Enron, one of the largest companies in the United States, was allowed to fail, and its consequences.

As editor, I am indebted to all who contributed articles to this book. Several of the chapters were presented at the 2002 annual meeting of the Financial Management Association in San Antonio, Texas, and at other venues. I also am indebted to Sherry Marshall who provided editorial assistance.

PART I

Historical and Current Perspectives

CHAPTER 1

Some Historical Perspectives on "Too Big to Fail" Policies

Charles G. Leathers and J. Patrick Raines

INTRODUCTION

The doctrine of laissez-faire seemingly has been revitalized as Republican and Democratic administrations alike now profess their firm commitment to policies of deregulation and "free markets" in the new global economy. The underlying theory that economic efficiency and growth are enhanced when firms and investors are free to choose the amount of risk in their pursuit of profit in a competitive market environment is deeply rooted in Adam Smith's rejection of mercantilist policies in *Wealth of Nations*. But Smith's laissez-faire doctrine also required that firms must be left to bear the discipline for failures meted out by market forces. Instead, large banks, large corporations, and highly speculative financial funds have been protected from market discipline on a selective basis.

The term *too big to fail* is commonly associated with actions by the FDIC (Federal Deposit Insurance Corporation) and the Federal Reserve to assist large banks in trouble. In 1984, the FDIC and the Federal Reserve Bank of Chicago rescued the failing Continental Illinois Bank. In 1991, the Bank of New England failed after the Fed had been lending heavily through its discount window for months and the U.S. Treasury had quietly funneled a billion dollars in tax and loan accounts to boost its liquidity. Ultimately, the FDIC rescued the bank, guaranteeing all deposits, including those over $100,000, and infused $750 million worth of capital notes into three bridge banks (Beckner 1996, p. 216). In 1998, the Federal Reserve Bank of New York organized financial assistance from private banks for the Long-Term Capital Management Hedge Fund to prevent what Alan Greenspan (1998) called a "firesale" of assets that result in a meltdown of financial markets. While Fed authorities emphasized that no public funds were involved, the Federal Reserve acted to assure plentiful reserves at low cost for the bank that had provided assistance to the hedge fund.

The term *government bailout* has been used when government has aided large corporations facing financial failure. In 1971, the federal government provided Lockheed with some $250 million in loan guarantees on grounds that its failure would imperil national defense and result in the loss of 60,000 high-wage jobs. In 1979, Chrysler received $1.5 billion in loan guarantees by the federal government, justified on the basis of the impact of that firm's failure on the national economy. In 1976, the bankrupt Penn Central Railroad was consolidated with parts of other failing railroads to create Consolidated Rail (Conrail) as a nationalized company. After spending some $7 billion in keeping Conrail afloat, the government sold it in 1987, realizing $1.9 billion. In 2001, the airlines received billions in government funds in the aftermath of the terrorist attack.

Our purpose is to provide some historical perspectives on the too big to fail policies. We begin with an examination of the special relationship between the British government and three large joint-stock companies in the eighteenth century. Under the mercantilist policies of Europe, government provided various types of assistance to companies that were deemed important to the economic strength of the country. In criticizing that aspect of mercantilism, Adam Smith (1976, p. 741) declared that large joint-stock companies were wasteful and inefficient and could survive only if given special government assistance, as evidenced by the examples of the South Sea Company and the East India Company. With banking being one of the few exceptions, Smith seemed to take a favorable view of the special relationship between the government and the Bank of England. In the next section, we review the reasons for British government's interest in those three companies, the types of assistance provided, and the outcomes.

We then focus on the American experience. While the War of Independence was in part a revolt against British mercantilist policies, the neomercantilist agenda of the Federalist Party that was formulated by Alexander Hamilton included a proposal for use of government credit to provide capital for private industry. Only a few of Hamilton's proposals were implemented by Congress, for example, the establishment of the First U.S. Bank, and beginning with the ascendancy of Thomas Jefferson's Democratic-Republican party the doctrine of laissez-faire soon came to define the general policy of the federal government toward assisting private companies. The several major exceptions to that doctrine in the nineteenth century were the founding of the Second U.S. Bank and the federal land grants and financial credit provided for construction of railroads after the Civil War. But even though the two U.S. Banks were established with federal charters and federal government participation and were clearly too important to be allowed to fail, the government caused the failures of both. And the federal subsidization of railroad construction resulted in national scandal and contributed to the long-term financial instability of railroads. While states initially played active roles in providing credit for private companies, by 1860 that practice was being banned by constitutional amendments in a number of states.

Thus, the real historical American antecedent of the modern too big to fail policies is Herbert Hoover's Depression-era Reconstruction Finance Corporation (RFC). Created in 1932 as a temporary agency to make emergency loans to banks, insurance companies, and railroads, the RFC survived for over 20 years and became both America's largest corporation and the world's biggest and most varied banking organization. Accordingly, it receives the bulk of our attention.

THE BRITISH GOVERNMENT AND THE "MONIED" COMPANIES

In the eighteenth century, the British government maintained a very close interest in the welfare of three large private joint-stock companies that went beyond the usual mercantilist policy of creating monopolies and providing subsidies to selected companies for the purpose of encouraging production and trade. Those were the Bank of England, the South Sea Company, and the United East India Company (henceforth, the East India Company), known colloquially as the "monied companies" (Sutherland 1952, p. 17). The commanding reason for the British government's involvement with both the Bank of England and the South Sea Company in the eighteenth century was a concern over what is generally called, in the histories of that time, the public confidence in the "public credit." In most cases, public credit referred to the debts of the British government. Indeed, both the Bank of England and the South Sea Company came into existence to make loans to the government and to undertake the task of reducing the cost of the government debt. But during times of financial crisis, public credit referred more broadly to the general credit conditions. When there was a loss of confidence in the public credit, creditors became reluctant to make loans to private borrowers as well as government borrowers.

Government and the Bank of England

From the very beginning, the interests of the English (subsequently British) government and the Bank of England were so intertwined that neither could allow the other to fail. At the heart of the relationship was the fact that financial failure of the government in the late seventeenth and throughout the eighteenth century was always a possibility. The expense of costly wars combined with the lack of broad-based taxes made public borrowing and funding of the debt a recurring problem.

The Bank of England was chartered as a corporation in 1694 for both commercial and political reasons. A bank was needed to receive deposits, make loans, and issue bank notes that were more secure than the goldsmith system. The government needed a source of borrowed funds as wars with France became increasingly expensive (Andreades 1966, pp. 45–59). The charter was granted in exchange for the Bank lending its entire capital to the government at 8 percent interest plus 4,000 pounds per year for management expenses. The Bank could then issue notes equal in value to the capital it had loaned to the government, but the notes were not legal tender. The charter was for 12 years and the government retained the right to pay off the debt in 1705 (Andreades 1966, p. 73).

The first crisis faced by the Bank was actually caused by the government. In 1696, Parliament passed an act calling for re-coinage of the English money, which had become badly debased. At the same time, Parliament sanctioned the creation of another joint-stock bank that proposed making a loan to the government based on the value of land in England and issuing paper notes equal in value to that land. While the proposed new bank was unable to attract enough subscribers, the threat of competition caused the prices of the Bank's shares to fall sharply. In addition, the re-coinage of money proved to be expensive and went so slowly that new coins were not issued as old coins were being withdrawn from circulation. When goldsmiths organized a run on the Bank, the shortage of coins forced it to limit the amounts that depositors could withdraw. In coming to the Bank's assistance by giving it temporary legal protection against depositors, the government was acting in its own self-interest since it needed a loan from the Bank to continue the re-coinage. To enable the Bank to make the loan, the government *required* the Bank to increase its capital and to accept depreciated tax bills in payment of the new subscription. That benefited the government's credit by reducing the number of tax bills, but at the Bank's expense. The Bank responded by demanding that it be given a banking monopoly and that all payments to the Government be made through the Bank. Secondary reforms included more efficient protection against possible counterfeiting of Bank notes (see Giuseppi 1966, pp. 26–32; Andreades 1966, pp. 111–113).

In 1707, a run on the Bank occurred that was partly in response to a panic induced by rumors of a French invasion and partly organized by private bankers attempting to destroy their greatest rival. The Bank survived by receiving funds from both the Queen and the government. As the war expenses grew, the government needed another large loan from the Bank, which was allowed to increase its capital by issuing new shares. It also agreed to put the government's Exchequer bills into circulation, buying them and receiving interest. While the 1697 act had given the Bank a monopoly, the act did not prohibit joint-stock companies from engaging in banking business. In 1709, a new act extended the Bank's charter and ended any serious competition to the Bank by prohibiting any institution with more than six owners to engage in issuing notes (Andreades 1966, pp. 119–122).

In other ways, the government assisted the Bank. In 1709, riots by Tory supporters threatened the Bank, which was identified with Whig interests. The Bank appealed to the secretary of state for protection, but no troops were available. The Queen showed her support for the Bank by sending her own troops to protect it, leaving herself unprotected rather than allow the Bank to be captured by rioters (Andreades 1966, pp. 125–126). In 1711, Parliament required the Bank to exchange all Exchequer bills for cash, but permitted it to raise the funds without having to use its capital stock for this purpose (Clapham 1970, p. 67). In 1716, Parliament exempted the Bank from usury laws in exchange for continued support of the public debt at 5 percent (Andreades 1966, p. 124).

The practice of the government demanding a loan from the Bank in return for periodically renewing its charter and monopoly on note issue continued through the 1700s. In *Wealth of Nations*, Adam Smith noted with evident approval the special relationship between the British government and the Bank of England.

The stability of the bank of England is equal to that of the British government. All that it has advanced to the publick must be lost before its creditors can sustain any loss. No other banking company in England can be established by act of parliament, or can consist of more than six members. It acts, not only as an ordinary bank, but also as a great engine of state. It receives and pays the greater part of the annuities which are due to the creditors of the publick, it circulates exchequer bills, and it advances to government the annual amount of the land and malt taxes, which are frequently not paid up till some years thereafter. In those different operations, its duty to the public may sometimes have obliged it, without any fault of its directors, to overstock the circulation with paper money. It likewise discounts merchants bills, and has, upon several occasions, supported the credit of the principal houses, not only of England, but of Hamburgh and Holland. (1976, p. 320)

The 1694 act that established the Bank had prohibited advances from the Bank to the government without express permission of Parliament. But in practice the Bank had routinely made relatively small advances against Treasury bills made payable to the Bank. When the expenses of government rose during the American Revolution, those advances had become much larger, which raised concern about their legality. In 1793, Parliament acted to grant Bank directors immunity from liability for those advances. But there was a political motive behind the act. By allowing the government to issue treasury bills that were payable at the Bank, the government could draw drafts on the Bank without limit, a power that was used actively as the war with France became ever more costly (Andreades 1966, pp. 190–191).

In 1797, the government came to the Bank's assistance in a major way. As the British government increased its subsidies to the continental allies in the war against France, a large amount of specie was being exported and the supply of treasury bills greatly increased. The drain on the Bank's specie reserve increased as country banks withdrew specie from London and the public hoarded specie in fear of a rumored French invasion. The Bank suspended payment of specie for its notes and turned to the government for assistance. Parliament responded by passing the Bank Restriction Act, which protected the Bank by making it illegal to make any cash payments to creditors and stating that payment of debts in Bank notes was deemed as payment in cash (Andreades 1966, pp. 201–202).

By the end of the war with France, the original reason for the British government's interest in the Bank no longer existed, as other ways had been found to obtain borrowed funds. As Schumpeter put it, the government "soaked" the joint-stock companies in the early part of the eighteenth century, but gradually released them from its grip (Schumpeter 1939, p. 249). At the same time, the public interest in the Bank as a supplier of paper currency had increased. In 1819, Parliament repealed the Restriction Act, providing for the return of specie payments for notes by the Bank. In 1826, an act by Parliament encouraged the establishment of joint-stock banks outside of London and took away the Bank's monopoly over note issue. The same act abolished notes of less than five pounds in denomination, which caused the Bank to have to redeem millions of one-pound notes that had been issued during earlier financial crises. In 1833, Parliament allowed joint-stock banks in London, but made the Bank's notes legal tender and exempted it from usury laws in discounting bills of less than three month's maturity. The act of 1844 divided the Bank into the issue department and the banking department. The issue department was allowed to issue notes against the government securities that it held, but any additional notes had to be against gold or bullion (Andreades 1966, pp. 241, 253, 284–294).

The South Sea Company

While Adam Smith expressed no disapproval of the government's relationship with the Bank of England, he was extremely critical of the other two monied companies. The South Sea Company and the East India Company were prime examples of the need for government assistance for large companies to succeed outside the limited fields of banking, insurance, canals, and supplying municipal water (1976, p. 756). In the case of the South Sea Company, Smith restricted his criticism to its trading operations, commenting that "The knavery and extravagance of their stock-jobbing projects are sufficiently known" (p. 745).

The British government played a role in the South Sea Company bubble by turning over portions of the public debt to the company. In 1711, Robert Harley, Chancellor of the Exchequer, proposed to incorporate the proprietors of the national debt, with the new company receiving an annual interest rate of 6 percent, secured by various duties. As an extra inducement, the incorporated company would be given a monopoly to carry on trade in the "South Sea," which was supposed to bring the riches of Peru and Mexico to England. In addition to the annual interest payment, the company would also receive an annual sum to compensate for management costs (Melville 1921, pp. 1–2; Carswell 1960, pp. 53–54).

The public was eager to subscribe, and remained so even though the Company's efforts at trade were largely unprofitable. As its trade endeavors failed to develop, the Company sought to enhance its importance by enlarging its financial operations. In 1719, it proposed to take over much of the rest of the government's debt. Again, the public was highly receptive and holders of government securities exchanged them for shares in the company. Despite the fact that its trading activities had not been profitable, the South Sea Company was perceived as being in fairly flourishing condition and its shares were trading at a premium in the secondary market (Melville 1921, p. 33). Since the government securities were received at par, not all of the new shares authorized were issued, and the company realized a profit from selling the surplus stock at market prices. That encouraged the directors to propose to emulate John Law in France by incorporating the funds of the Bank of England, the East India Company, and the Exchequer with the capital of the South Sea Company (p. 31). Although the government declined that proposal, a rumor spread in the autumn of 1719 that the Company was about to launch some great new project, and its shares started rising on the market, standing at 126 pounds at Christmas. The Company then came back with a proposal to take over all of the national debt (p. 34).

Indirectly, the government played a role in the speculative bubble in the Company's shares by various members of Parliament and government accepting shares in exchange for political support. In the debate in Parliament, a motion passed to have other proposals entertained, to which the Bank of England responded. For a time, the Bank of England and the Company competed by offering larger and larger sums to the Exchequer for the liberty to increase their stock and to accept lower interest rates on the debt assumed. In its second proposal, the Bank went much too far, offering to give 1,700 pounds in Bank stock for every 100 pound annuity (Carswell 1960, pp. 111–112; Melville 1921, pp. 39–40; Andreades 1966, pp. 129–130). Fortunately for the Bank, the Company's proposal was accepted. In Parliament, Robert Walpole warned that the Company's proposal rested on a continuing rise in the price of its stock in the market. Since the proposal contained no stated price for the stock, the Company could artificially raise the price of its stock by increasing dividends out of funds that would be inadequate for that purpose. His prediction of rampant speculation as a devious means to excite public interest in the stock proved to be very accurate (Melville 1921, pp. 42–43).

As soon as the public became aware of the Company's proposal, interest in the stock began to grow. Since the amount of stock to be exchanged for each annuity was not fixed, the higher the market price of the stock, the less stock the Company would have to issue for that purpose. Thus, the value of the Company's assets was artificially increased by the surplus stock that was left. As Walpole predicted, the Company directors began circulating rumors about the great profits that it was going to realize, and the public became frantic for its stock. That was further encouraged as the directors raised the dividend to 10 percent on all the stock, both old and new, and announced another subscription of stock at 400 pounds (100 pounds par). Seemingly unaware that the dividend was 10 percent of the 100 pounds par value of the stock, the public rushed to buy the shares. As the price continued to rise, the power of Company directors to bestow or withhold wealth by their allocations of stock that could be re-sold at once at higher prices made them courted, envied, and despised for their arrogance and conspicuous display of wealth (Melville 1921, pp. 53–74).

Even as the news of the collapse of the Mississippi Bubble in France arrived, the speculative mania in England continued. By early June, the South Sea stock was at 890, and would soon reach 1,000 (Andreades 1966, p. 131). The public demand was so great that the issue of capital stock was actually quadrupled. In addition, the Company began making loans secured by its own shares. As the speculative mania grew, the directors became concerned about the new companies that were being formed, whose shares the speculating public was eager to snap up. Their powerful influence on the government resulted in the Bubble Act, which was intended to eliminate competitors in the bubbling market for stocks. But it also pricked the bubble for the South Sea Company shares, and many prominent people who had speculated heavily on the stock suffered heavy losses as the price fell (Melville 1921, p. 114). Even though the price remained above par, tremendous public pressure was brought to bear on the King, the government, and Parliament to take action to minimize losses to those who had bought shares at higher prices.

The Bank of England became involved in the attempt to "restore the public credit" after the bubble burst. When the South Sea directors finally realized the extent to which the company faced financial ruin, they made secret overtures for amalgamation with the East India Company. Rejected there, they turned to the Bank of England, with the members of the government putting pressure on the Bank to meet with the Company's directors. The Company demanded assistance from the Bank, but the Bank indicated little interest in doing so. Bowing to government pressure, the Bank agreed to circulate 3 million pounds of South Sea bonds, with the Bank being paid in stock at a favorable (but unspecified) price. The Company announced that this was a done deal, and the price of stock rose from 130 to 320 before falling again when the Bank refused to follow through (Melville 1921, pp. 123–125; Carswell 1960, pp. 183–184).

With the public credit of England now essentially frozen, a financial crisis existed and confidence in the government was plummeting. The King was forced to hurriedly return from Germany, and the opening of Parliament was delayed for several weeks while the government attempted to formulate some scheme to restore the public credit. When Parliament began debating what to do, two views emerged. One group wanted to use Parliament's power to place the blame on the directors of the Company and turn their personal assets over to the Company for the benefit of the shareholders who had exchanged government annuities for shares. For that purpose, a committee of "secrecy" was established to pursue an investigation and recommend punishment of the directors. The other group wanted to avoid placing blame and instead proposed to restore the public credit by "ingrafting" nine millions of South Sea stock in both the Bank of England and the East India Company. Those who had exchanged government securities for an equal amount of South Sea stock could exchange that stock for an equivalent amount of stock in the other two monied companies. The terms of that exchange were not much different than if the South Sea stock had been sold and the shares in the other two companies purchased. But market transactions were impossible due to the lack of cash in the market. For the Bank of England and the East India Company, the ingrafting of South Sea stock would create the problem of maintaining dividends after a large increase in capital without any increase in assets or business, and neither was willing to accept it (Melville 1921, pp. 180–182).

A Parliamentary committee of secrecy was created to examine the books of the company, but the cashier of the company escaped from the country with the records (Melville 1921, p. 204). Parliament brought charges against the directors of the company, and took the personal assets of some to return to the Company. Ultimately, government ministers and members of Parliament were tried before the Commons sitting as a supreme court of justice for accepting stock in the Company for which they did not pay. While the secretary of treasury was acquitted, several others were expelled and sent to the Tower (Carswell 1960, pp. 226–244).

The government's rescue of the Company went more slowly. It faced payouts of over 14 million pounds and its cash position had been considerably weakened by loans and installments on subscriptions that would not be repaid and the payment of bribes and support of the market. The only asset against the 14 million obligations was the income of 2 million in interest payment from the government on the debt held by the Company. Half of the 14 million was owed to the government under the South Sea Act. Since the bulk of the shareholders were the former holders of government securities, a declaration of the Company's bankruptcy would be the equivalent of government defaulting on those securities. That justified government action to relieve the Company of some of its obligations.

Ultimately, Parliament provided direct financial assistance by waiving the seven million pounds that it was owed by the Company. The rest of the rescue plan was more like a modern bankruptcy, with private transactions rearranged by parliamentary fiat. Loans from the company were cancelled, with borrowers paying 10 percent of the amount borrowed to the Company, and the stock that had been deposited as collateral was transferred to the Company. (The borrowers included 138 members of Parliament.) Installments due on subscribed stock were reduced to money already paid in, and the surplus stock authorized by the original South Sea Act that had not been issued was divided proportionately among the shareholders (Carswell 1960, pp. 259–264; Melville 1921, pp. 249–250). In 1725, an act divided the Company's stock into trading stock and annuities. The trading activities ultimately proved unprofitable and the capital of the Company shrunk, until in 1854 it was converted into consuls and the Company went out of existence (Melville 1921, pp. 256–257).

THE EAST INDIA COMPANY

   The British government's assistance to the East India Company when it experienced financial difficulties merits special attention as a case in which the principle "with responsibility must go authority" was eventually applied. There was a unique element that developed in the special relationship between the government and the East India Company that was missing from its relationship with the other two monied companies. The East India Company was not only a monopolistic trading company with many influential people as stockholders. It became a private government in India, having acquired administrative control over Bengal and several other regions in India through military actions. In particular, the power to collect the revenues of local rulers gave the impression of access to large sums. The British government wanted a share, with some arguing that collection of revenue was a governmental function that should not be exercised by a private company. In light of recent scandals involving executives of corporations enriching themselves while the companies were plunging into bankruptcy, it is noteworthy that corruption and private trading by agents of the company at the expense of stockholders was a major factor in the financial difficulties of the Company.

   The East India Company, officially known as the United Company of Merchants Trading to the East Indies, was formed in 1709 by a merger between two predecessors that had become intense rivals for governmental favor in trade to the Far East. The new company was granted a monopoly on all English trade east of the Cape of Good Hope. By the early 1760s, the East India Company had grown in wealth and power until it stood with the Bank of England as the most powerful financial organizations in Britain (Sutherland 1952, p. 23). Although territorial acquisitions in India would later become the Company's primary source of income and power, at mid-century it was heavily dependent on profits from its exclusive trading rights. Tea, which became more popular than coffee in England, was the cornerstone of that trade, accounting for over 90 percent of the commercial profits. The Company encouraged a wider-spread consumption by lowering the price of tea so that those with low incomes could be consumers (Labaree 1964, pp. 58–59).

By the 1760s, the British government had increased the duty on tea until it equaled a 100 percent ad valorem. That encouraged smuggling from Holland, which cut into the Company's market. The Company used its political influence to get Parliament to reduce the inland duty on tea consumed in England in 1767 and provided a full rebate of the duty paid on tea entering England that was re-exported to the American colonies, as an experiment lasting five years. But Parliament also passed the Townsend Act, which imposed duties on a number of goods imported into the American colonies, including tea. While Company officials complained that government had given with one hand and taken back with the other, the price of East India tea in the colonies still had been reduced by Parliament's actions (Labaree 1964, pp. 60–63).

Despite the tax relief on tea imported for domestic consumption in England, the Company began experiencing serious financial difficulties. That was in part because smuggling continued to claim part of the market for tea and returned to its old level when the inland duties were restored in 1772. But in part the financial difficulties were also of the Company's own making. In 1766 and 1767, the annual dividend had been increased even though the Company was experiencing losses. Government intervention into Company affairs began when Parliament passed an act in 1767 that restricted the Company's dividend to 10 percent (which was raised in 1769 to 12.5 percent) in exchange for a requirement that the Company pay the government 400,000 pounds (Labaree 1964, p. 60).

In 1766, a wave of speculation began in the Company's stock that initially rested on expectations of an immediate and substantial increase in the Company's revenues based on its administration of Bengal. With speculative operations taking place in London, Amsterdam, and Paris in the form of dealing in futures and options, East India stock gained the reputation of being an unstable "gaming stock." Manipulation became a factor when groups of Dutch and English speculators who were "bulling" the stock in the market were able to intervene in the management of the Company to get the directors to pursue policies that furthered their ends, for example, increasing the dividend. In 1767, the Company resisted government encroachment into its affairs but was obligated to pay the government 400,000 pounds annually as the government's share of its revenues from India. In 1769, the Company's stock fell sharply on reports that the profits from Bengal were in jeopardy because of rumors of a French attack in India. Turmoil within the administration of the Company and a deteriorating situation in Bengal, where the Company had increasingly exercised political control, led the government to take an increasing interest in its affairs. Famine, corruption, and inefficiency in Bengal, combined with a decline in revenue from India, over-investment in the purchase of goods for London sales, and unexpected expenditures for military fortifications contributed to a chaotic situation (Sutherland 1952, pp. 141–147; Labaree 1964, p. 61).

By 1772, the government was ready to intervene to institute reforms in the Company's administration of Bengal. The opportunity for that intervention came in late fall 1772, when a financial panic following the failure of several important banking houses during the spring led to a general economic depression that lasted in both Britain and the continent for a year. By late fall, the Company was in serious financial trouble, unable to repay a large loan from the Bank of England, and having the Bank refuse to grant another extension. The Company owed an even larger amount to the government, partly in duties collected on tea and taxes on goods sold, and partly for payment for its monopoly status. But a substantial part was due to the government because its dividends had exceeded 6 percent, a provision of the Dividend Act of 1767. In March 1772, the Company had voted a 12.5 percent dividend, and thus owed the government (Labaree 1964, pp. 61–63).

When the Company threatened to suspend the regular semiannual dividend, alarm spread through London financial markets, and in November Parliament convened to look into the affairs of the Company. The directors of the Company requested a loan from the government for 1.5 million pounds, to be repaid at 4 percent interest over a four-year period. But the stockholders, led by the Duke of Richmond, balked at any concession and reforms. A compromise petition called for the loan in exchange for which the Company would limit its annual dividend to 6 percent until half the loan was repaid, then increasing it to 8 percent. When the loan was fully repaid, any surplus profits over 8 percent would be used to reduce the Company's bonded debt to 1.5 million pounds. After that, the Company would split any surplus profit equally with the government. In addition, the Company asked to be relieved of the obligation to pay the government 400,000 pounds whenever dividends exceeded 6 percent (Labaree 1964, pp. 62–63).

The government responded by proposing to reduce the loan to 1.4 million pounds and restrict dividends to 6 percent until it was fully repaid. After the bonded debt was reduced to 1.5 million pounds, the dividend could be increased to 8 percent, but the government would claim three-fourths of the surplus profits. In addition, the government would appoint the governor and council of Bengal and after six years would be free to take over full administration of Bengal. When the Company objected, the King suggested an act by Parliament that would prohibit the Company from paying any dividend for three years (Labaree 1964, pp. 63–65). Enacted by Parliament in 1773, the Regulation Bill made the loan from the government compulsory but deleted the reference to the government taking three-fourths of the surplus profits and the passage that suggested the Company's rights in Bengal would be limited to six years. But the East India Company henceforth ceased to be a master of its own house (see Sutherland 1952, pp. 240–268).

Despite the loan from government, the financial problems of the Company continued to attract Parliament's attention. The Company had on hand a large surplus of tea, which if it could be sold would go far toward solving the Company's problems. One proposal was to allow the tea to be sold on the continent at prices below those charged by continental sellers by rebating to all the British export duties to the Company. Even if the tea were sold at a loss, the Company would avoid the sizable charges for storage, deterioration, and interest on the capital invested. Under current law, the Company could sell tea only at its wholesale auctions in London. Parliament would have to grant permission to export abroad and provide a "drawback" of the duties on that tea. It was argued that since the surplus tea would not be sold at home, the government would lose no revenue (Labaree 1964, pp. 66–67).

While the original proposal said nothing about tea exported to America, the directors of the Company added a proposal to remove the Townsend duty. Problems with the proposed plan to sell surplus tea on the continent (selling tea to the continent would reduce supply in England, leading to higher prices, and give incentive to smuggle the shipped tea back to England) led the directors of the Company to focus on selling tea in America (in part because it would not be smuggled back to England). The hope was to be allowed to export surplus tea to the colonies free of all English duties and at rock-bottom prices, underselling the Dutch smugglers in that market. The final petition did not call for removal of the Townsend duties and also asked for permission to export tea to the continent. When the government made the proposal in Parliament, a member asked about removal of the Townsend duties, but the government was unwilling to oblige because the revenue was needed (even though little revenue had been collected). It was pointed out that part of the colonial resistance to the duties was the scarcity of money in the colonies. Proposals were made to remove the Townsend duties rather than the duties paid in England, but the government refused on political grounds. Thus, by the Tea Act of 1773, tea exported by the Company from England to the American colonies would pay no duties in England but would still be subject to the Townsend duties on imports in America (Labaree 1964, pp. 69–73).

In a curious historical development, this attempt to assist the financial status of the Company led to the Boston Tea Party. Political opposition was generated in America where it was thought that the strategy was to use the East India Company as an instrument by which the colonists could be made to accept those duties, establishing a precedent for additional levies (see Labaree 1964, pp. 88–90). In addition, colonial merchants were concerned that if the East India Company succeeded in establishing a monopoly over trade in one commodity, it would soon monopolize all the foreign commerce of America. Adding to the agitation was resentment on the part of influential colonial merchants who were not among those to whom the Company granted franchises for the sale of the tea (Labaree 1964, p. 91).

From Charleston to New York, organized efforts to prevent the landing of the tea succeeded in coercing agents for the Company to resign. But the agents in Boston, who were unpopular due to their reluctance to join the tax-resistance agreements, refused to resign (Labaree 1964, p. 104). Thus came the Boston Tea Party, with 150 men masquerading as Indians boarding three docked ships and dumping the Company's tea in the harbor (pp. 143–145). In addition to the loss of tea in Boston, the refusal of the tea in other American ports cost the Company over 3,000 pounds in shipping costs (p. 177). It asked the government for assistance in gaining compensation for the losses but did not request any punishment of the Bostonians responsible for dumping the tea (p. 173). But when the Bostonians refused to pay for the tea dumped into the harbor, the British government responded with the Coercion Act that contributed heavily to the Revolutionary War (pp. 183–184) by closing the port of Boston until the Company was compensated.

The aftermath of the government's interest in the East India Company was for the government to increasingly take over the administrative affairs in India, becoming the effective ruler of British India. By 1833, Parliament had ended the Company's trade monopoly, and after the Indian Mutiny of 1857–58, the government assumed direct control and the East India Company was dissolved.

GOVERNMENTAL ASSISTANCE FOR LARGE COMPANIES IN AMERICA

In the United States, the modern too big to fail policy has deep roots in the RFC, which was created in 1932. The RFC, in turn, had roots in the War Finance Corporation that was created in 1918. Prior to that, there were several isolated cases that merit attention. In the first half of the nineteenth century, the government caused the failure of the two U.S. Banks that were too important to be allowed to fail. In the last decade of the nineteenth century, an investment banker came to the financial assistance of the government. And in the first decade of the twentieth century, the failure of a large securities firm was prevented when the president exempted from antitrust enforcement the stock purchase by a large corporation that was controlled by that same investment banker.

The Two U.S. Banks

English mercantilism explained part of the assistance provided by British government to the Bank of England, the South Sea Company, and the East India Company, while the public debt and borrowing needs of the government explained the rest. In the early nineteenth century, neo-mercantilism endorsed by the Federalist Party resulted in limited government actions, notably the establishment of the First U.S. Bank and the building of the National Pike. Curiously, while the government created both the First and the Second U.S. Banks, both banks were brought down by government action because of a political perception that they were too big to be allowed to succeed. By mid-century, the federal government was adhering to a laissez-faire policy, although state governments continued to provide various types of assistance, less so, of course, after the state bankruptcies during the Panic of 1837. But in the 1860s, the federal government's subsidies for the construction of the transcontinental railroad resulted in the creation of the Credit Mobilier and the resulting scandal.

The First U.S. Bank was chartered by the federal government in 1791 as a joint venture of private enterprise and the federal government for a period of 20 years. While the government's share of the $10 million capital was $2 million, the actual control and management of the bank was in private hands, that is, a board of directors elected by the stock holders. In addition to serving as the depository for the federal government, the bank could hold deposits of state governments and private individuals, and could make loans to both levels of government and to private individuals. In 1811, Congress succumbed to political pressure from state banks that considered a federally supported bank as unfair competition and resented having their paper notes presented for redemption in specie when the U.S. Bank thought the issue had become excessive. The laissez-faire approach of the Republican-Democratic party led to a failure by Congress, which also played a role in opposing a powerful federally chartered bank.

That such an institution was needed became quickly evident when monetary and financial problems were greatly intensified by the War of 1812. The federal government borrowing from state banks resulted in excessive issues of state bank notes. Congress responded by chartering the Second U.S. Bank in 1816, again as a joint government-private enterprise venture with a 20-year charter. By the 1820s, the bank was acting as a de facto central bank, imposing discipline over the issue of state bank notes by presenting notes for redemption, which earned it the enmity of many state banks. The political opposition of Jacksonian Democrats, who viewed the Bank as the largest of the financial monopolies they despised, intensified when Andrew Jackson lost the presidential election of 1824 in the House of Representatives after receiving the largest number of popular votes. Jackson, who won the election of 1828, blamed his earlier defeat on the political influence of the U.S. Bank's president, Nicholas Biddle. When Biddle and his supporters made the mistake of asking Congress to renew the bank's charter four years early in 1832, Jackson vetoed the bill, then made that a major issue in his campaign for re-election that fall. Convinced by a landslide victory that the voters supported his antibank position, Jackson discontinued the deposit of federal funds. Biddle's attempt to respond with a restrictive credit policy, in the hope that the resulting financial distress would force Jackson to relent, only served to make the Bank more unpopular among the Jackson supporters. Without the federal funds, the bank could not survive and after taking out a state charter became defunct.

J. P. Morgan's Financial Assistance to the Federal Government

As a result of Jackson's actions, the United States had to cope with monetary problems and financial crises without the assistance of a central bank until 1914, when the Federal Reserve System became operational. In 1894, J. P. Morgan, as the leading investment banker on Wall Street, came to the financial aid of the federal government when it desperately needed gold reserves. The U.S. Treasury was experiencing a decrease in gold reserves as treasury certificates that had been issued in the purchase of silver were presented for redemption in gold. In addition, the Treasury was required by law to maintain a fixed amount of greenbacks in circulation. As quickly as greenbacks were redeemed in gold, the Treasury had to reissue more, which were immediately redeemed again for gold. The government was committed to maintaining the gold standard and thought a gold reserve of $100 million was necessary for that purpose. As the depression following the panic of 1893 deepened, the run on gold reserves intensified to the extent that reserves fell to only $66 million. A large sale of bonds to bankers raised the level above $100 million for a short time, but by late 1894, the reserves had fallen to $55 million. Again bonds were sold to acquire gold, with J. P. Morgan and Company taking the entire purchase. But the run on gold reserves continued, and President Cleveland agreed to a private bond sale to J. P. Morgan, who essentially guaranteed that the gold would not flow back out of the Treasury. Morgan later resold the bonds at a profit and refused to disclose the amount of that profit even when questioned by a congressional committee.

The Panic of 1907 and the Tennessee Iron and Coal Case

Before there was the Federal Reserve to bail out large banks, there was J. P. Morgan. The Panic of 1907 began when an attempt by two rogue speculators to corner the copper market was foiled. A bank controlled by one of the speculators suffered a run and had to close. Rumors quickly spread about weaknesses of other banks, and several others experienced runs and went under, including the Knickerbocker Trust Company, a pillar of the financial community. With a general banking panic under way, the financial community turned to J. P. Morgan for leadership, who summoned the leading bankers and financiers of New York City to his home to discuss what was to be done. In the meantime, the crisis had spread from banks to brokerage houses. As liquidity disappeared, traders began unloading their securities in desperate efforts to gain the needed cash.

When the two major banks, the Trust Company of America and Lincoln trust, experienced runs, Morgan decided that these were too important to be allowed to fail, and organized a pool of bankers to help create a cash fund to save the banks. As that effort went on for days, the public hoarded cash and there was a deluge of selling on the stock market as it suffered a liquidity crisis. The point came at which there was virtually no call money at the loan post on the floor, and the exchange faced closure. That was averted by Morgan again summoning the bankers and arranging for millions to be raised quickly for the exchange.

But the too big to fail aspect of the 1907 crisis is perhaps less well known. A leading brokerage house had pledged a large block of stock of the Tennessee Coal, Iron, and Railroad Company as collateral against loans and was being hard pressed for cash by the lending banks. Tennessee Iron and Coal was the largest competitor of the U.S. Steel Corporation that was controlled by Morgan and his syndicate. Through his representatives, who met privately with President Teddy Roosevelt, Morgan informed the president that unless U.S. Steel was permitted to purchase the stock of Tennessee Iron and Coal, the brokerage house would fail. That failure, in turn, would bring about a general collapse of the financial markets. Roosevelt agreed, and the purchase went through based on the understanding that the federal government would not file suit under the Sherman Antitrust Act against U.S. Steel for its acquisition. That gentlemen's agreement would later play a critical role in the eventual split between Taft and Roosevelt when the federal government brought antitrust action against U.S. Steel Corporation.

HOOVER'S RECONSTRUCTION FINANCE CORPORATION

In 1932, President Hoover convinced Congress to create the RFC as a temporary agency to make emergency loans to banks, insurance companies, and railroads experiencing liquidity problems. Instead of having a lifespan of one year, as originally planned, the RFC became America's largest corporation and the world's biggest and most varied banking organization and survived for over 20 years.

The War Finance Corporation

The predecessor to the RFC, the first step of the government in granting direct financial aid to private industry, was the War Finance Corporation (WFC), created during World War I. Owing to the financial uncertainty of the war period, commercial banks were unwilling to tie up a large part of their assets in securities or ineligible paper. There was also uncertainty over the position of the savings banks, since they could not be members of the Federal Reserve but faced the possibility of heavy withdrawals by their depositors. Congress created the WFC, with its stock subscribed by the U.S. Treasury and managed by a board of directors appointed by the president with the secretary of treasury as chairman. The WFC was empowered to grant loans to commercial banks, extending credit to borrowers whose operations were necessary to the war effort and to savings banks facing heavy withdrawals (Edwards 1938, p. 302).

The quality of the collateral for such loans was not carefully defined, and so the WFC was really an agency whose purpose was to grant loans for war purposes and to discount the ineligible paper for hard-pressed banking institutions. While little use was made of the WFC during the war, it extended advances to the railroads, due to the failure of the passage of the congressional appropriation bill that contained provisions for the governmental operation of the roads. In 1920, the WFC granted export credits to stimulate international trade and in 1921 it extended advances to finance agriculture. In 1925, it began the liquidation of its operations (Olson 1977, p. 12).

The National Credit Corporation

Hoover's initial response to the bank failures of 1930–31 was to persuade bankers to form a large credit association that would create a $500 million credit pool to discount the sound but frozen assets of banks. He argued at a private meeting with major bankers that large metropolitan banks should form a consortium that would provide rediscount facilities (on basis of sound assets) for the weaker banks who did not have commercial paper acceptable at the Federal Reserve Bank's discount windows (Barber 1985, pp. 127–128). The bankers rejected the private credit agency idea and called instead for the re-establishment of the WFC. Hoover threatened to create a federal credit agency unless a private one was created. The chairman of the Federal Reserve Board agreed. Finally, they agreed to a compromise. If the private credit agency failed to stabilize the economy, Hoover would ask Congress to revive the WFC. The bankers took this as a guarantee of federal help, which doomed the private agency before it was actually created.

Under the leadership of the governor of the New York Federal Reserve Bank, a group of leading bankers organized the National Credit Corporation (NCC). It was authorized to issue up to a billion dollars in debentures, with the nation's bankers subscribing at least half of that. Membership was offered to any bank that subscribed 2 percent of its net time and demand deposits to the association. It would then be eligible to ask for a loan. If the loan was approved, the national office of the NCC would forward the money, but only after an appropriate review of the application.

While there were delays at the start in processing the loan applications, by November 1931 bank failures were down and prices of both stocks and bonds had rallied. But more delays in processing loan applications and delivering the funds ensued. Privately, the leaders of the NCC hoped the agency could be dissolved without making any loans. To protect themselves in the case that loans had to be made, they set collateral requirements very high. U.S. government securities were accepted at only 75 percent of their market values, other securities were appraised at their depressed market values, and then loans were only made equal to 40 percent of the value of the collateral (Olson 1977, pp. 24–32). As another wave of bank failures occurred and securities prices fell again, Hoover realized that the private credit agency solution was a failure and asked the Chairman of the Federal Reserve Board to develop a proposal to be submitted to Congress to revive the WFC. What emerged from that was the RFC.

The Reconstruction Finance Corporation

In addition to providing funds to banks having liquidity problems, Hoover was concerned about railroad bonds. U.S. railroads had a spotty financial history but encountered new competition in the 1920s from auto and truck transportation. When a substantial number of railroads defaulted on interest payments on both short-term and long-term obligations, the prices of railroad bonds sank. This had a special impact on the financial community because for years railroad bonds had been important investment assets for banks, saving banks, and life insurance companies. Hence, the market value of their assets fell as railroads bonds became essentially frozen assets.

Hoover's economic rationale for the RFC was the famous "trickle down" theory. In his view, the essential economic problem was a lack of liquidity for the largest financial institutions. With much of their assets becoming illiquid, banks were facing suspension of withdrawals of deposits and, consequently, were pursuing defense strategies by attempting to maintain as much liquidity as possible. Insufficient lending to businesses and agricultural interests resulted in low investment, production, and employment. If bankers became more confident about their own liquidity, they would increase their lending activities and the economy would recover. Thus, funds flowing in at the top would trickle down to the entire economy.

In December 1931, Hoover asked Congress to enact a comprehensive legislative program aimed at stimulating economic recovery. One part of that program called for creating the RFC, which would offer government credit to a wide variety of financial institutions and to railroads in an attempt to liquefy their assets. Congressional response was mixed. Progressive Republicans and liberal Democrats bitterly criticized the program as government bailout of the rich while at the same time Hoover was refusing to offer any sort of government assistance for the growing masses of unemployed workers. Several clauses in the proposal had to be deleted. One was that the Federal Reserve banks would be permitted to discount the debentures and financial obligations of the RFC, which the administration had hoped would make RFC securities more marketable in the investment community. Instead, Hoover authorized the U.S. Treasury to purchase the RFC's securities. Another clause that was eliminated would have permitted the RFC to make direct business loans to industries needing credit in order to fulfill existing production contracts (Olson 1977, pp. 33–38).

The Reconstruction Finance Act of January 1932 provided for massive and direct governmental loans to commercial banks, savings banks, insurance companies, trust companies, building and loan associations, mortgage loan companies, credit unions, Federal Land banks, joint-stock land banks, Federal Intermediate Credit banks, agricultural credit corporations, livestock credit companies, receivers of closed banks, and railroads (Secretary of Treasury 1959, pp. 1–3). The federal government subscribed the initial capital of $500 million, and the RFC was authorized to borrow an additional $1.5 billion. The act required that the RFC would have to liquidate its operations on January 1, 1933, unless the president gave express written permission for it to continue operations for another year. Congressional authorization would then be necessary for the RFC to continue after January 1, 1934. Otherwise, the RFC was essentially independent of Congress both financially and in reporting. Its loans were to be kept confidential, both in terms of who received the loans and the amounts of the loans (Olson 1977, pp. 39, 43).

The RFC Board of Directors consisted of four Republicans and three Democrats, all appointed by the president. The chairman of the board was Eugene Meyer, who was also the chairman of the Federal Reserve Board. The secretary of treasury was an ex officio member of the board, as was the chairman of the Federal Home Loan Bank Board. Those three men represented the financial concerns of eastern bankers. The fourth Republican was Charles Dawes, head of a large Chicago bank and former vice president, who had been the architect of the Dawes Plan for German reparations in the 1920s. He was known to be hostile to Wall Street banking houses and eastern financial interests in general. The three Democrats were chosen for their conservative financial views and regional representation in the South, Southwest, and West. In philosophy, personnel, and organization, the RFC was very similar to the old WFC. Designed to be temporary emergency institutions with no rationale under normal economic conditions, their most important objective was to rejuvenate the private money market through massive government loans. A total of 33 agencies were opened around the country to receive loan applications. Those committees were staffed largely by the bankers who had assisted with the WFC in the 1920s (Olson 1977, pp. 39–41).

Hoover and the RFC directors believed that by assuring the public that the RFC would make loans only to banks whose assets were essentially sound, the public would respond by increasing deposits, allowing banks to deal with their deflated securities markets and capital problems in an atmosphere of relative calm. The RFC directors, like Hoover, did not want to create unfair competition with private institutions that normally loaned to the financial institutions, and purposely set the RFC interest rates at 6 percent, well above the prevailing money market levels. Strict requirements for collateral were imposed, essentially similar to those of the NCC. Only 80 percent of the market value of the highest-grade securities and not more than 50 percent of the market value of other securities would be accepted. A bank accepting an RFC loan had to deposit its most liquid assets at only a fraction of their previous value. The RFC also reserved the authority to demand increased collateral deposits in face of future declines in asset values. The loans were to have a maturity of not exceeding three years. The procedure for granting a loan required first a formal application together with detailed financial statements. Based on credit analysis, the loan was then approved by the RFC, the collateral was deposited, and the funds were then made available to the applying institution (Olson 1977, pp. 47–48).

Despite the stringent RFC requirements for granting loans, it received thousands of applications in its first month of operation. In February 1932, the RFC authorized $45 million to bank and trust companies (with $15 million of that going to the Transamerica Corporation in San Francisco to save the Bank of America, one of the nation's largest chains) and $25 million to railroads. By the end of March, 974 loans had been authorized, totaling $238 million, with $160 million to banks, $60 million to railroads, and the remaining $18 million to other financial institutions, including life insurance companies. Political controversy erupted over large loans to railroads, which had massive amounts of bonds and short-term notes coming due. When the RFC loaned the Missouri-Pacific Railroad almost $13 million, nearly half of that went as payments on earlier loans to three large Wall Street firms. The directors of the RFC who supported the pass-through payments to J. P. Morgan and Company, the Guaranty Trust Company of New York City, and Kuhn, Loeb, and Company were opposing the bonus payments for American veterans of World War I. Progressive Republicans and liberal Democrats agreed with Franklin Roosevelt's charge that Hoover and the RFC were only concerned with rescuing bankers and wealthy businessmen. Even some members of the RFC board thought that Meyer was too willing to help the largest banks even when assistance was not needed (Olson 1977, pp. 49–53).

At the same time, many bankers criticized the RFC for being too cautious in approving and authorizing loans. The RFC insisted all loans have short-term maturity, forcing many banks to repay loans long before their fundamental solvency had been restored and imposing additional pressures on them. Bankers believed the RFC directors' primary objective in setting high interest rates and collateral requirements was not to help banks but to prevent of a loss of government funds. With their best marketable assets pledged against RFC loans, banks would have to sell their less marketable assets at greatly deflated prices and additional liquidity was needed to meet withdrawals of deposits. That further eroded their capital and left the banks ineligible for future RFC loans because the value of their collateral would no longer cover the loans they needed (Olson 1977, p. 55).

A number of Federal Reserve officials also criticized the RFC, in part because they feared that a powerful RFC would surpass the Federal Reserve as the dominant public institution in the money market. Some worried that the RFC would become a permanent burden on the Federal Reserve and feared that Meyer would give the RFC priority and neglect the Federal Reserve. Federal Reserve officials insisted that it was the responsibility of the RFC as an emergency agency to prevent both bank failures and railroad receiverships. With that secondary role successfully carried out, the Federal Reserve would play the primary role of reviving commercial lending by lowering the discount rate and the reserve requirements and purchasing securities in the open market (Olson 1977, pp. 55–56).

As the situation deteriorated in 1932, both the Hoover Administration and the RFC directors began to blame the banks for not making loans. Instead, banks preferred to follow the defensive strategy of building up their liquidity against future demands for withdrawals by depositors. Federal Reserve officials blamed the high interest rates and stringent collateral requirements of the RFC for the failure of banks to increase their lending (Olson 1977, pp. 57–58).

By the end of May 1932, the RFC had authorized $500 million in loans. But the banking crisis was far from being over. In early June, some of the largest banks in Chicago began experiencing runs by depositors. Dawes resigned from the RFC board of directors because his Central Republic Bank and Trust Company was suffering from deflated assets due in part to the collapse of the Insull public utilities empire. The RFC authorized a loan of $90 million and took as collateral all the assets of the bank. Nevertheless, the bank had to suspend payments two months later, although without any public panic. Widespread criticism of the loan came from not only the progressive Republicans and liberal Democrats, but also from small bankers and the Mayor of Chicago, who had appealed for a federal loan of $70 million secured by city tax warrants to enable the city to pay its teachers and municipal employees. Even the Interstate Commerce Commission criticized the RFC as being too lenient with the railroads and the bankers holding the debt obligations of railroads (Olson 1977, pp. 58–59).

By July 1932, the RFC had authorized over 5,000 loans totaling over $1 million to 4,196 institutions. Approximately 65 percent of the loans had gone to banks and trust companies and 22 percent for railroads. While 70 percent of loans had gone to banks in small towns, over 40 percent of the funds had gone to large city banks. By the end of 1932, the RFC had loaned almost $1 billion to banks, with 26 of the largest banks receiving one-third of that amount (Olson 1977, pp. 60–61).

But as the Depression deepened, the administration came under increasing pressure to address the problems of unemployment, desperate poverty, and the problems of the urban areas. Hoover asked Congress to expand RFC responsibilities to provide loans to the states and cities to assist the unemployed and to finance self-liquidating public works such as toll roads and bridges, hydroelectric plants, public housing, and water and sewage works. In July 1932, the Emergency Relief and Construction Act extended RFC authority deep into state and local relief, public works construction, slum clearance, low income housing, reforestation, agricultural marketing, and agricultural finance. In his proposal, Hoover had called for giving the RFC the authority to make direct loans to businesses that had guaranteed orders for their products (which would make the loans self-liquidating). But that was opposed in Congress, and instead the act permitted Federal Reserve banks to make direct business loans to industries needing credit (Olson 1977, pp. 62–75).

At the end of 1932, the RFC employed 4,000 people and had authorized a billion dollars in loans to banks and over $330 million to railroads. Most of the latter went to 15 railroads, ten of which ultimately filed for bankruptcy. Ten percent of the banks that received loans failed anyway, and many banks had very weak capital positions. Hoover exercised his option and extended the authority to the RFC through January 1934. With another banking crisis occurring in February 1933, the Emergency Banking Bill passed in March 1933, authorizing the RFC to purchase the preferred stock or capital notes of banks. That was intended to both provide the banks with long-term investment funds and relieve them of short-term debts to the RFC. By April 1934, the RFC had purchased nearly $1.1 billion of preferred stock in over 6,500 banks, and owned stock in nearly half the nation's banks by September. When it discontinued the program in 1936, the RFC had provided nearly 6,800 banks with over $1.3 billion in new government capital. The RFC also bought the preferred stock of the Export-Import Bank (Olson 1977, p. 114; Jones 1951, pp. 33–34).

During the time that President Roosevelt was devaluing the dollar, the RFC was determined to have the legal authority to buy newly mined domestic gold or any foreign gold as a commodity, giving its notes in payment at the price of gold as set by the RFC. When Roosevelt banned the hoarding of gold coin, bullion, and certificates, the export of gold, and the gold-payment clauses in all contracts, there was no free market in the United States for newly mined domestic gold. The RFC agreed to create a market at the president's request. Over the next few months, it bought both newly mined domestic gold and foreign gold at rising prices, paying a total of $150 million in notes. The gold was subsequently turned over to the Treasury for cash, which was used to retire the notes. These were the first notes sold by the RFC to the public (Jones 1951, pp. 245–252; see also Secretary of Treasury 1959, p. 42).

In total, the Depression-era loans by the RFC amounted to $10.5 billion. Its defenders point out that all of the loans were repaid without any loss to the taxpayers. After paying the RFC's expenses and interest on the funds that it borrowed, there was actually a net revenue of one-half billion (Jones 1951, p. 4).

War-Time Activities of the RFC

During World War II, the RFC became a major source of credit for industrial expansion. Businessmen could borrow money from the RFC on very favorable terms to build war plants or factories for essential non-war goods. In addition, the RFC was authorized to acquire strategic and critical materials. It owned a pipeline, operated a tin smelter, and owned abaca plantations in Latin America and several plants that manufactured artificial rubber. The RFC was authorized to expend more than $34 billion. Of the $22.5 billion that was actually disbursed, $9.3 billion was unrecoverable. In 1948, the RFC was authorized to lend $1 billion for European redevelopment under the Marshall Plan (for detailed discussion, see Jones 1951, pp. 315–485).

In 1951, a Senate investigating subcommittee accused the RFC of using favoritism and political influence in some of its dealings. Reorganization followed and the RFC was placed under the supervision of a single administrator appointed by the president. The RFC Liquidation Act of 1953 provided for the liquidation of the RFC, allowing it to continue as an independent agency until June 1954. In 1954, Congress assigned the RFC's loan powers to the Small Business Administration and in 1957 abolished the RFC, transferring many of its functions to the Housing and Home Finance Agency (Secretary of Treasury 1959, pp. 169–183).

CONCLUSION

British government assistance to private companies essentially ended when the government no longer needed loans from those companies. In the case of the East India Company, government assistance ultimately was accompanied by government regulation. While modern government assistance to large banks and corporations in the United States has historical precedent in the RFC, there are several major differences. First, whereas the RFC was a well defined policy, there is no general policy today, which gives critics grounds for alleging that assistance may be reflective of lobbying power rather than genuine public interest. Second, the RFC operated within a policy environment of increased regulation. Critics of current policy can rightly argue that if government is going to be responsible for preventing the failure of large banks, corporations, and funds, there must be an effective policy of tighter regulation to prevent the problem of moral hazard.

REFERENCES

Andreades, A. (1966). *History of the Bank of England: 1640–1903*. 4th ed. 1909. Reprint, New York: Augustus M. Kelley.

Barber, William J. (1985). *From New Era to New Deal.* Cambridge: Cambridge University Press.

Beckner, Steven K. (1996). *Back from the Brink: The Greenspan Years.* New York: Wiley.

Carswell, John. (1960). *The South Sea Bubble.* Stanford: Stanford University Press.

Clapham, John. (1970). *The Bank of England,* Vol. I. Cambridge University Press.

Edwards, G. W. (1938). *The Evolution of Finance Capitalism.* New York: Longmans, Green and Co.

Giuseppi, John. (1966). *The Bank of England: A History from Its Foundation in 1694.* Chicago: H. Regnery Co.

Greenspan, Alan. (1998). "Private-Sector Refinancing of the Large Hedge Fund, Long-Term Capital Management." Washington, D.C.: The Federal Reserve Board, October 8.

Jones, Jesse H. (1951). *Fifty Billion Dollars: My Thirteen Years with the RFC.* New York: MacMillan.

Labaree, B. W. (1964). *The Boston Tea Party.* New York: Oxford University Press.

Melville, Lewis. (1921). *The South Sea Bubble.* London: Daniel O'Connor.

Olson, James Stuart. (1977). *Herbert Hoover and the Reconstruction Finance Corporation.* Ames: Iowa State University Press.

Secretary of the Treasury. (1959). *Final Report on the Reconstruction Finance Corporation.* Washington, D.C.: U.S. Government Printing Office.

Schumpeter, J. A. (1939). *Business Cycles.* Vol. 1. New York: McGraw-Hill.

Smith, Adam. (1976). *An Inquiry into the Nature and Causes of the Wealth of Nations.* Indianapolis: Liberty Classics.

Sutherland, Lucy S. (1952). *The East India Company in Eighteenth-Century Politics.* Oxford: The Clarendon Press.

CHAPTER 2

What Does Too Big to Fail Mean?

Benton E. Gup

INTRODUCTION

Banks, industrial concerns, and other organizations get into financial trouble periodically. The question is what, if anything, should governments and government regulators do about it? One choice is bankruptcy. The purpose of bankruptcy is to eliminate inefficient firms or to make them reorganize and improve their efficiency. However, bankruptcy may not be the best way to deal with very large complex organizations whose failure would have large-scale negative spillover effects. In such cases one-time government assistance policies may be used. The Continental Illinois Bank failure described below is one example of this type government bailout. A third alternative is longer-term government bailouts.

During the Great Depression, the government created the Reconstruction Finance Corporation (RFC) in 1932 to deal with widespread business failures, unemployment, and municipalities in financial distress.[1] The RFC was terminated in 1957. Another choice is to protect the companies from their competitors. On March 5, 2002, George W. Bush protected selected ailing steel companies from foreign competition by imposing tariffs on imported steel. Some argue that this was more a quest for votes in West Virginia and Pennsylvania than an action taken in the national interest.[2]

This chapter examines the issue of too big to fail (TBTF) as it applies to banks and to other types of organizations including airlines, cities, and railroads. The focus here is primarily on bailouts in the United States. The issue of bailing out governments is beyond the scope of this chapter. Such was the case when the International Monetary Fund and the U.S. Treasury came to the aid of Argentina, Brazil, Korea, Mexico, Russia, and other countries to pay off domestic and foreign lenders.[3] Similarly, the issue of bailing out the Japanese banks that have been in trouble since the early 1990s is not addressed here.[4]

THE TOO BIG TO FAIL DOCTRINE FOR BANKS

Continental Illinois Bank

The origin of the term TBTF can be traced back to Continental Illinois Bank in 1984 when bank regulators feared that the failure of this bank might cause a systemic crisis. Continental Illinois Corporation, the parent holding company for Continental Illinois National Bank and Trust Company, was known as an extremely aggressive wholesale bank during the late 1970s and early 1980s. With only one office in downtown Chicago, Continental grew into one of the largest ($45 billion in assets in 1981) banks in the country by selling large-denomination certificates of deposits to investors and using the proceeds to make corporate loans. For a time the strategy worked, and Continental experienced a rapid growth in earnings.

Unfortunately, Continental had two fundamental problems in its risk management system. First, its appraisal of credit risk was faulty, and second, it had almost no core deposits to tide itself over if it got into trouble.

In late 1981, problem loans and losses began to appear. Loan losses led to Moody's downgrading Continental's debt rating in March 1982 from AAA to AA. Fitch, however, kept it at AAA at that time.[5]

Disaster struck in July 1982 when Penn Square Bank, N. A., was closed. Penn Square was a small suburban bank in Oklahoma City with total deposits of $470 million. Penn Square sold to Continental more than $1 billion of oil and gas loans, some of which turned out to be fraudulent, and many of these loans went into default. In addition, Continental had non-performing loans to less-developed countries (LDC loans). The combination of the bad energy loans and the LDC debt crisis (August 1982) was fatal. As the story of its losses and downgrading became public, Continental experienced an erosion of its deposit base. Depositors with large-denomination deposits withdrew their funds (a silent run on the bank). The credit-quality problems became a liquidity crisis as depositors continued to withdraw funds.

Bank regulators feared that Continental's problems might spread to more than 1,000 other banks that had deposits and/or federal funds there and that they too might fail if Continental failed.[6] Accordingly, Comptroller of the Currency Todd Conover went before the U.S. Congress in 1984 to declare that Continental and 10 other of the nation's largest banks were "too big to fail." After a series of attempts to prop up the ailing bank, the Federal Deposit Insurance Corporation finally took control of Continental in 1984 (an action that has been referred to as the "nationalization" of the bank). Some assert that TBTF is an inaccurate term, and what is really meant is that the organization is "too big to liquidate."[7] What we are really talking about are government bailouts and when the government will step in to bail out an organization. Nevertheless, the term TBTF became widely used in the banking literature.

Bank regulators were concerned that the widespread failure of banks could lead to a drastic reduction in the money supply and have disastrous effects on economic activity. First, the monetary authorities rely on banks as a mechanism for the transmission of monetary policy by changing the quantity of loans made. Second, bank failures raise the cost of intermediation and can reduce aggregate demand. Finally, banks play a crucial role on the payments, clearance, and settlements systems. A breakdown of those systems would adversely affect the payments of goods and services, securities transfers, foreign exchange, and other international capital flows. Because of these concerns about the banking system's central role in the economy, Lindgren, Garcia, and Saal (1996) state that virtually no government will permit widespread bank failures, or forbear from intervening to support depositors in the event of systemic failures. In reality, the concept of bailouts is not limited to banks.

The Ohio Thrift Crisis

Lindgren, Garcia, and Saal (1996) were correct when they said that "virtually no government will permit widespread bank failures. . . ." The Ohio Thrift Crisis is one example of a state government providing aid. In 1985, the failure of EMS Government Securities Inc., a securities dealer located in Florida, created problems for Home State Savings Bank in Cincinnati, Ohio. Home State faced a loss of $145 million because of its dealings with EMS. That amount exceeded its capital and the $130 million of deposits insured by the Ohio Deposit Guarantee Fund (ODGF), which insured seventy Ohio financial institutions. When the news of the story was reported in the press, there were bank runs at Home State and other Ohio-ODGF insured institutions. On March 19, 1985, the Ohio legislature agreed to provide assistance, if needed, and required the institutions to convert to federal deposit insurance.[8]

The S&L Crisis

The savings and loan (S&L) crisis reveals a different aspect of government bailouts. As shown in table 2.1, interest rates soared in the late 1970s and early 1980s. The high interest rates paid on *new deposits* and the low interest earned on *outstanding long-term fixed-rate loans* resulted in losses for lenders. In 1979, S&Ls could pay a maximum of 5.5 percent on their deposits. The losses, restrictive regulations, declining real estate values, and poor management all contributed to the failure of massive numbers of banks and S&L

associations. Ricki Helfer, former Chairman of the FDIC, said, "From 1980 though 1994—1,617 banks failed or received financial assistance from the FDIC. . . . During the same period, nearly 1,300 savings and loans failed. These failures more than bankrupted the old savings and loan insurance fund and directly cost the taxpayers of America $125 billion, and billions more in indirect costs."[9] In this case, the financial institutions and the Federal Savings and Loan Insurance Corporation failed, and it was the depositors who were bailed out by the taxpayers.

A BROADER CONCEPT OF TBTF

While the term TBTF originated with failure of Continental Illinois bank in the United States, the concept of government bailouts is international in scope, and it also applies to nonfinancial industries, and even to cities. For example, in 1979, the Italian government enacted the *Amministrazione Straordinaria Grandi Imprese* (D.L.30.1.1979, n 26), a TBTF law that deals exclusively with nonfinancial firms.

In 1997, the Japanese government announced a series of measures to help support its troubled real estate industry. Property values had declined more than 70 percent during the previous six years. The rescue package used taxpayers funds to buy property from government agencies that had been repossessed from failed lenders, established real estate investment trusts to

Table 2.1
Selected Interest Rates

Rate Type	1975	1979	1980	1981
3-month Treasury Bills	5.78%	10.07%	11.39%	14.04%
Large CDs, 3-month	6.44	11.22	13.07	15.91
Bank Prime rate	7.86	12.67	15.26	18.87
HUD Series, Conventional mortgage-new home	9.01	11.15	13.95	16.52

Source: U.S. Department of Commerce, *Statistical Abstract of the United States 1993*, Washington, D.C., 1993, table 826.

facilitate the sale of real estate, and changed laws dealing with taxes and securitization.[10]

Examples of U.S. government bailouts of nonfinancial organizations include but are not limited to Penn Central Railroad (1974), Lockheed Aircraft (1971), New York City (1975), Chrysler Corporation (1979), and the U.S. domestic airlines (2001).

Penn Central Railroad

In May 1970, Penn Central Railroad was on the verge of bankruptcy and requested aid from the Nixon administration. Penn Central was the largest transportation company in the United States. It was formed in 1968 by the merger of the Pennsylvania and New York Central railroads. Competition from trucks and rising labor costs that exceeded low regulated rates resulted in large financial losses. Penn Central operated more than 20,000 miles of railroads in 16 states and Canada. Its service area encompassed 55 percent of the nation's manufacturing plants, and it carried more than 300,000 passengers per day.[11] A shutdown of service would have had a major negative impact on the economy.

Congress refused to provide aid, and Penn Central declared bankruptcy on June 21, 1970. It was the largest bankruptcy in the history of the United States. Penn Central filed for bankruptcy under Section 77 of the 1933 Bankruptcy Act. Section 77 of the Act states that railroad companies are not allowed to go out of business.[12] Penn Central continued to operate at a loss.

Penn Central was a major issuer of commercial paper, and it had more than $200 million outstanding. Commercial paper was considered almost risk-free because it was issued by creditworthy corporations. However, in early June 1970, creditors would not extend further credit to Penn Central without a 100 percent government guarantee. A group of banks asked the Federal Reserve Bank of New York to guarantee a loan of $225 million, and the Fed refused.[13] Nevertheless, recognizing the effects that the bankruptcy might have on the commercial paper market, the Federal Reserve Bank of New York encouraged the money center banks to lend to their customers who were unable to roll over commercial paper. The Federal Reserve Bank of New York kept its discount window open to make loans to the banks, and they borrowed $575 million. On June 22, 1970, Regulation Q interest rate ceilings on deposits of $100,000 or more were suspended to keep short-term rates from rising. Thus, the Federal Reserve acted as a lender of last resort and provided liquidity in order to allow the commercial paper market to function.[14]

At the same time that Penn Central Railroad was in trouble, Congress passed the Rail Passenger Service Act of 1970, authorizing the creation of the National Railroad Passenger Corporation in 1971. This company is generally known as "Amtrak," which blends the words "American" and "Track." Amtrak's mission is to operate a nationwide system of passenger rail transportation. Amtrak is funded by federal and state grants. For federal funds received before December 1997, Amtrak was required to issue preferred stock to the U.S. Secretary of Transportation. This government owned entity serves 46 states, but its largest volume stations are New York, NY (8.5 million boardings), Philadelphia, PA (3.7 million), Washington, DC (3.5 million), and Chicago, IL (2.1 million).[15] Part of the problem is that Amtrak serves many states where there is little profitable traffic. Nevertheless, congressmen want the railroad in their states to show constituents that they are doing something beneficial for them, even though it is operating at a financial loss. In 2002, Amtrak's losses were about $1.2 billion, and it threatened to shut down passenger service unless Congress bailed it out. Congress provided the bailout.

In January 1974, Congress passed the Regional Rail Reorganization Act to preserve rail service and to salvage the operations of financially distressed railroads and replace them with a new system. Penn Central and six other bankrupt railroads that operated in the Northeast and Midwest were reorganized into a government owned for-profit company, Consolidated Rail Corporation (Conrail), in order to "continue essential services."[16] The bankruptcy code and the Interstate Commerce Commission required unprofitable railroads to continue to provide services. To get Conrail started, the government invested over $2 billion. Conrail continued to operate at a loss, and an additional $5 billion was invested until it was sold in 1987. The stock was sold to CSX Corporation and Norfolk Southern for about $1.9 billion.

Lockheed Aircraft

In the mid 1960s, Lockheed Aircraft Corporation was trying to reduce its dependence on contracts with the Department of Defense (DOD) by reentering the market for commercial jets. The company had contract disputes with the DOD that it settled, but they resulted in before-tax losses of $484 million. Lockheed invested more than $1.4 billion for the development of the L-1011 wide-body passenger jet. Part of this investment included $400 million in bank loans. A slack economy and decreased demand for aircraft hurt Lockheed, and the L-1011 was not a commercial success.

To add to its woes, Rolls Royce, who supplied the engines for the L-1011, went into receivership in January 1971. The British government could not assure continued delivery of the engines unless it had assurance of continued L-1011 production.

The failure of Lockheed would have had major adverse economic consequences in California (a loss of 60,000 jobs) and the nation (a loss of GNP of $120–$475 million), as well as weakened our national defense capabilities.[17] Lockheed's failure would have reduced competition in the aerospace industry and left only Boeing and McDonnell to compete.

The basic problem was perceived to be a short-term liquidity issue. To provide the liquidity, Congress passed the Emergency Loan Guarantee Act in August 1971. The stated purpose of the Act was to provide emergency loan guarantees for any major business enterprise, and Lockheed Aircraft Corporation was the first recipient. The Act established the Emergency Loan Guarantee Board to operate under the Department of the Treasury. The Board was authorized to grant up to $250 million in loan guarantees and specified some of the conditions of the loans. In return, Lockheed paid loan guarantee and commitment fees to the board. The net income from the Board in fiscal 1972 and 1973 was $5.4 million.[18]

New York City

During the 1960s, New York City funded social programs, public employment, health care, and education by borrowing funds. While the expenses were increasing, New York's population base and tax base was shrinking. The population in New York City (NYC) declined from 7.9 million in 1970 to 7.1 million in 1980 as people migrated to the South and West.[19] The loss of population resulted in lower tax revenues, but the costs of running NYC were fixed, and the city had a financial crisis. By the mid 1970s, NYC was unable to borrow funds.

In June 1975, the State of New York provided financial aid and created the Municipal Assistance Corporation to refinance the city's debts and restore the confidence of the credit markets. It was believed that if NYC defaulted on its debts, the State of New York would be unable to borrow funds. In addition, 45 banks in 10 states had more than 70 percent of their net worth tied to NYC or the State of New York.[20] Finally, a default in NYC would negatively impact the nation's economic growth. In September 1975, the state enacted the Financial Emergency Act, creating an Emergency Financial Control Board that had oversight over NYC's fiscal affairs.

In December 1975, President Ford signed the New York City Seasonal Financing Act of 1975, providing up to $2.3 billion in loans to NYC. The intent was to provide "bridge financing" until NYC was restored to financial health. Under the bridge were 200–300 banks that held NYC securities, and they didn't want those banks to fail. The authorization to make loans expired in June 1978. Although the Treasury earned about $40 million in interest from those loans, NYC was still in financial distress in 1978. Accordingly, in August 1978, President Carter signed into law the New York City Loan Guarantee Act of 1978. This Act guaranteed the principal and interest on NYC debts bought only by the State of New York and NYC pension plans. The Treasury earned fee income from the guarantees, and the authority to guarantee loans expired in 1982. By that time, NYC was on the path to financial recovery.

Chrysler[21]

In every industry there are winners and losers, and they change places from time to time. The issue here is whether Chrysler was an economically viable concern. During the 1950s–1970s, Chrysler was a loser. It had higher operating costs than General Motors and Ford and was not successful as a multinational manufacturer, and it made poor marketing decisions. In the 1970s, rising energy prices and government safety, pollution, and fuel efficiency regulations added to its problems. In 1978 and 1979 it had losses of $218 million and $1.1 billion respectively. Chrysler was the 10th largest manufacturing company in the United States in 1978, and the 17th largest in 1979 when it asked the government for aid. It had 134,000 employees, most of whom were in the Detroit area. Detroit was already a high unemployment area.

Chrysler wanted to introduce its K-car, an intermediate size passenger car with a small four-cylinder fuel-efficient engine. It was hoped that this car would improve its competitive position and, equally important, reduce foreign competition.

In January 1980, the Chrysler Loan Guarantee Act was enacted, providing for up to $1.5 billion in loan guarantees. In addition, the government's aid was to be matched by U.S. and foreign banks, creditors, stockholders, suppliers, dealers, and others. Under terms of the agreement, the government had warrants to buy 14.4 million shares of Chrysler stock at $13 per share. At that time Chrysler stock was selling for $7.50 per share, and later it declined to $4 per share.

Chrysler was restored to financial health in 1982 when it showed a profit. Its stock price began to climb, and it reached $30 per share in July 1983. Subsequently, the government sold the warrants back to Chrysler in September 1983 for $311 million.

U.S. Domestic Airlines

The U.S. airline industry was in financial trouble before the September 11, 2001, terrorist attacks. The industry is inherently unstable because of its high levels of debt and high fixed costs for labor, fuel, and equipment. Labor accounts for about 40 percent of airline expenses and fuel for 10–15 percent. Relatively small changes in the volume of air travel and price changes in the cost of fuel have a major impact on profits. Thus, the downturn in economic activity and increase in fuel prices contributed to shrinking airline profits and the bankruptcy of many small airlines in 2000 (e.g., Tower Air, Pro Air Inc., Legend Airlines, National Airlines, Allegient Air, Access Air, and others), and TWA in January 2001 and Midway Airline in August 2001.[22] In the first half of 2001, United Airlines (the second largest in the U.S.) posted a loss of $605 million and a $2.1 billion loss for the year.[23]

Some argue that the air carrier deregulation that began in 1977 contributed to the instability in the industry.[24] Since then, the industry has grown in numbers, ticket prices have declined, and there has been an increase in industry concentration. Nevertheless, there are still slot restrictions at some airports and international open sky restrictions. For example, only four airlines are allowed to fly between London's Heathrow airport and the U.S.; all other UK and U.S. airlines are forbidden to do so.[25]

Within an hour of the September 11, 2001, terrorist attacks, the Federal Aviation Administration ordered a ground stop for all air carrier (passengers and air cargo) and general aviation flights (from September 11 to September 13). Revenue passenger miles flown by large certified air carriers declined from 67.5 billion miles in August 2001 to 38.2 billion in September.[26] The rebound was slow, and only 47.4 billion revenue passenger miles were flown in December.

On September 22, 2001, Congress passed and President Bush signed into law the Air Transportation Safety and System Stabilization Act (P.L. 107–42) to provide compensation to domestic air carrier for losses they incurred as a result of the mandatory grounding of aircraft in connection with the September 11, 2001, terrorists attacks and to maintain essential air carrier service. Title I of the Act includes $5 billion in compensation for direct losses incurred as a result of the federal ground stop, and up to $10 billion in loan guarantees or other federal credit instruments to such air carriers. It established the Air Transportation Stabilization Board (ATSB) to issue the credit instruments.[27] To compensate the Government for its risk in guaranteeing the loans, the ATSB will collect certain fees and receive warrants to participate in equity gains.

The compensation received by the airlines is based on their size. As of April 2002, American Airlines had received $583 million, United Airlines had received $644 million, and Delta Airlines had received $529 million.[28] At the other end of the size spectrum, Flying Eagle Aviation had received $273 thousand. A total of $3.9 billion had been paid to 348 air carriers.

Title II of the Act authorizes the Secretary of Transportation to reimburse air carriers for the increases in the cost of insurance since the terrorist attacks. It also limits the airline liability for losses in connection with the attacks to an aggregate of $100 million.

Title III delayed the payment of airline-related excise taxes from November 2001 until November 2002.

Even with the government compensation, the airlines' estimated losses from the 9/11 terrorist attacks are in excess of $7 billion, an increase of $4 billion over the losses expected from the downturn in economic activity.[29] In the first quarter of 2002, most of the major airlines (e.g., AMR, Delta, U.S. Airways, United) had reduced their seating capacity and suffered losses of more than $2 billion. Only Southwest had increased its seating capacity and showed a small profit.

As shown in table 2.2, America West Airlines, the nation's eighth-largest airline, was the first to apply for Federal loan guarantees and it received $379.55 million. In return, ATSB received warrants (nonvoting) that represent 33 percent of the airline's common stock on a fully diluted basis.[30] America West Airlines was unprofitable before the 9/11 attacks, and it owed millions of dollars in aircraft-lease payments and Federal ticket taxes.[31]

In June 2002, U.S. Airways, Inc., one of the nation's largest airlines, applied for a $900 million federal loan guarantee. In July 2002, the loan guarantee was approved contingent upon U.S. Air gaining concessions from labor and creditors. That did not happen and in August 2002, U.S. Airways filed for chapter 11 bankruptcy protection.

The ATSB rejected some of the loan requests. The rejections (as of August 13, 2002) included Frontier Flying Service and Vanguard Airlines.[32]

Not everyone agrees that the government bailout of these airlines is the right thing to do. Steven A. Morrison and Clifford Winston (2001) argue that "government is responsible for providing national security, as well as social insurance such as Social Security and Medicare. Should the protective goals that underlie these responsibilities be combined to form a new societal goal: protecting industries from suffering large losses because of unanticipated hostile actions by foreigners? And if we say yes to the airlines, what about insurance companies, hotels, rental cars, restaurants and other businesses that have been hurt?"

In review, the Air Transportation Safety and System Stabilization Act did provide limited funding for the airlines as a result of the ground stoppages in connection with 9/11. However, the ATSB did not bail out the airline industry. It provided guarantees to air carriers that were willing to make changes to their business models that the Board thought necessary, if they considered the air service essential to the commercial aviation system.

However, the story does not end here. In September 2002, the airlines again asked Congress for financial aid. Part of the aid was to help fund the additional security requirements imposed on them after 9/11. These requirements include both airport security (screening passengers, caterers, etc.) and aircraft security (e.g., bulletproof cockpit doors).[33]

Bailouts of the airlines were not limited to the United States. The European Commission did provide limited compensation following the terrorist attacks. In addition to the EC, some governments provided aid. The Swiss government provided a $1 billion bailout for Swissair and a $281 million loan to get its planes back in the air after the two day grounding.[34] Swissair Group, the parent company of Swissair, filed for bankruptcy in October 2002.

INTERVENTION

Gup (1998), in a previous study of TBTF, identified 23 methods of intervention with distressed institutions and firms that are summarized here. Most of these methods are used in connection with banks. They are listed in al-

Table 2.2
Selected Air Carriers Applying for Federal Loan Guarantees

Date of Application	Air Carrier
November 13, 2001	America West Airlines
December 6, 2001	Vanguard Airlines
January 29, 2002	Frontier Flying Service, Inc.
February 25, 2002	Evergreen International Airlines, Inc.
March 28, 2002	Spirit Airlines, Inc.
May 3, 2002	National Airlines
June 7, 2002	US Airways, Inc.
June 28, 2002	Aloha Airlines, Inc.
June 28, 2002	Frontier Airlines, Inc.
June 28, 2002	Ozark Airlines, Inc. (doing business as Great Plaines Airlines)
June 28, 2002	World Airways, Inc.

Source: Air Transportation Stabilization Board, 2002, http://www.ustreas.gov/atsb.

phabetical order, except where they are grouped together because of their logical connection.

(1) Assessability, (2) Double Liability, and (3) Source of Strength

Prior to the passage of the Banking Act of 1933, bank regulators could assess shareholders of a bank to provide additional capital up to the par value of the shares, and in some cases more. In addition, there was double and triple liability for the shareholders of failed banks in selected states. These rules no longer apply. However, the Financial Institutions Reform Act of 1989 requires all commonly controlled banks to be liable for the losses of affiliated banks. Simply stated, the banks in a holding company are liable for the losses of other banks in that holding company.

(4) Bad Banks

The nonperforming assets of a distressed institution can be removed from that institution and placed in another institution—called a *bad bank*—that was established for that purpose. The bad bank can be owned by other institutions or the government.

(5) Bridge Banks

Under the Competitive Equality Banking Act of 1987, the FDIC was granted the power to establish a *bridge bank* as a temporary means of dealing with large bank failures that may pose a threat to the insurance fund. It is a temporary form of conservatorship. The insolvent bank is merged into the bridge bank, and the bridge bank operates until the bank is sold. This method of resolution was used by First Republic Bank of Texas in 1988. Most of the assets were acquired by North Carolina National Bank (NCNB), which was the forerunner of what is now Bank of America.

(6) Delay, (7) Forbearance, (8) Holidays, and (9) State Aid

Under various circumstances, the government can order a "cooling off" period, or an injunction to delay certain actions.

Forbearance refers to not enforcing capital or other supervisory standards in problem financial institutions that are judged to be viable. It also includes instances in which the FDIC has an ownership position. In most cases, it means waiting before taking action.

When Franklin Roosevelt assumed the office of President in March 1933, there was a bank holiday to stop bank runs and restore confidence in the banking system. Similarly, in March 1986, Governor Richard F. Celeste of Ohio declared a mandatory closing for five days of all 70 state insured depository institutions in connection with the Ohio Thrift Crisis. As previously noted, the state promised financial assistance if it was needed.

(10) Deposit Insurance Transfer

The insured and secured deposits of a closed bank can be transferred to another bank that acts as an agent for the FDIC and assumes the responsibility for the payoff.

(11) Depositor Preference

The Omnibus Budget reconciliation Act of 1993 contains a provision that revised the priority of claims on failed depository institutions, making depositor liabilities come ahead of general and senior claims. This makes it less attractive for holders of general and senior liabilities to press for bankruptcy.

(12) Liquidation

Liquidation refers to the sale of a firm's assets. The market value of the dismantled assets may exceed the firm's value as a going concern.

(13) Liquidity

Liquidity can be in the form of loans, loan guarantees, or access to the Federal Reserve discount window.

(14) Monetary Policy Actions

During the 1990–2000 period in Japan, real estate values fell more than 70 percent. The Japanese monetary authority eased interest rates to stimulate economic growth. It did not work.

(15) Nationalization

Nationalization, as used here, refers to the government ownership or operation of banks. In 1984, the FDIC owned 80 percent of the parent corporation of Continental Illinois Bank. Some consider this nationalization, others use the term *conservatorship*.

(16) Open-Bank Assistance

The FDIC has the authority to provide financial assistance to keep a bank in operation when its continued operation is deemed essential to provide adequate banking services to the community. The assistance can be through loans and investments, net worth certificates for savings banks, capital forbearance, and conservatorship.

(17) Payoff

The FDIC can pay off the depositors of a failed bank up to the $100,000 limit.

(18) Persuasion

The Bank of England persuaded four banks to provide funds to support a gold bullion dealer. The Federal Reserve Bank of New York convened a meeting where various banks bailed out Long Term Capital Management (LTCM), a hedge fund that was in financial trouble.

(19) Privatization

Government owned entities could be privatized. In France, the government tried to sell Air France and Compagnie des Machines Bull, but their huge losses in the early 1990s made them unattractive for investors.

(20) Purchase and Assumption (P&A)

In a traditional P&A refers to the purchase of all or nearly all of a failed bank's assets and the assumption of its liabilities. The difference is covered by a payment from the FDIC to the acquiring insured bank.

(21) Restructuring

Restructuring refers to corporate reorganization, withdrawing from markets, selling divisions, and so on.

(22) Reorganization

Reorganization occurs under chapter 11 of the U.S. Bankruptcy Code.

(23) Stock Market Intervention

Following the stock market crash in 1987, the New York Stock Exchange imposed "circuit breaker" rules to halt trading during periods of large price declines. This action was taken at the suggestion of a Presidential Task Force report that indicated such rules were necessary for the efficient operation of the stock market.

The most commonly used methods include making long-term investments providing short-term liquidity, nationalization, selling all or part of the bank, payoff, and waiting.

Overview

Six methods of intervention appear to be common among the 23 methods examined here. These methods include (1) making long-term investments, (2) providing short-term liquidity, (3) nationalization, (4) selling all or part of the bank, (5) payoff, and (6) waiting. Some of the methods, such as a bridge bank or open-bank assistance, involve more than one method of intervention.

Delaying the Inevitable

Globalization has contributed to low cost imports and the demise of some domestic industries. The textile industry is one example, and another may be integrated steel mills that produce flat-rolled steel, steel bars, and tin mills.

In March 2002, President George W. Bush announced the imposition of steel tariffs and quotas that would protect such firms as U.S. Steel and Bethlehem Steel Corp., both of whom have been hurt by foreign competition from the European Union, Japan, and South Korea. The tariffs also help mini-mills that make steel out of scrap.

Various news articles argued that the tariff was politically motivated because the unionized steel companies are located in key electoral states—Pennsylvania and West Virginia.[35]

DRAWBACKS OF BAILOUTS

The TBTF policy creates a moral hazard problem when it is consistently applied in the banking industry, and elsewhere when organizations believe that they too may be bailed out if they are in distress. But bailouts are not always forthcoming. Consider the case of Superior Bank (a Federal Savings Bank), in Hinsdale, Illinois, which engaged in high-risk lending and failed in 2001. Superior had assets of about $2 billion when it failed. The owners of the bank, the Pritzker's, one of the nation's wealthiest families, and Alvin Dworman, a New York real estate developer, agreed to pay the FDIC $460 million and other considerations.[36]

In some countries, policymakers use banks as part of their industrial policy to support the growth of particular industries, and then bail out the banks when those industries are unable to repay their loans.

Demirguc-Kunt and Detragiache (1997) provide a list of drawbacks associated with bailouts. The drawbacks include the possible high costs of resolution; inefficient banks may remain in business; bailouts create the expectation of future bailouts; bailouts weaken managerial incentives; and loose monetary policy to prevent banking losses may stimulate inflationary pressures. In countries with exchange rate commitments, the loose monetary policy may trigger speculative attacks on the currency.

Finally, the U.S. airline bailouts following the September 11, 2001, terrorist attacks only delayed the inevitable failures for some airlines, but they also benefited the larger ones too.

CONCLUSION

Governments throughout the world intervene in the economy and bail out banks and other organizations when they believe that it is in national interest to do so. A U.S. General Accounting Office Study (1984) of bailouts of Chrysler, Conrail (Penn Central), Lockheed, and NYC listed the following national interest reasons for intervention:

- Maintaining service or product continuity (NYC, Chrysler, Conrail)
- Maintaining employment (NYC, Chrysler, Conrail, Lockheed)

- Maintaining a defense contractor (Lockheed, Chrysler)
- Maintaining technological capability (Lockheed, Chrysler)
- Preventing market penetration by foreign firms (Chrysler)
- Preventing industry concentration (Lockheed, Chrysler)
- Preserving good relations with our allies (Lockheed)
- Lessening adverse effects on financial markets (Chrysler, NYC, Conrail)
- Lessening regional, social, and economic costs (NYC, Chrysler, Conrail, Lockheed)

The airline bailouts were to ensure vital transportation services.

The TBTF doctrine has been applied to banks, industrial firms, and municipalities. Because banks are the primary channel for the transmission of monetary policy, and because of their crucial role in the payments mechanism, they are the most common recipient of the TBTF policy.

Feldman and Stern (2002) have identified six methods that governments can employ to reduce the use of TBTF. These methods include (1) rules or laws prohibiting bailouts of uninsured creditors, (2) penalizing policymakers for bailouts, or increasing the disincentives to provide protection, (3) reducing the incentives to provide bailouts, (4) appointing policymakers who are disinclined to make bailouts, (5) constructive ambiguity as to how policymakers might react.

In 2002, President George W. Bush added the use of tariffs and import quotas to protect the domestic steel industry as another way to delay failures of inefficient firms. The large U.S. integrated steel companies have received various forms of protection from foreign competition since 1969, when President Nixon forced Japan and Europe to accept voluntary export restraints to avoid U.S. import quotas.

NOTES

1. U.S. General Accounting Office, *Guidelines for Rescuing Large Failing Firms and Municipalities*, GAO/GGD-84-34, 29 March 1984.

2. Melloan (2002).

3. Meltzer (2002); Stiglitz (2002). For a discussion of problems with sovereign debt, see Boorman (2002); Spiegel (2002).

4. For a discussion of banking consolidation in Japan, see Gup (2002, chap. 7, "Bank Consolidation in Japan: What Can We Learn From It?"). The bailout was still going on in late 2002 (Pilling and Beattle 2002).

5. For additional details, see Davidson (1997), 235–257.

6. See Kaufman (1990); U.S. Department of Treasury, *Modernizing the Financial System* (1991).

7. Davidson (1997).

8. Federal Reserve Bank of Cleveland, *Annual Report 1985*.

9. Ricki Helfer (1997)

10. Dawkins (1997); Sapsford (1997).

11. United States House Report, *Regional Rail Reorganization Act*, 1973, 26.

12. This act was repealed under the Bankruptcy Act of 1978, Public Law 95–598.

13. Timlen (1977).

14. Mishkin (1991), 98–99.

15. Amtrak Facts, http://www.amtrak.com, cited 18 April 2002; Also see *Amtrak 2000 Annual Report*, National Railroad Passenger Corporation, (2001).

16. *Regional Rail Reorganization Act of 1973, Preliminary System Plan*. Vol. 1, Section 213, 26 February 1975.

17. U.S. General Accounting Office, *Guidelines for Rescuing Large Failing Firms and Municipalities*, GAO/GGD-84–34, 29 March 1984.

18. U.S. Department of the Treasury Emergency Loan Guarantee Board, *Second Annual Report*, (1973), 6.

19. U.S. Department of Commerce, *Statistical Abstract of the United States 1989*, table 39 and figure 1–2. Data include the five boroughs.

20. U.S. Senate, *Voluntary Municipal Reorganization Act of 1975, Report of the Committee on Banking, Housing, and Urban Affairs*.

21. The author is indebted to Lance Poole for his research assistance with this section.

22. "Airlines Industry Survey," *Standard & Poor's*, 29 March 2001.

23. Zuckerman (2001); "United Airlines' Parent Posts $510 Million Loss," (2002).

24. For a discussion of this issue, see Gowrisankaran (2002); Coy (2002). In 1977, Congress deregulated domestic cargo operations. In 1978, it passed the Airline Deregulation Act for domestic passenger operations. International air service is governed by bilateral treaties between nations, under the terms established in the Chicago Convention of 1944.

25. Bishop, "Government Are Not Nannies and Airlines Are Not Children."

26. U.S. Department of Transportation Bureau of Transportation Statistics, "Historical Air Traffic Data Monthly: Year 2001."

27. See http://www.ustreas.gov/atsb for details about the ATSB.

28. U.S. Department of Transportation (2002), http://www.dot.gov/affairs/carrierpayments.htm.

29. Hallett (2002); "United Airlines' Parent Posts $510 Million Loss" (2002).

30. "Air Transportation Stabilization Board Conditionally Approves Application by America West," in Treasury News (PO-890). The loan guarantee represents 85.3 percent of a $455 million financing package. On January 18, 2002, America West Airlines closed on a $429 million loan supported by the federal loan guarantee.

31. McWilliams and Dreazen (2001).

32. Frontier Flying Service, Inc., should not be confused with Frontier Airlines, Inc.

33. Miller (2002).

34. Olson (2001).

35. Matthews and King (2002); Allen and Blustein (2002).

36. FDIC Press Release, PR-90–2001. Details of the agreement can be found at the FDIC Web site, http://www.fdic.gov.

REFERENCES

"Airlines Industry Survey." *Standard & Poor's*, 29 March 2001.

"Air Transportation Stabilization Board Conditionally Approves Application by Amer-

ica West." In Treasury News (PO-890). 28 December 2001 [cited 9 April 2002].
    Available from http://www.ustreas.gov/press/releases/po890.htm; INTERNET.
Allen, Mike, and Paul Blustein. "O'Neill Criticizes Steel Tariffs." In Washington-
    post.com. 17 March 2002 [cited 17 March 2002]. A17. Available from http://
    www.washingtonpost.com; INTERNET.
Amtrak Facts. [Cited 18 April 2002.] Available from http://www.amtrak.com;
    INTERNET.
Amtrack 2000 Annual Report. Washington, D.C.: National Railroad Passenger Cor-
    poration, 2001.
Bishop, Sir Michael. "Governments Are Not Nannies and Airlines Are Not Children."
    In FT.com. 15 October 15 2001 [cited 24 October 2001]. Available from
    http://www.ft.com; INTERNET.
Boorman, Jack. "Globalization and Sovereign Debt." *The Ledger* (Georgetown Uni-
    versity), Summer-Spring 2002, 4–5.
Coy, Peter. "Deregulation Innovation vs. Stability." *Business Week*, 28 January 2002,
    108–109.
Davidson, Lee. "Continental Illinois and 'Too-big-to-fail,' " In *History of the Eighties,
    Lessons for the Future.* Vol. 1. 235–257. Washington, D.C.: Federal Deposit
    Insurance Corporation, 1997.
Dawkins, Willam. "Tokyo Package Aims to Spur Property Market." *Financial Times*,
    1 April 1997, 1.
Demirguc-Kunt, Asli, and Enrica Detragiache. "The Determinants of Banking Crises:
    Evidence from Developed and Developing Countries." Washington, D.C.:
    World Bank and IMF, unpublished paper, July 1997.
FDIC Press Release, PR-90–2001. "FDIC, OTS Announce Agreement with Holding
    Companies of Superior Bank." In FDIC Web site. 10 December 2001 [cited].
    Available from http://www.fdic.gov; INTERNET.
Federal Reserve Bank of Cleveland. *Federal Reserve Bank of Cleveland Annual Report
    1985.* Cleveland, OH, 1986.
Feldman, Ron, and Gary Stern. "Addressing the Too-Big-To-Fail Problem." In *Me-
    gamergers in a Global Economy*, edited by Benton E. Gup, 187–206. Westport,
    CT: Quorum Books, 2002.
Gowrisankaran, Gautam. "Competition and Regulation in the Airline Industry." *FRSB
    Economic Letter* (Federal Reserve Bank of San Francisco), No. 2002–01, 18 Jan-
    uary 2002.
Gup, Benton E. "Too-Big-To-Fail: An International Perspective." In *Bank Failures in
    The Major Trading Countries of the World: Causes and Remedies*, edited by B. E.
    Gup, 69–91. Westport, CT: Quorum Books, 1998.
Gup, Benton E., ed. *Megamergers in a Global Economy: Causes and Consequences.* West-
    port, CT: Quorum Books, 2002.
Hallett, Carol B. "State of the U.S. Airline Industry: A Report on Recent Trends for
    U.S. Air Carriers, 2002." Air Transportation Association. Washington, D.C., 6
    March 2002 [11 April 2002]. Available from http://www.airlines.org;
    INTERNET.
Helfer, Ricki. "Remarks by Ricki Helfer, Chairman, Federal Deposit Insurance Cor-
    poration." In *History of the Eighties, Lessons For the Future.* Vol. 2. 43–52. Wash-
    ington, D.C.: Federal Deposit Insurance Corporation, 1997.

Kaufman, George G. "Are Some Banks Too Large to Fail? Myth and Reality." *Contemporary Policy Issues* 8 (October 1990): 1–4.

Lindgren, Carl-Johan, Gillian Garcia, and Matthew I. Saal. *Bank Soundness and Macroeconomic Policy*. Washington, D.C.: International Monetary Fund, 1996.

Matthews, Robert Guy, and Neil King, Jr. "Imposing Steel Tariffs, Bush Buys Some Time for Troubled Industry." *Wall Street Journal*, 6 March 2002, A1, A8.

McWilliams, Gary, and J. Dreazen Yochi. "Government Board Gives Loan Guarantee to America West, but with Stiff Conditions." *Wall Street Journal*, 31 December 2001, A2.

Melloan, George. "Caving in to 'Big Steel' Tarnished Bush's Image." *Wall Street Journal*, 12 March 2002, A27.

Meltzer, Allan H. "Back to Bailouts." American Enterprise Institute (AEI). Washington, D.C., August 2002.

Miller, Leslie. "Airlines Seek Help From Congress." In washingtonpost.com. 24 September 2002 [cited 24 September 2002]. Available from http://www.washingtonpost.com; INTERNET.

Mishkin, Frederic S. "Asymmetric Information and Financial Crises: A Historical Perspective." In *Financial Markets and Financial Crises*, edited by R. Glenn Hubbard, 69–108. Chicago: University of Chicago Press, 1991.

Morrison, Steven A., and Clifford Winston. "Bailing Out the Airlines. Policy Matters 01–24, AEI-Brookings Joint Center for Regulatory Studies." September 2001 [cited 5 October 2001]. Available from http://www.aie.brookings.org; INTERNET.

Olson, Elizabeth. "Bailout Plan for Swissair Called Unfair By Rivals." In *The New York Times on the Web*. 24 October 2001 [24 October 2001]. Available from http://www.nytimes.com; INTERNET.

Pilling, David, and Alan Beattle. "Tokyo Hints that Troubled Banks May Get Extra Capital." *Financial Times*, 26 September 2002, 1.

Regional Rail Reorganization Act of 1973, Preliminary System Plan. Vol. 1, Section 213, 26 February 1975.

Sapsford, Jathon. "Japanese Panel Backs Creation of Real-Estate Investment Trusts." *Wall Street Journal*, 1 April 1997, A15.

Spiegel, Mark M. "Towards a Sovereign Debt Restructuring Mechanism." *FRSB Economic Letter*. Federal Reserve Bank of San Francisco, 2002–19, 28 June 2002.

Stiglitz, Joseph. "The Disastrous Consequences of a World without Balance." *Financial Times*, 23 September 2002, 15.

Timlen, Thomas M. "Commercial Paper—Penn Central and Others." In *Financial Crises: Institutions and Markets in a Fragile Environment*, edited by E. I. Altman and A. W. Sametz, 220–225. New York: John Wiley & Sons, 1977.

"United Airlines' Parent Posts $510 Million Loss." *Tuscaloosa News*, 20 April 2002, 5B.

U.S. Department of Commerce. *Statistical Abstract of the United States 1989*. Washington, D.C., 1989, table 39 and figure 1–2.

U.S. Department of Commerce. *Statistical Abstract of the United States 1993*. Washington, D.C., 1993, table 826.18.

U.S. Department of Transportation. [cited 6 May 2002]. Available from http://www.dot.gov/affairs/carrierpayments.htm; INTERNET.

U.S. Department of Transportation Bureau of Transportation Statistics. "Historical Air Traffic Data Monthly: Year 2001." Washington, D.C. [cited 5 May 2002]. Available from http://www.bts.gov; INTERNET.

U.S. Department of Treasury. *Modernizing the Financial System: Recommendations for Safer, More Competitive Banks.* Washington, D.C., February 1991.

U.S. Department of the Treasury Emergency Loan Guarantee Board. *Second Annual Report.* Washington, D.C., 1973, 6.

U.S. General Accounting Office. *Guidelines for Rescuing Large Failing Firms and Municipalities.* GAO/GGD-84-34, 29 March 1984.

U.S. House of Representatives. *Regional Rail Reorganization Act of 1973, Report of the Committee on Interstate and Foreign Commerce.* 93rd Cong., 1st sess. *House Reports.* Vol. 1–6. Washington, D.C., 1973.

U.S. Senate. *Voluntary Municipal Reorganization Act of 1975, Report of the Committee on Banking, Housing, and Urban Affairs.* 94th Cong., 1st sess. *Senate Reports.* Vol. 1–7, 15–23. Washington, D.C., 1975.

Zuckerman, Laurence. "United Airlines Ousts Chief." In *The New York Times on the Web.* 29 October 2001 [cited 29 October 2001]. Available from http://www.nytimes.com; INTERNET.

CHAPTER 3

Too Big to Fail, Government Bailouts, and Managerial Incentives: The Case of the Reconstruction Finance Corporation Assistance to the Railroad Industry during the Great Depression

Joseph R. Mason and Daniel A. Schiffman

Transportation infrastructure has long been thought to be important to economic growth and development. Hence, financial difficulties in the transportation industry have often been considered too big to fail and, as a result, elicited government assistance. Turnpikes, canals, railroads, and airlines have all received government assistance through United States history. However, it is unclear whether such assistance helps the target companies recover or just postpones their inevitable demise. The normative public policy bias toward transportation infrastructure seems to be "better too much of a public good (and hence assistance toward that public good) than too little." However, while that normative bias may at first glance appear reasonable, assistance has long been suspected of skewing investment incentives away from those that would obtain them in the absence of that assistance.

The pattern of boom and bust in the transportation sector has a long history. Much like today, when the earliest turnpikes, canals, and railroads became insolvent they often received various types of assistance in response. Ex post assistance has historically taken the form of loans, guarantees, investments, preferred stock, and/or legislative or judicial injunction.[1] For instance, Evans (1929, 1931) traces the origins of preferred stock as a financing vehicle back to state-level railroad assistance granted as early as the 1830s, typically used as a last resort after loans and guarantees failed to restore a railroad.

Martin (1974), tracing the evolution of reorganization procedures affecting railroads in the 1890s, illustrates how special judicial and legislative developments were adopted to resuscitate railroads in bankruptcy. Hence, by the Great Depression there existed a long history of policies that treated railroads as too big to fail.

As a result, it is not surprising that the first New Deal programs established by President Herbert Hoover in 1932 included assistance to the railroads. This chapter describes the agency charged with granting this assistance, the Reconstruction Finance Corporation (RFC), and its operations toward the railroad industry. More importantly, however, the paper illustrates that the assistance granted to the railroads often did not encourage incentives to maintain long-term solvency, leaving in place a shallow view toward short-term survival that entailed drastically reduced expenses on maintenance of capital goods like equipment and rights of way.

The sections that follow first describe the rationale for RFC intervention, the financial condition of railroads, and the RFC assistance targeted toward those railroads. Then the paper describes how and why maintenance and employment are routinely reduced in response to financial distress in the railroad industry. Finally, the chapter tests econometrically the effects of RFC assistance on maintenance expenditures and employment. The results illustrate that without meaningful debt restructuring and corresponding reduction of fixed charges, railroads did not resume maintenance and employment in an economically meaningful way. Railroads continued to operate with reduced maintenance after RFC assistance, holding down the value of the firms and working against long-term soundness and solvency. Incentives to healthy maintenance and employment practices were more strongly encouraged by the relief from high fixed charges that accompanied formal bankruptcy and reorganization.

RATIONALE FOR RFC ASSISTANCE TO RAILROADS

As the Great Depression deepened, President Hoover and others were concerned not only with preserving transportation infrastructure, but also with the effects that railroad difficulties placed on banks and other financial intermediaries. There are at least two important reasons, beyond the presence of externalities provided by transportation infrastructure, that railroads were considered too big to fail. First, railroads played a major role in the real economy. Second, financial markets and institutions held a substantial portion of railroad securities as investments.

On the financial side, because the federal government reduced significantly their outstanding debt during the 1920s, financial intermediaries of all types relied crucially upon blue-chip bonds, especially railroad bonds, as risk-free securities. Figure 3.1 illustrates that by 1929 railroads represented 11.8 percent of all long-term debt in the United States and 19.9 percent of all private,

Figure 3.1
Distribution of Long-Term Debts, December 31, 1929

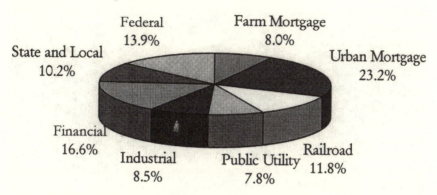

Source: Adapted from Evans Clark, *The Internal Debts of the United States,* New York: Twentieth Century Fund and the Macmillan Company, 1933.

nonfinancial long-term debt (Clark 1933). figure 3.2 shows that on December 31, 1931, insurance companies held 30.6 percent of outstanding railroad bonds and banks held 17.1 percent (Moulton 1933). Horton (1937) estimates that in 1932 the book value of railroad bonds comprised 16 percent; of bank assets and 23 percent of insurance company assets.

An important feature of the financial environment was the "legal list"—a list of permissible investments for banks and trusts that was binding in several states. Although each state maintained its own legal list, the concentration of institutional investors in New York State made that state's legal list especially influential within the financial community. Railroad bonds were legal in New York, as long as the issuing firm (a) had revenues exceeding fixed charges by at least 1.5 times in the previous year and in five of the previous six years,[2] and (b) had paid cash dividends equal to at least one-quarter of fixed charges in five of the previous six years. The second condition was waived if the coverage ratio condition had been met in nine of the previous ten years.

A number of states also stipulated a minimum firm size or scale of operation. Both New York and New Jersey required firms to operate at least 500 miles of railroad or generate at least $10 million in revenues annually. At the close of 1929, 36 percent of firms in the Interstate Commerce Commission's Class I (railroads with operating revenues over $1 million) failed to meet these size criteria (authors' calculation).[3]

The legal list contributed to major selloffs of railroad bonds and a massive collapse in their prices.[4] It also exacerbated the problem of refinancing maturing bonds. Railroads typically made no advance provisions for refinancing. Because of the flight to quality in the early 1930s, however, only the very strongest railroads could attract interest from potential investors and those

Figure 3.2
Holdings of Railroad Bonds, December 31, 1931

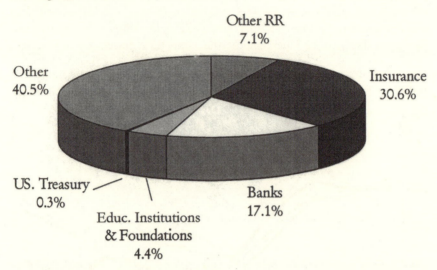

Source: Adapted from Harold Moulton and Associates, *The American Transportation Problem*, Washington, D.C.: Brookings Institution, 1933.

excluded from the legal lists faced even greater difficulty attracting funds. Hence, the solvency of both railroads and financial institutions was threatened when railroad bond performance declined.

The economic size and importance of the railroad sector in general, and its maintenance activities in particular, can readily be seen in Interstate Commerce Commission (ICC) data on Class I railroads. In 1929, Class I operating revenues (which comprised 98 percent of railroad industry operating revenues) accounted for 6.1 percent of GNP. Almost 3.5 percent of employed workers in the United States (almost 3.4 percent of the total labor force) worked for a Class I railroad.

Maintenance expenditures of Class I railroads accounted for 32.8 percent; of operating revenues (2% of GNP) and 45.7 percent of operating expenses. Maintenance workers comprised 51.6 percent of all railroad employees (1.74% of the U.S. labor force). Railroads were major purchasers of raw materials and manufactured products, spending 15.4 percent of their operating revenues (0.93% of GDP) on materials. Of this amount, approximately three-quarters were purchased for maintenance purposes (nearly 0.7% of GDP).[5]

For the railroad sector, 1929 was a fairly prosperous year. Class I operating revenues were $6.279 billion, the highest since 1923. Net income (income after taxes and interest) reached $1.589 billion, which was the best showing of any year in the 1920s. But in 1930, broader economic trends caught up with the railroads, and from the end of 1929 to the end of 1933, operating revenues declined by 50.7 percent (37.8% in real terms), maintenance of equipment by 50.2 percent (43.3%), maintenance of way by 62.3 percent (53.0%), and employment by 41.5 percent (see figure 3.3). Maintenance of way employment declined 51.3 percent, while maintenance of equipment employment declined 41.7 percent. At the same time, purchases of materials

Figure 3.3
Indices of Real Activity, Class I Railroads (1927 = 100)

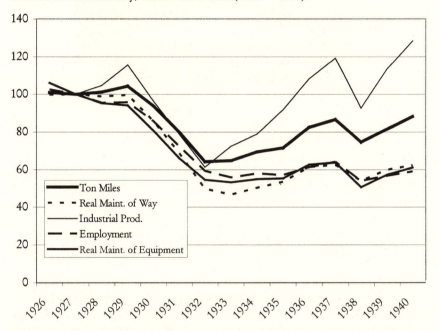

Sources and Notes: Ton Miles are from Association of American Railroads (1962). Real Maintenance of Way is computed by deflating nominal maintenance of way by the ICC's Railroad Construction Index. The index is a weighted average of labor and materials costs, and can be found in Interstate Commerce Commission (1962). Real Maintenance of Equipment is computed by deflating nominal maintenance of equipment by an index of maintenance of equipment costs. This index has been constructed by the authors as a weighted average of two indices: the index of hourly wages in the shopcrafts (75%) and the wholesale price index for metal and metral products (25%). The weights have been chosen to reflect the composition of maintenance of equipment costs (approximately 75% labor and 25% materials). The index of hourly wages is an annual average, and is taken from Bureau of Information of the Eastern Railways (1947); the (annual) metal price has been averaged from a monthly index, which can be found in the NBER Macro History Database (reproduced from Bureau of Labor Statistics publications; for details, see http://www.nber.org/databases/macrohistory/recdata/04/docs/m04066a.txt). Industrial Production from Federal Reserve Board (reproduced in Moody's Railroads 1941). Employment is from the ICC Statistics of Railways.

declined by 72.4 percent and net fixed investment by 86.9 percent (in nominal terms; appropriate deflators are not available).

Policymakers believed that increasing maintenance expenditures would put people back to work. This belief was probably reasonable, given the accepted rule of thumb that 50 percent of maintenance of way (track and structures) expenditures and 75 percent of maintenance of equipment expenditures went to labor. But despite the RFC's efforts, maintenance expenditures remained quite low until World War II—in 1937, maintenance of way and maintenance of equipment were still 42.1 percent and 31.3 percent below 1929 levels, respectively. The same is true of maintenance employment; in 1937, maintenance of way employment and maintenance of equipment employment were 43.2 percent and 30.9 percent below 1929 levels, respectively. Total railway employment also stagnated. In 1937, it reached a peak for the 1930s of 32.9 percent below 1929 levels (which was just 8% above 1932 levels).

By providing assistance, the RFC hoped to ameliorate these trends. Indeed, Jones (1951) claims that were it not for RFC assistance, the actual number of railroad bankruptcies would have been twice that actually experienced. As we will demonstrate, however, preventing bankruptcy may in fact have weakened managerial incentives to adopt policies of long-term investment that could more directly lead to the RFC's goals of restoring expenditures and increasing employment.

RFC ASSISTANCE AND THE FINANCIAL CONDITION OF RAILROADS

Historically, railroads have been the most failure-prone sector in the U.S. economy.[6] Waves of railroad bankruptcies accompanied the contractions of 1857–58, 1873–79, 1882–85, and 1893–94. The Great Depression, followed by the slow and incomplete recovery of railroad revenues, drove nearly one-third of U.S. railway mileage into bankruptcy by 1938 (figure 3.4). This unfortunate pattern resulted primarily from several peculiar structural attributes of the railroad industry. Railroad operations were characterized by (a) high fixed costs and economies of scale; (b) a highly cyclical pattern of revenues and profits; (c) sticky wages that were set by collective bargaining (labor costs accounted for nearly 60% of operating costs); and (d) regulation by the ICC. As the Depression deepened, the railroads appealed to the ICC for permission to increase rates and cancel unprofitable trains. For the most part, the ICC refused to grant its approval.

Railroad financial structures were characterized most prominently by condition (a) as a result of a decided emphasis on debt instruments over equity. Moreover, railroad debt was almost exclusively long term—much of it was in the form of 50-year mortgage bonds, secured by portions of railroad line. Railroads' high leverage led to heavy long-term fixed interest charges.[7]

Degrees of indebtedness differed significantly across firms, both prior to

Figure 3.4
Percentage of Mileage in Receivership or Trusteeship (All Classes)

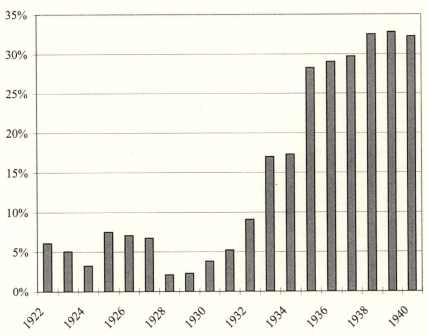

Source: Interstate Commerce Commission (1941).

and during the Depression. For example, the ratio of fixed charges to operating revenues ranged from almost 2 percent to over 46 percent, with a mean
of 16 percent. Similar results are obtained when other, less cyclical measures
of indebtedness are used. These differences among firms were almost certainly
generated by past financing decisions, and were not induced by the
Depression.[8]

Railroads' heavy fixed charges were exacerbated by small cash reserves and
low levels of accumulated retained earnings. Hence operating revenue was
the primary source of railroads' cash liquidity levels.

Since fixed charges remained fairly stable, there existed an inverse relationship between operating revenues and the ratio of fixed charges to operating
revenues. From 1929 to 1933, operating revenues fell 50.8 percent; at the
same time, the ratio of interest payments to operating revenues rose from 9.1
percent to 18.8 percent. The fixed charge coverage ratio (income available for
fixed charges divided by fixed charges) fell from 2.27 to less than one (see
figure 3.5).[9]

Financially troubled railroads that faced difficulties raising funds in bond
markets at economical rates typically resorted to short-term credit from

Figure 3.5
Interest Charges / Operating Revenues (Class I) and Times Fixed Charges Earned (All U.S. RR)

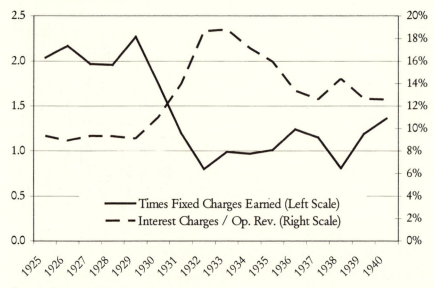

Sources: Interest Charges / Operating Revenues, Class I, from Moody's 1941. Times Fixed Charges Earned, from Interstate Commerce Commission, Statistics of Railways in the United States, 1941.

banks. The availability of bank credit, however, declined drastically during the early 1930s as banks came under tremendous pressure to increase the safety and liquidity of their assets (Calomiris and Wilson 1998). Banks refused to make new loans and called in many outstanding loans during that period.

Railroads often sidestepped these severe financial pressures in the short run by cutting out maintenance expenditures. In this manner, managers were able to improve their bottom line without suffering adverse consequences in the short run. But in the long run, there was no free lunch: Delayed maintenance often costs more to rectify later and too much neglect may lead to serious deterioration of the road, putting operating employees and passengers at increased risk of an accident.

When a firm could no longer borrow to cover its accumulated losses, or failed to refinance maturing bonds, it was forced to file for bankruptcy. Firms in bankruptcy were almost never liquidated. Operations continued under the direction of court-appointed receivers ("receivership"). To help them meet the firm's immediate obligations, the court authorized short-term financing through "receivers' certificates," which were senior to preexisting debts. Meanwhile, the firm's stakeholders worked out a reorganization plan. While reorganization was a lengthy, costly, and complex process, according to con-temporary analysts receivers often placed great importance on increasing maintenance expenditures in order to rehabilitate the road and prepare it to emerge from bankruptcy. We show below that RFC assistance did not lead to similar changes in maintenance expenditures or employment, suggesting that railroad managers did not view RFC assistance as an effective remedy that could help railroads avoid failure.

THE RFC'S EXPERIENCE WITH RAILROADS[10]

The RFC, under the provisions of section 5 of the RFC Act, was author-ized to make loans until February 1, 1935, or such earlier date as the pres-ident may fix by proclamation, upon approval of the ICC, to (1)(a) railroads and railways engaged in interstate commerce (b) to aid in the temporary financing to railroads and railways in the process of construction, and (c) to receivers of such railroads and railways, when, in the opinion of the board of directors of the RFC, such railroads and railways are unable to obtain funds upon reasonable terms through banking channels or from the general public and the Corporation will be adequately secured; (2) trustees of rail-roads that proceed to reorganize under section 77 of the Bankruptcy Act of March 3, 1933.

Table 3.1 details the purposes of railroad loans. Most RFC loans to railroads were for the purpose of paying debt interest and principal, and thereby prop-ping up the value of existing railroad securities. The second most popular type of loans to railroads were work loans (see table 3.2) and construction loans (see table 3.3). Work loans were for ". . . the construction, repair, and reha-bilitation of roadway and equipment," while construction loans were often more general in nature (Spero 1939, 38). The primary purpose of work loans was to maintain or increase employment rather than maintain or restructure the firm's finances. Work loans also carried two additional requirements: (1) the railroad had to repay the loan before granting any dividends, and (2) 75 percent of the money had to be spent rehiring furloughed labor. Moreover, work loans did not require ICC approval (Spero, 27, 38–41; Jones 1951, 118).

The RFC also purchased equipment trust certificates, that is, debt instru-ments for the purchase of operating equipment like locomotives or freight cars and secured by the same. The purchase of equipment trust certificates maintained employment in ancillary industries, and, as it later turned out, significantly smoothed the demand for increased production of railroad equip-ment on the eve of a high-demand period during World War II.

Under the act of January 31, 1935, that further extended the life of the RFC, the agency was empowered to purchase and guarantee the general ob-ligations of railroads and railways (Spero, 27). This extension of the RFC's powers was an acknowledgement that the Depression was now expected to

Table 3.1
Purposes and Amounts of Authorized RFC Loans to Railroads, January 22, 1932–October 31, 1937

Purpose	Jan. 22, 1932 - Oct. 31, 1932	Nov. 1, 1932 - Oct. 31, 1933	Nov. 1, 1933 - Oct. 31, 1934	Nov. 1, 1934 - Oct. 31, 1935	Nov. 1, 1935 - Oct. 31, 1936	Nov. 1, 1936 - Oct. 31, 1937
Bond Interest	$68,815,734	$34,399,942	$7,028,475	$8,906,800	$0	$0
Bond Maturities	54,144,460	15,073,000	10,597,575	6,757,000	-	218,861
Retirement of Bonds	-	-	-	-	12,405,667	18,007,500
Equipment Trust Maturities	21,829,181	16,212,305	4,611,000	-	5,000,000	573,000
Equipment Trust Interest	5,115,054	545,316	-	-	-	-
Short-term Maturities	40,702,413	-	43,000,000	-	-	-
Short-term Obligations, Interest	-	-	-	280,800	-	-
Payment of Short-term Loans (Notes)	-	-	-	-	-	310,639
Debenture Maturities	-	3,177,500	4,143,000	-	-	-
Debenture Interest	-	-	1,281,910	-	-	-
Purchase of Carriers' Securities	-	-	-	28,978,900	111,445,400	-
Mortgage Sinking Fund Payments	-	-	-	622,000	-	-
Purchase of Stock of Subsidiary Company	-	-	-	3,182,150	-	-
Interest on Leased Line Stock Certificates	-	-	-	195,200	-	-
Additions and Betterments	53,964,007	2,674,000	3,286,254	205,748	150,000	27,000
Bank Loans	39,803,100	-	-	-	-	-
Taxes	20,467,204	5,937,811	5,823,891	1,918,000	-	-
Audited Vouchers for Materials, Supplies, etc.	14,080,492	560,689	2,500,000	200,000	-	-
Rentals	7,050,059	-	-	-	-	-
Preferential Claims	6,986,742	1,500,000	-	-	-	-
Judgements	-	6,959,943	-	-	-	-
Equipment Repairs	-	2,500,000	-	-	-	-
Purchase of Property of Lessor Company	-	-	-	-	-	900,000
Working Capital	-	-	-	-	-	-
Miscellaneous	13,870,733	35,838	686,467	134,200	140,000	61,805
Total	$346,829,179	$89,576,344	$82,958,572	$51,380,798	$129,141,067	$20,098,805

Source: Interstate Commerce Commission, *Annual Report.*

Table 3.2
Authorized RFC Work Loans to Railroads, January 22, 1932–October 31, 1937

Carrier	Amount of Loan
Pennsylvania Railroad Company	$2,000,000
Central Railroad Company of New Jersey	500,000
Baltimore and Ohio Railroad Company	3,000,000
New York, New Haven & Hartford Railroad Company	700,000
Chicago & North Western Railway Company	1,000,000
New York Central Railroad Company	2,500,000
Southern Pacific Company	1,200,000

Source: Interstate Commerce Commission, *Annual Report,* cited in Spero (1939), p. 38.

last much longer than previously believed, and the philosophy of the RFC therefore adapted by providing long-term rather than short-term assistance.

In contrast with RFC assistance granted to other industries, only loans to railroads in *receivership* were required to be fully secured. Initially, the RFC paid ". . . little attention to the financial position and structure of (railroad and railway) applicants and their earning potentiality," (Spero, 2). This soon caused significant difficulties. It was not long before the RFC, as a principal creditor, was drawn into several large, and widely publicized, bankruptcy proceedings.

As a remedy, under the Emergency Railroad Transportation Act of June 6, 1933, the RFC Act was amended so that the agency could no longer make a loan to any railroad or railway that was in need of financial reorganization in the public interest. After 1935 the RFC was restricted to only those applicants ". . . who could demonstrate the fundamental soundness of their financial position and their ability to survive a reasonably prolonged period of depression" (Spero, 2).

A letter from Jesse Jones, chair of the RFC, to Vice President Garner dated November 6, 1934, is among the first evidence that the RFC had become concerned with the effects of their loans to the railroads, and the management quality of those railroads in which the RFC owned a stake (Jones 1951, 145). Eventually, the RFC began to insist on management changes and dividend restrictions as a condition of support. When the Pennsylvania Railroad borrowed 75 million dollars from the Corporation to electrify the lines between Boston, Massachusetts, and Washington, D.C., the RFC ordered that dividends be restricted until the loan was repaid. "When the debt was only a few months old and the dividend period was approaching, Pennsylvania Railroad, being proud of its [long, continuous] dividend record, chose to pay off the Reconstruction Finance Corporation loan instead of stopping the payment of

Table 3.3
Authorized RFC Construction Loans to Railroads, January 22, 1932–October 31, 1937

Carrier	Amount of Loan	Purpose
New York Central Railroad Company	$4,399,000	New freight line.
Pennsylvania Railroad Company	27,500,000	Electrify route from New York City to Washington, DC.
Cincinnati Union Terminal Company	10,398,925	New passenger terminal.
Denver & Rio Grande Western Railroad Company	3,850,000	Dotsero cutoff and acquisition of Denver & Salt Lake Western RR
Carleton & Coast Railroad Company	199,000	New extension.
Chesapeake Beach Railroad Company	395,000	Two new ferry terminals and boats.
The Quebec Extension Railway Company	3,000,000	New line.

Source: Interstate Commerce Commission, *Annual Report*, cited in Spero (1939), p. 38.

dividends" (Sullivan 1951, 23). Later, the RFC's loan to the Southern-Pacific Railroad was one of the first instances in which management concessions were used as a significant restrictive covenant. When the Southern-Pacific Railroad borrowed $23,200,000 in early 1937, the RFC ". . . ordered reduction of executives' salaries from ten percent to sixty percent" (43).

Even with such conditions, RFC loans to railroads only temporarily prevented a large number of insolvencies, prolonging the agony of impending bankruptcy. ". . . Prices of railroad bonds moved generally downward, intensifying the economic, banking, and credit difficulties," (Spero 1939, 143). "The underlying problems of the railroads, declining revenue, increased competition, and burdensome debt structures, were left untouched" (Olson 1972, 181).

Between February 1932 and October 1937, $638,597,795 was authorized to 75 railroads (see Spero, 33 for a complete list). "Of the twenty-one largest railroad borrowers from the RFC, nine were ultimately forced to file for bankruptcy, four underwent capital reorganization and judicial readjustment of their interest charges to avoid bankruptcy, and one was absorbed by a larger line. Only seven survived the depression and the RFC's loans unscathed" (see table 3.4) (Olson 1972, 182).

INCENTIVES AFFECTING RAILROAD MAINTENANCE AND EMPLOYMENT

Why did two-thirds of the largest twenty railroads that received assistance from the RFC fail anyway? We propose that the effects of RFC assistance can best be understood as distorting the incentives of railroad managers in a manner that did not reverse managerial policies adversely affecting maintenance and employment.

Our argument runs as follows: The government made loans in order to keep distressed railroads out of bankruptcy.[11] During financial distress, however, a railroad's first priority was to meet interest payments and stay out of bankruptcy. Hence, during financial distress managers had strong incentives to defer maintenance (and lay off maintenance employees), utilizing the cash "savings" to pay interest. But bankruptcy brought benefits. Although bankruptcy was costly, it also brought relief from high fixed charges that were often a principal cause of financial distress. Relieved of the high fixed charges, court-appointed receivers could physically rehabilitate the property by restoring maintenance, which not only increased the value of the firm, but also restored local employment and earnings. Hence, we argue that RFC loans often merely delayed the inevitable; had the government allowed these roads to enter bankruptcy earlier, the economy would have benefited from bankruptcy-related increases in maintenance and employment.[12]

Table 3.4
Major RFC Railroad Loans and Corporate Outcomes

Railroad	Loan Amount	Result	Date
Baltimore & Ohio	$82,125,000	Judicial Readjustment of Debt	9/3/1938
Boston & Maine	7,569,000	Judicial Readjustment of Debt	1/4/1940
Chicago & Northwestern	46,589,000	Bankruptcy	6/28/1965
Chicago, Milwaukee, & St. Paul	15,840,000	Bankruptcy	6/29/1935
Chicago & Rock Island	13,718,000	Bankruptcy	6/8/1933
Colorado and Southern	29,000,000	Judicial Readjustment of Debt	12/19/1940
Denver & Rio Grande	8,300,000	Bankruptcy	11/1/1935
Erie	16,582,000	Bankruptcy	1/20/1938
Ft. Worth & Denver	8,176,000	Merger	4/4/1932
Great Northern	105,422,000	OK	
Illinois Central	35,312,000	OK	
Lehigh Valley	9,500,000	Judicial Readjustment of Debt	10/11/1933
Missouri Pacific	23,134,000	Bankruptcy	4/1/1933
New York Central	27,500,000	OK	
New York, Chicago, and St. Louis	18,200,000	OK	
New York, New Haven, & Hartford	7,700,000	Bankruptcy	10/23/1935
Pennsylvania	29,500,000	OK	
St. Louis & San Francisco	8,000,000	Bankruptcy	11/1/1932
St. Louis & Southwest	18,790,000	Bankruptcy	5/17/1933
Southern Pacific	23,200,000	OK	
Southern Pacific	19,610,000	OK	

Sources: Loans from Spero (1939), p. 33. Results from *New York Times*, various issues, cited in Olson (1972), p. 207, *f* 21.

Determinants of Maintenance in Theory and Practice

We focus on two major categories of maintenance expenditure—maintenance of way (which includes both track and structures) and maintenance of equipment (locomotives and cars). Table 3.5 details the various types of maintenance activities in each major category (as defined by the ICC's standardized system of accounts).

Some of the listed activities are dependent on traffic volume (e.g., rail replacement, servicing engines). Others are seasonal or weather-dependent in nature, and independent of traffic volume (e.g., snow removal, replacement of wooden ties). Railway engineers noted this distinction, and made various estimates of *per cent variable*—the percentage of maintenance expenditures that varied with traffic. For example, the American Railway Engineering Association (1946) found that maintenance of equipment was 75 percent variable with traffic (25% fixed), while maintenance of way was one-third variable with traffic. Engineers therefore assumed that the desired elasticity of maintenance with respect to traffic is equal to per cent variable (Haber, Carroll, Kahn, and

Table 3.5
Typical Maintenance Activities, by Type

Maintenance of Way	Maintenance of Equipment
• Replace rail and ties • Drain water from tracks • Clean ballast (gravel and stones on which track rests) periodically–prevents track from becoming "dead" or rough-riding. Replace ballast when necessary • Burn weeds and mow grass • Clean and widen ditches, restore banks • Repair fences • Remove ice, snow and sand • Keep bridges/trestles/culverts/tunnels structurally sound • Maintain all buildings and structures (including facilities used for equipment maintenance) • Maintain roadway machines (but not other equipment) • Depreciation (insignificant until 1943, when the ICC changed its accounting requirements)	• Repair locomotives and cars. Includes the following activities: a. Running Repairs–under one man-hour of labor, performed in an enginehouse while the train is stopped b. Light Repairs–1 to 20 man-hours of labor, the equipment unit is removed from the train and serviced in a yard c. Heavy Repairs–over 20 man-hours of labor, performed in a shop on the "spot" system (which resembles an assembly line) • Repair work equipment • Repair power plant and shop machines • Depreciation (straight-line method) • Retirements

Source: Schiffman (2002).

Peck 1957, henceforth Haber et al.). (This is correct only under a special assumption—that physical depreciation is a linear function of traffic. See Schiffman 2000, 71.) For example, if traffic rose by 10 percent, maintenance of equipment was to be increased by 7.5 percent. By following such rules, engineers believed property would be kept in reasonably stable condition. This was the optimal policy from the vantage point of the engineers.

Most managers ignored engineers' decision rules and advice. Instead, managers typically followed a policy of linking maintenance expenditures (of both types) to operating revenues (not traffic), with an elasticity close to one. To demonstrate the differences between engineers and management, table 3.6 presents four different examples. Those examples assume that (a) managers use an elasticity of exactly one; (b) physical depreciation is a linear function of traffic; and (c) managers and engineers apply their respective rules in a symmetric manner. In case A, the ICC permits a rate increase of 10 percent, but traffic volume remains unchanged. In case B, traffic increases by 10 percent, while rates remain stable. Let cases A- and B- simply be the negatives of cases A and B. In cases A and A-, the engineers would advocate leaving maintenance unchanged, since traffic did not change. Managers would note the change in revenue, and adjust maintenance accordingly. In cases B and B-, both would agree that an adjustment is necessary, but would disagree re-

Table 3.6
Simulated Comparison of Incentives Provided Under Varying Elasticities of Maintenance Expenditures Relative to Operating Revenues

Case	Change in Revenues	Change in Traffic	Change in (Average) Rates on Traffic	Engineers' (Desired) Change in Maintenance of Way	Engineers' (Desired) Change in Maintenance of Equipment	Managers' Decision-- Change in Maintenance of Way	Managers' Decision-- Change in Maintenance of Equipment
A	10%	0%	10%	0%	0%	10%	10%
B	10%	10%	0%	3.33%	7.5%	10%	10%
A-	-10%	0%	-10%	0%	0%	-10%	-10%
B-	-10%	-10%	0%	-3.33%	-7.5%	-10%	-10%

garding its magnitude. From the standpoint of engineers, managers over-maintain in cases A and B, and undermaintain in cases A- and B-. Hence, managers permit excessive swings in maintenance and in the condition of the property.

As a result of the decision rules described, managers deferred maintenance when revenues were declining, then made it up as revenues picked up again. This policy was workable as long as revenues did not fluctuate too much. But if revenues declined drastically over several years (e.g., the Great Depression) a great deal of deferred maintenance would accumulate and the property might deteriorate to the point of danger.

Why did managers choose to vary maintenance with revenues? Unlike the engineers, managers focused primarily on the financial state of the road. Many railroad obligations were fixed, and did not vary with revenues. When revenues declined, roads needed to borrow money in order to keep up with interest payments, taxes, and other fixed expenses. Since external finance was not always easy to obtain, railroads needed an internal source of funds. The solution to this problem was to defer maintenance. In this way, they could generate internal funds by borrowing from the future.

Haber et al. describe this mechanism in detail (focusing on maintenance of way):

Railroad managements typically make maintenance of way activities serve as the balancing item in the total annual carrier budget. When revenues rise because traffic increases, maintenance of way operations pick up more than proportionately. When a management expects that a high level of traffic will be sustained for a while, it is even likely to permit some previously deferred maintenance to be undertaken. *When, on the other hand, traffic and therefore revenues fall, maintenance of way promptly suffers as the management tries to protect the road's cash position and make the customary dividend payments if that is possible* . . . [emphasis added].

What are present budget procedures on the railroads? Mr. Edward H. Bunnell, who was for many years the Vice President in Charge of Finance of the Association of

American Railroads, has outlined the typical procedure in a detailed volume on railroad practices.

A maintenance budget is prepared based on minimum safety-level appropriations and with provision for flexibility regarding other outlays. Mr. Bunnell discusses the desirability of "an approximately even balance between income and expenditures," and stresses the importance of up-to-the-minute forecasts of revenue to guide the budget officer in his release of funds for maintenance in excess of the level required for safety. The sample revenue forecast form, included in the appendix to Mr. Bunnell's work, shows the degree of importance attached to the immediate cash position of the railroad.

The typical budget procedure is apt to result in sudden revisions of maintenance plans irrespective of the physical programs (other than those involving safety) which might be considered desirable by the engineers in charge. Maintenance engineers have tried to convince their managements for years that the relationship between revenues and expenses is an "antiquated and improper yardstick [which] neither reflects the requirements nor does it reveal the efficiency of operation in performance of the work accomplished" (American Railway Engineering Association Proceedings 1953).

Why, it might well be asked, does the typical carrier undermaintain when revenues fall off and (sometimes) make up the deferral during periods when revenues rise? The most obvious answer is the correct one. *Most roads are not financially strong enough to resist the temptation to bolster falling revenues by deferring maintenance. They have usually been heavily burdened by fixed commitments. The maintenance account offers a hard-pressed comptroller one of his few avenues for curtailment when his cash position is endangered. It requires a substantial reserve position or a strong credit position, together with optimistic long-run expectations, for a management to continue outlays which might be pared down* [emphasis added].

It seems that managers had less freedom to defer maintenance of equipment. First, there was a "legal compulsion to maintain equipment" (Wood 1931). The ICC's Bureau of Locomotive Inspection made surprise visits and had the authority to order the removal of a piece of equipment from service. Second, equipment trusts (a special form of financing for new equipment) obligated the firm to keep the equipment in good shape. Third, cars were typically hired from one railroad to another. Fourth, and perhaps most important, continued undermaintenance would impair service and induce customers to take their business elsewhere.[13] Hence, maintenance of equipment was sometimes deferred due to financial distress, but given a choice, managers preferred to defer maintenance of way and avoid the riskier option of deferring maintenance of equipment.

The description found in Haber et al. (1957) and Wood (1931) is corroborated by the correspondence of railroad executives during the Depression.[14] The following example is quite instructive. On September 25, 1930, T. C. Powell, president of the Chicago & Eastern Illinois railroad, wrote to William Potter, a member of the company's Board of Directors, and reported that in August 1930, the road had lost money on operations and had failed to cover its fixed charges. He asked Potter to advise him on the following matter:

This railroad has been maintained in first class condition and reductions made this year are only in proportion to the reduction in revenue. The question that confronts me is whether I shall continue this policy or whether the maintenance and other expenses shall be cut to a point that might be difficult to overcome later on. (U.S. Congress 1935)

According to testimony given before the Senate on March 20, 1935, Wall Street investment bankers also exerted influence regarding maintenance decisions. Charles Beard, chairman of a Missouri Pacific Railroad bondholders' committee (and a noted historian at Columbia University), testified that the banking firms Chase Manhattan and Dillon Read forced maintenance cuts on the management of the St. Louis-San Francisco Railway. This was done in order to achieve earnings of $6.41 per share for the year 1930. Management protested that there were 25 broken rails every day, that unfit equipment was being used, and that safety was being impaired, but the bankers stubbornly refused to accept lower earnings. Although equipment maintenance shops were closed 182 days in 1930, dividends were declared for 1931 (U.S. Senate 1935).

Employees suffered the consequences of extremely cyclical maintenance expenditures. When traffic fell, workers were furloughed (temporarily laid off) according to seniority. Furloughed workers lost wages and could not accept another full-time job because they might be recalled if traffic recovered. Younger, less skilled workers were the first to be let go. They lost the opportunity to learn skills on the job, and, while unemployed, forgot the skills they had learned (Wood 1931).[15] Analysts believed that constant uncertainty and insecurity led to low worker morale and productivity.[16] The railroads suffered as well: Besides lower worker productivity and human capital deterioration, there was a tendency to purchase materials when they were most expensive. During slack periods, surplus materials had to be stored at a cost. Also, machinery deteriorated from lack of use. [17]

In the 1920s, both workers and management came to believe that sharp fluctuations in maintenance and employment were harmful to efficiency. On a number of major railroads, unions and management agreed on programs to stabilize employment. These agreements generally provided for a permanent staff, to be augmented by temporary workers when necessary. According to Wood (1931), these agreements were not "binding declarations," and it was understood by both parties that they might not be honored in an emergency situation. That is exactly what happened—beginning in 1930 firms notified their unions that furloughs could no longer be avoided.

The Effects of RFC Intervention

RFC assistance was offered to railroads in hopes that employees would be rehired and deferred maintenance would be made up. Did RFC assistance restore employment and maintenance and help restore the physical condition of the railroads, increasing their value?

We analyze this question using a panel data set drawn from the ICC's Statistics of Railways in the United States, and the RFC monthly reports (either published in the Congressional Serials or drawn from the national archives). We characterize purchases of equipment certificates and other types of RFC loans as assistance. Over 1932–40, total loans were \$891,336,960.[18]

Only 4.8 percent of RFC assistance money went to firms that were "small"—that is, firms that failed to meet the size criteria of the legal lists in New York and New Jersey—and only 12 of the 108 firm-years with positive RFC loans involve small firms. The very smallest (Class II and III) firms are excluded from the database, which generates some downward bias in our measurements.

Our tests utilize annual firm-level data to compare the maintenance and employment decisions of firms that received RFC aid with those who did not. We test for effects of RFC loans on maintenance and employment utilizing a version of the flexible accelerator model estimated in Schiffman (2002). We then examine if the behavior of RFC borrowers differs significantly from the behavior of nonborrowers. (Readers who are interested in further details should consult Schiffman 2002.) Ours is a neoclassical model in which two types of capital (way and equipment) are used to produce railroad service. The capital stocks may be adjusted by means of increasing or lowering maintenance expenditures subject to adjustment costs. At an optimum the marginal product of capital (for each type) is equated to its user cost. Because of the adjustment costs firms choose to follow a partial adjustment rule; each year they close a portion of the gap between the actual and desired capital stocks.

The model can be used to derive an equation that relates the log difference of maintenance to the log difference in revenues, the (economywide) rate of interest, log levels of maintenance in previous years, and an *error correction* term, which is the log of the previous year's maintenance to revenue ratio. The error correction term is negatively related to maintenance—if last year's maintenance to revenue ratio was high, this year's maintenance will be pushed downward (if all other variables are held equal). In practice, we experimented with some additional terms to capture the dynamics of maintenance better (such as the lagged log difference of sales). Those terms were not statistically significant and are omitted from the results reported here. Since maintenance workers accounted for more than half of all employees, it is reasonable to assume that employment and maintenance exhibit similar dynamics.

As it stands, the model assumes perfect (financial) capital markets. Firms may borrow and lend at a constant interest rate; if current revenues are insufficient to pay for the desired maintenance program, they will pay for it by borrowing. Suppose that capital markets are imperfect, due to information asymmetries between borrowers and lenders. This assumption is especially accurate for the Great Depression period (see Calomiris 1993 for detailed discussion and extensive references). Furthermore, suppose that the higher a firm's burden of debt, the greater its difficulties in obtaining external financing on reasonable terms. In such a case, firms with high preexisting debts and low current revenues may be unable to perform maintenance work at the desired level.

To capture the reality of imperfect capital markets, we assume that the difficulty of borrowing is proportional to the firm's leverage, defined as its ratio of fixed charges (primarily interest and property rents) to revenues in the previous year.[19] This ratio is added to the estimating equation. We then define the *leverage effect* as the effect of a one standard deviation increase from average railroad leverage on the log difference (or logarithmic rate of growth) of the dependent variable.

According to anecdotal evidence from a wide variety of sources, bankrupt firms showed a surge in maintenance expenditures. This reflected the desire of receivers and trustees to rehabilitate the property, in order to prepare for the firm's emergence from bankruptcy. Therefore, we add a bankruptcy dummy to the estimating equation, and define the *bankruptcy effect* as the effect of the bankruptcy dummy on the log difference (or logarithmic rate of growth) of the dependent variable.

The RFC sought to help credit constrained firms finance maintenance expenditures and employment in times of low and declining revenues. In fact, work loans were given with an explicit condition—the borrower had to bring back furloughed workers to perform the work. Since larger firms will tend to receive larger loans, we use a scale-free measure of loans that divides loan amounts by the amount of fixed charges in the previous year.[20] This variable, loans divided by fixed charges in the previous year, averaged 1.19 over the sample of 108 borrower firm-years. We define the *RFC effect* as the effect of a one standard deviation change from the mean level of RFC assistance to a railroad on the log difference (or logarithmic rate of growth) of the dependent variable.

Table 3.7 reports the results of our specification relating to growth in maintenance of way, maintenance of equipment, and employment.[21] Current period operating revenues are procyclical and statistically significant for maintenance and employment, as suggested by the maintenance literature. One-period lagged revenue growth is significantly related only to employment. We interpret these results as good indicators that our model relates revenue-driven managerial decisions in a manner similar to that suggested by the literature.

One-period lagged ratios of maintenance of way to operating revenues, one-period lagged stocks of maintenance of way, and one-period lagged ratios of fixed charges to operating revenue (leverage) are all negatively related to maintenance and employment and statistically significant (although leverage is not statistically significant in the employment model). Again, we interpret

Table 3.7
Panel Data Results Estimating Real Railroad Activities

	Dependent Variable: Log Difference of Maintenance of Way	Dependent Variable: Log Difference of Maintenance of Equipment	Dependent Variable: Log Difference of Employment
Log Difference of Operating revenues (t)	0.637*** (20.60)	0.575*** (16.30)	0.245*** (13.98)
Log Difference of Operating revenues (t-1)	0.051 (1.32)	-0.021 (-0.50)	0.046** (1.98)
Log Maintenance of Way (t-1) - Log Operating Revenues (t-1)	-0.444*** (-10.43)	-0.549*** (-11.74)	-0.131*** (-5.27)
Log Maintenance of Way (t-1)	-0.074* (-1.67)	-0.262*** (-5.76)	-0.141*** (-4.03)
Log Maintenance of Way (t-2)	0.032 (0.99)	0.038 (1.33)	-0.047 (-1.47)
(Fixed Charges/ Op. Rev.) (t-1)	-0.222*** (-3.21)	-0.135* (-1.72)	-0.042 (-1.07)
Bankruptcy (t) (Dummy)	0.083*** (4.25)	0.101*** (4.57)	0.024** (2.22)
RFC Loan (t)/ Fixed Charges (t-1)	0.003 (0.37)	0.000 (0.03)	-0.001 (-0.30)
Observations	1043	1043	1040
R-Sq. (within)	0.699	0.641	0.657
R-Sq. (between)	0.222	0.016	0.007
R-Sq. (overall)	0.553	0.072	0.053

Note: Variables included are those of Specification B in Schiffman (2002), plus the variable RFC Loan (t)/ Fixed Charges (t-1). Firm and year dummies and an intercept are included in the specification estimated, but are not reported. * indicates a significant difference at the 10 percent level, ** indicates a significant difference at the 5 percent level, and *** indicates a significant difference at the 1 percent level.

the results as capturing the appropriate accelerator effects hypothesized by the model.

The results most important to our analysis relate to the bankruptcy dummy and RFC loan variables. As suggested by anecdotal observation and historical accounts and previous work by, for instance, Rose (1990), the coefficient on the bankruptcy dummy variable is positive and significant for all measures of maintenance and employment. The coefficient on the RFC loan variable is statistically insignificant in all specifications.[22] Hence it appears that bankruptcy, by reducing the fixed charge burden on the firm, has beneficial effects of raising maintenance and employment. RFC loans did not resolve financial distress in a meaningful fashion, and therefore had little effect on maintenance and employment.

We also examine whether the leverage effects, bankruptcy effects, and RFC effects are economically, rather than statistically, significant. Table 3.8 compares the effects on maintenance and employment of a one standard deviation change in the leverage, bankruptcy, and RFC loan variables from their mean. Bankruptcy in table 3.8 carries with it an immediate 8.3 percent average increase in maintenance of way, a 10.1 percent average increase in maintenance of equipment, and a 2.45 percent average increase in employment. A one standard deviation increase in leverage in table 3.8 results in a 3 percent average decrease in annual growth of maintenance of way expenditures, a 1.8 percent average annual decrease in maintenance of equipment expenditures, and a 0.6 percent (statistically insignificant) average annual decrease in employment. Note that these effects are smaller than the bankruptcy effects, largely because leverage effects (unlike bankruptcy) accumulate over time.

The economic effect of RFC loans appears far smaller (notwithstanding statistical insignificance) than those for leverage and bankruptcy in table 3.8. Even if the RFC loan effect were statistically significant, a one standard deviation change in the ratio of RFC loans to (one-period lagged) fixed charges is associated with a 0.2 percent average increase in maintenance of way, a 0.01 percent average increase in maintenance of equipment, and a 0.07 percent average *decrease* in employment. Hence, again, it appears the effects of RFC loans on maintenance and employment, and therefore real structural adjustments associated with preventing railroad failures, paled in comparison with the effects of formal restructuring and debt realignment.

SUMMARY AND CONCLUSIONS

This paper provided historical and anecdotal evidence regarding railroad maintenance expenditures during a period of chronic financial distress. Railroad managers typically reduced maintenance and other "discretionary" expenditures during slow periods and increased these activities during periods of robust business activity. During normal cyclical swings, the described variations in maintenance and employment are relatively sanguine. However,

Table 3.8
Marginal Effects of Financial Factors on Real Activity (Percentage Points)

Effect	Dependent Variable: Log Difference of Maintenance of Way	Dependent Variable: Log Difference of Maintenance of Equipment	Dependent Variable: Log Difference of Employment
"Leverage Effect" One SD (0.135) Increase in (Fixed Charges/ Op. Rev.) (t-1)	-3.00*** (-3.21)	-1.82* (-1.72)	-0.57 (-1.07)
"Bankruptcy Effect" Bankruptcy (t) = 1	8.31*** (4.25)	10.10*** (4.57)	2.45** (2.22)
"RFC Effect" One SD (0.6278189) Increase in RFC Loan (t)/ Fixed Charges (t-1)	0.16 (0.37)	0.01 (0.03)	-0.07 (-0.30)

Note: * indicates a significant difference at the 10 percent level, ** indicates a significant difference at the 5 percent level, and *** indicates a significant difference at the 1 percent level.

during periods of chronic long-term financial distress, reduced maintenance and employment may become systemic effects that influence not only the supply of transportation services, but also the conditions under which those services are provided, and the income and consumption decisions of a large geographically dispersed portion of the workforce.

While the railroad industry may have been considered too big to fail during the Great Depression, economically meaningful assistance was not immediately forthcoming. In the meantime, we have demonstrated, maintenance and employment suffered in the presence of financial distress, which was prolonged by limited assistance offered to the industry.

The counterfactual is difficult to evaluate. As in some economies today, the industry in general and employment in particular may have been better served through speedy reorganization in bankruptcy. However, a more thorough investigation of that counterfactual will have to weigh the broad economic benefits of restored maintenance and employment expenditures against the potential for asset market pressures arising from faster debt downgrades and the liquidation of excess capacity. We leave these interesting and important questions for future research.

NOTES

1. We leave the discussion of ex ante incentives like railroad land grants aside.

2. In 1932, the state was forced to relax this requirement since many railroads were in violation; from then until April 1938 only railroads in default were excluded. Effective April 1, 1938, New York required a fixed charge coverage ratio of 1 during the previous year and five of the last six (*Moody's Governments* 1939).

3. We concentrate on Class I railroads for two reasons: (a) the data for Class I railroads are more detailed than for the smaller Class II and III railroads, and (b) very little is lost by omitting Classes II and III; Class I railroads accounted for 98.0 percent of total railroad employment and 98.6 percent of operating revenues (1927–40 average). Note that the requirement of $1 million in annual revenues for Class I status was not adhered to rigidly during the Depression. Between 1927 and 1929, there were two firms which repeatedly failed to reach the $1 million mark but remained in Class I.

4. Officially, New York's legal list applied (in a strict sense) to new investments only. For existing investments, the superintendent of banks had the discretion to decide whether to force banks to sell their holdings if the coverage ratio conditions were not met. In practice, this distinction was unimportant; banks hastened to sell bonds if the issuing railroad fell below the interest coverage threshold.

5. We do not have official data on the value of materials used in maintenance. However, we use available data to make a reasonable estimate, in the following way: Maintenance of way (track and structures) expenditures were approximately 50 percent labor, 50 percent materials, while maintenance of equipment expenditures were approximately 75 percent labor, 25 percent materials. Using these proportions, we find that in 1929, imputed materials spending in maintenance, as a percentage of total materials spending, was 75.4 percent. Since materials can be stored, and may be used after the year in which they are purchased, it is best to utilize a multi-year average. The 1923–29 average comes to 75.8 percent. See Schiffman (2002) for additional details of these estimates.

6. Over 1,100 railroad bankruptcies occurred from 1876–1970 (Altman 1971). This figure includes repeated bankruptcy episodes within the same firm.

7. These consisted primarily of interest on bonds and rent for leased lines. The latter was used to pay interest on the bonds of the lessor company.

8. For further details and supportive evidence, see Schiffman (2002) and the appendix to that paper, available upon request.

9. Income available for fixed charges is an after-tax measure of profits. It is the sum of after-tax operating income and nonoperating income.

10. Further historical details are available in Mason (2001).

11. Jesse Jones (1951) claimed that if not for the RFC's assistance, two-thirds of railroad mileage would have been in bankruptcy by the late 1930s (compared to the actual figure of one-third).

12. Bond and other asset prices, however, may have suffered due to the number of bankruptcies.

13. Equipment condition is also more visible to customers than track condition, because deteriorated track may be located far away from population and industrial centers. However, a series of accidents caused by poor track condition would become public knowledge and cause traffic losses for the firm.

14. In interpreting the quotations that follow, it is important to note that some managers (and analysts) failed to make an explicit distinction between maintenance of way and maintenance of equipment.

15. The lower-skilled employees were predominantly track workers. In 1928, the AREA Committee on Labor declared: "We do not believe that a track man is more than 50 percent efficient until he has served at least three months."

16. Wood (1931) places a lot of weight on this effect, but acknowledges that it is very difficult to measure.

17. In addition to cyclical instability, there were also huge seasonal swings in maintenance activity, which corresponded to a seasonal pattern of revenues. Revenues peaked during July to October and were lowest in December to January.

18. The Treasury's 1959 Final *Quarterly Report on the RFC* gives a figure of $786,604,805. The discrepancy is caused by equipment trust purchases, which our database counts but the Treasury did not. There is another difference, of relatively minor importance: Our database includes Class I railways only, while the Treasury data include railways of all classes.

19. Theoretically, other measures are possible. We selected this variable to follow the empirical work in Schiffman (2002).

20. Using current-year fixed charges would raise a simultaneity problem.

21. Firm and year dummies and an intercept are included in the estimated specification, but are not reported.

22. In additional work not reported here, we also ran specifications including interactions of the RFC loan variable with leverage and one-period lagged ratios of fixed charges to operating revenues. Neither specification yielded statistically significant coefficients on those variables or the raw RFC loan variable.

REFERENCES

Altman, Edward I. "Railroad Bankruptcy Propensity." *Journal of Finance*, May 1971, pp. 333–45.

American Railway Engineering Association. *Proceedings of the Annual Convention.* Vol. 47. Chicago: American Railway Engineering Association, 1946.

Anari, Ali, James W. Kolari, and Joseph R. Mason. "The Speed of Bank Liquidation and the Propagation of the U.S. Great Depression." Working Paper #02–35, Wharton Financial Institutions, August 2002.

Association of American Railroads. *Railroad Transportation: A Statistical Record, 1921–61.* Washington D.C., 1962.

Barger, Harold. *The Transportation Industries, 1889–1946: A Study of Output, Employment, and Productivity.* New York: National Bureau of Economic Research, 1951.

Bunnell, Edward H. *Railroad Accounting and Statistics: Research and Fact Finding as Aids to Management.* Chicago: Watson Publications, 1955.

Bureau of Information of the Eastern Railways. *Railroad Wages and Labor Relations: 1900–46.* New York: Bureau of Information of the Eastern Railways, 1947.

Calomiris, Charles W. "Financial Factors in the Great Depression." *Journal of Economic Perspectives,* Spring 1993, pp. 61–85.

Calomiris, Charles W., and Joseph R. Mason. "Contagion and Bank Failures during the Great Depression: The June 1932 Chicago Banking Panic." *American Economic Review,* December 1997, pp. 863–83.

Calomiris, Charles W., and Berry Wilson. "Bank Capital and Portfolio Management: The 1930's 'Capital Crunch' and the Scramble to Shed Risk." NBER Working Paper #6649, July 1998.

Clark, Evans. *The Internal Debts of the United States.* New York: Twentieth Century Fund and the Macmillan Company, 1933.

Evans, George Herberton, Jr. "The Early History of Preferred Stock in the United States." *American Economic Review,* March 1929, pp. 43–58.

Evans, George Herberton, Jr. "Preferred Stock in the United States, 1850–1878." *American Economic Review,* March 1931, pp. 56–62.

Haber, William, John Carroll, Mark Kahn, and Morton Peck. *Maintenance of Way Employment on U.S. Railroads.* Detroit: Brotherhood of Maintenance of Way Employees, 1957.

Horton, Donald C. *Long Term Debts in the U.S.* Washington, D.C.: U.S. Dept. of Commerce, 1937.

Interstate Commerce Commission. *Annual Report.* Washington, D.C.: U.S. Government Printing Office, Various Issues, 1929–41.

Interstate Commerce Commission. *Interstate Commerce Commission Activities, 1937–1962; Supplement to the 75th Annual Report.* Washington, D.C.: U.S. Government Printing Office, 1962.

Interstate Commerce Commission. *Statistics of Railways in the United States.* Washington, D.C.: U.S. Government Printing Office, 1941.

Jones, Jesse H. *Fifty Billion Dollars: My Thirteen Years with the RFC (1932–1945).* New York: The Macmillan Company, 1951.

Martin, Albro. "Railroads and the Equity Receivership: An Essay on Institutional Change." *The Journal of Economic History,* September 1974, pp. 685–709.

Mason, Joseph R. "The Determinants and Effects of Reconstruction Finance Corporation Assistance to Banks During the Great Depression." Ph.D. diss., University of Illinois at Urbana-Champaign, 1996.

Mason, Joseph R. "Do Lender of Last Resort Policies Matter? The Effects of Reconstruction Finance Corporation Assistance to Banks During the Great Depression." *Journal of Financial Services Research,* September 2000, pp. 77–95.

Mason, Joseph R. "Reconstruction Finance Corporation Assistance to Financial Institutions and Commercial & Industrial Enterprise in the U.S. Great Depression, 1932–1937." In *Resolution of Financial Distress,* edited by Stijn Claessens, Simeon Djankov, and Ashoka Mody, pp. 167–204. Washington: World Bank Press, 2001.

Moody's Governments and Municipals. New York: Moody's Investors Service, 1939.

Moody's Steam Railroads. New York: Moody Investors Service, 1941.

Moulton, Harold, and Associates. *The American Transportation Problem.* Washington, D.C.: Brookings Institution, 1933.

Olson, James S. "From Depression to Defense: The Reconstruction Finance Corpo-
    ration: 1932–1940." Ph.D. diss., State University of New York at Stony Brook,
    1972.
Report of Activities of the Reconstruction Finance Corporation. National Archives, Records
    of the Clerk of the House of Representatives.
Report of Activities of the Reconstruction Finance Corporation. Washington, D.C.: U.S.
    Government Printing Office.
Report of the Reconstruction Finance Corporation. Washington, D.C.: U.S. Government
    Printing Office, 1935–59.
Rose, Nancy L. "Profitability and Product Quality: Economic Determinants of Airline
    Performance." *Journal of Political Economy,* October 1990, pp. 944–64.
Schiffman, Daniel A. "Shattered Rails, Ruined Credit: Financial Fragility and Railroad
    Operations in the Great Depression." Ph.D. diss., Columbia University, 2000.
Schiffman, Daniel A. "Shattered Rails, Ruined Credit: Financial Fragility and Railroad
    Operations in the Great Depression." Working Paper, Bar Ilan University,
    2002.
Spero, Herbert. *Reconstruction Finance Corporation Loans to the Railroads, 1932–1937.*
    New York: Bankers Publishing Company, 1939.
Sullivan, Francis J. "Reconstruction Finance Corporation and Corporate Financial
    Policy." Thesis, George Washington University, 1951.
U.S. Senate Committee on Interstate Commerce. *Investigation of Railroad Financing.*
    Senate Resolution 71, 74th Congress, 1st sess. Washington, D.C.: U.S. Gov-
    ernment Printing Office, 1935.
U.S. Senate Subcommittee of the Committee on Banking and Currency. *Creation of a
    Reconstruction Finance Corporation.* Washington, D.C.: U.S. Government Print-
    ing Office, 1932.
Wood, Louis A. *Union-Management Cooperation on the Railroads.* New Haven: Yale
    University Press, 1931.

CHAPTER 4

Does Financial Liberalization Increase the Likelihood of a Systemic Banking Crisis? Evidence from the Past Three Decades and the Great Depression

Arthur E. Wilmarth, Jr.

INTRODUCTION

Over the past three decades, leading industrial nations and many developing countries have liberalized their financial markets by (a) removing foreign exchange controls, (b) deregulating interest rates paid on bank deposits, (c) expanding the powers of domestic financial institutions, and (d) creating greater opportunities for entry by foreign banks. Unquestionably, the deregulation of domestic and global financial markets has produced major benefits, including more efficient intermediation of financial resources, more rapid economic development, and faster growth in trade. However, banking crises have occurred with increasing frequency in international markets since 1973, and many crises have taken place in countries that deregulated their financial markets. This apparent linkage between deregulation and banking crises indicates that financial liberalization may have a dark side, because it tends to produce a banking system that is more vulnerable to systemic risk.

Several recent studies indicate that banking crises associated with deregulation occur in seven general stages. First, financial liberalization broadens the lending powers and permissible investments of banks, and deregulation also places greater competitive pressures on banks. As a result, banks have incentives to increase their profits by expanding their lending commitments and equity investments in the real estate and securities markets. Second, the expanded availability of debt and equity financing produces an economic boom.

Boom conditions are fueled by positive feedback between rising asset values and the willingness of creditors and investors to provide additional financing based on their belief that asset values will continue to rise. Third, asset markets ultimately overshoot and reach levels that cannot be justified by economic fundamentals (e.g., the cash flow produced by real estate projects and business ventures). Fourth, the asset boom becomes a bust when investors and creditors (1) realize that market prices for real estate and securities have diverged from economic fundamentals, and (2) engage in a panicked rush to liquidate their investments and collect their loans.

Fifth, the asset bust creates adverse macroeconomic effects, because it (a) impairs the liquidity and market value of assets held as investments or pledged as collateral for loans, and (b) discourages investors and creditors from making new investments or extending additional loans, thereby depressing economic activity and reducing the ability of borrowers to pay their debts. Sixth, the continuing fall in asset values and rise in nonperforming loans inflict large losses on many banks. Those losses impair the confidence of depositors and threaten a systemic crisis in the banking sector. Seventh, to prevent such a crisis, governmental authorities spend massive sums to protect depositors and recapitalize banks.

In sum, deregulated financial markets generally promote faster growth rates by providing more extensive financing to consumers and business firms during economic expansions. However, by encouraging a greater reliance on external funding, deregulation creates a higher risk that consumers and firms will become overextended and insolvent if external funding sources shut down during economic contractions. Thus, financial liberalization tends to amplify the business cycle, and it therefore creates a difficult tradeoff between (1) the important policy goal of creating better conditions for economic expansion and (2) the equally important objective of minimizing the risk of a severe economic downturn.[1]

The first part of this chapter considers evidence that financial liberalization has increased the likelihood of systemic banking crises since the early 1970s. Particular attention is given to the Japanese banking crisis of the 1990s, the U.S. banking and thrift crisis of 1980–92, and the potential threat to banks posed by the boom-and-bust cycle in U.S. securities markets during 1996–2002. The second part describes the expansion of bank involvement in the U.S. real estate and securities markets during the 1920s, and the apparent links between the collapse of those markets and the systemic banking crisis of the Great Depression. The concluding section offers some general observations about the evidence presented in the first and second parts.

FINANCIAL LIBERALIZATION AND BANKING CRISES SINCE THE 1970S

Banking Crises in International Markets

In the early 1970s, the breakdown of the Bretton Woods system of fixed exchange rates, together with dramatic increases in energy prices, brought an end to the postwar period of relative stability in global financial markets. By the late 1970s, advances in information technology and the creation of innovative financial instruments (including securitized debt and "junk bonds") were undermining legal and institutional barriers that separated banks from nonbank financial intermediaries in many countries. Over the next two decades, government officials in both developed and developing countries progressively deregulated their banking systems by abandoning foreign exchange controls, tearing down geographic barriers to entry, and removing restrictions on mergers and product diversification.

The competitive forces unleashed by innovation and deregulation created financial markets that were dynamic and more efficient, but also more interdependent, volatile, and fragile. As a consequence, international markets have witnessed a series of financial crises since 1973. More than 130 countries encountered serious banking problems during 1980–96, and East Asia and Russia experienced devastating banking crises in 1997–98. In many nations, financial crises occurred in conjunction with a boom-and-bust cycle in the general economy. In reviewing such crises, analysts frequently concluded that a poorly supervised deregulation of the banking sector had encouraged financial institutions to pursue aggressive lending and investment policies, thereby creating an unsustainable economic boom. In many cases, a rapid growth in financing was linked to speculative valuations of illiquid assets (e.g., real estate and corporate securities) that banks used for investments or as collateral for loans.[2]

Numerous countries incurred losses ranging from 4–40 percent of their gross domestic product (GDP) in coping with financial disruptions. For example, the governments of Finland, Indonesia, Japan, Mexico, Norway, South Korea, Sweden, and Thailand responded to systemic banking crises by protecting all depositors against loss, and they also spent massive amounts to recapitalize major banks during the 1990s. Mexico and South Korea each committed $100 billion or more for this purpose, while Japan has spent or budgeted $550 billion to support its deeply troubled banking system. The International Monetary Fund (IMF) assisted many of these bank rescue programs. During the 1990s, the IMF and its member nations supplied $250 billion of assistance to debtor countries, including programs totaling $145 billion for Indonesia, Mexico, and South Korea.[3]

Japan's banking troubles since 1990 provide a particularly striking example of the apparent linkage between financial deregulation, asset booms, banking crises, and impaired macroeconomic performance. In the last half of the 1980s, the Bank of Japan's lax monetary policy fostered a large increase in bank lending that produced a "bubble economy." Credit expansion led to rapid increases in market values for Japanese real estate and securities, which in turn encouraged banks to make further loans based on speculative valuations of land and stock used as collateral. Japanese banks also built up huge portfolios of corporate shares, due to their desire to profit from the booming stock market and to maintain strong cross-shareholding relationships with nonbank firms that were members of the banks' *keiretsu* (corporate groups). Japanese banks had two additional incentives to make real estate loans and equity investments. First, real estate loans helped to offset a decline in corporate lending that occurred when financial liberalization enabled large Japanese companies to obtain credit through the Japanese bond market and the Eurobond market. Second, Japanese regulators and the Basel Capital Accord of 1988 permitted Japanese banks to use unrealized capital gains from their stock portfolios to satisfy a significant portion of their capital requirements.

The Bank of Japan tightened its monetary policy significantly in 1990 to discourage further expansion of the bubble economy. In response to more restrictive credit conditions, the Japanese real estate and stock markets both collapsed in the early 1990s, with values in each sector falling by more than two-thirds. Two of the twenty largest Japanese banks failed, and several other major banks were driven to the brink of insolvency. Two major securities firms and three large insurance companies also failed. By the fall of 2002, Japanese banks had written off more than $600 billion of nonperforming loans, but private sector analysts estimated that the banks' remaining bad debts still exceeded $1 trillion. Japanese banks also held severely depreciated stock portfolios that impaired their ability to satisfy capital requirements. Japan's government failed to revive the economy after spending more than $1 trillion on economic stimulus programs. The government also failed to restore the financial system despite spending $200 billion and budgeting an additional $350 billion to support Japanese banks.

Japan's banking crisis has crippled the Japanese economy in two ways. First, banks have been reluctant to collect or charge off loans owed by failing companies, because aggressive collection efforts would trigger a wave of corporate bankruptcies, and the required charge-offs would seriously erode the capital of many banks. Second, the banks' huge burden of uncollectible debts has undermined their ability and willingness to make new loans to viable Japanese businesses. The Japanese government's financial capacity to resolve the crisis remained doubtful in the autumn of 2002, because Japan was already saddled with a huge public sector debt burden that exceeded 150 percent of its GDP.[4]

U.S. Banking and Thrift Crises during 1980–92

The banking and thrift industries in the United States were severely shaken during the 1980s and early 1990s by a systemic crisis that was associated with deregulation and a boom-and-bust cycle in the U.S. economy. Beginning in 1980, federal and state governments greatly expanded the real estate lending powers of banks and thrifts. Federal and state officials encouraged consolidation by liberalizing geographic restrictions on branching and relaxing antitrust rules governing mergers. Federal and state officials also permitted thrifts to make large investments in junk bonds, commercial real estate projects, and a wide array of other ventures. Nor did federal regulators object when banks made extensive loans to energy producers and corporations engaged in leveraged buyouts (LBOs).

Legislators and regulators believed that deregulation would help banks and thrifts to overcome a significant erosion that was occurring in their traditional lending businesses. Corporate borrowers increasingly bypassed banks by selling commercial paper and issuing junk bonds in the credit markets. At the same time, inflation and securitization created a residential mortgage market that was more competitive, more volatile, and less profitable for thrifts. Government officials concluded that deregulation would enable banks and thrifts to modernize their operations and "grow out of their problems." Congress expanded deposit insurance coverage from $40,000 to $100,000 per depositor, while federal deposit insurers charged flat-rate premiums that failed to take account of the risk profile of each insured institution. Due to the low-cost funding opportunities provided by flat-rate deposit insurance and a nationwide network of deposit brokers, aggressive banks and thrifts had strong incentives to use insured deposits to finance their risky loans and investments.

In combination, deregulation and financial innovation produced a rapid expansion of private sector credit for real estate development, energy production, LBO transactions, and other corporate takeovers. Between 1980 and 1989, outstanding junk bonds increased from $30 billion to $210 billion, and junk bonds' share of the corporate debt market grew from 13 percent to 27 percent. During the same period, nonfinancial corporate debt rose by $1.6 trillion, and real estate developers obtained financing to build more than $1 trillion of commercial projects. Bank lending to business firms and real estate developers more than doubled during the 1980s, while thrift lending to such borrowers expanded at a comparable rate until 1986. By 1990, banks held about $250 billion of commercial real estate loans and $150 billion of LBO loans, while thrifts held more than $100 billion of commercial real estate loans and $12 billion of junk bonds.

The real estate, energy production, and LBO markets all collapsed by the end of the 1980s, with devastating consequences for banks, thrifts, and the U.S. economy. During 1980–94, U.S. regulators spent almost $200 billion of deposit insurance funds and taxpayer revenues to resolve the failures of 2,900 banks and thrifts, which collectively held more than $900 billion of assets. U.S. officials protected all insured depositors in failed banks and thrifts, and they also protected *uninsured* depositors and payments system creditors in several "too big to fail" (TBTF) banks that failed or were threatened with failure during 1980–92. Some of the most aggressive and fastest-growing banks and thrifts of the 1980s (e.g., Bank of New England, Continental Illinois Bank, First City, First Republic Bank, CenTrust Savings, Imperial Savings, and Lincoln Savings) became prominent casualties by the end of the decade. Regulators also granted extensive forbearance to some very large troubled banks, including Bank of America and Citicorp.

The banking and thrift crises of the 1980s produced a prolonged "credit crunch" that had significant adverse effects on U.S. economic growth during the early 1990s. Bank and thrift failures disrupted credit relationships with many borrowers. Surviving institutions were generally reluctant to extend new loans until they had repaired their balance sheets and the economy had shown clear signs of recovery from the recession of 1990–91. Bank lending to businesses and real estate developers declined in each year during 1990–92, and did not show any significant recovery until 1994.[5]

The Recent Boom-and-Bust Cycle in U.S. Securities Markets

During the 1990s, Congress and federal regulators adopted deregulatory measures that encouraged large commercial banks to expand geographically and diversify their lines of business. In 1994, for example, Congress removed all legal barriers to interstate bank mergers and acquisitions. The new nationwide banking regime promoted a consolidation movement that enabled the ten largest banks to increase their combined share of U.S. banking industry assets from 26 percent to 49 percent during the 1990s. In addition, by 1998 federal regulators and the courts had allowed banks to make substantial inroads into the securities and insurance sectors by exploiting loopholes in two statutes—the Banking Act of 1933, popularly known as the "Glass-Steagall Act" (G-S Act), and the Bank Holding Company Act (BHC Act)—that previously had been viewed as strong legal barriers to bank entry into the securities and insurance fields. Congress ratified this diversification of banking powers when it passed the Gramm-Leach-Bliley Act of 1999 (GLB Act), which authorized banks to affiliate with securities firms and insurance companies by establishing financial holding companies. In confirming this grant of "universal banking" powers to financial holding companies, the GLB Act repealed several provisions of the Glass-Steagall Act and the BHC Act.

By the time Congress adopted the GLB Act, Citigroup, J. P. Morgan Chase, and Bank of America had already established large investment banking operations that competed with the "big three" Wall Street firms (Goldman Sachs, Merrill Lynch, and Morgan Stanley) and three major European universal banks (Credit Suisse, Deutsche Bank, and UBS).[6] As domestic and foreign banks entered the securities business, they offered generous loan commitments to attract customers for securities underwriting and merger advisory work. The major Wall Street firms responded by offering their own "package deals" that included lending, underwriting, and advisory services. This fierce competition for investment banking clients fostered a huge expansion in debt and equity financing for business firms in the United States. The annual volume of syndicated loans rose from less than $400 million in 1993 to more than $1 trillion in each year during 1997–2000. Similarly, the annual volume of underwritten public offerings of corporate debt and equity securities grew from less than $900 billion in 1992 to more than $1.8 trillion in each year during 1998–2000.[7]

A similar surge of debt financing occurred in the consumer sector. Large banks, securities firms, and finance companies created a nationwide market for securities backed by consumer debt. The growth of securitized consumer credit accelerated after federal courts issued decisions that effectively destroyed state-law limitations on maximum interest rates for consumer loans. By 2002, commercial and investment banks had sold asset-backed securities representing some $7 trillion of consumer debt.[8]

The competition for market-based financing among banks, securities firms, and finance companies has resulted in a dramatic increase in leverage and risk for both corporate and consumer borrowers. During 1990–2002, the outstanding debt of U.S. nonfinancial firms rose from $2.4 trillion to $4.9 trillion. Outstanding junk bonds tripled during the same period and reached $600 billion. During 1995–2001, total U.S. consumer debt (including home mortgage loans) grew from $4.5 trillion to $7.2 trillion. Banks and nonbank lenders increasingly marketed credit services to higher-risk "subprime" consumer borrowers, and those borrowers held a third of all credit card loans and a tenth of all home mortgages and home equity loans by 2002. As a result of this rapid growth in private sector credit, (a) U.S. corporate debt rose to record levels as a percentage of both GDP and corporate profits, and (b) U.S. household debt exceeded annual household income for the first time in postwar economic history.[9]

Rising debt levels and a slowing U.S. economy have produced a sharp rise in troubled corporate and consumer loans. By 2002, a record $880 billion of corporate bonds were either in distress or in default, including 45 percent of all outstanding junk bonds. The volume of syndicated loans criticized by bank examiners rose to $240 billion, a fivefold increase since 1998. Delinquencies on consumer loans (including mortgage loans) reached their highest level since the recession of 1990–91. Growing consumer debt burdens also produced a large increase in personal bankruptcy filings, which rose from 700,000 in 1990 to more than 1.3 million in each year during 1997–2001.[10]

The greatest excesses of the financing boom of the 1990s occurred in the information technology (high-tech) and telecommunications (telecom) industries. The Telecommunications Act of 1996 and the implementing rules adopted by the Federal Communications Commission deregulated the telecom industry and encouraged new firms to enter markets that had long been dominated by the regional Bell companies. Banks, securities firms, and venture capital funds provided debt and equity financing to a myriad of high-tech and telecom firms, including many unproven, start-up ventures. During 1996–2001, the telecom industry received $1.3 trillion in debt financing from syndicated loans and bond offerings, as well as hundreds of billions of dollars in equity financing from initial public offerings (IPOs). By 2000, new entrants into the telecom business included 6,000 Internet providers, 250 local telephone companies, and a half-dozen long distance carriers.

However, in early 2000 it became clear that these "new economy" firms would fall far short of their optimistic forecasts for revenues and earnings, because they had created operating capacity that far exceeded customer demand. For example, telecom firms installed millions of miles of fiber-optic cables with the expectation that Internet traffic would double every hundred days. Instead, Internet use grew at a much slower rate, and less than 3 percent of the installed fiber-optic lines were actually needed to meet customer demand. As a result of this glut of excess capacity, telecom firms suffered an estimated negative cash flow of $60 billion in 2000. When market participants realized the magnitude of the telecom industry's problems, they rapidly sold off shares of high-tech and telecom companies, and the debt and equity markets virtually shut down for those firms.[11] Investors similarly dumped the stocks of large energy companies that had aggressively expanded their energy trading operations after federal and state agencies deregulated energy markets in the 1990s.[12]

The collapse of high-tech and telecom stock prices triggered a broad downturn in U.S. equity markets during 2001–02. Investors manifested a general loss of confidence, due in part to stunning disclosures of fraudulent financial reporting and other serious misconduct at some of the most glamorous corporate stars of the 1990s (e.g., Adelphia, Enron, Global Crossing, Qwest, Tyco, and WorldCom). Between March 2000 and September 2002, the NASDAQ market index (representing primarily the stocks of high-tech and telecom firms) fell by more than three-quarters, while the broader S&P 500 index declined by almost one-half. In the process, investors lost an estimated $8 trillion in paper wealth.[13]

Like their U.S. counterparts, European equity markets experienced a prolonged slump in 2000–02. The end of the high-tech and telecom booms created economic hardships for a wide range of companies on both sides of the Atlantic. The U.S. economy struggled through a recession and a slow recovery, while economic growth in the European Union ground to a virtual halt. In both the United States and Europe, the prospects for a strong economic recovery appeared very doubtful in late 2002. Observers concluded that the surge of debt and equity financing in the late 1990s had created significant problems with overcapacity in many economic sectors.[14]

The bursting of the stock market bubble in 2000–02 has been blamed on a variety of factors, including (a) "irrational exuberance" that impaired the judgment of too many investors, (b) "infectious greed" that tempted too many corporate executives, and (c) conflicts of interest that undermined the effectiveness of too many outside monitors of corporate performance, including public accountants, securities analysts, and credit rating agencies.[15] This chapter will focus on allegations that large commercial and investment banks promoted transactions that involved excessive risks to investors, the financial system, and the broader economy.

By the autumn of 2002, government officials and private litigants had filed legal claims asserting that the following financial institutions had committed serious misconduct:

Citigroup, J. P. Morgan Chase ("Chase"), and Merrill Lynch allegedly helped Enron's fraudulent reporting schemes by entering into prepaid commodity forward transactions with Enron and with offshore entities that were established and controlled by the banks. These three-party derivatives contracts allegedly provided $8 billion of debt financing to Enron but were recorded on Enron's financial statements as commodity trades, thereby materially understating Enron's debt and overstating its trading revenues.

During 1997–2000, Citigroup's Salomon Smith Barney unit became the leading investment bank for the telecom industry. During this period, Citigroup earned an estimated $1 billion in fees and raised $190 billion of debt and equity financing for its telecom clients. Jack Grubman, Citigroup's main telecom analyst, played a key role in arranging financing and merger deals for many of the most aggressive firms in the telecom industry. Citigroup rewarded senior executives of its clients by allowing them to buy underpriced shares in IPOs underwritten by Citigroup. Grubman was also one of the most bullish cheerleaders for the telecom industry in his reports for investors. Ten large companies that Grubman advised and recommended to investors—including Global Crossing, Winstar, and WorldCom—filed for bankruptcy by mid-2002. Grubman failed to give timely warnings to investors about the grave problems confronting these firms, despite the knowledge he reportedly gained through his close ties to senior management.

In May 2001, Citigroup and Chase acted as lead underwriters for an $11.8 billion public bond offering by WorldCom. That offering enabled WorldCom to pay off outstanding loans owed to Citigroup, Chase, and other banks. The offering also allowed WorldCom to satisfy its working capital needs in 2001 without requesting additional bank loans. WorldCom suddenly defaulted on its bonds and filed for bankruptcy in 2002, while disclosing that it had overstated its profits by more than $7 billion since 1998. Bondholders alleged that (a) the self-interest of Citigroup and Chase as leading lenders to WorldCom conflicted with their duties as underwriters, and (b) the banks failed to act with due diligence in ensuring that WorldCom's financial statements were accurate when WorldCom made its bond offering.[16]

Credit Suisse, Merrill Lynch, and other major financial institutions allegedly adopted promotion and compensation policies that pressured their securities analysts to issue strong recommendations in favor of existing or potential investment banking clients, without regard to the clients' actual financial condition or prospects. In addition, Credit Suisse and Goldman Sachs reportedly allocated underpriced shares in IPOs to executives of clients and venture capital firms for the purpose of winning investment banking deals.[17]

In sum, critics charged that the entry of large commercial banks into the investment banking business in the 1990s had (a) created structural conflicts of interest that impaired the objectivity of lending decisions, securities underwriting, and investment advice, and (b) promoted a highly competitive, deal-oriented culture that encouraged both banks and Wall Street firms to offer loans and underwrite securities that were not justified by any reasonable assessment of the long-term viability of the enterprises being financed.[18] Press accounts indicated, for example, that the quest for investment banking fees had produced the following perverse behavior among banks: (1) encouraging clients to endorse wildly optimistic business plans that would justify bigger mergers and larger securities offerings, (2) offering loans only to clients that agreed to retain the banks for underwriting or merger advisory services, and (3) threatening to cut off research coverage for firms that were former IPO clients but failed to retain the banks for continuing services.[19]

As of October 2002, the stock market slump and economic slowdown in the United States and Europe had not yet produced a severe banking crisis. However, 27 U.S. banks and thrifts, holding combined assets of nearly $7 billion, failed during 1999–2002, a failure rate that was significantly higher than the comparable figures for 1995–98.[20] In addition, leading U.S. and European financial conglomerates—including ABN-Amro, Allianz-Dresdner, J. P. Morgan Chase, Commerzbank, Credit Suisse, Deutsche Bank, Fleet-Boston, Merrill Lynch, and Morgan Stanley—reported steep declines in earnings during 2001–02, due to problems with nonperforming loans, lower demand for investment banking services, and large losses on equity investments. Analysts warned that major banks on both continents would probably confront much higher loan default rates if their economies endured a prolonged slump, because business firms and consumers were dangerously overburdened with debt.[21] Observers also cautioned that U.S. and European economies were particularly vulnerable to a downturn in their housing markets, because consumers were relying heavily on increased home equity values to support their spending habits and offset declining shareholder wealth.[22]

Some commentators maintained that major banks did not face a significant threat in late 2002, because banks had transferred many of the risks of their lending and underwriting activities to institutional investors, including insurance companies, mutual funds, and pension funds. It is true that large banks have used risk management vehicles—including syndicated business loans, securitized consumer loans, financial derivatives, and credit derivatives—to transfer a wide variety of risks to institutional investors. However, the complex terms and/or proprietary nature of these transactions have made it much harder for regulators and the financial markets to evaluate the true risks and liabilities retained by banks. In addition, because banks are increasingly transferring their risks to other investors, analysts have questioned whether banks currently have short-term incentives for generating transactional fees that outweigh their long-term reputational interest in making prudent judgments about the creditworthiness of borrowers.

Yet another problem is that the liquidity, market value, and enforceability of risk management vehicles have been subject to sudden adverse changes during financial crises of the 1980s and 1990s. During those disruptions, many syndications, securitizations, and derivatives failed to perform as anticipated, because (a) their liquidity and market values were impaired by the actual or threatened default of either banks or their counterparties, or (b) counterparties challenged the ability of banks to enforce these arrangements because of alleged violations of disclosure duties or other legal obligations. As a consequence, some observers have argued that major banks confront serious risks that are *not* accurately reflected on their financial statements and also are *not* adequately controlled by capital rules or other supervisory requirements.[23]

FINANCIAL LIBERALIZATION AND THE GREAT DEPRESSION OF 1929–33

The Expansion of Bank Involvement in the Real Estate and Securities Markets after World War I

Prior to 1900, national banks were prohibited from making real estate loans and were also largely barred from underwriting, dealing, or investing in securities.[24] In response to changing competitive conditions, federal authorities granted significantly broader powers to national banks during the first three decades of the twentieth century. The Federal Reserve Act of 1913 permitted national banks headquartered in small cities and rural areas to make loans secured by farm land. In 1916, Congress authorized all national banks to make loans secured by any type of real estate with terms of up to one year. The McFadden Act of 1927 allowed all national banks to make real estate loans with terms of up to five years, provided such loans did not exceed 25 percent of a bank's capital and surplus or 50 percent of its time deposits.[25]

In the early 1900s, the Office of the Comptroller of the Currency (OCC) informally allowed national banks to establish bond departments, which could underwrite, sell, and invest in debt securities issued by federal, state, and local governments and corporations. The McFadden Act of 1927 ratified the legality of the OCC's policy on bond departments. The McFadden Act did not authorize national banks to underwrite, sell, or invest in corporate stocks. However, as a practical matter, this omission did not significantly restrain the securities activities of national banks. Since 1908, national banks had circumvented statutory restrictions by organizing affiliated corporations, which engaged in a full range of underwriting, selling, and dealing activities involving both bonds and stocks. Prior to the Great Depression, federal authorities did not interfere with these securities affiliates.[26]

Federal authorities expanded the real estate lending and securities powers of national banks because they wanted national banks to compete more successfully with state-chartered banks and trust companies (which enjoyed similar or greater powers under state law). Both national banks and state banks had strong incentives to enter the real estate and securities markets after World War I. Commercial banks had been the primary providers of credit to large corporations before 1920. During the 1920s, however, major corporations greatly reduced their borrowing from banks and instead turned to the securities markets for most of their external financing. Commercial banks saw the real estate and securities markets as attractive new profit sources to offset the decline in their traditional corporate lending business.[27]

Federal officials also liberalized the deposit-taking powers for national banks to give them greater parity with state banks. Prior to 1900, national banks could accept only deposits that could be withdrawn on demand. In 1903, the OCC began allowing national banks to accept time (savings) deposits so that national banks could compete more effectively with state-chartered commercial banks and mutual savings banks. The Federal Reserve Act of 1913 expressly authorized national banks and state banks that were members of the Federal Reserve System to accept time deposits. The act (as amended in 1917) also made time deposits a very attractive funding source for member banks, because it prescribed reserve requirements for time deposits that were much lower than the reserve requirements applicable to demand deposits.[28] Time deposits in national banks almost tripled during 1919–29, and time deposits increased from 34 percent of total member bank deposits in 1921 to 46 percent of such deposits in 1931.[29] The longer maturities and higher yields for time deposits encouraged banks to invest those deposits in longer-term and less liquid assets that had a higher perceived potential for earnings, such as real estate loans, loans on securities, and investments in corporate and foreign securities.[30]

In sum, the liberalization of bank powers after 1900 was fueled by (a) competition for bank charters between federal and state authorities, and (b) rivalry between the banking and securities industries. Commercial banks rapidly expanded their presence in the real estate and securities markets after 1918. Commercial banks more than tripled their real estate loans between World War I and the Great Depression. During the same period, national banks' real estate loans grew by a factor of ten. Most of this increase in real estate lending occurred in urban markets, which enjoyed boom conditions during most of the 1920s. In contrast, bank loans secured by farm land showed very little growth after 1920, due to the agricultural economy's slump after World War I.[31]

During the 1920s, commercial banks greatly expanded three types of securities-related activities. First, bank loans on securities grew from $5.2 billion to $13.0 billion during 1919–30, with the consequence that loans on securities rose from 24 percent to 38 percent of total bank loans during that period.[32] Second, banks greatly increased their investments in more risky, higher-yielding securities and shifted away from safer, lower-yielding U.S. government bonds. The total securities investments of commercial banks grew from $8.4 billion to $13.7 billion during 1921–30. Four-fifths of this growth represented additional investments in state and municipal bonds, corporate bonds, and foreign securities. As a result, the percentage of U.S. government bonds held in the securities portfolios of commercial banks declined from 35 percent to 26 percent.[33]

Third, commercial banks greatly expanded their involvement in securities underwriting during the 1920s, and they reached competitive parity with investment banks by the end of the decade. The number of commercial banks engaged in securities underwriting through bond departments or securities affiliates more than doubled, rising from 277 in 1922 to 591 in 1929. Banks and their affiliates originated 22 percent and participated in 37 percent of all bond issues in 1927. By 1929, banks and their affiliates originated 45 percent and participated in 51 percent of all bond issues.[34] The leading bank securities affiliate was National City Company (NCC), which was established in 1911 by National City Bank (NCB). By 1929, NCC had built the world's largest securities distribution network, which included more than 50 U.S. offices and sales representatives working in NCB's 89 foreign branches. NCC's market power was demonstrated by (a) its origination or participation in offerings for a fifth of all domestic and foreign bonds issued in the United States during 1921–29, and (b) its status as the largest distributor of domestic and foreign bonds issued in the United States during 1927–31. Chase established the second largest securities affiliate, Chase Securities Corp. (CSC). By acquiring Harris Forbes & Co. in 1930, CSC built a selling network that also included more than 50 domestic offices and numerous foreign locations.[35]

Large-scale entry by commercial banks into the real estate and securities markets caused a dramatic change in their balance sheets. Real estate loans and loans on securities accounted for only 30 percent of commercial bank loans in 1919 but rose to half of such loans in 1929.[36] As previously noted, the investment portfolios of commercial banks grew by more than $5 billion during the 1920s, and four-fifths of this growth was concentrated in higher-risk and less liquid securities.[37] While the primary assets of commercial banks in 1918 had been short-term, self-liquidating commercial paper and U.S. government securities, by 1929 the principal assets of commercial banks were "loans and investments whose liquidity depended on general capital values" in the securities and real estate markets.[38] The heavy reliance of banks on the health of the real estate and securities markets proved to be disastrous during the Great Depression.

The Impact of Financial Liberalization on the Asset Boom of the 1920s and the Banking Crisis of 1930–33

Senator Carter Glass, Representative Henry Steagall, and other proponents of the G-S Act were convinced that banks had played a significant role in promoting unsustainable booms in the real estate and securities markets during the 1920s. As adherents of the "real bills doctrine," Glass and his principal banking advisor, Professor H. Parker Willis, maintained that commercial banks should restrict their operations to the acceptance of demand deposits and the extension of short-term, self-liquidating loans to finance the production and sale of goods by business firms. Glass and Willis believed that these restraints on commercial bank activities would (a) maintain a basic equilibrium between prudent bank lending and legitimate business needs for credit, and (b) prevent banks from financing illiquid and speculative investments that were likely to produce a boom-and-bust cycle in the general economy.[39]

As one of the principal architects of the Federal Reserve System, Glass believed that the Federal Reserve Banks should (a) provide appropriate liquidity services to member banks by discounting short-term commercial paper, and (b) discourage speculative activities by member banks, including loans or investments that facilitated "stock gambling." By 1931, Glass and Willis concluded that the Federal Reserve System had failed to provide the liquidity needed by banks and had also been derelict in restraining speculative activities by banks. Glass and Willis therefore pushed for legislation that would prevent member banks from using the Federal Reserve discount window for speculative purposes, and would also separate commercial banks from the investment banking business.[40] In advocating such legislation, Glass, Steagall, and their supporters argued that (1) banks had made unsound loans and investments that encouraged an "overbuilt" real estate market and an "immense over-expansion of real estate values,"[41] (2) banks had made imprudent investments in securities that undermined their solvency after the stock market crashed,[42] and (3) banks had made excessive loans to finance the purchase of securities, and their affiliates had underwritten too many unsound and speculative issues, thereby contributing to the "overinvestment" in securities that jeopardized banks, investors and the general economy.[43]

Beginning in the 1980s, several prominent scholars challenged the factual premises and policy justifications for the G-S Act.[44] In adopting the GLB Act in 1999, Congress determined that the G-S Act's constraints on affiliations between banks and securities firms had become "unsuitable and outdated."[45] A comprehensive analysis of the merits and shortcomings of the G-S Act is beyond the scope of this chapter. I plan to address that topic in a future work.

For present purposes, I wish to make three points. First, bank involvement in the real estate and securities markets during the 1920s was associated with unsustainable asset booms in both markets. Second, excessive exposure to real estate loans, loans on securities, and investment securities was a major factor in many bank failures during the 1930s. Third, many of the largest and most devastating bank failures during the 1930s involved institutions that were heavily involved in either the real estate market or the securities market or both. These large bank failures had severe macroeconomic effects that compelled the federal government to undertake a massive recapitalization program through the Reconstruction Finance Corporation (RFC) and a comprehensive deposit insurance program through the FDIC.

The Contribution of Banks to Boom Conditions in the Real Estate and Securities Markets

The involvement of banks in the real estate and securities markets helped to produce spectacular booms in both sectors during the 1920s. Commercial banks more than tripled their real estate lending during the 1920s, and securities affiliates of banks also competed with investment banks in issuing mortgage bonds to investors. By 1929, outstanding debts secured by real estate included $37 billion of urban mortgages and some $6–$8 billion of mortgage bonds. Commercial banks held more than 10 percent of these obligations as assets on their balance sheets. Due to this massive influx of real estate financing, the volume of new construction activity rose from less than $4 billion in 1921 to more than $54 billion during 1922–28. Nearly $35 billion was invested in building new homes during the 1920s, and many apartments, hotels, and office buildings were also constructed. Analysts concluded that many urban real estate markets had become "overbuilt" and highly speculative by 1929.[46]

The boom in the securities markets was even more remarkable. Annual offerings of debt and equity securities by U.S. corporations nearly tripled, rising from $2.8 billion in 1920 to an average of $7.6 billion during 1927–29. Annual offerings of foreign stocks and bonds more than doubled, growing from $600 million in 1920 to an average of $1.4 billion during 1924–28. The number of shares traded annually on the New York Stock Exchange (NYSE) more than quadrupled, increasing from 230 million in 1920 to 1 billion in 1928–29.[47] Based on a widespread belief among investors that the U.S. economy had entered a "new era" of permanent economic growth, the Dow Jones Industrial Average (DJIA) skyrocketed from 64 in August 1921 to 382 in September 1929. The price-earnings ratio for the S&P Composite Index of stocks multiplied by a factor of six during the 1920s and reached 32.6 in September 1929, a record that lasted until the peak of the bull market in early 2000.[48]

Several scholars have concluded that the stock market boom produced a speculative bubble during its final, frenzied stage in 1928–29.[49] Those are the same two years during which (a) commercial banks and their affiliates accomplished the most spectacular growth in their securities underwriting and retail selling activities, and (b) securities firms responded by organizing and selling units in hundreds of investment trusts (similar to today's mutual funds) to small investors.[50]

Speculative activities during the 1920s produced a rapid buildup of consumer and business debt, which left the U.S. economy in a highly leveraged state on the eve of the Great Depression. Mortgage loans and bonds on urban real estate quadrupled to almost $40 billion by 1929, with half of that amount owed by homeowners. Consumer non-mortgage debt more than doubled to

$7.6 billion, as merchants encouraged consumers to buy cars, household appliances, and other durable goods on installment credit. Banks financed a significant portion of this growth in consumer credit by purchasing installment paper from merchant creditors.[51] Banks also provided most of the loans on securities, including broker call loans. During the 1920s, loans on securities more than doubled to $16 billion, which "represented 18 percent of the value of all listed stocks [in 1929], an enormous proportion to be held on credit."[52] U.S. corporations issued nearly $30 billion of bonds during the 1920s, increasing their total indebtedness to almost $90 billion by 1929.[53] Debt service relative to GDP reached 9 percent for the United States in 1929, compared to only 3.9 percent for Canada. This high degree of leverage in the U.S. economy—which was spurred by rosy expectations of continued economic growth—exposed consumers, business firms, banks, and institutional investors to devastating financial shocks during the Great Depression.[54]

Bank Failures Resulting from Exposure to the Real Estate and Securities Markets

Losses from real estate loans and securities investments were major causes of bank failures during 1930–33. Default rates rose rapidly for both residential and commercial mortgages and reached crisis proportions by 1931–32. Real estate values in many urban areas fell by 25–40 percent during 1929–31, and a large number of urban real estate markets were essentially frozen by 1932. Banks often could not liquidate nonperforming loans by foreclosing on them, because no buyers were available to pay any reasonable price for the underlying property. For national banks, real estate loans as a percentage of capital and surplus rose from 24 percent in 1926 to 44 percent in 1930 and 57 percent in 1932. During 1930–32, the capital funds of national banks declined from $3.9 billion to $3.1 billion. The illiquid status of defaulted real estate loans was evidently a significant factor explaining the loss of bank capital during the early 1930s.[55] Moreover, as described in the next section, several of the largest clusters of bank failures occurred in urban areas that had the heaviest concentrations of bank real estate loans and investments.

Many banks were also devastated by depreciation in their securities portfolios. The market values of corporate and foreign bonds with less than an "A" rating fell sharply during 1930–32. Investor losses on South American and Eastern European bonds were especially severe, because three-quarters of those bonds defaulted during the 1930s.[56] One analysis of closed New York state banks found that their securities portfolios had suffered an average loss in market value of 37.5 percent. Similarly, a study of closed Michigan state banks determined that depreciation in their bond portfolios (especially with regard to real estate bonds) was a primary reason for their failure.[57] During 1929–32, the percentage losses suffered by national and state member banks on their securities investments exceeded their percentage losses on loans.[58]

Smaller country banks suffered the greatest percentage losses, because they had generally invested a larger share of their funds in higher-risk securities. Some commentators blamed country bankers for their imprudence in pursuing higher yields without regard to risk. However, members of Congress and other observers condemned securities firms and securities affiliates of banks for encouraging unsophisticated country bankers to buy high-risk securities.[59]

Securities affiliates of banks did not escape the carnage. For example, the affiliates of NCB and Chase produced major losses for themselves and their sister banks. After making profits of $25 million during 1925–29, NCC incurred net losses of more than $100 million during 1930–33, including heavy losses on its equity investments. For its part, NCB held (a) $80 million of frozen "bridge loans" extended to NCC's customers in expectation of bond offerings that were never completed, and (b) several million dollars of unpaid loans obtained by NCB's officers for the purpose of buying NCB's stock. NCB recorded total losses of $170 million during 1930–34, amounting to two-thirds of its shareholders' equity at the end of 1929.[60]

Similarly, CSC wrote down its capital by $80 million during 1930–33, reflecting heavy losses on its equity investments. Chase's losses for 1930–34 exceeded $130 million, reducing its book value per share by 54 percent since the end of 1929. More than half of Chase's losses resulted from (a) loans made to the Republic of Cuba to support of CSC's Cuban underwriting activities, and (b) loans and equity investments supporting General Theatres Equipment, a bankrupt company that had been a major client of CSC. The boards of directors of NCB and Chase dismissed the executives (Charles Mitchell and Albert Wiggin) who had led the banks into the securities business, and both banks liquidated their securities affiliates in 1934. NCB and Chase survived the Great Depression, even though they suffered tremendous reputational damage and their stock prices declined more than most of their peer institutions.[61] As discussed in the next section, many of their regional competitors did not fare so well.

Major Bank Failures Related to Real Estate and Securities Activities

A comprehensive discussion of bank failures during the 1930s is beyond the scope of this article. However, the following failures or near-failures of major banking organizations can be tied to their heavy involvement in the real estate and/or securities markets:

Caldwell and Co. (CAC) established a large financial and industrial empire that included (1) a securities firm that underwrote municipal bonds, real estate bonds, and industrial revenue bonds throughout the South, (b) the largest chain of banks and the largest insurance group in the South, with combined assets of nearly $450 million, and (c) newspapers and industrial companies. In early 1930, CAC merged with BancoKentucky Co., which controlled a chain of banks with total assets of $130 million. The entire structure was financially unsound and collapsed in November 1930. CAC's demise precipitated the failures of more than 130 banks and inflicted a severe economic shock on several Southern states (including Arkansas, Kentucky, North Carolina, and Tennessee).[62]

Bank of United States (BUS), a large New York City bank with over $200 million of assets, failed in December 1930. BUS expanded rapidly during the 1920s by purchasing five other banks, and it also established a large network of real estate and securities affiliates. BUS and its real estate affiliates made large loans to real estate developers and invested in real estate bonds. BUS also made substantial loans to its officers and securities affiliates to finance trading in its stock. BUS was determined to support its stock price because of price guarantees it had issued to many shareholders. BUS failed when the real estate and stock markets slumped in 1930. While there has been scholarly debate over the macroeconomic effects of the failure of BUS, its demise probably had a significant adverse impact on public confidence in banks. A small New York bank and a medium-sized Philadelphia bank failed shortly thereafter, and the New York Clearing House was forced to defend Manufacturers Trust against a potential depositor run.[63]

In 1931 banking panics occurred in Chicago, Pittsburgh, Philadelphia, and several cities in the Cleveland district (including Akron, Toledo, and Youngstown). Most of these failures occurred because of the banks' heavy exposure to defaulted real estate loans and depreciated real estate bonds. Each panic was brought to an end by collective action (including forced mergers) organized by the leading banks in each community. For example, the First National Bank of Chicago acquired Foreman State Bank and two other threatened Chicago banks were merged together to form Central Republic Bank. Similarly, the New York Clearing House helped Manufacturers Trust to acquire the Chatham Phoenix Bank and several smaller New York City banks.[64]

In 1932, a full-scale banking panic broke out in Chicago. Central Republic Bank was faced with imminent failure after the Insull utility empire collapsed, because half of Central's capital was tied up in loans that were collateralized by Insull securities. Central's problems threatened the city's two largest banks—Continental Illinois and First National—because they had also made extensive loans secured by Insull interests and their securities affiliates had underwritten Insull debentures. Chicago banks also confronted severe real estate lending problems, as $1 billion of Chicago property was already in foreclosure. The RFC made an emergency loan of $90 million to Central, which enabled Central to transfer its deposits and offices to a newly chartered bank and liquidate its remaining assets in an orderly manner. The RFC's action effectively protected Central's depositors and thereby forestalled a likely depositor run on the other big Chicago banks. Similarly, the RFC headed off a threat to Bank of America, the largest bank in California, which was heavily burdened with nonperforming real estate loans. The RFC boosted Bank of America's liquidity by lending $90 million to the bank and its affiliated mortgage company.[65]

A nationwide banking panic was triggered by the failure of Detroit's two largest bank holding companies in February 1933. Detroit Bankers Corp. (DBC) and Guardian Detroit Union Group (Guardian) controlled four-fifths of the Detroit area's banking assets. DBC and Guardian grew rapidly by acquiring numerous banks during the 1920s, and both companies had active securities affiliates. Both companies and their banks had heavy concentrations in real estate loans, real estate bonds, and loans secured by their own stock. The severe slump in the automotive industry after 1929 devastated the Detroit economy and exposed both organizations to severe losses. The RFC tried to rescue Guardian and DBC, but its lending capacity was limited by its statutory mandate to obtain good collateral for its loans. Henry Ford refused to provide financial support for Guardian, and he threatened to pull his deposits out of DBC. Federal and state authorities therefore closed all of DBC's and Guardian's banks, and the Michigan governor declared a statewide bank holiday. The Michigan disaster rapidly spread to other states. For example, the two largest banks in Cleveland collapsed shortly after the Michigan debacle, due largely to their heavy exposure to failed corporate and real estate ventures promoted by the Eaton and Van Sweringen interests. By early March, nearly every state had imposed a general moratorium or other restrictions on deposit withdrawals. Upon his inaugural, President Franklin Roosevelt declared a nationwide bank holiday.[66]

The foregoing bank failures had a severe macroeconomic impact in two respects. First, bank failures had adverse monetary effects because (a) depositors increasingly converted their deposits into currency as major bank failures multiplied after 1930, and (b) about $7 billion of bank deposits were frozen in closed or suspended banks by 1933. Commercial bank deposits declined by over 42 percent of $18 billion during 1929–33, which depressed the nation's money supply.[67] Second, bank failures also had serious nonmonetary effects, because they (1) disrupted lender-borrower relationships; (2) discouraged surviving banks from extending loans to smaller firms, which faced much greater risks to their viability in comparison with large corporations; and (3) encouraged banks and other institutional investors to invest only in U.S. government bonds and the securities of the largest and safest corporations. In short, banks sought to survive the Great Depression by shifting from loans to safe government securities, bond spreads between highly rated firms and lower-rated firms grew to unprecedented levels and smaller firms were essentially shut out of the credit markets.[68]

It is noteworthy that thousands of small rural banks had failed during the 1920s (primarily due to the severe slump in agricultural markets after World War I), but those failures did not have a material impact on the national economy. Most studies have found that severe monetary effects (including currency hoarding) and nonmonetary effects (including widespread business failures) began with the failures of large banks that commenced in late 1930 and continued through the bank holiday of 1933 and the long resolution process that followed.[69] For a variety of reasons, the Federal Reserve Bank failed to act effectively as lender of last resort to the banking system in the early 1930s. By 1933, collective action by banks and loans by the RFC could no longer prevent a nationwide banking crisis. The federal government restored the banking system and depositor confidence only by (a) recapitalizing banks with RFC purchases of preferred stock and (b) instituting a national deposit insurance scheme.[70]

CONCLUSION

International banking crises since the 1970s and the U.S. experience during the Great Depression manifest a number of common elements. Financial deregulation encourages banks to expand their involvement in the securities and real estate markets, and it also intensifies competition between banks and nonbank financial intermediaries. As a result, financial liberalization typically increases the vulnerability of the banking system to sudden collapses in asset values. For these reasons, deregulation has been associated with boom-and-bust cycles and banking crises in many countries since the 1970s, and the same was true of the United States during the Great Depression. Systemic bank crises have serious monetary and nonmonetary effects on the general economy that are difficult and expensive to overcome. While government officials often proclaim their adherence to "market discipline" before a banking crisis occurs, the experiences of the Great Depression and more recent events have convinced most authorities that systemic banking crises cannot be left to run their course. The conventional response since the 1970s has been to take the same course that U.S. authorities adopted after 1933—namely, to recapitalize large banks and protect depositors against loss. Given the virtual certainty of massive governmental intervention when systemic banking crises occur, regulators must give greater attention to the potential long-term economic risks of financial liberalization programs.

NOTES

1. For discussion of lessons to be drawn from the apparent correlation between financial liberalization and economic crises since the early 1970s, see Ben Bernanke & Mark Gertler, "Monetary Policy and Asset Price Volatility," 84 Economic Review No. 4 (Fed. Res. Bank of K.C., MO), 4th Qtr. 1999, at 17, 17–21; Claudio Borio & Philip Lowe, "Asset Prices, Financial and Monetary Stability: Exploring the Nexus," Bank for International Settlements Working Paper No. 114, July 2002 (available at http://www.bis.org); E.P. Davis, *Debt, Financial Fragility, and Systemic Risk* 152–278 (Clarendon Press, 1992); International Monetary Fund, World Economic Outlook, May 2000: Asset Prices and the Business Cycle (available at http://www.imf.org hereinafter cited as 2000 IMF World Economic Outlook]), ch. 3; Luc Laeven, Daniela Klingebiel, & Randy Kroszner, "Financial Crises, Financial Dependence, and Industry Growth," World Bank Policy Working Paper 2855, June 2002 (available at http://econ.worldbank.org); Hal S. Scott & Philip A. Wellons, *International Finance: Transactions, Policy, and Regulation* 12–32 (Foundation Press, 8th ed. 2001).

2. For discussion of the links between deregulation, asset price booms, and crises in international financial markets since the 1970s, see, Roberto Chang & Andres Velasco, "A Model of Financial Crises in Emerging Markets," 116 *Quarterly Journal of Economics* 489 (2001); Davis, supra note 1, at 216–41, 256–73; Benton E. Gup, ed.,

International Banking Crises passim (Quorum Books: Greenwood Pub. Group, Inc. 1999); Ari Hyytinen, "The Time Profile of Risk in Banking Crises: Evidence from Scandinavian Banking Sectors," 12 *Applied Financial Economics* 613 (2002); George G. Kaufman, "Banking and Currency Crises and Systemic Risk: Lessons from Recent Events," *Economic Perspectives* (Fed. Res. Bank of Chi., IL), 3d Qtr. 2000, at 9 [hereinafter cited as Kaufman, "Banking Crises"]; Henry Kaufman, *On Money and Markets: A Wall Street Memoir* (McGraw-Hill, 2000) [hereinafter cited as Kaufman, *On Money and Markets*], at 46–83, 122–35, 242–46, 287–321; Carl-Johan Lindgren et al., *Bank Soundness and Macroeconomic Policy* passim (International Monetary Fund, 1996); Ronnie J. Phillips & Richard D. Johnson, "Regulating International Banking: Rationale, History, and Future Prospects," in Benton E. Gup, ed., *The New Financial Architecture: Banking Regulation in the 21st Century* (Quorum Books: Greenwood Pub. Group, 2000), at 1, 1–8; Arthur E. Wilmarth, Jr., "How Should We Respond to the Growing Risks of Financial Conglomerates?", in Patricia A. McCoy, ed., *Financial Modernization after Gramm-Leach-Bliley* (LexisNexis Group, 2002), at 65, 68–70, 85–90; *2000 IMF World Economic Outlook*, supra note 1, at 77–78, 91–107.

3. See Hyytinen, supra note 1, at 613, 616–17; Kaufman, "Banking Crises," supra note 1, at 11–18; Allan H. Meltzer, "Back to Bailouts," *Wall Street Journal*, Aug. 7, 2002, at A14; Arthur E. Wilmarth, Jr., "The Transformation of the U.S. Financial Services Industry, 1975–2000: Competition, Consolidation, and Increased Risks," 2002 *University of Illinois Law Review* 215 [hereinafter cited as Wilmarth, "Transformation"], at 308–11. See also Charles A.E. Goodhart, *The Central Bank and the Financial System* 350–410 (1995) (finding, based on an analysis of 104 major bank failures in international markets during 1973–93, that governmental authorities I[a] provided financial assistance or arranged mergers to rescue 73 of those banks without any loss to depositors, and [b] protected all or most of the depositors in 20 of the 31 remaining cases).

4. For discussion of Japan's "bubble economy" and its resulting financial crisis, see Alan Ahearne et al., "Preventing Deflation: Lessons from Japan's Experience in the 1990s," International Finance Discussion Paper No. 729, Bd. of Governors of Fed. Res. Sys., June 2002 (available at http://www.federalreserve.gov); Tamim Bayoumi & Charles Collyns, eds., *Post-Bubble Blues: How Japan Responded to Asset Price Collapse* passim (International Monetary Fund, 2000); Lynn E. Browne, "Does Japan Offer Any Lessons for the United States?", 2001 *New England Economic Review* No. 3 (Fed. Res. Bank of Boston, MA), at 3; Allan D. Brunner & Steven B. Kamin, "Bank Lending and Economic Activity in Japan: Did 'Financial Factors' Contribute to the Recent Downturn?", 3 *International Journal of Finance and Economics* 73 (1998); Takeo Hoshi & Anil Kashyap, "The Japanese Banking Crisis: Where Did It Come from and How Will It End?", in Ben Bernanke, ed., 1999 *NBER Macroeconomics Annual* 129; Wilmarth, "Transformation," supra note 3, at 308, 451–53. For analysis of Japan's continuing economic and financial problems in the autumn of 2002, see Ken Belson, "A Sick Banking System Resists Therapy," *New York Times*, Oct. 29, 2002, at C1; James Brooke, "Fears of a Hard Landing Rattle Tokyo," *New York Times*, Oct. 10, 2002, at W1; Akio Mikuni & R. Taggart Murphy, "Trapped in Japan's Bank Crisis," *New York Times*, Oct. 29, 2002, at A31; Adam Posen, "For Japan, It's Every Which Way but Back," *Washington Post*, Oct. 20, 2002, at B5.

5. For discussions of the causes and consequences of the banking and thrift crises of the 1980s and early 1990s, see Edward Chancellor, *Devil Take the Hindmost: A History*

of Financial Speculation 255–82 (1999); Kaufman, *On Money and Markets,* supra note 1, at 273–81, 347–49; L. William Seidman, *Full Faith and Credit: The Great S&L Debacle and Other Washington Sagas* 139–97, 229–39 (Times Books: Random House, 1993); Wilmarth, "Transformation," supra note 3, at 313–16, 327–28, 355–57, 412; Federal Deposit Insurance Corp., *History of the Eighties: Lessons for the Future* (1997), Vol. 1, at 137–88, 235–54, 291–378. For narrative descriptions of major bank failures, and for data regarding bank and thrift failures and resolution costs during 1980–94, see Federal Deposit Insurance Corp., *Managing the Crisis: The FDIC and RTC Experience* 509–704, 794–99, 807–09, 860–63 (1998).

6. In both 2000 and 2001, the foregoing nine institutions and Lehman Brothers were the top-ranked global underwriters of stocks and bonds. See "2001 Underwriting Rankings: Global Stocks and Bonds," *Wall Street Journal*, Jan. 2, 2002, at R19 (also showing that those 10 institutions accounted for 75 percent of all global underwriting proceeds in 2000–01). For a discussion of the consolidation of the U.S. banking industry and the entry of U.S. and foreign banks into the securities and insurance businesses during the 1990s, see Wilmarth, "Transformation," supra note 3, at 225–27, 250–56, 318–32, 418–21, 427–28, 438–50.

7. Emily Thornton et al., "The Breakdown in Banking," *Business Week*, Oct. 7, 2002, at 40 [hereinafter cited as Thornton et al., "Breakdown in Banking"], at 41; Wilmarth, "Transformation," supra note 3, at 326–28, 378–81, 411–12; *Securities Industry Association, 2001 Securities Industry Fact Book*, at 12, 24–25.

8. Keith Athreya, "The Growth of Unsecured Credit: Are We Better Off?," 87 *Economic Review* No. 3 (Fed. Res. Bank of Richmond, VA), at 11, 11–15; Thornton et al., "Breakdown in Banking," supra note 7, at 41; Wilmarth, "Transformation," supra note 3, at 388–90. Federal courts have held that two federal statutes—12 U.S.C. §§ 85 & 1831d—allow national banks and state banks that are insured by the Federal Deposit Insurance Corporation (FDIC) to export interest rates from any state in which they are located to borrowers residing in other states. Based on these decisions, large banks have avoided restrictive state usury laws by locating their consumer lending operations in states (e.g., Delaware and South Dakota) that are willing to attract those operations by abolishing all limitations on consumer lending rates. See *Marquette National Bank v. First of Omaha Service Corp.*, 439 U.S. 299 (1978); *Smiley v. Citibank (South Dakota), N.A.*, 517 U.S. 735 (1996); *Greenwood Trust Co. v. Massachusetts*, 971 F.2d 818 (1st Cir. 1992), *cert. denied*, 506 U.S. 1052 (1993).

9. Carrick Mollenkamp, "Credit-Card Scrutiny Hits Lenders and Threatens to Damp Spending," *Wall Street Journal*, Aug. 19, 2002, at A1; Wilmarth, "Transformation," supra note 3, at 232, 383–85, 392–96, Heather Timmons, "Surprise! The Little Guy Loses," *Business Week*, July 8, 2002, at 42; Gregory Zuckerman, "Debtor Nation: Borrowing Levels Reach a Record, Sparking Debate," *Wall Street Journal*, July 15, 2000, at C1; "Dicing with debt," *Economist*, Jan. 26, 2002, at 22.

10. Patrick Barta, "Signs of Strain: After Long Boom, Weaknesses Appear in Housing Market," *Wall Street Journal*, Oct. 3, 2002, at A1; Richard Cowden, "Large, Syndicated Loan Problems Rise," 79 BNA's *Banking Report* 599 (Oct. 14, 2002); Peter Coy et al., "Consumer Credit: A Crunch May Be Coming," *Business Week*, Aug. 12, 2002, at 32; Loretta J. Mester, "Is the Personal Bankruptcy System Bankrupt?", *Business Review* (Fed. Res. Bank of Phila., PA), 1st Qtr. 2002, at 31, 33 (Figures 1 & 2); Thornton et al., "Breakdown in Banking," supra note 7, at 41–42; Wilmarth, "Transformation," supra note 3, at 382–85, 394–98.

11. For discussion of the rapid expansion and collapse of the telecom industry during 1996–2002, see Yochi J. Dreazen, "Behind the Fiber Glut: Telecom Carriers Were Driven by Wildly Optimistic Data on Internet's Growth," *Wall Street Journal*, Sept. 26, 2002, at B1; Remarks by Alan Greenspan, Chairman of the Federal Reserve Board ("FRB"), "World Finance and Risk Management," Sept. 25, 2002 (available at http://www.federalreserve.gov [hereinafter cited as Greenspan, "Risk Management"]); Steven Pearlstein, "Fiber-Optic Overdose Racks Up Casualties," *Washington Post*, May 2, 2002, at A1; Steve Rosenbush & Heather Timmons, "Telecom Lenders: Standing in Line for What?", *Business Week*, Feb. 11, 2002, at 62; Jacob M. Schlesinger, "The Deregulators: Did Washington Help Set Stage for Current Business Turmoil?", *Wall Street Journal*, Oct. 17, 2002, at A1; Arthur E. Wilmarth, Jr., "Controlling Systemic Risk in an Era of Financial Consolidation," in Roy C. Baban, ed., *Current Developments in Monetary and Financial Law* (International Monetary Fund, 2003), Vol. 3 (forthcoming) [hereinafter cited as Wilmarth, "Systemic Risk"), Part II(C)(3)(a); *Special report: The telecoms crisis: Too many debts; too few calls, Economist*, July 20, 2002, at 59.

12. Peter Behr, Dynegy Ends Power-Trading Operations, *Washington Post*, Oct. 17, 2002, at E1; Schlesinger, supra note 11; Energy trading: Prepare to be shocked, *Economist*, May 18, 2002.

13. Anthony Bianco, "The Angry Market," *Business Week*, July 25, 2002, at 32; E.S. Browning, "Industrials Fall to 4-Year Low, Close Below 7600," *Wall Street Journal*, Oct. 1, 2002, at C1; Greenspan, "Risk Management," supra note 11; Joseph Nocera et al., "System Failure: Corporate America Has Lost Its Way," *Fortune*, June 24, 2002, at 62.

14. For example, James C. Cooper & Kathleen Madigan, "Business Outlook: Why this Recovery Feels Like a Recession," *Business Week*, Oct. 28, 2002, at 31; Craig Karman, "Stock Market Quarterly Review: Led by U.S. Tribulations, Third Quarter Held More Pain for World Markets," *Wall Street Journal*, Oct. 1, 2002, at C13; Pam Woodall, "The unfinished recession: A survey of the world economy," *Economist*, Sept. 28, 2002 (following p. 52); "Europe's tumbling stockmarkets: Feeling for the floor," *Economist*, Sept. 28, 2002, at 67.

15. See Robert J. Shiller, *Irrational Exuberance* (Princeton Univ. Press, 2000), quoting Alan Greenspan's statement that the U.S. stock market exhibited "irrational exuberance" in late 1996, id. at 3, and offering reasons for the excessive optimism of investors during the "most dramatic bull market in U.S. history," id. at 5; *Federal Reserve Board's Semiannual Monetary Policy Report to the Congress: Testimony of FRB Chairman Alan Greenspan before the Senate Committee on Banking, Housing, and Urban Affairs*, July 16, 2002 (available at http://www.federalreserve.gov), at 5 (stating that "corporate governance checks and balances" broke down during the late 1990's because "the rapid enlargement of stock market capitalizations . . . arguably engendered an outsized increase in opportunities for avarice" and thereby fostered an "infectious greed [that] seemed to grip much of our business community"). For evidence that a speculative "bubble" existed in the U.S. stock market in early 2000, which could not be justified by economic fundamentals, see Shiller, supra, at 5–16, 183–93; 2000 *IMF World Economic Outlook*, supra note 1, at 79–88, 110–12. For evidence that conflicts of interest impaired the objectivity and reliability of securities analysts, public accounting firms and credit rating agencies during the late 1990s, see, Wilmarth, "Systemic Risk," supra note 11, Part II(C)(2); "Financial Oversight of Enron: The SEC and Private-Sector

Watchdogs," Report of the Staff of the Senate Committee on Governmental Affairs, Oct. 8. 2002 [hereinafter cited as Senate Private-Sector Watchdog Report], at 26–28, 69–127.

16. For discussion of the claims described in the preceding three paragraphs, see Charles Gasparino, "New York Sues Telecom Executives over Stock Profits," *Wall Street Journal*, Oct. 1, 2002, at A1; Paula Dwyer et al., "Merrill Lynch: See No Evil?", *Business Week*, Sept. 15, 2002, at 68; Steve Rosenbush et al., "Inside the Telecom Game," *Business Week*, Aug. 5, 2002, at 34; Emily Thornton et al., "Crisis at Citi," *Business Week*, Sept. 9, 2002, at 35; Wilmarth, "Systemic Risk," supra note 11, Part III(C); Senate Private-Sector Watchdog Report, supra note 15, at 84–85.

17. Susanne Craig, "Massachusetts Claims CSFB Stock Reports Led Investors Astray," *Wall Street Journal*, Oct. 22, 2002, at C1; Burton Malkiel, "Remaking the Market: The Great Wall Street?", *Wall Street Journal*, Oct. 14, 2002, at A16; Gretchen Morgenson, "Market Place: Documents Suggest Credit Suisse Linked Banking and Stock Ratings," *New York Times*, Oct. 8, 2002, at C1; Randall Smith, "Goldman Gave Hot IPO Shares to Top Executives of Its Clients," *Wall Street Journal*, Oct. 3, 2002, at A1; Randall Smith et al., "Something Ventured and Something Gained?", *Wall Street Journal*, Oct. 17, 2002, at C1; Ben White, "CSFB E-Mails Link IPO Shares, Banking Business," *Washington Post*, Oct. 22, 2002, at E1; "Face value: Ex-friends of Frank," *Economist*, Sept. 28, 2002, at 62; Senate Private-Sector Watchdog Report, supra note 15, at 80–89.

18. For example, Gretchen Morgenson, "Banks Are Havens (And Other Myths)," *New York Times*, July 28, 2002, § 3 (Money & Bus.), at 1; Jathon Sapsford & Paul Beckett, "Loss Leader: Linking of Loans to Other Business Has Perils for Banks," *Wall Street Journal*, Sept. 19, 2002, at A1; Schlesinger, supra note 11; Thornton et al., "Breakdown in Banking," supra note 7; "Flawed Financial Giants," *Business Week*, Sept. 9, 2002, at 156 (editorial).

19. Kathleen Day, "Banks' Risky Reversal: As Industry Focuses on More Profitable Securities Business, 'Tying' Loans to Other Transactions Becomes a Hot Topic," *Washington Post*, Nov. 18, 2001, at H1; Jeffrey A. Eisenach, "The Real Telecom Scandal," *Wall Street Journal*, Sept. 30, 2002, at A16; Rosenbush et al., supra note 16; Jathan Sapsford, "Leading the News: NASD Probes Issue of Bank 'Tying'," *Wall Street Journal*, Sept. 20, 2002, at A3; Sapsford & Beckett, supra note 18; Randall Smith & Geeta Anand: "Cleaning Up Wall Street: Piper Jaffray Is Fined for Research Threat," *Wall Street Journal*, June 26, 2002, at C1; White, supra note 16.

20. Federal Deposit Ins. Corp., "Quarterly Banking Profile," 2d Qtr. 2002, at 17 (Tbl. IV-C). Compare Federal Deposit Ins. Corp., "Quarterly Banking Profile," 4th Qtr. 1998, at 17 (Tbl. IV-C) (showing that 18 banks and thrifts, with combined assets of less than $2 billion, failed during 1995–98).

21. Matthew Bishop, "Capitalism and its troubles: A survey of international finance," *Economist*, May 18, 2002 (following p. 54), at 9–11, 16–18; Vanessa Fuhrmans, "Deutsche Bank Posts Quarterly Loss," *Wall Street Journal*, Nov. 1, 2002, at A6; Anita Greil & Marcus Walker, "Credit Suisse Expects Large 3rd-Period Loss," *Wall Street Journal*, Oct. 3, 2002, at C5; John Plender, "After the Binge: The Financial System Has Avoided a Crisis over Mounting Debt but It Is Still Not in the Clear," *Financial Times* (London, U.K.), April 17, 2002, at 14; Marcus Walker, "Allianz Is Saddled with Dresdner's Woes," *Wall Street Journal*, Oct. 14, 2002, at C1; Marcus Walker & Eric Portanger, "Is the Selloff in Europe's Big Banks Justified?", *Wall Street*

Journal, Oct. 10, 2002, at C1; Wilmarth, "Systemic Risk," supra note 11, Part I(A); Wilmarth, "Transformation," supra note 3, at 378–402; Woodall, supra note 14, at 3–5, 18–28.

22. Patrick Barta, "Signs of Strain: After Long Boom, Weaknesses Appear in Housing Market," *Wall Street Journal*, Oct. 3, 2002, at A1; Shawn Tully, "Is this house worth $1.2 million?", *Fortune*, Oct. 28, 2002, at 58; "Special Report: House prices: Going through the roof," *Economist*, Mar. 30, 2002, at 59.

23. For example, Bishop, supra note 21, at 9–13, 16–18; Peter Coy et al., "Where the Risk Went," *Business Week*, Oct. 28, 2002, at 98; Kaufman, On *Money* and Markets, supra note 1, at 46–83, 122–35, 287–321, 327–49; Thornton et al., "Breakdown in Banking," supra note 7, at 41–42; Heather Timmons, "Everybody Out of the Risk Pool?", *Business Week*, Sept. 2, 2002, at 86; Wilmarth, "Transformation," supra note 3, at 316–407, 454–75. Chairman Alan Greenspan has praised financial derivatives, credit derivatives, securitization, and other risk management vehicles for accomplishing a beneficial "dispersion of risk" from banks to nonbank investors. See "World Finance and Risk Management," remarks by Chairman Greenspan at Lancaster House, London, U.K., Sept. 25, 2002, at 2–4 (available at http://www.federalreserve.gov). However, it is worth recalling that the FRB did not recognize the risks posed to global financial markets by Long-Term Capital Management (LTCM), a hedge fund which held massive and highly speculative investments in financial derivatives, until LTCM informed the FRB that it was about to collapse in 1998. Indeed, Chairman Greenspan had reassured Congress, shortly before the LTCM crisis began, that bank derivatives dealers were applying effective credit discipline to their hedge fund counterparties. See Wilmarth, "Transformation," supra note 3, at 346–50, 358–59, 370–72.

24. H. Parker Willis & John M. Chapman, *The Banking Situation* 199, 536 (Columbia Univ. Press, 1934); W. Nelson Peach, *The Securities Affiliates of National Banks* 38–51 (John Hopkins Univ. Press, 1941).

25. C. D. Bremer, *American Bank Failures* 97 (Columbia Univ. Press, 1935); Willis & Chapman, supra note 24, at 199, 585–89.

26. Peach, supra note 24, at 39–43, 50–70; Willis & Chapman, supra note 24, at 176–87, 536–37. In 1911, the solicitor general of the United States submitted an opinion to the attorney general declaring that securities affiliates were illegal under the National Bank Act. However, the attorney general did not take action based on the solicitor general's opinion. Similarly, Congress and the OCC did not take any formal steps to restrict the activities of securities affiliates of national banks until the Great Depression occurred. See Peach, supra note 24, at 143–51; Edwin J. Perkins, "The Divorce of Commercial and Investment Banking: A History," 88 *Banking Law Journal* 483, 488–96 (1971).

27. Bremer, supra note 25, at 121–22; Harold van B. Cleveland & Thomas F. Huertas, Citibank, 1812–1970, at 127–28, 140–53 (Harvard Univ. Press, 1985); Raymond W. Goldsmith, *The Changing Structure of American Banking* 55, 60–67, 72–98, 130–45 (George Routledge & Sons, Ltd., 1933); Peach, supra note 24, at 22–31, 150; Willis & Chapman, supra note 24, at 192–93, 199–200, 527–32, 546–62, 610–21.

28. Bremer, supra note 25, at 97–98; Willis & Chapman, supra note 24, at 180–81.

29. Willis & Chapman, supra note 24, at 244 (Tbl. 48) (showing that time deposits at national banks grew from $2.8 billion to $8.1 billion during 1919–29); Goldsmith, supra note 27, at 41–43 (providing data from member bank deposits).

30. Cleveland & Huertas, supra note 27, at 119–20; Goldsmith, supra note 27, at 77; Willis & Chapman, supra note 24, at 180–81, 193, 199.

31. See Goldsmith, supra note 27, at 72–78, 293 (Tbl. 6) (stating that real estate loans made by all commercial banks increased from $1.4 billion to $5.0 billion during 1919–29); Willis & Chapman, supra note 24, at 552 (Tbl. 118), 558–59, 591–602 (reporting that real estate loans made by national banks increased from $150 million to $1.6 billion during 1915–32).

32. Goldsmith, supra note 27, at 86–87, 293 (Tbl. 6).

33. Bremer, supra note 25, at 115–16 (including Tbl. 26); James S. Olson, *Saving Capitalism: The Reconstruction Finance Corporation and the New Deal, 1933–1940*, at 5 (Princeton Univ. Press, 1988); Willis & Chapman, supra note 24, at 535, 546–47.

34. Peach, supra note 24, at 83 (Tbl. I), 109 (Tbl. III), 110 (Tbl. IV). See also Vincent P. Carosso, *Investment Banking in America: A History* 279 (Harvard Univ. Press, 1970) (stating that, by 1929, banks and their securities affiliates were "equal in importance to all investment bankers in the distribution of long-term capital and in the facilities and value of their [securities underwriting] business").

35. Cleveland & Huertas, supra note 27, at 139, 140 (Tbl. 8.1), 152–53, 385 n.15; Goldsmith, supra note 27, at 137; Peach, supra note 24, at 86–97.

36. Goldsmith, supra note 27, at 293 (Tbl. 6).

37. See supra note 33 and accompanying text (discussing changes in investment portfolios of commercial banks during the 1920s); Goldsmith, supra note 27, at 298 (Tbl. 12) (showing that national banks' investments in corporate, foreign, state and local securities rose from $1.5 billion to $3.6 billion during 1919–30, while their holdings of U.S. government bonds declined from $3.2 billion to $2.8 billion).

38. Olson, supra note 33, at 5.

39. Peach, supra note 24, at 9–15, 151–61, 169, 177; Perkins, supra note 26, at 497–505, 517–25.

40. Peach, supra note 24, at 12, 151–54; Perkins, supra note 26, at 497–505. See also 75 Congressional Record ("Cong. Rec.") 9883–85 (1932) (remarks of Sen. Glass, arguing that the Federal Reserve System had failed to carry out the purposes of the Federal Reserve Act); 77 Cong. Rec. 3725 (1933) (remarks of Sen. Glass, declaring that the "main purpose" of his bill "was to prevent . . . the use of Federal Reserve facilities for stock-gambling purposes"); id. at 3835 (remarks of Rep. Steagall, stating that the bill would "call back to the service of agriculture and commerce and industry the bank credit and the bank service designed by the framers of the Federal Reserve Act," and would prevent banks from engaging in "speculation, in stock gambling, and in aid of wild and reckless international high finance").

41. Senate Report No. 77, 73d Cong., 1st Sess. (1933) (hereinafter cited as 1933 Senate Report), at 3, 7.

42. Id. at 6–7, 8, 11, 16; 77 Cong. Rec. 3835 (1933) (remarks of Rep. Steagall).

43. 1933 Senate Report, supra note 41, at 3–4, 6–7, 8–10, 16–18; 75 Cong. Rec. 9883–85 (1932) (remarks of Sen. Glass); id. at 9904–06 (remarks of Sen. Walcott); id. at 9909–13 (remarks of Sen. Bulkley); 77 Cong. Rec. 3835–36 (1933) (remarks of Rep. Steagall); id. at 3907 (remarks of Rep. Kopplemann).

44. For example, George J. Benston, *The Separation of Commercial and Investment Banking: The Glass-Steagall Act Revisited and Reconsidered* (Oxford Univ. Press, 1990); Jonathan R. Macey, "Special Interest Groups Legislation and the Judicial Function: The Dilemma of Glass-Steagall," 33 *Emory Law Journal* 1 (1984); Eugene N. White,

"Before the Glass-Steagall Act: An Analysis of the Investment Banking Activities of National Banks," 23 *Explorations in Economic History* 33 (1986) [hereinafter cited as White, "Glass-Steagall"].

45. Senate Report No. 106–44, at 3–6 (1999). See also H.R. Report No. 106–74 (Part 1), at 97–98 (1999).

46. Lester V. Chandler, *America's Greatest Depression*, 1929–41, at 16–17 (Harper & Row Publishers, 1970); Goldsmith, supra note 27, at 77–79, 105, 296 (Tbl. 10); Willis & Chapman, supra note 24, at 587–600, 608; 1933 Senate Report, 3, 7.

47. Carosso, supra note 34, at 243 (Exh. 7), 244 (Exh. 8); Ilse Mintz, *Deterioration in the Quality of Foreign Bonds Issued in the United States*, 1920–30 (National Bur. of Econ. Res. 1951), at 9 (Tbl. 1).

48. Chancellor, supra note 5, at 191–213; J.T.W. Hubbard, *For Each, the Strength of All: A History of Banking in the State of New York* 190–96 (New York Univ. Press, 1995); Shiller, supra note 15, at 8–9, 103–07.

49. See John K. Galbraith, *The Great Crash*, 1929, at 12–92 (Houghton Mifflin Co., 3d ed. 1972); J. Bradford De Long & Andrei Shleifer, "The Stock Market Bubble of 1929: Evidence from Closed-end Mutual Funds," 51 *Journal of Economic History* 675 (1991); Eugene N. White, "The Stock Market Boom and Crash of 1929 Revisited," 4 *Journal of Economic Perspectives* No. 2, Spring 1990, at 67.

50. Carosso, supra note 34, at 278–99; Galbraith, supra note 49, at 49–70; Goldsmith, supra note 27, at 130–46; Peach, supra note 24, at 89–110; 75 Congressional Record 9910, 9913 (1932) (remarks of Sen. Bulkley).

51. Chandler, supra note 46, at 8–9, 15–17, 73; Goldsmith, supra note 27, at 61–64, 72–77; Martha L. Olney, "Avoiding Default: The Role of Credit in the Consumption Collapse of 1930," 114 *Quarterly Journal of Economics* 319, 320–23 (1999).

52. Barrie Wigmore, *The Crash and Its Aftermath: A History of the Securities Markets in the United States*, 1929–33, at 27 (Greenwood Press, 1985). See also Goldsmith, supra note 27, at 297 (Tbl. 11).

53. Carosso, supra note 34, at 243 (Exh. 7); Chandler, supra note 46, at 8 (Tbl. 1–5).

54. Ben S. Bernanke, "Nonmonetary Effects of the Financial Crisis in the Propagation of the Great Depression," 73 *American Economic Review* 257 (1983) (hereinafter cited as Bernanke, "Nonmonetary Effects"), at 260–66; Charles W. Calomiris, "Financial Factors in the Great Depression," 7 *Journal of Economic Perspectives* No. 2, Spring 1993, at 61, 73–77; Chancellor, supra note 5, at 191–99, 207–11; Eugene N. White, "Banking and Finance in the Twentieth Century," in Stanley L. Engerman & Robert E. Gallman, eds *Economic History of the United States*, (Cambridge Univ. Press, 2000), Vol. 3, at 693, 752–63.

55. Chandler, supra note 46, at 73; Goldsmith, supra note 27, at 79–84; Elmus Wicker, *The Banking Panics of the Great Depression* 16 (Cambridge Univ. Press, 1996); Wigmore, supra note 52, at 228–29, 308, 317, 430–31; Willis & Chapman, supra note 24, at 126 (Tbl. 1), 598 (Tbl. 139), 599–609. See also Mintz, supra note 47, at 46–48 (describing R. J. Saulnier's study of urban mortgage lending by life insurance companies, which found that, by the end of 1934, lenders had foreclosed on 24 percent of mortgages made during 1920–24 and 41 percent of mortgages made during 1925–29).

56. Goldsmith, supra note 27, at 103–07; Mintz, supra note 47, at 8–11, 29–43, 51–52; Wigmore, supra note 52, at 287–293, 302–05, 394–417.

57. Willis & Chapman, supra note 24, at 537–40 (describing study of 34 failed New York state banks); Robert G. Rodkey, "State Bank Failures in Michigan," 7 Michigan

Business Studies 101, 101–02, 130–39 (1935–36) (presenting study of 163 failed Michigan state banks).

58. Wicker, supra note 55, at 13–14 (showing that, during 1929–32, member banks lost $6.84 for every $100 of investments, compared to $5.09 for every $100 of loans); Goldsmith, supra note 27, at 302 (Tbl. 16) (reporting that member banks reported $470 million of losses on securities during 1929–31, compared to $630 million of losses on loans).

59. Milton Friedman & Anna J. Schwartz, *A Monetary History of the United States, 1867–1960,* at 312–13, 319, 355–57 (Princeton Univ. Press, 1963); Goldsmith, supra note 27, at 105–07, 190–91; Mintz, supra note 47, at 63–86; Wicker, supra note 55, at 13–15; Wigmore, supra note 52, at 291–93, 322–23, 394–95. See also 75 Cong. Rec. 9883 (1932) (remarks of Sen. Glass, claiming that "the great banks in the money centers choked the portfolios of their correspondent banks from Maine to California with utterly worthless investment securities"); 77 Cong. Rec. 4416 (1933) (remarks of Sen. Wheeler, citing a Montana bank that failed after suffering defaults on bonds it bought from New York banks).

60. Cleveland & Huertas, supra note 27, at 159–61, 171, 191, 390 n.44, 391–92 n.4.

61. Carosso, supra note 34, at 329–35, 346–48; Cleveland & Huertas, supra note 27, at 172–88, 197–98; Goldsmith, supra note 27, at 139–42; Peach, supra note 24, at 113–39, 157–65; Wigmore, supra note 52, at 121, 173–75, 220–21, 238, 357–60, 468, 469 (Tbl. 14–6) (showing that, in 1933, the stock prices of Chase and NCB fell to 6 percent and 3 percent of their 1929 peak values).

62. Goldsmith, supra note 27, at 225–26; John B. McFerrin, *Caldwell and Company: A Southern Financial Empire* passim (Vanderbilt Univ. Press reprint, 1969); Wicker, supra note 55, at 32–36, 43–59.

63. Friedman & Schwartz, supra note 59, at 308–12; Goldsmith, supra note 27, at 227–28; Joseph L. Lucia, "The Failure of the Bank of United States: A Reappraisal," 22 *Explorations in Economic History* 402 (1985); Paul B. Trescott, "The Failure of the Bank of United States, 1930," 24 *Journal of Money, Credit, and Banking* 384 (1992); Wicker, supra note 55, at 36–59; Wigmore, supra note 52, at 223–28.

64. Goldsmith, supra note 27, at 81–84, 158–59, 163–64, 227–32; F. Cyril James, *The Growth of Chicago Banks* (Harper & Bros., 1938), Vol. 2, at 992–1006; Wicker, supra note 55, at 62–104; Wigmore, supra note 52, at 218–21.

65. Goldsmith, supra note 27, at 91, 151 n.1, 175–76, 195–200; James, supra note 64, at 1030–41; Marquis James & Bessie R. James, *Biography of a Bank: The Story of Bank of America* 313–17, 337–38, 350–54 (Harper & Bros., 1954); Wicker, supra note 55, at 112–14; Wigmore, supra note 52, at 152–54, 247, 321, 344–48, 353–54, 360.

66. Goldsmith, supra note 27, at 81–84, 91, 168–70, 235–36, 238 n.2; Olson, supra note 33, at 27–30; Wicker, supra note 55, at 116–29; Wigmore, supra note 55, at 433–45; 77 Cong. Rec. 4034–36 (1933) (remarks of Rep. Truax).

67. For example, Friedman & Schwartz, supra note 59, at 310–52; Wicker, supra note 55, at 19–23, 155–65.

68. For example, Bernanke, *Nonmonetary Effects,* supra note 54; Calomiris, supra note 54.

69. For example, Bernanke, supra note 54; Calomiris, supra note 54; Patrick J. Coe, "Financial Crisis and the Great Depression: A Regime Switching Approach," 34 *Journal of Money, Credit, and Banking* 76 (2002); Friedman & Schwartz, supra note 59, at 308–59; Goldsmith, supra note 27, at 7–8, 207–35; Wicker, supra note 55, at 5–19.

70. The RFC purchased $1.3 billion of preferred stock in more than 6,000 banks during 1933–34. By 1934, the RFC held stock in half of all U.S. banks, and RFC contributions accounted for one-third of the total equity capital of U.S. banks. The RFC also made $2 billion in loans to more than 8,000 open and closed banks during 1932–34. According to the RFC's chairman, Jesse Jones, only 20 of the banks selling preferred stock to the RFC did *not* need capital assistance. The new federal deposit insurance program effectively prevented further depositor panics and was the "structural change most conducive to monetary stability" after 1933. Friedman & Schwartz, supra note 59, at 421–42 (see id. at 427 n.4, as to Jesse Jones's remark, and id. at 434, 440–42, as to the authors' opinion regarding the benefits of federal deposit insurance). See also Olson, supra note 33, at 69–82 (describing the RFC's role in restoring the banking system after the national bank holiday of 1933).

CHAPTER 5

The Federal Home Loan Bank System and the Farm Credit System: Historic Parallels and Implications for Systemic Risk

David Nickerson and Ronnie J. Phillips

INTRODUCTION

Historically the single largest participant in domestic financial markets, the U.S. federal government currently provides a stock of nearly one trillion dollars of credit, through direct lending, subsidies, and loan guarantees, to targeted recipients.[1] Directed credit and guarantee programs have most often been undertaken in response to perceptions of adverse selection and other informational failures in debt markets, as well as in response to externalities, distributional effects, and distortions caused by other public programs. Although no rigorous measure of the net benefits of such programs has been made, the annual efficiency costs of such programs have been estimated to be over a third of U.S. gross domestic product (GDP) (Gale 1991). These cost estimates, however, have excluded costs imposed through suboptimal risk bearing by taxpayers.

Inefficient public risk bearing can occur whenever directed lending by public credit institutions is guaranteed by the federal government, without risk-adjusted pricing of the put option implicit in such a guarantee or the implementation of equivalent capital requirements. The failures and subsequent recapitalizations of the Farm Credit System (FCS) and the thrift industry in the last two decades illustrate the realized costs of government provision of such guarantees. Kaufman (1995) estimates costs to the taxpayers of these failures were at least $250 billion, even in the presence of explicit a priori limits on government guarantees for debt holders.

Despite the historical experience with the FCS and the thrift industry, Congress has recently expanded directed credit programs to mortgage markets, through the reorganization of the Federal Home Loan Bank System (FHLBS) under the Financial Institutions Reform, Recovery, and Enforcement Act of 1989 (FIRREA) and the Gramm-Leach-Bliley Act of 1999 (GLBA). Congress established the FHLBS in 1932 to increase liquidity and the volume of lending in the market for residential mortgages by serving as a lender to thrift institutions (savings and loan associations and savings banks.) Although subsequent legislation modified minor aspects of the FHLBS during the succeeding decades, FIRREA and GLBA significantly changed both the structure and the mission of the FHLBS. FIRREA extended access to FHLBS lending to commercial banks and credit unions that held at least ten percent of their assets in mortgage-related securities. GLBA subsequently eliminated this 10 percent constraint for community banks, allowed a wider variety of loans (including small business and farm loans) to serve as collateral for FHLBS loans, relaxed restrictions on the admissible portfolios of the 12 Federal Home Loan Banks (FHLBanks) comprising the FHLBS, altered capital regulations for these member Banks and encouraged the Banks to directly participate in both primary and secondary markets for mortgages. Combined with subsequent financial innovations pursued by the member institutions of the FHLBS and their ratification, without legislative review, by the FHLBS regulator, the Federal Housing Finance Board (FHFB), concern has arisen, among academics, policymakers, and the business press, over the possibility of systemic risk posed by the FHLBS to financial markets and to the liability of the federal government.

The Farm Credit System (FCS) is, like the FHLBS, an example of a government-sponsored enterprise (GSE), and is organized as a mutual system.[2] The FCS is composed of member lending institutions, the Federal Land Banks. Owing both to deregulation and unanticipated declines in the value of the agricultural mortgage loans that the Federal Land Banks held as assets, the FCS suffered severe financial distress and required recapitalization by government during the 1980s.

There are several economic parallels between the present structure of the FHLBS and that of the FCS that pertain to the solvency risk of the member institutions of each system and, conditional on the explicit and implicit guarantees offered on lending by participants in the FHLBS by the U.S. Treasury, on the efficiency costs of the systemic risk posed by the FHLBS. The purpose of this paper is to explore these parallels and to analyze whether the current structure of the FHLBS, on the basis of these parallels, poses significant systemic risk to financial markets in the United States and abroad.

The paper is organized into seven sections. The second section describes four important parallels between the historical structure of the FCS and the current structure of the FHLBS in the aftermath of the GLBA. The third section examines the economic aspects of the first of these parallels, the provision of joint and several liability for debt among the respective member institutions of the FCS and the FHLBS. The fourth section examines the second parallel, that of the capital structure and the nature of borrower equity as capital. The fifth section examines the effects of deregulating portfolio restrictions, and in particular the range of new risk-sharing agreements, such as the MPF program of the FHLBS, on the risk of the FHLBanks and the Federal Land Banks, and specifies the incentives to shareholders of the members of each System. The sixth section considers the effects of legislative restrictions on diversifying mortgage lending in geographical terms. Concluding remarks appear in the final section.

ECONOMIC PARALLELS BETWEEN THE FCS AND THE FHLBS

Four important economic parallels exist between the historical structure of the FCS and the current structure of the FHLBS:

1. *Joint and Several Liability:* The FHLBS issues system-wide debt for which each bank is jointly and severally liable, as did the FCS after 1971 and, in exactly the same manner as the FCS, operates under an implicit external guarantee of its debt provided by the U.S. government

2. *Capital Regulations:* Like the FCS, the capital structure of the FHLBS relies almost exclusively upon non-traded "borrower stock," valued at par, which circumscribes the ability of investors and regulators to assess the solvency risk of FHLBanks

3. *Portfolio Deregulation:* GLBA has relaxed portfolio restrictions for the FHLBanks, much as Congressional legislation did for the members of the FCS in the 1980s

4. *Diversification Risk:* Both the Federal Land Banks belonging to the FCS in the 1980s and the present-day FHLBanks are geographically restricted in their lending portfolio[3]

The historical parallels between the FCS and the FHLBS are not surprising when the origins of each system are considered (Irwin 1985, Freshwater 1997, and General Accounting Office 1993). Both represented a Congressional response to a perceived failure of mortgage markets to serve politically important constituencies on desirable terms.

The FCS emerged, as discussed by Hoag (1976) and Furlong and Pozdena (1985), from the concerns of Congress that the volume of credit to agriculture supplied by private financial institutions (mostly commercial banks and life insurance companies) was insufficient to satisfy, at reasonable yields, the credit demand of farmers and, because of additional contractual structure and covenants, imposed an unacceptable financial burden to mortgagors. Prior to 1916, as documented, the only available agricultural mortgages, supplied by farm mortgage brokers and life insurance companies, were three- to five-year, non-amortizing (bullet) loans, with callability provisions and substantial renewal fees (Atack and Passell 1994). The 12 Federal Land Banks, created by

Congress in the Federal Farm Loan Act of 1916, were intended to enhance liquidity in the market for agricultural mortgages by having each Land Bank lend advances to local mortgage originators. These originators were local farm credit associations, and each such association was required to belong to a Land Bank in order to receive advances, and to purchase stock in the regional Land Bank as a proportion of the advances received. Each Federal Land Bank was capitalized with $750,000 through an initial stock purchase by the U.S. Treasury. The Federal Land Banks, through their member Federal Land Bank Associations, began making loans of up to 40 years, with most between 20 and 35 years (Barry et al. 2000, 488, and Hoag 1976, 46). The Land Banks were intended to equalize rates throughout the country and thus were restricted to making loans at 6 percent and paying no more than 5 percent on the bonds they issued.

The onset of the Great Depression led to illiquidity for many banks and thrift institutions, and, ultimately, a large number of lender insolvencies. Concerned by both these losses and their implications for the availability of mortgage credit, Congress passed the 1932 Federal Home Loan Bank Act, which created 12 FHLBanks and, as their supervisory agent, the Federal Home Loan Bank Board (FHLBB). The purpose of the FHLBanks was to be an alternative source of long-term funds for the thrift institutions that specialized in residential mortgage lending. Funds for the FHLBanks came from both the issuance of debt obligations and the capital contributions of member thrifts. Subsequent legislation increased the regulatory scope of the FHLBB and enhanced the value of the FHLBS charters. In 1933, the Home Owners' Loan Act authorized the FHLBB to charter and regulate thrift institutions, and the National Housing Act of 1934 created deposit insurance for these institutions. The FHLBB could grant federal charters, as the Office of the Comptroller of the Currency (OCC) did for national banks; provide deposit insurance, as did the Federal Deposit Insurance Corporation (FDIC) for banks; and act as a lender of last resort, as did the Federal Reserve. The FHLBB, consequently, served as a single regulator for an entire industry, rather than for only some part of the division of the functions that characterize commercial banking.

The FHLBanks, like the Federal Land Banks of the FCS, historically received additional explicit and implicit advantages from their public charter. Consolidated obligations of the FHLBanks were exempt from SEC regulation and FHLBank earnings were exempt from federal, state, and local taxation, and both obligations and earnings retain this status today. The Department of the Treasury, at its option, is explicitly authorized to purchase up to $4 billion of FHLBank debt and is widely perceived to act as an implicit external guarantor of the debt of the entire FHLBS, as the government did for the FCS in the 1980s. FHLBS debt issues currently trade at yields that are just a small spread over the yields on comparable Treasuries.[4]

THE ECONOMICS OF JOINT LIABILITY

Legislation creating both the FCS and the FHLBS, as mutual organizations, maintained "joint and several liability" for debt among their respective members. This liability condition means that liabilities issued by any one member of the respective systems are the liabilities of all system members. Under certain circumstances, including liquidation, lending, and debt issuance strategies coordinated to maximize the joint value of all system members, such a provision effectively reduces investor concern about the default risk posed by the liabilities of any specific system member (Stiglitz 1990; Ghatak and Guinnane 1999).

The provision of joint liability has been a feature of the FCS since its creation in the Federal Farm Loan Act of 1916 (FFLA). Prior to the Great Depression, when the various institutions in the FCS issued their own bonds, the joint and several liability condition was imposed in the case of the insolvency of the Federal Farm Land Bank of Spokane. The other 11 banks, which were reorganized in 1927, assumed the debt of the Spokane bank, repaying its creditors, while examination and supervision standards were subsequently enhanced (O'Hara 1983, 437). Any enhancement of solvency provided by joint liability within the FCS was, however, insufficient to cope with the Great Depression. The Reconstruction Finance Corporation (RFC), a government owned corporation created under President Hoover in 1932 and capitalized with taxpayer funds, led the reform of the FCS through the creation of 12 Regional Agricultural Credit Corporations (RACCs) that made operating loans to farmers and ranchers. The passage of the Emergency Farm Credit Act and the Farm Credit Act in 1933 liquidated the private joint stock Land Banks and the RACCs, and reorganized the FCS (Hoag 1976, 232, 241; Stokes 1973, 6; Todd 1992). Joint and several liability was, however, retained for the Federal Land Banks and the regional Banks for Cooperatives.

Analogous to the FCS, the FHLBS maintains joint and several liability between the member FHLBanks. In the event of financial distress on the part of one FHLBank, the equity capital of all other FHLBanks would be legally at risk in order to satisfy outstanding debt obligations of the distressed member.[5] Also analogous to the FCS after its 1971 reorganization, debt of each FHLBank is issued through a central agent, the Federal Home Loan Banks Office of Finance. The Office of Finance is a cooperative venture by the FHLBanks, which issues debt upon individual FHLBank request.[6] The volume and nature of the debt contracts it issues is determined by individual member requests for debt issuance, rather than by a centralized strategy of collective value-maximization.[7] Debt issued by the FHLBS is commonly believed to be fully, if implicitly, guaranteed by Treasury, as evidenced by the minimal yield spread of FHLBS debt over comparable Treasury debt (Leggett and Strand 1997; Stojanovic, Vaughan, and Yeager 2001).

Risk and Incentives under Joint and Several Liability

The economic rationale for borrowers to endogenously form a group that shares joint and several liability in issuing debt is based upon a reduction in borrowing costs, owing to one or more of the following features: (1) diversification and its role in reducing the default risk perceived by debt holders; (2) delegation of monitoring, by debt holders, to peers within the group sharing joint liability, who are assumed to have superior information about the credit risk of group members than do debt holders; and (3) internalization, within the group, of benefits from asset selection and, if necessary, liquidation of members. These features at least partially mitigate the traditional incentive, on the part of shareholders in limited liability institutions, to expropriate wealth from debt holders under conditions of moral hazard.[8]

When debt holders can costlessly observe the risks generated by assets acquired by an individual borrower, the yield paid by that borrower will adjust, in an efficient market for debt, to reflect the risks of default posed to these debt holders. Under circumstances in which debt holders cannot fully ascertain this risk, owing to issues of either selection or incentives on the part of borrowers, required yields will be higher, and the volume of credit lower, than under complete information. If debt holders perceive diversification benefits in the pooling of default risk across assets held by different borrowers, then, analogous to traditional insurance, the required risk premium on debt issued under a joint liability arrangement will be lower than that required of a single borrower. When the costs of assessing the risks posed by selection or moral hazard are higher for external debt holders than for members of a group of borrowers, then mutual assumption of repayment liability by these members, with a suspension of further borrowing by any member until the debt of all is repaid, can result in the same allocation of risk to debt holders as would occur if assessment was costless, with a corresponding reduction in the yield they require to lend to the group. If, in addition, group members can coordinate their investments and exposure to risk through contracts internal to the group, then, in a symmetric equilibrium, members will each choose investment strategies that maximize the market value of their joint debt, and will also more promptly liquidate defaulting members, since joint liability allows the group to capture gains from such prompt liquidation that would, under individual debt issuance, otherwise accrue to external creditors.[9]

Joint liability also, however, imposes costs. The extension of implicit put options by one member to another, through the assumption of such liability, can increase the risk faced by each member. Since the return to each member on its investment is reduced, in expectation, by the probability of repayment of the liability of other members, it also inevitably creates an incentive for each member to free ride on either the effort or reputation of the other members. If the ability of each member to assess the risk posed by other members is imperfect or the ability of each member to sanction deviant investment behavior on the part of others is limited, then, under plausible circumstances, these adverse effects will almost surely outweigh the gains in reducing default risk obtained from pooling liability, and the required yield on group debt will increase (Che 2002). If, in addition, the group bears only partial liability for its debt, with an external guarantor extending, on favorable terms, an explicit or implicit guarantee on debt jointly issued by the group, the increase in yield required by private debt holders is reduced or eliminated, and each member enjoys an additional enhancement of his incentive to free ride and invest in riskier assets.

Joint Liability among Banks

Although analyses of joint liability almost invariably consider agrarian lending to individual farmers in developing economies, our analysis focuses on groups of banks (FHLBanks or Federal Land Banks in the FCS) in a developed economy, sharing joint liability on issues of debt to investors in efficient bond markets. The representative bank holds a portfolio of assets and liabilities, with both of these securities being in the form of debt, and the difference between these assets and liabilities serves as the equity capital of the bank. The market values of assets and liabilities are random and each will be differentially affected by various types of economic events. A representative member bank, for example, bears default risk in holding collateralized loans to individuals or corporations as assets. If some economic event reduces the value of the collateral (such as agricultural property) below the value of the balance remaining on the loan, the borrower may rationally choose to default. In this case the bank institutes foreclosure proceedings, and may also choose to pursue additional compensation through the court system under the conditions of the promissory note accompanying the original loan. If the value of the collateral has declined substantially, however, and if the wealth of the borrower was concentrated in that collateral, then the value of the asset may be substantially less than the balance of the loan. This loss to the bank in the value of its asset is exacerbated by the costs, in both money and time, of legal proceedings.[10] If a common regional or macroeconomic event causes similar declines in the value of the collateral of many borrowers of the bank, the resulting defaults and loss of asset value can cause the bank itself to become insolvent.

Investors from whom the bank borrows funds, and to whom it issues its debt liabilities, are aware of the risk posed to their own investment by such default risk on the debt assets of the bank. Relative to par, the value such investors will bid for the bank's liabilities will fall, the greater is the perceived risk of the assets held by the bank, and the higher, consequently, are the interest rates that the bank must pay in order to borrow from these investors. To the extent that investors' perceptions are unable to differentiate degrees of risk posed by different banks, they will rationally assume that bank owners will take advantage of this inability, selecting relatively risky portfolios of loans and expending less effort to monitor loan performance. Relatively less risky banks, consequently, will be unable to "signal" their prudence to investors under such circumstances, and will pay higher rates than would be economically efficient. This causes a loss to both investors and to the owners (shareholders) of the relatively less risky banks.

This poses a trade-off to the shareholders of the bank. Ownership of the bank is equivalent, in economic terms, to holding a call option on the assets of the bank (Merton 1974). Such an option increases in value as the riskiness of the portfolio of assets held by the bank increases and, consequently, bank owners experience an increase in the value of their shares as the bank selects riskier borrowers to whom to loan funds. Such increased riskiness, however, leads to the bank paying higher interest rates to investors who perceive such additional riskiness, which reduces the value of equity held by the shareholders. In addition, increased portfolio risk exposes shareholders to the potential loss of their "charter value" (Keeley 1990). These considerations may give the shareholders, acting through the bank manager, a countervailing incentive to temper asset risk by diversifying loans across classes of borrowers whose collateral values are relatively independent, in a statistical sense, from the effects of adverse economic events.

Although a single bank may be limited in the extent to which it can diversify its assets and lower the risk of default perceived by the investors to whom it issues its liabilities, the reduction achieved by diversifying liability across a set of individual banks may be much higher. This will occur if the value of the assets held by each bank in the set is relatively uncorrelated with the value of those assets held by other member banks, if the members can more easily monitor each other's investments than can debt holders, and if the investment and debt issuance strategies of the member banks can effectively be coordinated, through peer sanctions or through commitment to investment and borrowing on a system-wide basis by a centralized agency. These functions, in which the default risk posed to a lender to any individual bank is reduced by requiring that all banks in the set bear liability for repayment to this lender, are motivation for the "joint and several liability" feature of both the FCS and FHLBS. Under ideal conditions, each bank will pay lower borrowing costs to fund their acquisition of assets by belonging to such a system than by operating independently.

Financial Options and Mutual Loan Guarantees

The reduction in borrowing costs to each member of a mutually insuring system occurs through the diversification, across all members, of the default risk inherent in the assets each member holds in portfolio, and through the coordination of investment and borrowing strategies of members made possible by peer monitoring and the ability of the system to sanction a member deviating from this equilibrium.[11] The benefits of joint and several liability status of a system of banks can be examined in terms of the options a member bank receives from, and grants to, other banks in the system. When other banks assume liability for the debt issued by a specific member bank, that member bank receives a partial loan guarantee, or put option, on its liabilities from all other member banks, acting collectively through the system. This put option allows the shareholders of the specific member bank to borrow at lower cost from its own lenders. This occurs because, when the value of that specific bank's assets is lower than the value of its outstanding debt, it can "put" the balance of the repayment to other member banks, forcing them to repay its debts out of their equity capital. The specific member bank, however, must also grant or "write" an analogous put option to every other member of the system, promising its own equity capital to repay the balance of outstanding debt to other members' creditors, should those other members experience a decline in the value of their assets.

Like call options, the value of put options increases as the riskiness, or volatility, of the assets upon which they are written increase. The put option granted to each member bank in the System is written, in essence, upon the value of the assets held by that bank. This put option is value accruing to the owners of the bank, exactly in the same sense as the net present value of future portfolio returns accrues to those owners, or "residual claimants," as equity capital. The shareholders of a specific member bank will, as a consequence, have an incentive to increase the riskiness of the loans their bank makes, in order to increase the value of the put option implicit in their loan guarantee from the system, if doing so is unobserved by other member banks.

Each bank, of course, also grants such a put option to every other member of the System. To the extent that the banks collectively hold liability for their joint debt, and to the extent that the riskiness of each member's portfolio of assets can be observed or monitored by the other members, the incentives inherent in such reciprocity will lead each bank to choose a relatively moderate level of risk in the portfolio of loans it makes.[12] This moderation is enhanced, to the extent that the system as a whole, or an outside agency, can coordinate member bank decisions, such as through sanctions and peer monitoring, or by having a centralized manager or regulatory that places restrictions on the types of loans or other assets that are admissible for the members to hold.[13]

Moral Hazard and "Racing to the Bottom"

Assuming debt holders cannot readily monitor bank portfolios, then, given these characteristics of a joint liability system, prerequisites for a *moderate* level of solvency risk to be chosen by each member can be identified. The first is that the degree of risk posed to the system by the assets held by any one member bank can be observed or inferred in a timely manner by all the other members of the system, or, alternatively, by a centralized manager. The second is that the investment and debt issuance strategies of the members be coordinated, either in a decentralized fashion, as in a symmetric (Nash) equilibrium, or, alternatively, by the manager. In either case, such coordination depends, in realistic circumstances, on the feasibility of imposing sanctions on members deviating from the coordinated strategies. Diversification of asset holdings across members will, of course, further contribute to lowering the default risk of the system as a whole, which is the primary concern to debt holders.

If, however, these prerequisites are unsatisfied, the incentive to free ride created by a joint liability arrangement is likely to increase the solvency risk of the system beyond that of a single borrower, under otherwise similar circumstances. Assuming peer monitoring is costly, each member will act to increase the implicit value of its equity shares, by increasing the value of its put option or communal guarantee on the risk of its loan portfolio. If, for example, the shareholders of a specific member bank knew that the loans the bank made or purchased, such as mortgages, were relatively "opaque," and their risk imperfectly unobservable to outsiders, they would rationally perceive that they could increase the value of the put option they held, in the form of the system's guarantee of their bank's debt liabilities, without incurring a reciprocal response, or a system sanction (in the form of a regulatory response) from other members, by increasing the credit and interest rate risk of the their portfolio. If each bank perceives itself to be in this situation, the total risk of all the member bank portfolios will increase, as each attempts to take advantage of its peers in the system. Apart from a regulatory response from an external agency, such as government, the only consideration inhibiting continual increases in the asset risk selected by the shareholders of each member bank is the ultimate response by debt holders lending to the member banks as a whole. Since all the member banks must compete for funds with other financial institutions and other investment opportunities, an increase in system-wide risk perceived by external lenders to the member banks will limit the ultimate expansion in asset risk, albeit at a suboptimally high level.

This situation is exacerbated by the presence of an external guarantor. The demand by external lenders to the member banks for additional compensation, induced by the increased risk inherent in each member's portfolio, depends upon the system as a whole actually bearing liability for the total debt issued by the system. If an external guarantor of the debt grants the system a put option on this debt, and each member is not charged for its contribution to the solvency risk of the system as a whole, then external lenders will realize that the debt of each bank enjoys a more substantial guarantee than the system itself will generate. Consequently, they will lend to member banks at lower interest rates. Moreover, if the external guarantor charges each member bank a fee less than the market value of this option to each member, the shareholders of those member banks will again rationally wish the bank manager to further increase the default risk of the loans the bank extends as assets. The removal of liability for its collective debt from the members of the system will then reduce consequences of free-riding to each member, and lead to a simultaneous and possibly substantial increase in the riskiness of each member's loan portfolio, as each member "races to the bottom" in pursuing returns from assuming greater portfolio risk. This, consequently, increases the riskiness of the system as a whole. If the external guarantor is the federal government, this increase in risk is borne by taxpayers, and represents an inefficient transfer of wealth from taxpayers to the shareholders of the member banks.[14]

Historical Problems with Joint and Several Liability in the Farm Credit System

The historical experience of the FCS provides an illustration of the potential for moral hazard and increased risk-taking in a system with joint and several liability, an implicit external guarantee of system-wide debt, and an absence of transparency in regard to the issuance of debt.

Although FCS bonds were originally issued by individual Federal Farm Land Banks, Congress changed this in the 1971 Farm Credit Act. The 1971 act allowed banks to issue FCS-wide securities, ostensibly in order to improve creditor perceptions of liability and reduce issuing costs (Peoples et al. 1992, 13). These changes led, as one might predict, to a significant increase in borrowing by members of the FCS and, eventually, to a response by investors in bond markets. During the farm crisis of the 1980s, given joint and several liability, a substantial spread in yields between farm credit securities and comparable Treasury securities was observed (Freshwater 1997, 215).

Although Congress hailed the 1971 act as providing a more competitive FCS, both the capacity for moral hazard by FCS members and their attempts to restrain it through cartelization of agricultural credit was observed at the time. According to Freshwater (1997, 225):

As long as joint and several liability is in place, a fairly strong incentive to mute competition exists, but it could be overwhelmed by pressure to increase market share or maintain loan volume in a low-demand period. As a result, the FCS may soon experience its own version of the tragedy of the commons if individual banks determine their share of the exposure to losses is less than the potential gains from predation.

The explicit effect on bank risk-taking, induced by the moral hazard inherent in the FCS system, was noted, shortly after the 1971 act, by Irwin (1985, 98):

With many separate pools of capital, but with joint bank liability to protect Systemwide securities, conflict develops in trying to provide assistance to a distressed financial institution. Although capital preservation and loss sharing agreements exist, they are not always effective at ensuring continued viability of an institution. Nearly half the capital is in the form of borrower stock. The local nature of ownership leads to local resistance to such assistance. Borrowers have become especially aware that in their effort to ensure local autonomy in lending, they lack risk control on the other lenders with which they are jointly liable. This capital is also less permanent from an investor viewpoint, because loan repayments usually results in retirement of the stock.

Implications of the FCS experience after the 1971 Farm Credit Act for the FHLBS, in the aftermath of the analogous Gramm-Leach-Bliley Act in 1999 and the FHFB approval of the MPF and MPP mortgage programs in 2000, seem obvious. Three aspects of the post-GLBA FHLBS are parallel to those of the FCS after the 1971 act. First, the FHLBS is a system invoking joint and several liability on debt issued by any member. Second, a common perception exists among investors that the solvency of the FHLBS is externally guaranteed by the U.S. Treasury. Third, the FHLBS exhibits a lack of transparency about both the ability of individual FHLBanks to influence the issuance of System-wide debt and, in light of the decentralization of solvency stress testing to individual FHLBanks by the FHFB, about the individual riskiness of each of the member FHLBanks.

CAPITAL REGULATIONS FOR THE FHLBS AND THE FCS

Capital Regulations of the FHLBS

Similar to other regulated intermediaries, each FHLBank has traditionally been required to hold capital in order to protect its creditors in the event of financial distress and to protect any guarantor of its debt. Assets comprising this capital are retained earnings and non-traded equity shares. This latter asset is the primary source of capital for each FHLBank and for the FHLBS as a whole.[15]

The 1999 GLBA changed both the specific capital requirements for the FHLBanks and the nature of the equity shares that the FHLBanks could issue to their members in order to comply with these new requirements. The new capital regulations require each FHLBank to satisfy both a minimum leverage requirement and a risk-based capital requirement. Under the GLBA, the FHFB was charged with drafting the specific details of the capital requirements and with supervisory oversight in regard to their implementation by each FHLBank. The FHFB was also responsible for issuing specific regulations regarding how FHLBanks could use the new form of equity shares issuable by each FHLBank, as mandated under GLBA, to comply with the FHFB capital regulations.[16]

The leverage-based capital requirements specified by the FHFB resemble similar requirements for U.S. banks and thrifts.[17] They require the ratio of each FHLBank's capital to assets, measured in book value terms, to meet or exceed a specified minimum level. The nature of the capital used to meet this leverage requirement, in the form of the new types of equity shares to be issued by each FHLBank as mandated in GLBA, however, necessitates a relatively more complex measure of compliance than would apply to U.S. banks or thrifts. In contrast to the minimum leverage requirements, the risk-based capital requirements are explicitly based on statistical stress tests for both credit and interest rate risk, rather than the additive classifications for asset risk used, under the 1988 Basle Accord, by U.S. banks and thrifts.

Compliance with both the minimum leverage and risk-based capital requirements depend, as described in GLBA, on two new classes of non-traded equity shares issued by the FHLBs, which are respectively termed Class A and Class B shares.[18] Class A shares are specified to have a par value and issue price of $100 and to pay a dividend to holders that has priority over any dividend payments of Class B shares. Although these shares cannot publicly trade in stock markets, they are redeemable, at their par value, upon a maximum of six months written notice to the issuing FHLBank. Like Class A shares, Class B shares are unable to trade publicly, but are also redeemable at their par value, in this case at a maximum of five years written notice. Unlike Class A shares, the FHFB has proposed that FHLBanks can, at their discretion, issue Class B shares at a price higher than their par value. Class B shares can also pay a dividend to holders, subordinate to the dividend on Class A shares from the same institution.

The minimum leverage requirement for FHLBs is formulated on two alternative measures of capital: *permanent capital* and *total capital.* Permanent capital is comprised of the sum of the amounts paid in for Class B stock plus retained earnings of the FHLB. Total capital consists of permanent capital plus amounts paid in for Class A stock, plus general loss allowances.

The FHFB requirements for minimum leverage are calculated by two alternative methods. The first method requires that "weighted" permanent capital—permanent capital (the amount paid in for Class B stock plus retained earnings) multiplied by a weighting factor of 1.5—equal a minimum of 5 percent of total assets. The second method requires that total capital—permanent capital plus amounts paid in for Class A stock plus general loss allowances—equal at least 4 percent of total assets.

In contrast to its traditional formulation of the minimum-leverage requirement, the FHFB has introduced three novel features into its regulation for risk-based capital requirements. First, the risk-based capital requirement for each FHLBank will explicitly be based on a statistical stress testing procedure, rather than the Basle-type risk-based capital regulations used by U.S. bank regulators. Second, risk-based capital is to be based on both credit and interest rate risk, again in contrast to Basle-type regulations, which focus on only the former source of risk. Finally, and perhaps most importantly, the FHFB decentralized the actual design and implementation of the stress tests to each individual FHLBank, which were then to be ratified by the FHFB.[19] These tests must satisfy the legislative requirement that each FHLB must " . . . maintain 'permanent capital' . . . sufficient to meet the credit and interest rate risk to which the [FHFB] is subject, with the [measure of] risk being based on a stress test established by the Finance Board that tests for changes in certain specified market variables."[20] Issues of transparency, with respect to public information about the tests employed by individual FHLBanks, and of moral hazard, created by the ability of FHLBank members to redeem the equity shares that comprise the measures of permanent and total capital, are not explicitly addressed in FHFB regulations.

Rights of stock redemption are also an important parallel between the capital regulations of the FHLBS and that of the FCS. As with the FCS, the nature of the equity issued by the FHLBS is problematic for both FHLBS capital regulations and in the capital regulations governing each of its members. While FHLBank stock is held by each member bank or thrift, the book value of these shares is counted as capital for each FHLBank by the FHFB and, simultaneously, owing to its accounting status as an asset, also essentially counted as capital for each member bank or thrift by bank/thrift regulators (OCC/OTS/FDIC).[21]

Rights of redemption and double-counting have three immediate implications for solvency risk throughout the FHLBS. First, if an FHLBank is perceived as entering a period of financial distress, members of that FHLBank would clearly have an incentive to request redemption of their shares, and it would be politically difficult for the bank, regulators, or courts to deny such redemption on the grounds of financial exigency. Second, these members would potentially be joined by member banks and thrifts of other FHLBanks, owing to the externality borne by them through the joint and several liability feature of the FHLBS. An FHLBank can experience a "run" on its shares, consequently, just like private banks could, in the absence of deposit insurance, experience a run on their debt, and this could be contagious across the entire FHLBS. Stanton notes that the FHLBank stock "exhibits many of the characteristics of 'borrower stock' with a powerful constituency that will argue that it should be protected against losses" (1995, 33). This bears close similarity to the events in the FCS, also a cooperatively owned GSE, in the mid-1980s, as discussed below. Finally, if an FHLBank experienced actual insolvency, remaining capital on the books of that FHLBank would be depleted from each of its member banks and thrifts on a one for one basis, transferring the resulting insolvency risk directly to the FDIC.

Historical Capital Regulations of the FCS

The current capital regulations of the FHLBanks bear strong similarities to the historical capital structure of the Farm Credit System. Barry et al. (2000, 490–91) describe the ownership structure of the FCS:

The basic ownership structure of the Farm Credit System reflects cooperative principles and exhibits a tiered approach to ownership and management. The farmer/borrower/patron of a lending association acquires an ownership interest in the local association and participates in the selection of management by voting for the association's board of directors. In turn, the association either obtains its funds from or serves as a lending agent of the district Farm Credit Bank (Land Bank). As a part of the funding and ownership arrangement, the local association then acquires an ownership interest in the district Farm Credit Bank and participates in the selection of its management by voting for the bank's board of directors. Similarly, the members of co-operatives who hold stock in a Bank for Cooperates elect the board of directors of their respective banks. In general, then, the ownership interests in the FCS institutions originate from the bottom up, in contrast to the ownership structure of a multi-bank holding company, for example.

The Federal Land Banks established in 1916 were, as noted, capitalized by funds from the U.S. Treasury.[22] When farmers borrowed from the banks they were required to subscribe to one share of capital stock for each $100 borrowed. The par value of each share of stock was $5. The capital was subscribed through the local farm association, who in turn subscribed to the capital of the Federal Land Bank. The Federal Land Bank paid dividends on this stock and when the loan was paid off, the par value of the stock was paid to the farmer/borrower. This additional capital served as security for the loan, represented ownership of the local farm association, and kept the Federal Land Banks replenished with capital. The farmer/borrower was liable for twice the amount of his shares, and this clause presumably insured diligence in the operation of the association:

Shareholders of every national farm loan association shall be held individually responsible, equally and ratably, and not one for another, for all contracts, debts and engagements of such association to the extent of the amount of stock owned by them at the par value thereof, in addition to the amount paid in and represented by their shares. (Wright 1923, 66–67)

This double liability clause was eliminated in the reforms of the New Deal era.

Under the Great Depression reforms, 12 Production Credit Corporations (PCCs) were created and capitalized by Treasury funds. The purpose of the PCCs was to help organize local Production Credit Associations (PCAs) that would provide the mechanism for farmers to borrow from the PCAs and eventually own the Farm Credit System. Capital for the PCAs was in the form of either class A or class B stock. When the PCAs were organized, the PCCs subscribed to the class A stock of each PCA within its district. Additional class A stock could be sold to the public, though such sales were not typically successful. Class A stock was required to be at least 20 percent of the amount of loans made by the association. Class B stock could only be held by borrowers or people eligible to borrow from the PCA. This stock carried voting privileges, but it entitled the holder to only one vote regardless of the amount of shares owned. Class B stock could only be transferred to another farmer borrower or to an individual eligible to borrow, and then only after the transfer had been approved by the board of directors of the PCA. Further, within two years after a holder of class B stock ceased to be a borrower, the stock must be sold (to an eligible borrower) or exchanged for class A stock (American Institute of Banking 1934, 297).

The events of the Great Depression demonstrated the undercapitalization of the FCS from 1917–33. Whereas initially the capital contribution of the U.S. Treasury was $9 million, to stave off the total collapse of the FCS, Congress allocated $125 million to the banks through the RFC, but even this could not bring them anywhere near solvency (O'Hara 1983, 438).[23] The failure to adequately capitalize in the period prior to 1933 was in large part due to the cooperative associations paying dividends to their members instead of investing in the capital of the Federal Land Banks.[24]

In 1968, the FCS repaid the last of the government capital that had been part of the 1930s rescue by the Reconstruction Finance Corporation. In 1969, the Farm Credit Board appointed a commission to study the FCS and suggest possible reforms (Hoag 1976, 263). Many of the commission's suggestions were then incorporated into the Farm Credit Act of 1971. The reforms were designed to increase the profitability of the FCS and to reduce the need for future federal investment (Peoples et al. 1992, 13). As in 1916, this legislation set into place structural reforms of the FCS that were later to aggravate agricultural problems.

DEREGULATION OF PORTFOLIO RESTRICTIONS

Legislative History of the FHLBS and the THRIFT Crisis

Since its creation in 1932, the Federal Home Loan Bank System has undergone continual legislative changes in its organization and mission. In response to financial innovations by banks and other financial institutions like mutual funds, which created liquid assets that offered higher rates of return, the Depository Institutions Deregulation and Monetary Control Act (DIDMCA) of 1980 began the process of portfolio deregulation for FHLBank members. This act released several portfolio restrictions on member thrift institutions, but without taking into account the potential for interest rate risk posed to such institutions by the disparate maturities of their assets and liabilities.

A rise in interest rates in 1980–81 led to effective insolvency of many thrifts and exhausted the deposit insurance fund for this industry. Interest rates on three-month Treasury bills rose from 4 to 16 percent, and long-term rates rose from 6 to 13 percent, and eventually by 1982, 85 percent of all savings and loans were insolvent on the basis of book or market value (Kaufman 1995, 11). Regulatory forbearance and inadequate resources added to the problems so that eventually the FHLBB became a creditor for troubled institutions through the income-capital certificate program. In order to encourage the private sector to invest in thrift liabilities, FSLIC became a partner. This meant that an individual could buy into a thrift for a small investment. The Garn-St. Germain Act liberalized the investment policies of thrifts that were further liberalized in California, Texas, and Florida.

Beginning in 1982, interest rates began to decline and the staff of the FHLBB was reduced (Kane 1989, 100–101). Beginning in 1985, the FHLBB made attempts to stem the growing losses of thrift institutions, but conflicts between the regulators and the members of Congress persisted. It also became apparent that FSLIC could not cover the projected thrift losses. The debate on recapitalizing FSLIC continued through 1987 when FSLIC was declared insolvent. The Competitive Equality Banking Act provided $10.8 billion to recapitalize FSLIC and placed the "full faith and credit of the U.S. government" behind the bank and thrift insurance funds.

Resolution of the FSLIC problem fell to the Bush administration. The Financial Institutions Reform, Recovery, and Enforcement Act (FIRREA) of 1989 provided another $50 billion while at the same time ending forbearance and the liberal investment policies of thrifts.

FIRREA had several direct implications for the FHLBS. It expanded the financial institutions that were eligible for membership in the FHLBS to include all federal and state chartered thrift institutions, commercial banks, credit unions, and insurance companies that have at least 10 percent of total assets in residential mortgages loans and meet minimum regulatory standards. It abolished FSLIC and created the Savings Association Insurance Fund (SAIF) under the FDIC, which carried "prompt corrective action" provisions for the members of the FHLBanks.[25] It also created the Resolution Trust Corporation (RTC) to resolve failed thrifts and the Office of Thrift Supervision (OTS) in the Treasury Department to regulate the thrifts that survived. Finally, it required FHLBanks to finance earlier federal expenditures in the resolution of failed thrifts, through annual payments to the Resolution Funding Corporation, and to subsidize low and moderate income housing.[26]

Portfolio Deregulation in the FHLBS

Although DIDMCA and Garn-St Germain both had the effect of deregulating portfolio restrictions on members of each FHLBank, neither those acts nor FIRREA directly affected existing legislative restrictions, as embodied in the FHLB Act of 1932, on the assets eligible to be held by the FHLBanks themselves. This was, however, accomplished, by legislation, in the GLBA of 1999 and also by regulatory fiat, by the approval of the MPF and MPP mortgage programs by FHFB in 2000. To understand the implications of this deregulation, we must consider the balance sheets of the FHLBanks prior to these events.

The FHLBanks have traditionally acted as sources of short-term credit for member institutions, which primarily held portfolios of long-term residential mortgage loans, by providing those members with advances, which were short-term loans collateralized with residential mortgages held by the members.[27] Owing to their short maturity and to the collateralization provisions, advances were relatively immune to either credit or interest rate risk. These collateralization requirements included the requirement that members purchase FHLBank stock in proportion to the value of their advance, and, in addition, the FHLBank enjoyed priority status as a creditor in the event of default.[28] The relatively low risk of advances as FHLBank assets is illustrated by the historical absence of default on any FHLBank advance.[29]

The Gramm-Leach-Bliley Act (GLBA) of 1999 had several effects on the FHLBank System. First, GLBA dropped the requirement that residential mortgage loans represent at least 10 percent of assets for some member financial institutions. In particular, insurance companies and "community financial institutions," defined as institutions with federal deposit insurance with less than $500 million in average total assets over the three preceding years, are no longer bound by the requirement. Second, as detailed above, GLBA replaced previous requirements that member institutions partially collateralize their advances by purchasing FHLBank stock in proportion to their advances. GLBA expanded the permissible assets that can be used to collateralize advances from residential mortgages to small business, small farm, and agri-business loans as well. Finally, GLBA effectively deregulated the range of assets FHLBanks can hold in portfolio by allowing FHLBanks to engage in risk-sharing arrangements, through implicit swaps and puts on residential mortgages, with their member institutions.

In 2000, the FHFB, chaired by Bruce Morrison, extended the relaxation of historical portfolio restrictions on FHLBanks by its ratification of the Mortgage Partnership Finance Program (MPF), created by the Federal Home Loan Bank of Chicago, and the related Mortgage Purchase Program (MPP) of the Federal Home Loan Banks of Cincinnati, Indianapolis, and Seattle, and by its subsequent lifting of caps on mortgage holdings in FHLBank portfolios (Rehm 2000; McTague 2000). The MPF program was originally conceived as a means of arbitraging the difference in the risk weights assigned by the Basle capital regulations to loan guarantees (direct credit substitutes) versus residential mortgages held in portfolio.[30] The program allows the sponsoring FHLBank to acquire long-term, fixed interest rate residential mortgages and to hold them as assets in portfolio, while offsetting a portion of the credit risk of such mortgages through the purchase of a guarantee, on a certain portion of the potential loss from default, from the originating member.[31]

Although based on a potential comparative advantage of the mortgage originator (the member bank or thrift) in mitigating adverse selection among residential mortgage borrowers and that of the FHL Bank in mitigating interest rate and credit risk, the ultimate effect of the MPF and MPP programs is to allow the shareholders of member banks or thrifts of the sponsoring FHLBank to increase the value of their equity by having pools of residential mortgages they originate appear as assets on the balance sheets of the sponsoring FHLBank, rather than on the balance sheet of their bank or thrift, and in return to receive fees for taking second-tranche exposure to default risk on these pools. This exposure, interpreted by U.S. bank regulators as a "direct credit substitute," carries, under the Basle risk-based capital rules, a substantially lower capital charge than would retention of these mortgages in portfolio, despite a potential for substantial exposure to default risk (Office of the Comptroller of the Currency 1999). While this is a source of wealth to these shareholders, this risk-sharing arrangement also exposes each participating FHLBank to credit and interest rate risk to which it had not, prior to the FHFB ratification of the programs, been exposed. This exposure, in turn, increases the risk borne by taxpayers through the U.S. Treasury, as the implicit guarantor of FHLBS debt, and enhances the value of this guarantee to the same shareholders.[32]

Equally important in terms of the incentives of the FHLBank managers, the advent of the MPF and MPP programs, and subsequent regulatory accommodation of these programs, sets a precedent for future expansion of the range of risk-sharing agreements between FHLBanks and their member institutions, such as the current FHLBS proposal to engage in large-scale securitization of residential mortgages (Federal Home Loan Bank System 2002). Such programs serve to increase the share value of the member banks and thrifts of each FHLBank, by rearranging assets and liabilities from the balance sheets of member institutions to the balance sheet of the FHLBank, where the advantages of joint and several liability provisions and additional external debt guarantee can be optimally utilized. Each of these programs can and will be rationalized in terms of additional liquidity provided to primary mortgage lenders, in exactly the same way that deregulation of covenants on the Federal Land Banks of the FCS were rationalized after the 1971 Farm Credit Act.

Legislative History of the FCS and the Farm Credit Crisis of the Eighties

Like the FHLBS, the organization and mission of the FCS evolved substantially since its inception in 1916. This was accompanied by a simultaneous decentralization of regulatory authority and an easing of restrictions on admissible transactions by the Farm Credit Banks and other FCS members.

The major post-Depression reforms began with the Farm Credit Act of 1971. One major change was that the FCS received an updated charter that decentralized power and decision-making in the system. Many authorities and responsibilities were removed from Congress and vested in the Federal Farm

Credit Board (FFCB). In turn, many of the FFCB's powers were given to district Farm Credit Boards, and local Associations were given powers that were formerly held by district Boards. The FFCB was given additional authority to delegate to the Farm Credit Banks and to the district Farm Credit Boards (FCB). The FCBs were "given authority to delegate additional powers to the Federal Land Banks and Production Credit Associations and their boards of directors" (Hoag 1976, 268–9).

Foreshadowing the GLBA of 1999 and the FHFB regulatory waivers in 2000, the 1971 act, in addition, deregulated the FCS in the following ways:

1. it raised the loan-to-value ratio to 85 percent of appraised or current market value (as opposed to the lower "normal" value) for FCS lenders;
2. it allowed the Land Banks and PCAs to make loans to nonfarm rural home owners; and
3. in order to be eligible for a loan from the Bank for Cooperatives, it reduced the requirement for the percentage of a cooperative to be composed of farmer-members to 80 percent (in 1976, this was reduced to 70 percent).

In September 1985, the Governor of the FCS announced that the system would lose money and it might require in excess of $13 billion in government assistance (Peoples et al. 1992, 76–7). The concern on Wall Street was that the problems of allowing a GSE to fail might critically impact the housing market, where other GSEs were involved (such as Fannie Mae and Freddie Mac), as well as causing overall instability in financial markets, where the perception of a federal guarantee of FCS debt was strongly held. Treasury officials and Congress believed that failing to reassure bondholders in the case of the FCS would have a contagious impact on the housing market (Peoples et al. 1992, 77–80). Accordingly, Congress amended the act, in 1985, incorporating these features:

1. the FCA was restructured as an "arm's length" regulator with increased supervisory power;
2. the Capital Corporation was rechartered as a specialized bank to deal with non-performing loans for the entire FCS;
3. a backstop line of credit was authored to assure that financial markets would be protected in the event the FCS was unable to meet its obligations.

Additional amendments, in 1986, added the following:

1. the FCA would no longer have the authority to approve interest rates charged by System institutions;
2. FCS banks could, in certain circumstances, depart from generally accepted accounting principles (GAAP) and defer recognition of interest expenses associated with some high-coupon bonds;

3. FCS institutions could, under certain circumstances, depart from GAAP and defer recognition of required provisions for loan losses.

These legislative attempts to amend the Farm Credit Act in 1985 and 1986, nominally intended to relieve the financial distress of System members, did not resolve the farm crisis (Peoples et al. 1992, 81.) In response, Congress created a Farm Credit System Financial Assistance Corporation (FAC) in 1987 that was authorized to sell up to $4 billion in U.S. government bonds to assist FCS institutions. The FAC ultimately issued $1.26 billion in bonds (Ely 1999, 8). The 1980s legislation trimmed the FCA board, promoted consolidation within the FCS, reduced the minimum stock purchase requirement for member-borrowers from 5 percent of the amount borrowed to the lessor of 2 percent of the amount borrowed or $1,000, and created the Farm Credit Insurance Fund. The FCS went from total loans outstanding of $81.9 billion in 1983 to $50.4 billion in 1989. Its lending share dropped accordingly.

RESTRICTIONS ON GEOGRAPHICAL DIVERSIFICATION

The tension between specialization and diversification of a bank's portfolio has stretched over the entire U.S. financial history. Going back to the debates over the First Bank of the United States, there has been a strong constituency for the belief that financial institutions should serve local interests, which of course inherently restricts diversification of a loan portfolio. In the case of agriculture, the wave of failures by small banks in the Midwest that specialized in agricultural loans demonstrated that such portfolio restriction, and geographical constraints due to prohibitions on interstate banking and branching, could exacerbate financial difficulties. It was not until the Riegle-Neal Interstate Banking and Branching Act of 1994 that full interstate banking and branching was permitted in the United States (subject to any provisions that individual states might impose).

Both the FCS and the FHLBS reflect the belief that asset and geographic restrictions are desirable because they presumably assure that the institutions will serve the interests of the communities within which they are located. The cooperative nature of the ownership structure in both systems (borrowers are owners) necessarily implies geographic restriction. The problem with this structure, for regulators, is that it makes the institutions susceptible to regional economic downturns, increasing solvency risk that is either implicitly or explicitly assumed by the government. In recent years, the FCS has sought to expand these geographic restrictions in recognition of this problem and the need for the institutions of the FCS to seek a broader geographic base.

In November 1998, the FCA put forth a proposed rule to eliminate the "notice and consent" requirement on existing FCS institutions that wish to lend outside of their chartered territory. In April 2000, a final rule was published that deleted requirements for an FCS institution to provide notice to or seek consent from any other FCS institution when it buys certain participation interests in loans originated outside its chartered territory (Reyna 2000, 3–4.) Thus FCS institutions can enter into loan participations with non-System lenders, including community and commercial banks, but the notice and consent requirements for direct lending were not removed. On March 8, 2000, the FCA announced plans to remove geographic barriers by granting national charters to FCS direct lender associations that apply for them. The primary reason for removal of the geographic barriers is to allow greater diversification of FCS institutions, and through this diversification, reduce overall risks.

A lack of geographical diversification, per se, will, of course, not adversely affect an economy that is already efficient. When financial markets are complete and individual investors can "span" the relevant sources of future uncertainty with their portfolios, such investors would prefer the managers of firms, including the managers of banks and thrifts in which they hold shares, to simply maximize the value of those shares, without regard for the provision of diversification (Merton 1974). When, however, an external guarantee on the debt of a firm is provided at a cost to shareholders other than the efficient, no-arbitrage price for that guarantee, the volatility of the assets held by the firm are germane to both the value of the guarantee provided by the government and, more broadly, to overall economic efficiency.[33] If the firm in question is a Federal Land Bank or a Federal Home Loan Bank, and the manager strives to increase the value of the shares of the members of his Bank, his natural incentive is to increase the riskiness of the portfolio of assets held by his Bank, increasing the value of the put option that represents the guarantee on his Bank's liabilities. The guarantor, in this case the U.S. Treasury, has diametrically opposed interests to that of these shareholders, and will strive to create regulatory incentives for the Bank manager to reduce the riskiness of the Bank's portfolio. Geographical restrictions on diversification restrict the regulator's ability to accomplish this, while simultaneously reducing the benefits of competition to regional mortgage borrowers.[34]

CONCLUDING REMARKS

The FHLBS was created during the Great Depression, with a mission of enhancing liquidity for residential mortgage lenders by providing a ready source of advances to members of each FHLBank. The FCS was created two decades earlier, but with an analogous mission. In both cases, the economic rationale for the creation of a public system of banks was founded on a perceived failure in mortgage markets, resulting in a lack of capital despite the potential existence of efficient lending opportunities. Both systems shared several features during their respective histories, including the provision of joint liability, a lack of transparency regarding the individual portfolios of their members, a mutual ownership structure relying upon non-traded borrower stock for capital, and an implicit or explicit external guarantee on system debt, provided by the federal government to the shareholders/owners of members of the institutions comprising each system.

Both systems also experienced legislative deregulation of restrictions on the type of assets held by their members, and of their ownership structure. Less than a decade after a major deregulation of the FCS, the 1971 Farm Credit Act, the FCS experienced substantial financial distress and a substantial government recapitalization and reorganization of the FCS was carried out. Concern has arisen over a similar fate, on the basis of this historical experience, for the FHLBS, following their analogous deregulation by legislation, in the 1999 Gramm-Leach-Bliley Act, and by regulatory fiat, in the 2000 ratification of the MPF and MPP mortgage programs by the FHFB.

Several decades after their respective foundings, the economic rationale for the maintenance of either the FCS or the FHLBS, in terms of a failure of capital markets to provide sufficient liquidity to mortgage lenders, is very difficult to accept. Financial markets are integrated globally, investors have access to pricing data for fixed-income securities of all types, and extensive credit histories and other information have diminished problems of adverse selection in both primary and secondary mortgage markets.

Arguments that an expanded role for the FHLBS would provide additional competition in secondary mortgage markets also appear largely specious. The very nature of lending networks in an intermediated market implies that economic efficiency is attained not by additional entry, which, in the presence of fixed costs, is socially wasteful, but rather by increasing the number of participants both borrowing from and lending to each other through the incumbent intermediaries (Glosten and Milgrom 1985; Stahl 1988).

While the two systems may not enhance economic efficiency, they do continue to contribute to the overall risk the public bears, through the perceived or real guarantee that the U.S. Treasury extends to the collective debt of both systems. This is an inefficient transfer of wealth from taxpayers to the shareholders/owners of the institutions belonging to the respective member banks of the FCS and the FHLBS. Unless such a guarantee is priced efficiently, this cost will be borne by taxpayers regardless of whether an actual bailout occurs.

Based on the historical parallels between the features of the FCS and the FHLBS, four specific areas of concern exist regarding the potential for the FHLBS to destabilize U.S. and international financial markets and to necessitate recapitalization by Treasury. These are (1) joint and several liability; (2) the nature of capital regulations for the FHLBanks; (3) legislative deregulation of portfolio restrictions on the FHLBanks; and (4) restrictions on the ability of FHLBanks to diversify their portfolios and on members of each FHLBank to diversify across different Banks.

Joint and several liability of the FHLBanks is problematic in the presence of an external guarantee on their collective debt, an ability of each FHLBank to influence the issuance of new debt, and an absence of transparency about the solvency risk of each FHLBank, both to external investors and to other FHLBanks. The scope for moral hazard on the part of each FHLBank will inevitably increase the incentives for each Bank to increase value to the shareholders of their members by increasing the riskiness of their portfolios. Capital regulations required by GLBA and implemented by the FHFB fail entirely to address the issue of transparency, while simultaneously increasing the externality created by joint liability by specifying redeemable stock as the primary form of capital held by each FHLBank. Relaxation of the restrictions on the portfolios of the FHLBanks, which have given rise to innovations such as the MPF and MPP programs, exacerbate the scope for moral hazard by allowing the FHLBanks to hold increasingly risky assets. Finally, restrictions on the ability of individual FHLBanks to geographically diversify their holdings of risky mortgages will, in a second-best environment, diminish economic efficiency, through both restricting the regulatory incentives to diminish portfolio risk and by reducing competition among the extant FHLBanks.

NOTES

1. Based on data from the Budget of the United States Government (1996–2000), direct lending programs, which have traditionally focused on agricultural, small business, and rural sectors, had 170 billion dollars of credit outstanding at the end of 1999, while primary and secondary loan guarantees and other forms of subsidies to private lenders, which primarily target housing markets and agricultural borrowers, have doubled, in real terms, since 1970, with a 1999 stock of over 800 billion dollars in primary guaranteed loans. Gale (1990) and Li (1998) survey federal credit programs in the United States.

2. The FHLBS is not itself a mutual system, but rather is composed of FHLBanks which are themselves mutuals.

3. Diversification through membership of a single bank or thrift in multiple FHLBanks is currently being reviewed by the Federal Housing Finance Board, primarily in response to the petition of the Federal Home Loan Bank of Dallas on behalf of the single largest thrift, Washington Mutual Bank FA, currently a member of the San Francisco Federal Home Loan Bank. See Federal Housing Finance Board, http://www.fhfb.gov/PressRoom/Rules/WAMU.htm.

4. See "Federal Home Loan Bank System Overview," FHLBanks Office of Finance, http://www.fhlb-of.com/about/introduction.htm. ("All debt securities issued by the FHLBank System carry the highest credit ratings awarded by both Standard & Poor's and Moody's rating services: AAA/Aaa and A-1/P-1.") Given the extraordinary degree of leverage exhibited by the FHLBanks, this is prima facie evidence of a market perception of a government guarantee on FHLBS debt. Stojanovic, Vaughan, and Yeager (2000, 2001) discuss FHLBS yield spreads, subsidies and the increased risk posed to the FDIC by FIRREA and GLBA liberalization of criteria for FHLBank membership.

5. See Federal Housing Finance Board, CFR Part 910, Allocation of Joint and

Several Liability on Consolidated Obligations among the Federal Home Loan Banks (available from http://www.fhfb.gov/PressRoom/press/PR99–23.htm).

6. Centralized debt issuance is useful to partially mitigate moral hazard implicit in a joint and several liability system, but only if the timing and volume of debt issued serve to maximize the value of the system as a whole, and members of the system cannot extensively influence the debt issued on an individual or discretionary basis. These conditions are not satisfied by the FHLBS. Debt instruments issued by the FHLB Finance Office include short term discount notes, zero-coupon (TAP) bonds and coupon-bearing bonds (including bonds with both put and call provisions as well as bonds denominated in foreign currencies, issued under the FHLBS Global Debt Program), and so-called master notes with adjustable yields. See http://www.fhlb-of.com/about/ for a description of system debt issuance and brief descriptions of each of these bond categories.

7. Individual FHLBanks retain full control of both their investment and debt strategies, despite the adverse implications this has under joint debt liability. Pollock (2001) points out, as an example, that the Federal Home Loan Bank of San Francisco follows a policy of extreme concentration in its asset holdings, with over 80 percent of its loans to only three members, and other FHLBanks are powerless to influence this portfolio strategy.

8. Ghatak and Guinnane (1999) survey, in detail, the economic rationales for joint liability contracts, including (1) adverse selection (Ghatak 2000, Armendariz de Aghion and Gollier 2000, and Gangopadhyay and Lensink 2001), (2) moral hazard (Stiglitz 1990; Varian 1990; Banerjee, Besley, and Guinnane (1994); and Conning 2000), and (3) collateral and contract enforcement (Besley and Coate 1995). Selection of group members with similar risk characteristics, in the first case, and peer monitoring and peer sanctions, in the latter two cases, play crucial roles in assessing the net benefits of joint liability schemes.

9. Virtually all models of debt issuance under joint liability assume that group members can contract with each other, under conditions of complete information, to coordinate their selection of investments and effort in generating returns on those investments, and can costlessly sanction members deviating from the selection and effort strategies in those contracts. Che (2002) shows that relaxation of this assumption generally leads to the inefficiencies associated with externalities between members outweighing the efficiency gains from lower probabilities of default, except in the limiting case of infinitely repeated play among group members.

10. Banks also bear risk to the value of their equity capital posed by fluctuations in short- and long-term interest rates. If the respective loans comprising assets and liabilities feature coupon payments or other cash flows at disparate frequencies, interest rate movements can cause assets to decline in value more than do liabilities. Such movements can, in extreme circumstances, reduce equity capital to zero, leading to default. This source of risk is not easily diversifiable across member banks in the same economy, however, and both the Federal Land Banks and the FHLBanks have historically exhibited periods of serious duration and convexity mismatch in their portfolios.

11. Mutual systems may, under certain circumstances, also be relatively efficient, even when the flow of information among members is imperfect, as long as the investment strategies of members are effectively coordinated through a centralized manager. If members of a mutual system differ in their inherent probability of defaulting

on their liabilities, the relatively low-risk members may be able to "signal" their status to the manager of the mutual system, relative to their higher-risk peers, by sharing risk with the system as a whole. One method of signaling would be to accept less of a reduction in the cost of borrowing funds and to simultaneously contract to receive shares of ownership in the system which specified periodic payments of dividends that varied across adverse economic events that posed risk to the system as a whole. A relatively low-risk member might usefully communicate that status by accepting such dividend payments when the system has jointly suffered an adverse event that has reduced the total value of its assets. Although inapplicable to the FHLBS, which invokes joint liability over individualized debt issuance but which lacks centralized management and is not a true mutual ownership system, Smith and Stutzer (1990), building on the adverse selection models of Besanko and Thakor (1987, "Competitive Equilibrium"; 1987, "Collateral and Rationing"), Smith and Stutzer (1989), and Azariadis and Smith (1989), use this signaling capability to explain the mutual ownership nature of Federal Land Banks in the FCS. The incentives facing each shareholder of a Federal Land Bank or FHLBank, in his role as both shareholder and borrower from that bank, and the incentives he has in his role as a shareholder in the FCS or FHLBS as a whole, however, will differ, since the member bank in which he holds shares does not borrow from other banks in the System, but rather from external creditors/investors, and to the extent that the bank in which he owns shares can place a greater extent of liability for debt repayment on other banks in the system, or on an outside guarantor, such as the U.S. Treasury.

12. This situation can be analytically modeled, as described in Nickerson and Phillips (2002), as the Nash equilibrium of the game played between member banks, in which the strategy of each bank is to select a level of effort or risk (represented, for example, by a mean-preserving spread) in its portfolio of assets, and in which the equity value of the FHLBank depends on the expected value of its assets, priced in an efficient economy (that is, one possessing a unique equivalent martingale measure), the value of its own liabilities, and the put options it respectively holds on, and has written for, all the other members of the FHLBS.

13. Such restrictions were enforced in the FCS until 1971 and in the FHLBS, which historically held most assets in the form of heavily collateralized short-term advances to member banks, until many portfolio restrictions were legislatively loosened by GLBA in 1999 and the Federal Housing Finance Board, under the leadership of Bruce Morrison, granted regulatory approval in 2000 to the Mortgage Partnership Finance program, initiated by the Federal Home Loan Bank of Chicago, and the related Mortgage Partnership Programs of the Federal Home Loan Banks of Seattle and Indianapolis, which generate revenue for FHLBanks through retention of interest rate and residual credit risk in portfolios of residential mortgages. Such so-called Acquired Member Asset (AMA) programs, which may soon include securitization of residential mortgages (Miller et al. 2002), provide examples of new and potentially risky assets for each FHLBank.

14. The inefficiency created by moral hazard and an external guarantee cannot be offset by risk-based capital regulations, as shown by Hellman, Murdock, and Stiglitz (2000). Van Order (2000) discusses capital regulations and subsidy issues for GSEs.

15. Retained earnings in the FHLBank System are a small source of capital. For example, there was $30.6 billion of FHLBank stock, which equals 4.8 percent of the total assets of the FHLBanks, on 30 September 2000, while, on the same date, there

was $0.7 billion of retained earnings, which equals 0.11 percent of total assets. See FHLBank Office of Finance, http://www.fhlb-of.com/financial/. This primary role of FHLB equity raises measurement difficulties in comparing the capital of FHLBs with other GSEs, as well as with banks and other intermediaries. Member financial institutions of each FHLBank own the stock of that FHLBank and the capital stock of the FHLBanks is an asset on the books of the member financial institutions. FHLB equity is, consequently, double counted, once as capital for the FHLBanks and once as capital for the member financial institutions, as discussed below.

16. A useful summary of both the new types of equity issuable by FHLBanks and their role in complying with FHFB capital regulations appears at http://www.fhfb.gov/ PressRoom/press/capfacsheet.htm. Historically, institutions belonging to an FHLBank were required to purchase stock valued at 5 percent of their total level of FHLBank advances or one percent of their total mortgage assets, whichever was greater. This "subscription" system paralleled that of the Federal Land Banks in the FCS and, given the relatively narrow class of assets legally held by each FHLBank prior to GLBA, resulted in both substantial capitalization of each FHLBank and, in combination with mandated payments to the REFCorp, AHP, and CIP programs of the Federal Home Loan System, a lower value of membership accruing to shareholders of each institution belonging to an FHLBank. The GLBA mandates that shares purchased under this subscription system be replaced with new Class A or Class B shares issued by the FHBanks. See http://www.fhfb.gov/ for details of this redemption plan.

17. Further details of these new capital requirements appear in the FHFB publication, "Capital Requirements for Federal Home Loan Banks: Final Rule," *Federal Register* 66 FR 8262, issued on 30 January 2001, and are summarized at http:// www.fhfb.gov/PressRoom/press/OF-QandAs.htm.

18. The specific FHFB specification of the Class A and Class B shares mandated by GLBA, which replace the previous "subscription shares" held by member banks and thrifts of each FHLBank, can be found at http://www.fhfb.gov/PressRoom/press/cap-facsheet.htm, page 2. Under current FHFB regulations, an FHLBank can issue either, or both, types of equity shares. In addition, an FHLBank has discretion over the issue price of a Class B share, relative to the par value at which the share can be redeemed.

19. After the issuance of the Final rule on 30 January 2001, individual FHFBs had 270 days to submit their capital plans to the FHFB for approval, and three additional years to satisfy compliance requirements. Although all FHLBank capital plans were approved by September 2002, after public hearings, it is interesting to note that FHFB, during the drafting of its capital regulations, had only one staff member with expertise (doctoral training or research publications) in quantitative finance, and, since mid-2001, has had none to provide internal expertise on the plans submitted during the ratification period.

20. "Capital Requirements for Federal Home Loan Banks: Final Rule," *Federal Register*, 66 FR 8262 (30 January 2001) at 8264. This rule does not, however, mandate transparency by requiring either the FHFB or the Finance Board to make public the structure of the FHFB's internal test, nor does it address the potential for systemic risk created by the incentives of individual FHFB members to redeem their stock, withdrawing capital from the FHFB and from the System as a whole. The option of members to redeem their stock at par is a feature of the FHLB System that differentiates it from the other GSEs and from banks, and, in the presence of asymmetric information, will directly affect the overall risk posed by the FHLBs to international financial markets.

21. Currently, OTS and OCC regulations grant a risk-weight of only 20 percent to respective thrift and bank holding of FHLBank shares and, under the Basle RBC guidelines adopted by both regulatory agencies, thrifts and banks need hold only 8 percent of the book value of their "risk-adjusted assets" in capital. A thrift or bank then, consequently, needs to hold only 1.6 percent of the par value of a share of FHLBank Class A or B stock in equity on their balance sheet.

22. The capital structure of the Federal Intermediate Credit Banks (FICB) was also initially provided by the Treasury, as was the capital for the Banks for Cooperatives (BC). The FICBs then made loans to the PCAs and the BCs made loans to local farmer cooperatives. In 1956, the process of merging the PCAs and FICBs began and was completed by 1968 when both became fully farmer/borrower owned (Hoag 1976, p. 28).

23. By Executive Order of 27 March 1933, President Franklin Roosevelt changed the name of the Federal Farm Board to the Farm Credit Administration (FCA). The agency retained its statutory mandate to make loans to farm cooperatives and all existing federal agricultural credit organizations were consolidated under the FCA. Major overhaul of the farm credit system was achieved by the passage of the Farm Credit Act passed 16 June 1933. The act established the FCA as an independent government agency.

24. Currently, the FHLBanks pay out dividends at a very high rate (over 7 percent) but keep retained earnings, part of capital, at a very low rate.

25. Notably, GLBA and the Federal Housing Finance Board Regulations for the year 2000 are silent on this provision for the FHLBanks themselves: FHFB regulations do not provide for any "prompt corrective actions" by the FHFB nor, given the current size of the agency, is this practical.

26. LBA amended FIRREA by replacing the annual REFCorp payment from $300 million to 20 percent of each FHLBank's net earnings, and, in this way, shifted costs from the FHLBanks to taxpayers through the put option implicit in this risk-sharing arrangement. See "Capital Requirements for Federal Home Loan Banks: Proposed Rule," *Federal Register*, Vol. 65, No. 135 (13 July 2000) at 43434. The channel of FHLBanks subsidies to affordable housing are through two programs, Affordable Housing Program and the Community Investment Program, details of which can be found at http://www.fhfb.gov/FHLBProg/FHLBP_housing_affordable.htm.

27. Approximately $438 billion in advances were outstanding by the end of 2000, with 58.2 percent of the advances being lent to thrifts, and 39.3 percent to commercial banks.

28. More specifically, an FHLBank claim as a creditor had legal priority over every other claim, including those of the FDIC, which substantially exacerbates the moral hazard problem faced by the FDIC and the risk exposure of its insurance funds. Stojanovic, Vaughan, and Yeager (2000) discuss the implications of this priority rule for the FDIC.

29. Documentation of this repayment history can be found at the FHLBank Office of Finance, "Financial Information," http://www.fhlb-of.com/financial/. Although originally intended to provide a source of liquidity to solvent primary mortgage lenders, the provision of advances has not been unequivocally beneficial in an economic sense: in the presence of book-value accounting by thrifts and regulatory forbearance by the FHLBB, the ability of near-insolvent thrifts to obtain funding from the FHLBank System made the savings and loan crisis worse and increased the losses inflicted on taxpayers through the deposit insurance system.

30. The dependence of the profitability of the MPF program on this arbitraging of the Basle capital regulations for banks and thrifts was explicitly recognized by U.S. regulators at the time of its proposal by the Federal Home Loan Bank of Chicago: see Nickerson (1998).

31. Essentially, the sponsoring FHLBank advances funds to a participating member bank or thrift, which then originates a pool of residential mortgages. The shareholders of the member bank or thrift can increase their equity value by avoiding the high risk weight charged on the mortgages, by swapping them for an origination fee and the "credit enhancement" fee received from writing a put option to the sponsoring Federal Home Loan Bank. This put obligates the bank or thrift to assume a portion of the default losses on the mortgage pool over a threshold level. The put option or "direct credit substitute" carries only a 20 percent risk-based capital charge under the 1988 Basle regulations, as opposed to a 50 percent charge on a first-lien residential conforming mortgage.

32. That is, it transfers wealth directly from taxpayers to the shareholders of the member banks or thrifts, since these shareholders do not pay a price for this guarantee commensurate with the risk their institution, through the FHLBank to which it belongs, poses to the FHLBS as a whole.

33. Although Merton (1977) was the first to analytically model the value of the put option implicit in loan guarantees and deposit insurance, Keeley (1990) points out that the charter value of a bank or other financial intermediary, reflecting the current value of intermediation services under restrictions on entry, can attenuate the incentives of bank shareholders to maximize the value of the call and put options embedded in their equity ownership of a firm enjoying a mispriced loan guarantee on its liabilities. Consequently, the issue of diversification may be of direct importance to shareholders and to overall economic efficiency through more than the value of the government loan guarantee: shareholders may wish bank managers to diversify their loan portfolios to preserve the bank charter value against unanticipated insolvency and the solvency of the bank may be important in terms of its role as a delegated monitor (Diamond 1984) and the externalities implicit in informationally intensive lending. See Freixas and Rochet (1997) for a survey of this latter issue.

34. The MPF and MPP programs have the potential to create some degree of geographical diversification in FHLBank portfolios, since an FHLBank can retain mortgages originated anywhere in the United States under either of these programs. Of all FHLBanks, only the Federal Home Loan Bank of Chicago, however, has purchased a geographically diverse set of mortgages

REFERENCES

American Institute of Banking. *Farm Credit Administration*. Washington, D.C.: American Bankers Association, 1934.

Armendariz de Aghion, B., and Christian Gollier. 2000. "Peer Monitoring in an Adverse Selection Model," *Economic Journal* 110 (2), 632–43.

Atack, Jeremy, and Peter Passell. 1994. *A New Economic View of American History from Colonial Times to 1940*. 2d ed. New York: W.W. Norton & Company.

Azariadis, C., and B. Smith. 1989. "Adverse Selection in the Overlapping Generation Model." Working paper, Economics Department, University of Western Ontario.

Banerjee, A., Timothy Besley, and Timothy Guinnane. 1994. "Thy Neighbor's Keeper: The Design of a Credit Cooperative with Theory and a Test." *Quarterly Journal of Economics* 109 (2), 491–515.

Barry, P., and J. Brake. 1990. "Competition within the Farm Credit System: Concepts and Options." Unpublished study prepared for the Farm Credit Administration.

Barry, Peter J., Paul N. Ellinger, C. B. Baker, and John A. Hopkin. 2000. *Financial Management in Agriculture*. 6th ed. Danville, Ill.: Interstate Publishers, Inc.

Barth, James. 1991. *The Great Savings and Loan Debacle*. Washington, D.C.: American Enterprise Institute.

Bartholomew, Philip F. 1990. *Reforming Federal Deposit Insurance*. Congressional Budget Office, Washington, D.C., September.

Bartholomew, Philip F. 1993. *Resolving the Thrift Crisis*. Congressional Budget Office, Washington, D.C., April.

Bartholomew, Philip F., and Gary Whalen. 1995. "Fundamentals of Systemic Risk." In *Research in Financial Services*, edited by George G. Kaufman. Vol. 7, pp. 3–17.

Benjamin, Gary L. 1985. "An Overview of Financial Stress in Agriculture." *Proceedings of a Conference on Bank Structure and Competition*. Federal Reserve Bank of Chicago, 72–92.

Besanko, David, and Anjan Thakor. 1987. "Collateral and Rationing: Sorting Equilibria in Monopolistic and Competitive Credit Markets." *International Economic Review* 28, 671–89.

Besanko, David, and Anjan Thakor. 1987. "Competitive Equilibrium in the Credit Market under Asymmetric Information." *Journal of Economic Theory* 42, 167–82.

Besley, Timothy, and Stephen Coate. 1995. "Group Lending, Repayment Incentives and Social Collateral." *Journal of Development Economics* 46 (1), 1–18.

Boehlje, Michael D. 1985. "Agricultural Policy and Financial Stress." *Proceedings of a Conference on Bank Structure and Competition*. Federal Reserve Bank of Chicago, 120–45.

Brenton, C. Robert. 1985. "A Rural Banker's Viewpoint." *Proceedings of a Conference on Bank Structure and Competition*. Federal Reserve Bank of Chicago, 146–49.

Che, Yeon-Koo. 2002. "Joint Liability and Peer Monitoring under Group Lending." *Contributions to Theoretical Economics* 2 (1), 1–26. Available from http://www.bepress.com/bejte; INTERNET.

Conning, Jonathan. 2000. "Monitoring by Delegates or by Peers? Joint Liability Loans under Moral Hazard." Williams College, Williamstown, Mass.

Cotterman, Robert, and James Pearce. 1996. "The Effects of the Federal National Mortgage Association and the Federal Home Loan Mortgage Corporation on Conventional Fixed-Rate Mortgage Yields." In *Studies on Privatizing Fannie Mae and Freddie Mac*, U.S. Department of Housing and Urban Development, Office of Policy Development and Research, May, 97–168.

Diamond, Douglas. 1984. "Financial Intermediation and Delegated Monitoring." *Review of Economic Studies* 51 (3), July, 393–414.

Ely, Bert. 1999. *The Farm Credit System: Reckless Past, Doubtful Future*. Alexandria, Va.: Ely & Company, Inc.

Federal Home Loan Bank System. 2002. *AMA Securitization Feasibility Study*. Presented at FHLBS Bank President's Conference, 10 September.

"Federal Home Loan Bank System Overview." In FHLBanks Office of Finance. Available from http://www.fhlb-of.com/about/introduction.htm; INTERNET.

Federal Housing Finance Board. 2001. "Capital Requirements for Federal Home Loan Banks: Final Rule." *Federal Register* 66, FR 8262. 30 January.

Freixas, X., and J. C. Rochet. 1997. *Microeconomics of Banking.* Cambridge: MIT Press.

Freshwater, David. 1997. "Competition and Consolidation in the Farm Credit System." *Review of Agricultural Economics* 19 (1), 219–27.

Freshwater, David. 1999. "Can Continuation of GSE Status for the Farm Credit System Be Justified?" *Journal of Public Budgeting, Accounting & Financial Management* 11 (1), 35–55.

Furlong, Frederick, and Randall Pozdena. 1985. "Farm Credit System." Federal Reserve Bank of San Francisco. *FRBSF Weekly Letter.* December 20.

Gale, William G. 1990. "Federal Lending and the Market for Credit." *Journal of Public Economics* 8, April, 107–21.

Gale, William G. 1991. "Economic Effects of Federal Credit Programs." *American Economic Review* 81 (1), March, 133–52.

Gangopadhyay, Shubashia, and Robert Lensink. 2001. "Joint Liability Lending: A Note." Research Report 01E09, Research School Systems, Organization and Management (SOM), University of Groningen, Netherlands.

General Accounting Office. 1993. *Federal Home Loan Bank System: Reforms Needed to Promote Its Safety, Soundness, and Effectiveness.* GAO/GGD-94–38.

General Accounting Office. 1999. *Capital Structure of the Federal Home Loan Bank System.* GAO/GGD-99–177R.

Ghatak, Maitreesh. 2000. "Screening by the Company You Keep: Joint Liability Lending and the Peer Selection Effect." *Economic Journal* 110 (2), 601–31.

Ghatak, Maitreesh, and Timothy Guinnane. 1999. "The Economics of Lending with Joint Liability: Theory and Practice." *Journal of Development Economics* 60 (1), 195–228.

Glosten, Lawrence, and Paul Milgrom. 1985. "Bid, Ask and Transaction Prices in a Specialist Market with Heterogeneously Informed Traders." *Journal of Financial Economics* 14, 71–100.

Gregorash, George M., and James Morrison. 1985. "The Lean Years: Trends in Agricultural Banking." *Proceedings of a Conference on Bank Structure and Competition.* Federal Reserve Bank of Chicago, 101–19.

Hellman, Thomas, Kevin Murdock, and Joseph Stiglitz. 2000. "Liberalization, Moral Hazard in Banking and Prudential Regulation: Are Capital Requirements Enough?" *American Economic Review* 90 (1), 147–65.

Hoag, W. Gifford. 1976. *The Farm Credit System: A History of Financial Self-Help.* Danville, Ill.: Interstate Publishers.

Horsefield, J. Keith. 1960. *British Monetary Experiments, 1650–1710.* Cambridge: Harvard University Press.

Irwin, George D. 1985. "The Role of the Farm Credit System." *Proceedings of a Conference on Bank Structure and Competition.* Federal Reserve Bank of Chicago, 93–100.

Jensen, Farrell E. 2000. "The Farm Credit System as a Government Sponsored Enterprise." *Review of Agricultural Economics* 22 (2), 326–35.

Jones, Jesse H. 1951. *Fifty Billion Dollars: My Thirteen Years with the RFC (1932–1945).* New York: The Macmillan Company.

Kane, Edward J. 1977. "Good Intentions and Unintended Evils: The Case against Selective Credit Allocation." *Journal of Money, Credit, and Banking* 9 (1), February, 55–69.

Kane, Edward J. 1985. *The Gathering Crisis in Federal Deposit Insurance*. Cambridge, Mass.: MIT Press.

Kane, Edward J. 1989. *The S&L Insurance Mess*. Washington, D.C.: The Urban Institute Press.

Kane, Edward J. 1999. "Housing Finance GSEs: Who Gets the Subsidy?" *Journal of Financial Services Research* 15 (3), May, 197–209.

Kaufman, George G. 1995. "The U.S. Banking Debacle of the 1980s: An Overview and Lessons." *The Financier: ACMT* 2 (2), May, 9–26.

Keeley, Michael. 1990. "Deposit Insurance, Risk and Market Power in Banking." *American Economic Review* 80 (5), December, 1183–1200.

Lamb, Ellen Clair. 2000. "Federal Home Loan Bank Modernization: How Has It Fared?" *Community Banker* 9 (12), December, 30–33.

Leggett, Keith, and Robert Strand. 1997. "The Financing Corporation, Government-sponsored Enterprises, and Moral Hazard." *Cato Journal*, Fall, 179–87.

Li, Wenli. 1998. "Government Loan, Guarantee and Grant Programs: An Evaluation." Federal Reserve Bank of Richmond. *Economic Quarterly* 84 (4), Fall, 25–51.

McTague, Jim. 2000. "House Odds: Critics Say Home Loan Banks' Mortgage Program Puts System at Risk." *Barron's*, 2000.

Merton, Robert. 1974. "On the Pricing of Corporate Debt: The Risk Structure of Interest Rates." *Journal of Finance* 29, May, 449–70.

Merton, Robert. 1977. "An Analytic Derivation of the Cost of Deposit Insurance and Loan Guarantees." *Journal of Banking and Finance* 1, June, 3–11.

Miller, M., et al. 2002. "AMA Securitization Feasibility Study." Presentation to the FHLBS Bank Presidents' Conference, 10 September.

Nickerson, David. 1998. "The Economics of the MPF Program of the Federal Home Loan Bank of Chicago." Internal Memorandum, Economic Analysis Division, Office of Thrift Supervision.

Nickerson, David, and Ronnie Phillips. 2002. "Risk-taking in a Joint Liability System with External Debt Guarantees: A Game of Strategic Complements." Mimeographed, Colorado State University.

Office of the Comptroller of the Currency. Federal Reserve Board, Federal Deposit Insurance Corporation and Office of Thrift Supervision. 1999. Letter to Peter Gutzmer of the Federal Home Loan Bank of Chicago, 19 July.

O'Hara, Maureen. 1983. "Tax-Exempt Financing: Some Lessons from History." *Journal of Money, Credit and Banking* 15 (4), November, 425–41.

Peoples, Kenneth L. et al. 1992. *Anatomy of an American Agricultural Credit Crisis: Farm Debt in the 1980s*. Lanham, Md.: Rowman and Littlefield Publishers, Inc.

Phaup, Marvin. 1985. Government-Sponsored Enterprises and Their Implicit Federal Subsidy: The Case of Sallie Mae. Washington, D.C.: Congressional Budget Office. December.

Phillips, Ronnie. 1994. "An End to Private Banking: Early New Deal Proposals to Alter the Role of the Federal Government in Credit Allocation." *Journal of Money, Credit and Banking*, 26 (3), pt. 2, 552–68.

Pollock, Alex. 2001. Private communication. Office of the CEO, Federal Home Loan Bank of Chicago.

Rehm, Barbara. 2000. "Finance Board Head Waiting for 'Thank You.'" *American Banker*, 30 June, 4–7.

Reyna, Michael. 2000. Remarks and Testimony before the Committee on Financial Services, U.S. House of Representatives. 3 October.

Rhodes, J. 1987. "Competition Among Cooperatives." *Cooperative Theory: New Approaches*. Washington, D.C.: U.S. Department of Agriculture, ACS Rep. 18, July.

Rhodes, J. 1983. "The Large Agricultural Cooperative as a Competitor." *American Journal of Agricultural Economics* 65, December, 1090–95.

Roll, Richard. 2000. "Benefits to Homeowners from Mortgage Portfolios Retained by Fannie Mae and Freddie Mac." Anderson Graduate School of Management Working Paper, UCLA. *Journal of Financial Services Research*, forthcoming.

Russell, Steven. 1991. "The U.S. Currency System: A Historical Perspective." Federal Reserve Bank of St. Louis. *Review* 73 (5), September/October, 34–61.

Seiler, Robin, et al. 1991. Controlling the Risks of Government-Sponsored Enterprises. Washington, D.C.: Congressional Budget Office. April.

Smith, Brian. 2000. "Looking at FHLB Modernization." *Community Banker* 9 (2), Feb, 36–37.

Smith, Bruce D., and Michael J. Stutzer. 1989. "Adverse Selection and Mutuality: The Case of the Farm Credit System." *Journal of Financial Intermediation* 1 (2), June, 125–49.

Stahl, Dale. 1988. "Bertrand Competition for Inputs and Walrasian Outcomes." *American Economic Review* 78, 189–201.

Stanton, Thomas H. 1995. "Government-Sponsored Enterprises and Changing Markets: The Need for an Exit Strategy." *The Financier* 2 (2), May, 27–42.

Stiglitz, Joseph. 1990. "Peer Monitoring and Credit Markets." *World Bank Economic Review* 4 (3), 351–66.

Stock, James H. 1984. "Real Estate Mortgages, Foreclosures, and Midwestern Agrarian Unrest, 1865–1920." *Journal of Economic History* 44, 89–105.

Stojanovic, Dusan, Mark Vaughan, and Timothy Yeager. 2001. "Do Federal Home Loan Bank Membership and Advances Lead to Bank Risk-Taking?" Working paper, Federal Reserve Bank of St. Louis.

Stojanovic, Dusan, Mark Vaughan, and Timothy Yeager. 2000. "Is Federal Home Loan Bank Funding a Risky Business for the FDIC?" Federal Reserve Bank of St. Louis. *Review* 73 (5), September/October, 34–61.

Stokes, W. N., Jr. 1973. *Credit to Farmers: The Story of Federal Intermediate Credit Banks and Production Credit Associations*. Washington, D.C.: The 12 Federal Intermediate Credit Banks.

Thayer, Theodore. 1953. "The Land-Bank System in the American Colonies." *Journal of Economic History* 13 (3), Spring, 145–59.

Todd, Walker. 1992. "The History of and Rationales for the Reconstruction Finance Corporation." *Economic Review*. Federal Reserve Bank of Cleveland 28 (Quarter 4): 22–35.

Trechter, David D. 1987. Assisting the Farm Credit System: An Analysis of Two Bills. Washington, D.C.: Congressional Budget Office, December.

U.S. Secretary of the Treasury. 1990. Report of the Secretary of the Treasury on Government Sponsored Enterprises. Washington, D.C.: U.S. Department of Treasury. May.

Van Order, Robert. 2000. "The U.S. Mortgage Market: A Model of Dueling Charters." *Journal of Housing Research* 11 (2), 233–55.

Varian, Hal. 1990. "Monitoring Agents with Other Agents." *Journal of Institutional and Theoretical Economics*, 153–74.

Wright, Ivan. 1923. *Farm Mortgage Financing*. McGraw-Hill: New York.

Acknowledgments

We would like to thank Zvi Bodie, Benton Gup, Art Hogan, Paul Kupiec, Stephen Ledbetter, David Malmquist, David Nebhut, Peter Nigro, Alex Pollock, William Segal, Ken Spong, Rick Sullivan, Walker Todd, Robert Van Order, Mark Vaughan, and seminar participants at the Financial Management Association Annual Meetings for helpful comments and correspondence. The first author would like to thank the Economic Research Department of the Office of Thrift Supervision and the Division of Housing Economics and Financial Research at the Federal Home Loan Mortgage Corporation, where he was a visiting scholar and financial economist while the first draft of this paper was written. The opinions expressed here are those of the authors and do not necessarily reflect the views of OTS or Freddie Mac.

CHAPTER 6

Too Big to Fail in the Banking Industry: A Survey

Marcelo Dabós

INTRODUCTION

The too big to fail (TBTF) doctrine states that governments will intervene in order to prevent failures of large institutions, mainly banks.[1] This article surveys the literature about this doctrine in the banking industry and mainly in the United States. In the United States, the TBTF doctrine developed primarily as the policy of protecting uninsured depositors in large bank failures in order to prevent adverse effects on the financial system. This is often referred to as the TBTF doctrine (see "Economic Implications," 1991). This is a narrow definition.

In a number of other countries, authorities are widely believed to follow a TBTF policy, although it is rarely admitted in public. The severe negative macroeconomic effects of the failure of a large financial institution, including the possible contagion to other banks, makes TBTF an issue that needs to be considered by the government in each country. This issue exists even in the absence of a specific deposit insurance program (see Roth, 1994). In other words, the economic and political consequences of the failure of a large bank may be so big that governments are forced to bail them out, which obviously generates moral hazard, since the managers of these large banks can thus take excessive risks.

Obviously, Central Banks would never admit ex ante that they adhere to this view. They have tried to put forward a less clear-cut policy of "constructive ambiguity," which is supposed to maintain some uncertainty about the criteria actually used for deciding whether to bail out a failing bank. Examples of bailouts of large insolvent banks by governments (such as Continental Illinois in the United States in May 1984 and others) have persuaded the public that some banks are "too big to fail."[2]

REVIEW OF THE LITERATURE

Rochet and Tirole (1996) lay some theoretical foundations for this doctrine in a model in which the Central Bank wants to promote peer monitoring among commercial banks. Rochet and Tirole refer to the propagation of an agent's economic distress to other agents linked to that agent through financial transactions. They stress the link via interbank lending. They analyze the interbank lending and systemic risk. In the paper, a bank's failure may trigger a chain of subsequent failures and therefore force the Central Bank to intervene to nip the contagion process in the bud. It is widely believed by banking experts and by the markets that industrialized countries adhere to a TBTF policy of protecting uninsured depositors of large insolvent banks, whose failure could propagate through the financial system although authorities rationally refuse to corroborate this belief.

Authorities talk (as it was said) of a policy of constructive ambiguity when discussing their willingness to intervene.

While the authors' work emphasizes contagion in the banking system through interbank transactions, financial distress may alternatively propagate through an informational channel. Namely, in a situation in which financial markets are imperfectly informed about the Central Bank's willingness to bail out failing banks, the Central Bank's refusal to support a troubled bank may signal that other banks may not be supported either in the future and may thus precipitate their collapse.

Thus, the policy of TBTF is one used to deal with the problem of systemic risk in a financial system. An alternative method of prevention of systemic risk mentioned in Rochet and Tirole (1996) consists of centralizing a bank's liquidity management. A case in point is a payment system in which the Central Bank acts as a counterparty and guarantees the finality of payments. To the extent that the Central Bank bears the credit risk if the sending bank defaults, the default cannot propagate to the receiving bank through the payment system.

The authors analyze whether one can build an articulate theoretical argument for why TBTF policy may exist in the first place, and study how one might protect Central Banks while preserving the flexibility of the current interbank market in the United States.

They deemphasize the concept of size in TBTF by viewing TBTF as a policy in which a borrowing bank bail-out substitutes for direct assistance to its lenders. This viewpoint may be surprising, but they made three points in defense of it. First, they notice that size per se cannot be the cause of TBTF; Drexel and BCCI (which were allowed to fail) were large institutions whose failure created little risk of contagion as they were somewhat disconnected from the rest of the system. Here one must remark that the authors present a model that stresses interbank lending and systemic risk. Second, even if one accepts their position, TBTF may not be a misnomer given that large banks often borrow in the United States from smaller deposit-collecting banks, and thus there is a correlation between size and rescue operations. Third, the latter correlation may have alternative explanations; for instance, a political economy explanation may be that the failure of a large bank makes national headlines while that of small banks goes almost unnoticed in the media.

In their model, there is the possibility that a slightly higher liquidity shock for any of the banks implies a complete breakdown of the banking system, whereas a slightly lower liquidity shock for any of the banks would, on the contrary, entail no failure at all. This can be interpreted as showing the existence of unstable situations where the failure of a single bank can propagate to the entire banking system. This situation means that the single bank that fails can be considered as a TBTF bank. This is an interesting theoretical point.

TBTF IN THE UNITED STATES

The reasons why the TBTF policy is a controversial issue are that it is costly to the Federal Deposit Insurance Corporation (FDIC), increases tax-payer exposure, discourages market discipline, increases moral hazard, and the more emotional issue of fairness to depositors of large versus small banks.[3]

On the other hand, the prevention of systemic risks that can overwhelm the banking and financial system is the primary argument made in support of the TBTF doctrine. Systemic risk include "potential spillover effects leading to widespread depositor runs, impairment of public confidence in the broader financial system, or serious disruptions in domestic and international payment and settlements systems."[4]

An important source of systemic risk relates to the risk of depositor runs on banks if confidence in the banking system is shaken. These runs can affect both healthy and unhealthy banks and lead to significant short-run credit availability problems and banks failures.

The primary justification for TBTF policy is the avoidance of systemic risks associated with large bank failures. However, there are some undesirable economic consequences. The principal consequences following Moyer and Lamy (1992) are:

(a) The moral hazard issue: under TBTF, large banks have a greater incentive to increase risk.

(b) The moral hazard issue also has implications for the structure of the banking industry. The structural implication is that large banks have an incentive to maintain lower capital-to-asset ratios than small banks. Also depositors of large banks have little incentive to monitor the riskiness of banks. If the bank fails, the FDIC is obligated to protect small ($100,000 and under) depositors, and large depositors can rely on the FDIC to extend coverage in accordance with the TBTF doctrine.

(c) A TBTF policy also can have a negative effect on the economic efficiency of banking. The uncontrollable economic conditions in a particular banking market may be so severe as to cause a bank to be unprofitable or suffer a large run and ultimately to fail. Such "bad luck" can result in the failure of both efficient and inefficient banking firms. The optimal system is one where regulators are able to determine which are efficient and inefficient banking firms. The TBTF policy does not provide the incentive to force inefficient banks out of business.

After giving empirical evidence of the negative consequences of TBTF policy, the authors analyze the 1991 Federal Deposit Insurance Corporation Improvement Act (FDICIA)[5] (fundamental deposit insurance and prudential regulatory reform) and give alternatives to the TBTF doctrine. Popular alternative approaches to the TBTF policy are co-insurance or deposit "haircuts," increased capital ratios, use of subordinated debt, and private insurance schemes. They concluded that each of these alternatives improves upon the TBTF policy by providing incentives to capital markets to monitor and discipline banks based upon risk. They said that creating incentives for private monitoring would align the interests of regulators, stockholders, and large depositors and significantly reduce the moral hazard problem that arises with TBTF.

In addition, the TBTF policy is basically unfair because large banks that are considered to be too big to fail are provided with additional effective insurance that they do not pay for. This policy thus puts small banks at a competitive disadvantage because their large depositors (above the $100,000 ceiling) run a risk of losses, while large depositors at big banks are immune from losses (see Mishkin, 1992).

Mishkin also said that giving regulators the discretion to engage in a TBTF policy creates incentives for large banks to take on too much risk, thus exposing the deposit insurance fund and taxpayers to large potential loses. Nevertheless, he does not advocate giving up a discretionary use of the TBTF policy if there are highly unusual, unforeseen circumstances. He recommends, however, that with a TBTF policy in place, there is a greater need to reduce the incentives for large banks to take on risk through other means. This position does not agree with the policy of elimination of the TBTF policy recommended by the Shadow Financial Regulatory Committee (1991).

O'Hara and Shaw (1990) investigated the effect on bank equity values of the Comptroller of the Currency's announcement that some banks were too big to fail and that for those banks total deposit insurance would be provided. Using an event study methodology, they found positive wealth effects accruing to TBTF banks, with corresponding negative effects accruing to non-included banks. They demonstrated that the magnitude of these effects differed with bank solvency and size.

Black et al. (1997) determine whether the market's perception of bank riskiness declined for banks other than those considered TBTF. To test this hypothesis, they examined the stock market reaction to changes in dividend cuts and omissions as an indication of whether the market perception of bank holding company riskiness has fallen since the Comptroller's statement (see note 2 in this chapter). They observed the market reactions to bank holding company dividend cuts and omissions from 1974 through 1991, bracketing the TBTF announcement. If the market expected regulators to expand TBTF coverage to banking firms below the eleven largest in 1984, it should have formed probabilities about which banks would receive TBTF coverage. They examined the stock market's reaction to dividend cuts and omissions to determine whether the market changed its value of dividends as a signal of bank riskiness after the TBTF announcement. They found that the 1984 TBTF announcement changed the market's interpretation of bank dividend cuts and omissions. They said that the regulatory broadening of the TBTF doctrine encouraged institutional investors to seek the shares of these firms in a superior risk-return trade-off and caused the stock market to reduce its reliance on dividends as a signal of firm value. They concluded that the market did not confine the coverage of TBTF only to those banks included in the Comptroller's announcement. By examining the market's reaction to dividend cuts and omissions before and after the TBTF announcement, they found that the price response by the market is stronger in the pre-TBTF period. Before the TBTF doctrine, the results show that the market reaction to dividends cuts and omissions by Banking Holding Companies (BHC) is stronger for larger banks and for banks with relatively low institutional coverage. In the post-TBTF period, neither bank size nor institutional involvement is important. They further examined the role of institutional investors by comparing the percentage of shares held by institutions for a random sample of financial institutions and S&P 500 firms. The results show that institutions significantly increase their ownership of BHC stocks following the TBTF doctrine, relative to the control sample. Consequently, the passage and expansion of the TBTF doctrine is interpreted as reducing the market's perception of the riskiness of banking organizations that were not originally considered too big to fail.

Swary (1986) notes a downward revision in the market values of banks considered outside the protection of the TBTF doctrine.

Athavale (2000) examined the changes in the deposit regimes that occurred in 1984 and 1991 using a time series of observations on the interest rates applicable to uninsured certificates of deposit. Their analysis suggests that the actions of policymakers and regulators over time have reduced the default risk on bank liabilities, and investors believe that the FDIC would continue to apply the TBTF policy to the uninsured deposits of large banks.

TBTF can also have other impacts. For example, under a discretionary policy, the benefit of requiring banks to issue subordinated debt is that the market price of the subordinated debt securities provides regulators with additional, market-derived information. It is uncertain, however, that the subordinated debt price will clearly reflect investors' appraisal of bank risk taking because it might also reflect their guesses about regulator response. Offsetting the dubious benefit of providing regulators with additional information would be the additional cost imposed on banks that currently do not find it in their interest to issue subordinated debt or to issue as much as the policy would prescribe. The largest banks will be at a relative advantage not only because they would pay a smaller illiquidity premium and bear lower issuance costs than banks with smaller issues, but also because they might benefit from a lower risk premium based on their too big to fail status (Maclachlan, 2001).

Still another problem has to do with identifying the correct model of the determination of subordinated debt yields. The implicit model in many studies is that subordinated investors price the securities according to the perceived level of risk of the bank's assets and activities (see Flannery, 1998, for a review of the literature). It is also plausible to suppose, however, that investors price the risk that regulators will close the bank. The two hypotheses are not necessarily equivalent, for at least two reasons. First, any discrepancy between regulators and investors in their capability and motivation to detect excessive risk taking could cause the implications of the two theories to diverge. Second, as investors perceive that regulators are concerned with systemic risk, those investors will be less likely to discipline a bank considered too big to fail (Maclachlan, 2001).

TBTF IN OTHER COUNTRIES

Roth (1994) studied the German Likobank Approach. On June 26, 1974, a private bank of about $900 million in assets, the Bankhaus I.D. Herstatt KgaA in Cologne, Federal Republic of Germany, failed because it had lost more than $400 million in foreign exchange trading. This unexpected collapse left many foreign banks exposed and temporarily paralyzed the world foreign exchange market. While Herstatt was allowed to fail, steps were taken to protect the German banking system against future instabilities. Within a month, regulations were approved to prevent excessive foreign exchange dealings. In September 1974, the Liquiditats-Konsortialbank GmbH (Likobank) was formed on the initiative of the Deutsche Bundesbank. The stockholders' equity of the bank totaled DM 250 million and was provided by the Deutsche Bundesbank (30%), commercial banks (30%), the saving bank sector (27%), the credit cooperatives sector (11%), and several other banking institutions. By 1992 the stockholders' equity had grown to DM 372 million. If called, the stockholders have a contingent obligation to provide further capital of up to DM 1,860 million. The Likobank's task is to ensure the due settlement of domestic and external payments through banks. Thus, the function of the Likobank is to support sound banks with temporary short-term liquidity on an emergency basis rather than to help banks in severe financial difficulties. Already, just because of its existence, the Likobank has increased confidence in the soundness of the banking system. In September 1974, the formation of the Likobank led to a calming of the markets after the Herstatt crisis. The Bundesbank Act prohibits the Bundesbank from acting as the lender of last resort for deposit protection schemes. Such an arrangement protects the Bundesbank from political pressure to help an insolvent bank continue operations. It also helps to avoid a conflict between the Bundesbank's task to maintain price stability and to ensure the soundness of the banking system. Thus, it is not the Bundesbank's task to solve a TBTF problem. The Bundesbank states that if a bank failure overtaxes the resources of a guarantee fund or even jeopardizes the existence of the banking system as such, it is up to the government or Parliament to decide how to address the too big to fail problem with the economic and fiscal policy instruments available. Such action should not be predictable.[6]

Roth (1994) compares the deposit insurance schemes, the banking systems, and the methods of handling a banking crisis in Canada, France, Germany, Italy, Japan, the United Kingdom, and the United States. All seven countries offer deposit insurance programs. The characteristics of a national banking system determine its inherent stability to a large degree. One factor is government ownership of banks. In Germany , the savings bank sector is owned by states and municipalities that are by law the ultimate guarantors of all liabilities of their banks. In this context, the deposit insurance fund for savings banks functions only as an additional protection. Government ownership of banks also occurs in France and Italy. An example of the stabilizing effect of government ownership occurred in March 1994 when troubled Credit Lyonnais, a bank with assets of $340 billion, was rescued by its main shareholder, the French government, which injected $850 million in new capital and assumed the risk for $7 billion in questionable loans. A detailed description of how banking crises have been handled in foreign countries is given in U.S. Department of the Treasury (1991).

TBTF IN THE PRESENT AND IN THE FUTURE

Soper (2001) examined the rising importance of international M&A activity and problems of added moral hazard and too big to fail in the context of emerging megabanks and large, complex financial service firms—many of which cross international borders. Repeal of many provisions of the Glass-Steagall Act and structural changes in banking imply that many banks will either consolidate with other banks or converge with non-bank financial firms. Whether the focus is on the United States alone or with Europe added to the equation, the issue of too big to fail banking organizations and rising moral hazard concerns must be addressed.

Due to recent megamergers and the emergence of large, complex banking entities, do we now find ourselves in a state of elevated moral hazard where too big to fail becomes a dominant concern? Soper's opinion is based in recent research by Moore and Siems (1998). These two authors indicate that merger activity is not the source of too big to fail problems. In their words, "some of the recent megamergers are combinations of banks that are already too big to fail. Those mergers are not creating a new TBTF institution. That's worth remembering because some people claim that the desire to become too big to fail is driving the current megamergers" (Moore and Siems, 1998, 13).

Soper's opinion is in fact that the Federal Reserve and the International Monetary Fund may have more to do with creating moral hazard than anything done by merged megabanks. The Fed's role in engineering the fall 1998 bailout of Long-Term Capital Management has been acknowledged by Chairman Greenspan as an example of moral hazard. And the IMF's actions to extend international liquidity to states that had defaulted on private-sector loans moves moral hazard to a new plane. Blaming megabanks for creating moral hazard problems seems to make little sense when Central Banks like the Fed and international lending agencies such as the IMF are manufacturing moral hazard on a much larger scale (Soper, 2001).

NOTES

1. It is interesting to note that the TBTF doctrine is not unique to the banking industry. In 1971, Lockheed's L-1011 Tri-Star commercial jet program was rescued by a $250 million government loan guarantee for funds needed to complete development of the plane. Similarly, when Chrysler teetered near bankruptcy, the firm sought and received $1.2 billion of U.S. government loan guarantees, which had the effect of lowering its financing costs while it tried to resolve its operating and financial difficulties (see Moyer and Lamy, 1992). Also Penn Central Rail Road, New York City, and most recently the airline industry have been bailed out.

2. In the wake of the Continental Illinois bank liquidity crisis, the Comptroller of the Currency testified to Congress on September 19, 1984, that some banks were just "too big to fail," and in these cases total deposit insurance protection would be provided, rather than enforcing the statutory $100,000 per account limit. In his testimony, the Comptroller admitted that banks included in the TBTF policy were the 11 largest. The next day, the *Wall Street Journal* identified these banks as BankAmerica, Bankers Trust, Chase Manhattan, Chemical Bank, Citibank, Continental Illinois, First Chicago, J. P. Morgan, Manufacturers Hanover Trust, Security Pacific, and Wells Fargo (see Moyer and Lamy, 1992). As is clear from the bailout of the thirty-third largest U.S. bank, the Bank of New England, in January 1991, the TBTF policy applies to big banks which are not even among the eleven largest. (Mishkin, 1992). Also, the failure resolution packages for First Oklahoma Bank in 1986, First Republic Bank in

1988, and MBank in 1989 indicate that TBTF coverage has been applied to smaller banks (Black et al., 1997).

3. Moyer and Lamy (1992).

4. Moyer and Lamy (1992) and John P. LaWare, Member, Board of Governors, Federal Reserve Board, hearing before the Subcommittee on Economic Stabilization of the Committee on Banking, Finance and Urban Affairs, House of Representatives, May 9, 1991. The purpose of the hearing was to review in detail the economic justifications for a too big to fail policy and the proposed changes to this policy. All in the framework of Congress's ultimate goal that is to reform the banking industry in a way that will restore vitality to the banking industry, benefit consumers, and avoid another taxpayer bailout. To reach that goal, the too big to fail issue must be resolved (see "Economic Implications," 1991, 2). Congress was analyzing the Treasury's proposal for the most thorough overhaul of the banking regulatory system since the Great Depression: the FDIC Improvement Act of 1991 (see Benston and Kaufman 1997, and Athavale 2000).

5. Under the FDICIA (established effective January 1, 1995), the FDIC is prohibited from protecting uninsured depositors or creditors at a failed bank if it would result in an increased loss to the deposit insurance fund. However, there is an exemption from this requirements for banks that regulators judge to be too big to fail and where imposing losses on their depositors or creditors would have serious adverse effects on economic conditions or financial stability. But this exemption requires the determination by the secretary of the treasury upon the written recommendation of two-thirds of both the FDIC Board of Directors and the Board of Governors of the Federal Reserve System and after consultation with the president of the United States. Moreover, any loss incurred by the FDIC from protecting insured claimants must be recovered with a special assessment on all insured banks based on their total assets. Since this assessment impacts large banks proportionately more, it is doubtful that the protected bank's competitors would be overly supportive of such a rescue. Finally, the U.S. General Accounting Office must review the basis for the decision. Given these procedural hurdles, compared to the pre-FDICIA situation the TBTF exemption is likely to be used rarely, if at all (Benston and Kaufman, 1997, 150). In contrast to the pre-FDICIA policies, it appears that the FDIC did not favor depositors at larger banks in its 1992 through 1996 resolutions. Uninsured depositors have been put on notice that their funds are at risk and this has brought an element of market discipline back into banking (Benston and Kaufman, 1997, 155). See also the related literature about FDICIA: Barnett (1992), Carow and Larsen (1997), Garcia (1995), Jones and King (1995), Kaufman (1995), Madura and Bartunek (1995), Peek and Rosengren (1997), and Wall (1993).

6. Deutsche Bundesbank, "Deposit Protection Schemes in the Federal Republic of Germany," Monthly Report of the Deutsche Bundesbank, July 1992, 31.

REFERENCES

Athavale, Manoj. "Uninsured deposits and the too-big-to-fail policy in 1984 and 1991." *American Business Review* 18 (2), June 2000, 123–28.

Barnett, Robert E. "FDICIA-hardly a 'narrow' act." *The Bankers Magazine*, July/August 1992, 53–55.

Benston, George, and George Kaufman. "FDICIA after five years." *The Journal of Economic Perspectives* 11 (3), Summer 1997, 139–58.

Berry, J. M. "Can we do without the 'Too-Big-to-Fail' doctrine?" *Financier,* April 1991.

Black, Harold A., M. Cary Collins, and Breck L. Robinson. "Changes in market perception of riskiness: The case of too-big-to-fail." *Journal of Financial Research* 20 (3), Fall 1997, 389–406.

Carow, Kenneth A., and Glen A. Larsen, Jr. "The effect of FDICIA regulation on bank holding companies." *The Journal of Financial Research* 20, 1997, 159–74.

"Economic implications of the too-big-to-fail policy." Hearing before the Subcommittee on Economic Stabilization of the Committee on Banking, Finance and Urban Affairs, House of Representatives, 102nd Congress, First session, 9 May 1991.

Flannery, M. J. "Using market information in prudential bank supervision: A review of the U.S. empirical evidence." *Journal of Money, Credit, and Banking* 30 (3), 1998, 273–305.

Freixas, Xavier, and Jean-Charles Rochet. *Microeconomics of Banking.* Cambridge: M.I.T., 1997, 286–7.

Garcia, Gillian. "Implementing FDCIA's mandatory closure rule." *Journal of Banking and Finance,* 1995, 723–5.

Grant, James. "Too big to fail? Walter Wriston and Citibank." *Harvard Business Review* 74 (4), July/August 1996, 146–51.

Jones, David, and Kathleen K. King. "The implementation of prompt corrective action: An assessment." *Journal of Banking and Finance* 19, 1995, 491–510.

Kaufman, George. "FDICIA and bank capital." *Journal of Banking and Finance* 19, 1995, 721–2.

Maclachlan, Fiona C. "Market discipline in bank regulation." *Independent Review* 6 (2), Fall 2001, 227–34.

Madura, Jeff, and Kenneth Bartunek. "Valuation effects of the FDIC Improvement Act." *Applied Financial Economics* 5, 1995, 191–8.

Mishkin, Frederic S. "An evaluation of the Treasury plan for banking reform." *Journal of Economic Perspectives* 6 (1), Winter 1992, 133–53.

Moore, Robert, and Thomas Siems. "Finding meaning in mergers." *Financial Industry Issues,* Federal Reserve Bank of Dallas, 1998.

Moyer, R. Charles, and Robert E. Lamy. "Too-big-to-fail: Rationale, consequences, and alternatives." *Business Economics* 27 (3), July 1992, 19–24.

O'Hara, Maureen, and Wayne Shaw. "Deposit insurance and wealth effects: The value of being too-big-to-fail." *The Journal of Finance,* 45 (5), December 1990, 1587–1600.

Peek, Joe, and Eric Rosengren. "Will legislated early intervention prevent the next banking crisis?" *Southern Economic Journal* 64, 1997, 268–80.

Rochet, J. C., and J. Tirole. "Interbank lending and systemic risk." *Journal of Money, Credit, and Banking* 28 (4), 1996, 733–62.

Roth, Michael. "Too-big-to-fail and the stability of the banking system: Some insights from foreign countries." *Business Economics* 29 (4), October 1994, 43–50.

Shadow Financial Regulatory Committee. "The Treasury's deposit insurance reform recommendations." Statement No. 65, mimeographed, 11 February 1991.

Soper, John C. "What's next for consolidation in banking?" *Business Economics* 36 (2), April 2001, 39–43.

Swary, I. "Stock market reaction to regulatory action in the Continental Illinois crisis." *Journal of Financial and Quantitative Analysis* 59, 1986, 451–74.

U.S. Department of the Treasury. "Modernizing the financial system: Recommendations for safer, more competitive banks." Washington, D.C., February 1991.

Wall, Larry D. "Too-Big-to-Fail after FDICIA." *The Federal Reserve Bank of Atlanta Economic Review*, January/February 1993, 1–14.

CHAPTER 7

Too Big to Fail in U.S. Banking: Quo Vadis?[1]

George G. Kaufman

INTRODUCTION

Too big to fail (TBTF) is a term frequently used in banking to describe how bank regulators may deal with severely financially troubled large banks. At least in the United States, it is also a much misunderstood term. Except for a brief period in the 1980s, TBTF did not and does not now mean what it clearly appears to be saying. Banks were and are now failed in terms of terminating the interests of the shareholders and generally also senior management, but some uninsured depositors and creditors may be protected. In usage, TBTF pertains to two issues: one, what parties to protect in insolvencies and two, if shareholders are not protected and the bank is legally failed, how to reorganize or liquidate (unwind it).[2] The term came into common usage in 1984, when the regulators were faced with the economically insolvent Continental Illinois National Bank in Chicago, which was both the seventh largest bank in the country at the time and the largest correspondent bank, having interbank deposit and Fed funds relationships with more than 2,200 other banks. Although the poor financial condition and potential insolvency of Continental was widely known both to the comptroller of the currency from its examination reports and to the public from newspaper articles, the failure caught the regulators unprepared. They did not have a plan on the shelf ready for immediate use for resolving such a large and important bank. Rather than fail the bank legally, appoint a receiver, sell its assets, protect insured deposits by having them assumed at par by another bank, and permit uninsured depositors and other unsecured creditors to share in any losses, which was the resolution procedure that the FDIC (Federal Deposit Insurance

Corporation) had started to apply to smaller banks shortly before, the federal regulators did not legally fail or close the bank, and protected all uninsured depositors and creditors of both the bank and its parent holding company against loss. In addition, at least initially, the old shareholders were not completely ousted.

The regulators resolved the institution by providing funds to the Continental's parent holding company, the Continental Illinois Corporation, in the form of preferred stock to be downstreamed to the bank as equity capital. This served to recapitalize both institutions and keep the bank solvent and the holding company out of bankruptcy.[3] The FDIC also purchased $3.5 billion of bad loans from the bank. Both institutions were permitted to continue to operate, but under FDIC control. The FDIC chose new senior management. The interest of the old shareholders, although not terminated altogether, was greatly reduced. They received a residual claim on the non-performing loans purchased by the FDIC (Federal Deposit Insurance Corporation [FDIC], 1998b). The bank was effectively nationalized. When, after five years, losses from resolving these loans exceeded the amount specified in the financing agreement, the old shareholders' interests were declared worthless and the change in control was complete. The FDIC slowly reprivatized the bank by periodically selling its shares to the public. The last shares were sold and the bank completely reprivatized in 1991. In 1994, the bank was bought by BankAmerica Corp. The total cost of the rescue operation was estimated by the FDIC to have been some $1.1 billion on a nonpresent value basis, or about 3 1/4 percent of the bank's assets as of the date of resolution (FDIC, 1998b). The estimated loss is understated by not present valuing recoveries at later dates, but is smaller if computed as a percent of assets one year before resolution before a run reduced Continental's asset size by nearly 20 percent. On the whole, the final loss is not greatly different from the loss rate estimated at the time of resolution.

The Continental was resolved in this way in part because the regulators believed that, particularly because of its large size and broad interconnections with other banks, failing the bank and/or its parent bank holding company and imposing losses on its uninsured depositors and creditors would have had serious adverse effects on other banks, financial markets, and the macroeconomy (House, 1984; FDIC, 1998b; and Sprague, 1986).[4] Rightly or wrongly, and the evidence on the existence of serious contagion and systemic risk is open to differing interpretation, the regulators perceived that such widespread devastation could result from failing a large bank for a number of reasons, including that bank deposits provide the large share of the country's money supply; banks are the largest lenders to households, businesses, and governments; banks operate much of the payments system; and, particularly in the case of Continental, banks are closely interconnected to each other through interbank deposits and loans, so that losses at any one bank may cascade down the chain to other banks and beyond to financial markets and the macroeconomy and drive otherwise solvent units into insolvency (Kaufman, 1994 and 1996).[5] Thus, adverse shocks from bank failures were perceived to be more strongly and widely felt than similar shocks from the failure of nonbank firms of equal size, and the larger the bank the more serious and widespread the damage.

The fear is evident in the statement of C.T. Conover, who was the Comptroller of the Currency at the time of the Continental Illinois National Bank failure in 1984, in his testimony to Congress at the time that

had Continental failed and been treated in a way in which depositors and creditors were not made whole, we could very well have seen a national, if not an international, financial crisis, the dimensions of which were difficult to imagine. None of us wanted to find out. (Conover, 1984, p. 288)

John LaWare, a former governor of the Federal Reserve System, was more specific about the dimensions of this crisis in later testimony before Congress when he was governor. He noted that

it is systemtic risk that fails to be controlled and stopped at the inception that is a nightmare condition that is unfair to everybody. The only analogy that I can think of for the failure of a major international institution of great size is a meltdown of a nuclear generating plant like Chernobyl.

The ramifications of that kind of failure are so broad and happen with such lightning speed that you cannot after the fact control them. It runs the risk of bringing down other banks, corporations, disrupting markets, bringing down investment banks along with it. . . . We are talking about the failure that could disrupt the whole system. (LaWare, 1991, p. 34)

In addition, at least the Chairman of the House Banking Committee, Congressman St. Germain, believed that "had the Continental Illinois been allowed to fail . . . all those people [would have been] put out of work and all those corporations out of money" (see appendix and House, 1984, p. 299). His concern that failed banks physically disappear down a black hole with all hands aboard and that the bank is totaled, so that uninsured depositors lose all their funds, is probably widely shared by the public. Large segments of the public also appear to fear that, even if the bank does not disappear physically, access to depositor accounts is totally or partially frozen for a lengthy period, which greatly increases adverse effects.

The remainder of the paper traces the history of TBTF as it applies to commercial banks and analyzes the changes in its application through time by both the regulators and legislation. The paper does not consider explicit or implicit intervention by bank regulators to protect financial markets from perceived serious shocks originating from nonbank sources such as the commercial paper default by the Penn Central Railroad in 1971, the stock market collapse in 1987, and the Russian default and the Long-Term Capital Management debacle in 1998.

HISTORY OF TBTF

TBTF has changed considerably in concept and implementation from both the periods before and immediately after the Continental failure. Before the introduction of deposit insurance in 1934, very big banks did not often become insolvent and fail, even in periods of widespread bank failures and macroeconomic difficulties, such as 1893, 1907, and the early 1930s. For example, between 1921 and 1931, only two of the near 60 banks with loans and investments in excess of $50 million in 1921 failed and they represented only 0.02 percent of all bank failures in this period. In contrast, 7,000 of the 19,000 banks with loans and investments of under $0.5 million failed (Federal Reserve Committee, 1933). Even if more large banks had become insolvent, government regulators had little, if any, authority or resources to assist them. Banks failed either when they were unable to meet depositor claims or when the appropriate regulator believed that their capital was negative and they would default. The banks were forced to suspend operations and were either recapitalized by their old or new owners or liquidated. Assistance to larger banks perceived to be experiencing liquidity, but not solvency, problems was frequently provided by the local clearinghouse of which they were a member, financed by the other member banks. Such assistance was not provided to banks perceived to be insolvent and full repayment unlikely. Thus, the New York Clearing House did not provide assistance to the medium-sized Knickerbocker Trust in 1907 and the Bank of United States in 1930 and both were liquidated (Friedman and Schwartz, 1963; Sprague, 1910; O'Brien, 1992; and Trescott, 1992).

But things changed with the introduction of federal deposit insurance, which gave the federal government an implicit financial interest in the solvency of insured banks and a greater role in bank failure intervention. For its first 40-plus years through the 1970s, although there was a de jure coverage ceiling on insured deposits, de facto the FDIC acted to protect all depositors, although not shareholders, at nearly all failed banks. It did so primarily by merging the failed banks with solvent banks and effectively assuming some or all of the bad loans or paying the assuming banks for any losses they incurred in the transaction.[6] Such a procedure (termed *purchase and assumption*) was used to resolve the Franklin National Bank (New York) in 1974, which was the twentieth largest bank in the country at the time and the first large bank, although still a regional bank but with both an international presence and international ownership, to become insolvent in the post–World War II era. It was failed and sold after an attempt to continue the bank in operation after it became insolvent with funding through large-scale borrowing from the Federal Reserve Bank of New York discount window at below market rates, which eventually accounted for one-half of the bank's total funding, failed to restore it to profitability (Garcia and Plautz, 1988; Spero, 1980). Shareholders' interests were wiped out, but all depositors were fully protected. The FDIC experienced a moderate loss.

In 1980, the First Pennsylvania Bank (Philadelphia), which was the oldest chartered bank in the United States and then the twenty-third largest bank in the country, became insolvent after taking large interest rate bets and losing. Because it was difficult to find an eligible buyer for the bank, given the prohibition against interstate banking at the time, and a deposit payoff would drain the FDIC's funds, the FDIC provided "open bank" assistance. Additional financial support was provided by the Federal Reserve and a consortium of large banks. In contrast to most earlier rescues, the shareholders were left intact, although the FDIC made some management and director changes. When interest rates declined in the next few years, the bank repaid the loans and regained solvency at little net cost to the FDIC, which had included stock warrants in the rescue package and profited from their sale back to the bank in 1983 and 1985 (FDIC, 1998b; Sprague, 1986).

Regulatory rescue operations in which insolvent banks were not legally failed at the time and kept in operation with all depositors, although not necessarily stockholders, protected are referred to as open bank assistance. If the bank could not be merged because of an absence of eligible and suitable partners, direct assistance to the bank required a determination by the FDIC that the bank was "essential" to the community.[7] The First Pennsylvania Bank was deemed to be essential because of its large size (FDIC, 1998b; Sprague, 1986). But protection of all depositors effectively eliminated concern and discipline by de jure uninsured depositors. The FDIC began to view this as a problem.

To incentive large depositors to once again monitor and discipline their banks and reduce the costs of failure to itself, the FDIC experimented in 1983–84 with failing banks and not protecting uninsured depositors (FDIC, 1997). However, all the banks resolved in this fashion (termed *modified payoff*) were reasonably small. The uninsured depositors shared in any loss with the FDIC on a prorata basis. But rather than being forced to wait for their funds to be collected and paid by the receiver from the sale of the bank assets, which could take many years to complete, uninsured depositors were for the first time paid advance dividends by the FDIC at the time of resolution effectively equal to the estimated prorata recovery amount.[8] This amount was made available at the bank that assumed the insured deposits at par value. This important innovation minimized the adverse effects from the loss of liquidity to these depositors. Because often the fear of bank failures is based more on the inability to access one's account rather than the credit loss in its value, by liquifying the deposits, advance dividends effectively made resolutions with losses to uninsured depositors both economically and politically more feasible (Kaufman, 2002; Kaufman and Seelig, 2002).[9] But the Continental caught the regulators unprepared to deal with such a large institution and caution overrode experimentation.[10] As Sprague noted, "what were the real reasons for doing the . . . bailouts? Simply put, we were afraid not to" (Sprague, 1986, p. 10).

The decision to protect the Continental Bank after permitting smaller banks to fail and not protecting their uninsured depositors drew sharp criticism from some legislators, particularly on the basis of fairness of treatment from those representing the local areas that had recently suffered small banks failures. In defending the action in testimony before the House Banking Committee, Todd Conover, comptroller of the currency at the time, was drawn into stating that the regulators were unlikely to permit any one of the 11 largest multinational banks to fail, although he tried to argue that "it isn't whether a bank fails or not. It is how it is handled subsequently to its failure that matters" (see appendix and House, 1984, pp. 299–300).[11] Although the newswires did not highlight this exchange, the next day (September 20, 1984), the *Wall Street Journal* headlined a lengthy article on the hearings "U.S. Won't Let 11 Biggest Banks in Nation Fail—Testimony by Comptroller at House Hearing Is First Policy Acknowledgement" (Carrington, 1984). And so, the term TBTF was born! Using event study methodology, O'Hara and Shaw (1990) found that the market awarded positive excess returns to these 11 banks on September 20.

The FDIC attempted to restore market discipline after the Continental failure by progressively narrowing the stakeholders it protected in large bank failures. In 1986, it did not protect the creditors of a bank holding company, the First Oklahoma Corporation, when its lead subsidiary bank, the First National Bank of Oklahoma City, became insolvent, so that the holding company, although not the bank, failed and filed for bankruptcy. Holding company creditors were not protected and shareholders were wiped out. The bank was sold at a loss to the FDIC to a newly chartered Oklahoma subsidiary of First Interstate Bankcorp (California). In 1988, the FDIC failed banks owned by the FirstRepublic Corporation (Dallas). However, it protected all depositors and creditors of these banks when it sold the banks, including the lead bank, the First Republic National Bank, to a newly chartered FDIC operated bridge bank, which was, in turn, sold shortly afterwards to the NCNB Corporation, the parent holding company of the former Nations Bank in North Carolina (FDIC, 1998b; Siedman, 1993).[12]

In 1989, the FDIC permitted some uninsured depositors, nondeposit creditors, and off-balance sheet counterparties, although not uninsured nonaffiliated depositors, to experience losses when many but not all of the subsidiary banks of MCorp (Dallas) were failed (FDIC, 1998b). For purposes of interbank deposits among MCorp banks, the FDIC effectively treated the separately chartered holding company bank subsidiaries as a branch bank and charged the solvent banks for losses at the insolvent banks. Thus, by 1990, TBTF no longer meant what it did in 1984, but basically only that a bank was "too big to impose losses on most uninsured depositors" (Kaufman, 1990). Indeed, the term TBTF in terms of not permitting a bank holding company to legally fail applied basically only to the Continental and a few other holding companies from 1984 through 1986 and to banks for only two more years through 1988.

However, while the definition of "fail" was narrowed, the definition of "big" to protect uninsured depositors was broadened and progressively reduced to eventually include even the $2 billion of National Bank Washington (D.C.), which was only about the 250th largest bank in the country and apparently more "too political to fail" than TBTF. In addition to protecting all depositors at its domestic offices, the FDIC also protected all deposits at the bank's off-shore office in the Bahamas.[13]

FDICIA AND SYSTEMATIC RISK EXEMPTION

The high costs of the large number of bank failures and, in particular, the S&L failures of the 1980s and early 1990s, the great overuse and widely perceived serious misuse of TBTF in the 1980s, and the perceived inequitable treatment of uninsured depositors at failed banks differing in size or political influence led Congress, over the objection of many regulators, to reform the structure of deposit insurance, including procedures for resolving insolvencies, in the FDIC Improvement Act (FDICIA) of 1991. The act introduced regulatory prompt corrective action (PCA) and least cost resolution (LCR) that supplemented regulatory discretion with progressively harsher mandatory sanctions if these sanctions were ineffective and a bank's financial condition continued to deteriorate and more timely resolution when a bank's equity declines to less than a minimum of 2 percent of its on-balance sheet assets at least cost to the FDIC. The purpose of these provisions was "to resolve the problems of insured depository institutions at the least possible long-term loss to the deposit insurance fund" (*Federal Deposit Insurance Corporation Improvement Act*, 1991, p. 19). In contrast to before FDICIA, the computation procedure for estimating least cost was spelled out.[14] To help achieve LCR, the act explicitly prohibited the FDIC from protecting uninsured depositors and other nondepositor bank stakeholders, unless doing so represents the least costly resolution. They must share in the loss with the FDIC in accordance with legal priorities. But an exemption was provided. The FDIC could partially or fully protect any noninsured stakeholder and violate LCR if not doing so "would have serious adverse effects on economic conditions or financial stability; and . . . [doing so] would avoid or mitigate such adverse effects." In 1993, the FDIC was specifically prohibited from assisting shareholders in the RTC Completion Act. Thus, TBTF became the systemic risk exemption (SRE) and encompasses only the possibility of protecting partially or fully some or all nonshareholder stakeholders of insolvent banks.

The new SRE was also made significantly more difficult to invoke than the old TBTF. It requires a retained documented determination by the secretary of the treasury in consultation with the president in response to a written recommendation by two-thirds of both the Board of Directors of the FDIC and the Board of Governors of the Federal Reserve System that such action is necessary because in their judgment the above adverse preconditions specified exist and that not taking action that may violate LCR would validate these effects. The secretary must provide written notice of the determination to the Senate and House Banking Committees. If, after these hurdles, SRE is invoked, other provisions kick in. The comptroller general of the General Accounting Office must review the basis for the determination, the purpose of any actions taken, and the likely effects on the behavior of the banks and uninsured depositors and the findings reported to Congress. By increasing transparency and accountability, such ex post congressional and public reviews should serve to reinforce the greater ex ante hurdles in increasing the hesitancy of the regulators to request SRE and the Treasury to grant it (Mishkin, 1997). In addition, moreover, any loss to the FDIC resulting from protecting uninsured depositors and other creditors must be repaid "expeditiously" by a special assessment on all insured banks scaled to their total assets. This provision should make such action less popular with competing large banks and intensify opposition to its invocation.

Indeed, concurrent changes in the deposit insurance structure that made insurance basically privately funded, although still government managed, further reduced the likelihood of SRE and the cost to the public if and when it is invoked (Kaufman, 2002; Kaufman and Wallison, 2001). Unlike earlier, FDICIA requires the FDIC to increase premiums whenever losses from failures not stemming from protecting uninsured depositors drive the FDIC's reserve to insured deposits ratio below 1.25 percent to recover the shortfall within one year or impose very high premiums. Thus, the government's liability for losses is sharply reduced to effectively only after the aggregate capital of the banking system as a whole is or is almost wiped out and the banks cannot pay the premiums. The cost of paying for all FDIC losses should further incentize the healthy premium paying banks to prevent the FDIC from riding to the rescue of uninsured depositors at large banks.

Regulators now may also be more reluctant to support invoking the SRE than earlier both because of greater experience with and knowledge about resolving large institutions and because of the better understood adverse effects of moral hazard behavior by the banks. For example, Federal Reserve Chairman Alan Greenspan has recently stated that

the issue is an organization that is very large is not too big to fail, it may be too big to allow to implode quickly. But certainly, none are too big to orderly liquidate. . . . What you want to avoid is the quick reaction. And that we can do. But not to protect shareholders. And presumably, not to protect non-guaranteed deposits from loss. (Greenspan, 2000, p. 14)

The potential for greater market discipline at large institutions is substantial. (Greenspan, 2001, p. 7)

Moreover, as noted by Greenspan, "the least-cost resolution exemption does not require that all uninsured creditors be made whole, but rather that they be made no worse off than they would have been if the bank were liquidated" (Greenspan, 2001, p. 7). Thus, regulators also have the flexibility to keep uninsured depositors at risk, but to limit their exposure to loss to less than the full amount of the loss and thus presumably limit any spillover collateral damage. That is, the uninsured depositors could be subject to partial loss sharing with the FDIC rather than full loss sharing. In addition, to the extent losses are charged first to unsecured creditors and depositors at foreign branches, the uninsured depositors at domestic offices are also likely to be protected wholly or partially. To the uninsured domestic depositors, these subordinated funds serve as capital.

It is interesting to note that the inclusion of provisions in FDICIA requiring least cost resolution and increasing the difficulty of obtaining permission to protect uninsured depositors in TBTF resolutions, which reflected Congress' dissatisfaction with the FDIC's frequent practice of protecting all depositors at high cost, was not the first time that Congress expressed dissatisfaction with this practice and attempted to limit it. In 1950, in response to the FDIC's practice in the 1940s of protecting all depositors through assisted mergers with solvent banks, Congress amended the FDI Act. It restricted the FDIC's ability to protect all depositors only to resolutions in which an assisted merger is less costly than a deposit payoff or when a merger with a suitable partner is not possible but the bank is declared to be "essential" to the community. In his book, Sprague quotes Senator Paul Douglas of Illinois as suggesting at the time that the FDIC's practice was creating "a moral obligation upon the Government to protect all deposits and not merely insured deposits" (1986, p. 25). Nevertheless, Sprague noted that "despite the fact that Congress made it clear in the 1950 act that the FDIC was not created to insure all deposits in all banks, in the years since . . . the regulators have devised solutions that protect even the uninsured in the predominance of cases" (p. 32).

CONCLUSION

TBTF has changed greatly in both definition and application since protection of at least some claimants of large banks become possible with the introduction of deposit insurance in the 1930s. The concept was broadest in the resolution of the Continental Illinois Bank in 1984, when all claimants of the bank and all creditor claimants of its parent holding company were protected fully against loss and the bank was continued in operation. But, even then, the shareholders of the holding company were effectively wiped out and senior management of both the bank and bank holding company was changed by the FDIC. Since then, the number and type of claimants protected have progressively been significantly narrowed, even before the enactment of FDICIA in 1991. Nevertheless, the high cost and perceived unfairness of TBTF resulted in opposition to its continued use. FDICIA transformed TBF into SRE and greatly raised the barriers to its use. Partially as a result, since

1992, uninsured deposits have been protected only in a few resolutions of very small banks, where the uninsured deposits were apparently sold to an assuming bank at a sufficient premium to satisfy the LCR test, that is, to reduce the estimated cost to the FDIC below that of paying the uninsured depositors the present value of the prorata estimated recovery value.[15] Although the total number of resolutions has been small and no very large banks have failed, uninsured depositors have not been protected in any of the largest commercial banks that were resolved and in which the FDIC incurred losses. SRE was never invoked. Thus, the system remains to be tested for the resolution of a large complex bank. But the combination of the substantial barriers imposed by FDICIA to invoking SRE, the ability of the FDIC to avoid freezing uninsured deposits at failed banks and provide near-instant liquidity to the depositors, the higher direct cost to surviving banks from paying for any FDIC losses, and the apparent greater reluctance of some regulators to invoke SRE than in the past may significantly reduce the probability of its use in the future.[16] In addition, any uncertainty about the use of the SRE will center on which, if any, depositors and other creditors to fully or partially protect and not on legal failure.

APPENDIX

Comptroller Conover and the Birth of TBTF

CHAIRMAN ST. GERMAIN. Mr. Conover, where does Continental Illinois' rank in size among the banks of the United States of America? Is it 11th, 10th, 9th, 8th?

MR. CONOVER. It seems to be moving.

CHAIRMAN ST. GERMAIN. Where was it?

MR. CONOVER. It was eighth, approximately.

CHAIRMAN ST. GERMAIN. Number eight?

MR. CONOVER. Yes.

MR. WYLIE. You have 11 multinationals?

MR. CONOVER. Right.

CHAIRMAN ST. GERMAIN. All right. Ever see the fellow who is painting himself into that corner? He doesn't realize there is no door back there. And there is less floor for him to walk over. I got news for you. You are painting yourself in a corner because my question now is: Can you foresee, in view of all the reverberations internationally that you described, had Continental Illinois been allowed to fail, and all those people put out of work and all those corporations out of money and all those other banks that would have failed, in view of that, you can ever foresee one of the 11 multinational money center banks failing? Can we ever afford to let any one of them fail?

MR. CONOVER. The answer to that, Mr. Chairman, is that we have got to find a way to. In order—

CHAIRMAN ST. GERMAIN. You are not answering.

MR. CONOVER. In order to have a viable system.

CHAIRMAN ST. GERMAIN. Mr. Conover, you said you don't have in your hip pocket the solution for the small banks, and you are never going to have it. The fact of the matter is, as a practical matter, neither you nor your successors are ever going to let a big bank the size of Continental Illinois fail.

MR. CONOVER. Mr. Chairman, it isn't whether the bank fails or not. It is how it is handled subsequent to its failure that matters. And we have to find a way. I admit that we don't have a way right now. And so, since we don't have a way, your premise appears to be correct at the moment.

CHAIRMAN ST. GERMAIN. That is one of the prime reasons for these hearings. We have quite a few, but one of our principal reasons is we have to make a decision. Do we allow, ever, a large bank to fail?

MR. CONOVER. I think it is important that we find a way to do that.

MR. BARNARD. Thank you.

MR. MCKINNEY. Would Mr. Barnard yield for a moment so I could follow through on the chairman's statement?

MR. BARNARD. I want to follow through too, if you don't mind.

MR. MCKINNEY. With all due respect, I think seriously, we have a new kind of bank. And today there is another type created. We found it in the thrift institutions, and now we have given approval for a $1 billion brokerage deal to Financial Corporation of America.

MR. CHAIRMAN, let us not bandy words. We have a new kind of bank. It is called too big to fail. TBTF, and it is a wonderful bank.

Source: House, 1984, pp. 299–300.

NOTES

1. Earlier versions of this paper were presented as the Distinguished Scholar Lecture at the annual meeting of the Midwest Finance Association in Chicago (March 2002) and to the Chicago Association of Business Economists (June 2002), the Western Economic Association (July 2002), and the Financial Management Association (October 2002), and will be published in the *Quarterly Review of Economics and Finance*, summer 2002, pp. 423–36. I am indebted for helpful comments on earlier drafts to Bill Bergman and Douglas Evanoff (Federal Reserve Bank of Chicago), Richard Carnell (Fordham University), Christian Johnson (Loyola University Chicago), and Edward Kane (Boston College), as well to the audiences at these meetings. The views

presented are those of the author and do not necessarily represent those of the Federal Reserve Bank of Chicago or the Federal Reserve System.

2. I am indebted to Edward Kane for this point.

3. In the United States, chartered banks are legally failed and resolved by their primary federal regulator or state chartering agency and the FDIC under provisions of the FDI Act. In contrast, bank holding companies and nonbank subsidiaries are failed and resolved under the general corporate bankruptcy code like any other corporation.

4. In part, the parent holding company was protected and not forced into bankruptcy because of legal covenants in some of the debt obligations that prohibited the issuance of additional equity in the bank to anyone other than the holding company. This restriction was perceived by the regulators to have made it more difficult to provide financial assistance to the bank directly (Sprague, 1986). On the other hand, the FDIC argues that had the bank alone had been protected, the holding company had sufficient deposits at the bank to repay its maturing debt and avoid bankruptcy (FDIC, 1998b).

5. For example, even long after the failure of the Continental Bank, the FDIC argued that "the failure of one bank would set off a chain reaction, bringing about other failures. Sound banks frequently failed when large number of depositors panicked and demanded to withdraw their deposits, leading to 'runs' on the bank" (FDIC, 1998b, p. 212). Likewise, focusing on the payments system, the Federal Reserve believes that "if an institution participating on a private large-dollar payments network were unable or unwilling to settle its net debit position . . . the institution's creditors on that network might . . . then be unable to settle their commitments. . . . Serious repercussions could spread to other participants in the network, to other depository institutions and to the nonfinancial economy generally" (Coleman, 2002, p. 68).

6. In 1950, at its request, Congress authorized the FDIC to provide assistance to banks by making loans, purchasing assets, assuming liability, or making contributions to insured banks in danger of default or that lessen the risk to the FDIC (FDIC, 1984).

7. In days when interstate and, in some states, even intrastate banking was restricted, it was difficult at times to find acquiring banks.

8. In 1982, the FDIC had resolved the medium-sized Penn Square Bank (Oklahoma City) with losses to uninsured depositors but through a deposit payoff, when its large and uncertain off-balance sheet contingent obligations made it difficult for the FDIC to sell the bank quickly. Up to that time, it was by far the largest bank failure resolved with losses to uninsured depositors. These depositors received receivership certificates and were paid only through time as the FDIC, as receiver, liquidated the bank assets (FDIC, 1998b). The final payments were made and the receivership ended in 1996. Uninsured depositors received nearly 90 percent of the par value of their deposits on a non-present value basis.

9. Quick payment of depositors at closed banks to reduce the loss in liquidity has an interesting history in the United States. It was included in the form of a question in a questionnaire mailed to bankers and bank supervisors by the National Monetary Commission in 1908, proposed by Senator Carter Glass in 1931 as a superior strategy to federal deposit insurance, attempted by the Federal Reserve Bank of New York in 1932, and actually implemented by both the New York State Banking Department and the Reconstruction Finance Corporation in 1933 (Kaufman, 2002).

10. In addition, at the time,

There also was a belief at the FDIC that, while market discipline for investors and shareholders was desirable, depositor discipline was more of a mixed blessing. In practice, depositor discipline generally affected only unsophisticated depositors. Sophisticated depositors, who really should have provided depositor discipline, generally were already out of failing institutions by the time it was closed (FDIC, 1998b). However, because the Continental Bank was basically a single office unit bank, it conducted mostly a wholesale business and most deposits at the date of resolution were uninsured. Although there had been a significant run on the bank in the year before its resolution, the failure of all uninsured depositors to flee, in part, reflected a series of nonbinding assurances provided by federal regulators other than the FDIC to protect these depositors.

11. The complete transcript of the exchange between Conover and the Committee is shown in the appendix.

12. The FDIC also permitted the bank's parent holding company—FirstRepublic Bank Corporation (Dallas)—to file for bankruptcy by extending loans directly to the subsidiary banks rather than to the holding company (FDIC, 1998b). The significance of this was noted by William Seidman, who was Chairman of the FDIC at the time, as follows:

Unlike Continental Illinois, we gave our guarantee and our money directly to two of the banks owned by the company (the Dallas and Houston banks), but not to the holding company itself and its bond—and stockholders. This difference was of great significance. It removed the safety net from the billions of dollars of holding company dept. It reduced our insurance losses, disciplined the creditors of the holding company for their bad investment, and stabilized the banking system. (Siedman, 1993, p. 150).

13. This rescue drew unusual attention that hastened the end of TBTF for two reasons. One, a conflict between the FDIC and the Fed about protecting the offshore deposits. According to William Siedman, Chairman of the FDIC at the time, the FDIC was forced to protect the foreign deposits by the Federal Reserve, which claimed that not doing so would trigger a run against foreign deposits at offshore offices of other U.S. banks and threaten domestic financial stability (Bacon, 1990). Two, a minority owned and oriented bank—the Freedom National Bank in Harlem, New York, organized by baseball star Jackie Robinson in 1964—failed shortly afterwards, but uninsured depositors, many of whom were minority charities and churches, were not protected. Although the Freedom Bank was considerably smaller than the Continental Bank, a number of New York City congressmen vocally questioned the fairness of the policy (Bacon, 1990).

14. Before FDICIA, the FDIC frequently used highly creative and publicly undocumented methods for estimating the loss in uninsured depositor payoff resolutions. This cost was almost always found to be far greater than for bank assistance and justified the use of purchase and assumption in which all deposits were assumed by another bank par.

15. Uninsured depositors may have been fully protected in some failures in which the FDIC eventually reported a meaningful loss because the FDIC had originally overestimated the recovery value (underestimated the loss rate) and accepted a bid from the assuming bank that offered a premium that was larger than the estimated loss rate at the time but smaller, in retrospect, than the loss rate actually realized and reported.

16. Whether SRE will be invoked by the government and whether large noninsured depositors will assume it may not be invoked and therefore monitor their banks more carefully also depends in part on the public perception of the probability of its use. Some analysts remain highly skeptical that, when push comes to shove, it will not be invoked and leave uninsured depositors and creditors unprotected. For example, in reviewing the Senate hearings on the confirmation of Donald Kohn as a member of the Board of Governors, a central bank electronic newsletter wrote

Kohn . . . recommended that banks should be allowed to go bust if they fail the market test. "No depository institution should be insulated from market forces by being considered too-big-to-fail." Perhaps fortunately, nobody in the markets actually believes that doctrine, but political correctness never did have much to do with the real world, did it? (Mander, 2002)

REFERENCES

Bacon, Kenneth. "Failures of a Big Bank and Little Bank Bring Fairness of Deposit-Security Policy into Question." *Wall Street Journal*, 5 December 1990, p. 18.

Carrington, Tim. "U.S. Won't Let 11 Biggest Banks in Nation Fail." *Wall Street Journal*, 20 September 1984, p. 2.

Coleman, Stacy P. "The Evolution of the Federal Reserve's Intraday Credit Policies." *Federal Reserve Bulletin*, February 2002, pp. 67–84.

Conover, C.T. Testimony. *Inquiry into the Continental Illinois Corp. and Continental Illinois National Bank: Hearing before the Subcommittee on Financial Institutions Supervision, Regulation, and Insurance of Committee on Banking, Finance, and Urban Affairs*. 98–111. U.S. House of Representatives, 98th Cong., 2d Session. 18–19 September and 4 October.

Federal Deposit Insurance Corporation. *Resolutions Handbook*. Washington, D.C.: 1998a.

Federal Deposit Insurance Corporation. *Managing the Crisis*. Washington, D.C.: August, 1998b.

Federal Deposit Insurance Corporation. *History of the Eighties: Lessons for the Future*. Washington, D.C.: 1997.

Federal Deposit Insurance Corporation Improvement Act of 1991. See U.S. House. 1991.

Federal Deposit Insurance Corporation. *The First Fifty Years*. Washington, D.C.: 1984.

Federal Deposit Insurance Corporation. *Deposit Insurance in a Changing Environment*. Washington, D.C.: 1983.

Federal Reserve Committee on Branch, Group, and Chain Banking. *Bank Suspensions in the United States, 1921–1931*. Vol. 5. Washington, D.C.: Board of Governors of the Federal Reserve System, 1933.

Friedman, Milton, and Anna J. Schwartz. *A Monetary History of the United States: 1867–1960*. Princeton, N.J.: Princeton University Press, 1963.

Garcia, Gillian, and Elizabeth Plautz. *The Federal Reserve*. Cambridge, Mass.: Ballinger, 1988.

Greenspan, Alan. "Banking Evolution." *The Changing Financial Industry Structure and Regulation*. Chicago: Federal Reserve Bank of Chicago, May 2000, pp. 1–8.

Greenspan, Alan. "The Federal Safety Net." *The Financial Safety Net*. Chicago: Federal Reserve Bank of Chicago, May 2001, pp. 1–8.

Holland, David S. *When Regulation Was Too Successful: The Sixth Decade of Deposit Insurance*. Westport, Conn.: Praeger, 1998.

Kaufman, George, G. "Depositor Liquidity and Loss-Sharing in Bank Resolutions." *Contemporary Economic Policy*, 2004 (forthcoming).

Kaufman, George G. "Bank Failures, Systemic Risk, and Bank Regulation." *Cato Journal*, Spring/Summer 1996, pp. 17–45.

Kaufman, George G. "Bank Contagion: A Review of the Theory of Evidence." *Journal Financial Services Research*, April 1994, pp. 123–150.

Kaufman, George G. "Are Some Banks Too Large to Fail: Myth and Reality." *Contemporary Policy Issues*, October 1990, pp. 1–14.

Kaufman, George G. "FDIC Reform: Don't Put Taxpayers Back at Risk." *Policy Analysis*, Cato Institute, no. 432, 16 April 2002.

Kaufman, George G., and Steven A. Seelig. "Post-Resolution Treatment of Depositors at Failed Banks." *Economic Perspectives* (Federal Reserve Bank of Chicago), 2Q, 2002.

Kaufman, George G., and Peter Wallison. "The New Safety Net." *Regulation*, Summer 2001, pp. 28–35.

LaWare, John. Testimony. *Economic Implications of the "Too-Big-to-Fail" Policy: Hearing before the Subcommittee on Economic Stabilization of Committee on Banking, Finance, and Urban Affairs*. U.S. House of Representatives, 102d Cong., 1st Sess. 9 May 1991.

Mander, Benedict. "Bernanke and Kohn Accepted." In *Newsmakers-Central Bankers in the News*. 9 August 2002. Available from http://www.centralbanknet.com; INTERNET.

Mishkin, Frederic S. "Evaluating FDICIA." In *FDICIA: Bank Reform Five Years Later and Five Years Ahead*, edited by George G. Kaufman. Greenwich, Conn.: JAI Press, 1997, pp. 17–33.

O'Brien, Anthony P. " The Failure of the Bank of United States." *Journal of Money, Credit, and Banking*, August 1992, pp. 370–374.

O'Hara, Maureen, and Wayne Shaw. "Deposit Insurance and Wealth Effects: The Value of Being Too Big to Fail." *Journal of Finance*, December 1990, pp. 1587–1600.

Siedman, L. William. *Full Faith and Credit*. New York: Random House, 1993.

Spero, Joan E. *The Failure of the Franklin National Bank*. New York: Columbia University Press, 1980.

Sprague, Irvine H. *Bailout*. New York: Basic Books, 1986.

Sprague, O.M.W. "History of Crises under the National Banking System." In *National Monetary Commission*. Vol. 5 (Document No. 538; 61st Congress, 2d sess.), Washington, D.C.: Government Printing Office, 1910.

Trescott, Paul B. "The Failure of the Bank of United States, 1930." *Journal of Money, Credit, and Banking*, August 1992, pp. 384–399.

Upham, Cyril, and Edwin Lamke. *Closed and Distressed Banks*. Washington, D.C.: Brookings Institution, 1934.

U.S. House Committee on Banking, Finance, and Urban Affairs. *Inquiry into Continental Illinois Corp. and Continental Illinois National Bank: Hearings*. 98th Cong., 2d Sess. Washington, D.C.: 18–19 September and 4 October 1984.

U.S. House. *Federal Deposit Insurance Corporation Improvement Act of 1991*. Report 102–907. Washington D.C.: 27 November 1991.

CHAPTER 8

The Fall and Rise of Banking Safety Net Subsidies

Joe Peek and James A. Wilcox

INTRODUCTION

Several longstanding federal government programs and policies are intended to operate as financial safety nets. Financial safety nets reduce the likelihoods and severities of financial crises that have macroeconomic externalities. Safety nets also improve shorter-term and longer-term macroeconomic performance by reducing the expected effects of disruptions in financial intermediation or the payments system. Historically, safety net policies generally directly pertained to commercial banking. The most frequently recognized and analyzed safety nets have been the "traditional triad" of FDIC deposit insurance, the Fed's discount window, and the Fed's electronic payments system (Fedwire).

While safety nets are intended to confer benefits on the macroeconomy, their designs and implementation also are likely to confer benefits disproportionately on identifiable segments of the macroeconomy, such as banking and bank depositors. We distinguish between safety net benefits and subsidies. A standard definition is that a subsidy in some way transfers resources from one group to another. A subsidy often drives a wedge between the (lower) price paid by consumers and the (higher) social cost of production. Subsidies are often conferred on banking by the mispricing of the financial services associated with safety nets.[1]

Safety nets may confer benefits without conferring subsidies. While benefits likely flow from the presence of safety nets, subsidies stem from their mispricing. Ely (1999) and Jones and Kolatch (1999) point out that fairly priced deposit insurance confers no subsidies. By contrast, the reduction in interest rates that banks pay to depositors on insured deposits would considerably overstate the subsidy associated with deposit insurance. The reduction typically consists not only of any subsidy, but also of the benefit attributable to a government having a cost advantage over the private sector in supplying deposit insurance to the very large banking industry. Inefficient design and implementation of safety nets may hamper their long-term efficacy, subsidize banks and their deposit and loan customers, and generally misallocate resources.

We first illustrate how safety nets can provide benefits and subsidies to banking. We delineate (1) the difference between benefits and subsidies and (2) the difference between (a) the cost to government, (b) the value to banks and their customers, and (c) the misallocation of resources associated with subsidies. Next, we discuss how existing estimates correspond to those benefits and subsidies. We also discuss the difficulties involved in aggregating different subsidies and ascribing and measuring costs that would reduce the net subsidy associated with some or all the components of safety nets.

Then, we make the case that banking safety net subsidies declined after the late 1980s, rose starting in the middle of the 1990s, and may well rise further in the early part of the 2000s. Reforms that reduced banking safety net subsidies include the introduction of risk-based deposit insurance premiums, restricting discount window borrowing to solvent institutions, and instituting fees for Fedwire daylight overdrafts. Since the middle of the 1990s, however, other significant developments have almost certainly *raised* banking safety net subsidies.[2] For example, the recent growth of the size and activities of the Federal Home Loan Banks (FHLBs) is very likely to have raised the size of the safety net subsidy already and will do so further in the coming years.[3]

SAFETY NET BENEFITS vs. SUBSIDIES

In this section, we distinguish the benefits from the subsidies attributable to banking safety nets. The first section considers the case of government provision of financial services to banks. The U.S. Treasury's supply of a line of credit to the FDIC, the discount window, the Fed's supply of intraday credit on its Fedwire electronic payments system, and the implicit government credit guarantee on the debt of the FHLBs are examples of government supplies. Government provision of financial services at prices that fully cover its costs of supplying them is likely to provide banks with benefits without aggregate or cross-subsidies, avoid resource transfers across groups, and be efficient, in that it would not misallocate resources. In contrast, government provision at prices below its costs typically generates aggregate and cross-subsidies and misallocates resources.

The second section analyzes the benefits and the subsidies specifically associated with the government provision of deposit insurance. Deposit insurance affects banks' demands for deposits and households' (and others') supply of deposits to banks. We model deposit insurance premiums that banks pay as a fixed share of deposits. As is the case for many government subsidies, the government subsidies attributable to the underpricing of deposit insurance are likely to be shared with depositors (and bank customers more generally). In response to the subsidy, banks raise the deposit interest rates that they pay.[4] In doing so, banks transfer some of the government subsidy to depositors.[5]

Subsidies in Markets with Government Supply of Financial Services

There are many privately provided financial services that provide banks (and other financial institutions) with safety nets. In essence, all risk-sharing financial services may be conceived as safety nets. Any bank may purchase lines of credit or derivative products to reduce risk of failure. That these financial services may not completely protect banks from financial distress does not mean that they do not serve as safety nets. At the same time, government safety nets may be designed to reduce the risks to the macroeconomy, but typically would not be expected to completely insulate individual financial institutions or their customers from risks.

Figure 8.1 shows demand for and supply of a financial service that provides a safety net (e.g., a line of credit). The downward sloping demand curve reflects that banks (as consumers of safety net services) value the first units of protection highly, but are less willing to pay for protection against more remote risks. The private supply of this financial service may be expected to be upward sloping. Agents willing to supply risk reduction will expect more compensation as they take on additional amounts of risk. Absent government, a private equilibrium occurs at point (P) with associated price (P_P) and quantity (Q_P). Point P shows that some financial services that entail safety nets may be

Figure 8.1
The Market for Government-Provided Financial Services

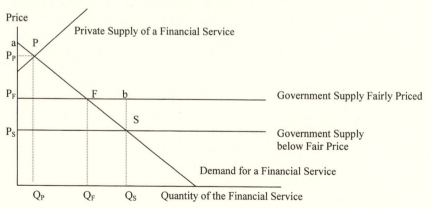

privately provided. The existence of this service yields a consumer surplus
(aPP$_P$) that is retained by banks and that may be associated with the benefits
they receive from the existence of this service. For instance, the knowledge
that a line of credit will be available in times of distress may permit banks to
hold fewer liquid assets, to receive better terms from other creditors, or to
engage in some higher-yielding riskier activities.

Public provision of this financial service is possible at costs that are lower
than available through private provision. This is plausible, since agents holding larger volumes of assets and liabilities that are more diversified may be
expected to absorb individual risks with a much smaller increase in overall
portfolio risk. Thus, individuals may choose to self-insure for smaller risks
(such as a refrigerator breakdown) and not purchase maintenance plans. In
turn, individuals typically do not self-insure for larger, more long-term risks
(such as death) and purchase life insurance policies. A small private insurance
company may provide life insurance to individuals profitably by pooling their
risks, since the incidence of deaths in a population can be predicted easily for
even small populations and is unlikely to suddenly increase by large amounts.

Other types of claims are less predictable (such as casualty insurance for
houses against tornadoes) and require larger insurance companies with more
geographically diversified assets, and eventually even re-insurance companies
that diversify their risks internationally. Along these lines, the government (of
a large and stable country) might be viewed as an agent with assets that are
more diversified and more capable of bearing risks and temporary losses for
longer than any other domestic company, in part because of its larger wealth
that includes the valuable assets of being able to command resources by printing money and imposing taxes. Thus, it appears likely that governments may
be able to provide safety net financial services at a lower cost and in larger
amounts than the private sector. In a sense, the government has "better technology," and thus there can be a benefit from the government entering the
market.

Figure 8.1 includes a supply of government financial services that is sold
fairly priced (i.e., at marginal cost). The intersection of fairly priced government supply and the demand curve yields a "fairly priced" equilibrium point
(F) with an associated price (P$_F$) and quantity (Q$_F$). The supply curve of government fairly priced financial services included in figure 8.1 is represented
as a horizontal line, with average cost equal to marginal cost. It is likely, in
practice, that this supply curve would not be perfectly horizontal, since larger
volumes of insured deposits would increase the risk imposed on the government. However, the slope is likely to be close enough to zero that a horizontal
supply curve closely approximates reality.

To the extent that this supply curve does represent a fairly priced financial
service (i.e., demanders pay fees that cover the government's cost of production), there are no subsidies involved. There is, however, a measurable (net)
benefit from the provision of this financial service. The triangle aFP$_F$ repre-

sents the benefits to banks attributable to the introduction of government-supplied, fairly priced financial service. (The extra benefit of having the government rather than the private sector supply fairly priced financial service is measured by the difference between this larger triangle (aFP_F) and the smaller triangle (aPP_P)). As in the case of private provision of safety net related financial services, the increased quantity of lower-priced lines of credit, for example, may tilt bank portfolios toward less-liquid assets and better borrowing terms from other creditors.

However, government provision of financial services can indeed lead to subsidies, transfers across groups, and the misallocation of resources. Consider the case of the government providing a safety-net related financial service below its fair price. In figure 8.1, this is shown as a supply curve at the subsidized price of P_S (lower than P_P).[6] At this lower price, the subsidized equilibrium point (S) is associated with increased use of this financial service by banks (from Q_F to Q_S). At lower prices, banks indeed receive an additional gain that we may call a subsidy and that would be represented by the trapezoid P_FFSP_S. Along with this subsidy, banks could be expected to again reduce their holdings of liquid securities, to receive (perhaps) even better terms from other creditors, and to engage in further riskier activities. However, this additional risk taking is likely to impose costs in the form of bank failures or defaults on obligations that will have to be borne by the issuer of the credit lines (i.e., the government). By construction, the rectangle P_FbSP_S represents the extent of the underpricing of the financial service, and thus the costs imposed by it. Since the costs (P_FbSP_S) that providing this subsidy impose on government (and thus on taxpayers) exceed the subsidy received by banks (P_FFSP_S), the mispricing of this financial service leads to the misallocation of resources and to social waste in the amount of triangle Fbs.

Subsidies in Markets with Government Programs: The Case of Deposit Insurance

In this section, we show that fairly priced deposit insurance premiums provide benefits to banks and depositors alike, and, if government subsidies are provided to banks through the underpricing of deposit insurance, those subsidies may be shared with depositors. However, mispriced premiums generate subsidies, redirect resources across groups, and misallocate resources.

Let figure 8.2 represent the market for deposits. In this market, households supply deposits as a positive function of interest rates with the intercept determined, for instance, by the risk of losing their deposits in a bank failure (as well as by the rates of return and risks on other investments). Banks demand deposits (to be lent out) as a negative function of interest rates with a vertical intercept determined, for instance, by the noninterest costs of deposits (and the rates required by other creditors). In the absence of a deposit insurance system, the equilibrium would occur at point A, with a level of deposits D_A

Figure 8.2
Deposit Insurance and the Supply of and Demand for Deposits

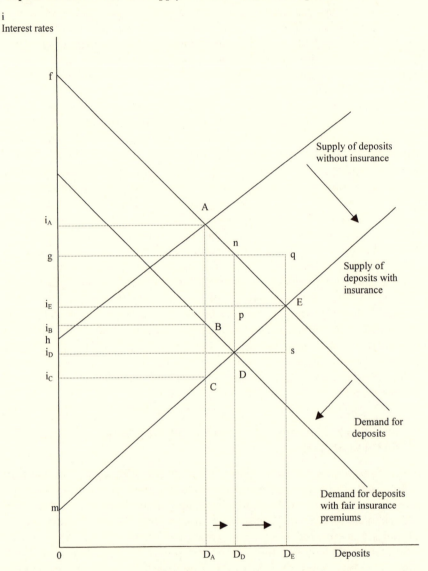

and an interest rate (i_A) that would incorporate the default-risk premium demanded by depositors and would not incorporate the (noninterest) costs of
participating in the deposit insurance system. Even in the absence of a credible
deposit insurance system, the willing participation of private banks and depositors implies that there are benefits from the existence of a banking system.

In particular, the benefit to banks may be represented by their consumer surplus (fAi_A) and the benefit to depositors by their producer surplus (i_AAh).

Fairly Priced Deposit Insurance

Credible deposit insurance involves shifting the risk of bank defaults from depositors to an outside party. Since this risk was a determinant of the supply of deposits, the introduction of deposit insurance shifts the supply of deposits downward. Since deposit premiums are a constant share of deposits, the supply shifts parallel. At the original level of deposits D_A, the vertical distance AC ($= i_A - i_C$) is the difference between the interest rates that depositors would demand with and without insurance, and thus represents the default-risk premium.

A fair deposit insurance premium charged by a risk-neutral government would equal the sum of expected deposit losses plus any administrative costs. If this fair premium per unit of deposits were imposed on banks, the demand for deposits would shift down to incorporate this noninterest cost. At the original level of deposits D_A, the vertical distance AB ($= i_A - i_B$) represents the difference between the interest rates that banks would pay if they bore the full costs of deposit insurance compared to bearing none of the costs.

We assume that the per-unit cost of providing deposit insurance does not vary across different banks, across aggregate amounts of deposits, or across time. Below we discuss the possibility that different banks have different risks of default. To allow for increasing aggregate amounts of deposits increasing risk to the deposit insurer, we could have the supply curve in figure 1 slope upward. If insuring more deposits imposed more risks, and thus costs per unit of deposits, the distance between the two demand curves (i.e., the fairly priced premium) would increase as deposits rose.[7] We also assume that the distribution of expected losses due to bank failures is stable enough for the deposit insurer to calculate fairly priced, ex ante deposit insurance premiums.

In figure 8.2, the downward shift in the supply curve combined with a downward shift in the demand curve leads to a new equilibrium point (D). This equilibrium will be associated with unambiguously lower interest rates to be received by depositors (falling from i_A to i_D). This is not surprising, since depositors would no longer demand a default-risk premium (AC) and banks have new noninterest costs (AB = nD). The level of deposits (D_D) associated with the new equilibrium could theoretically be higher or lower than D_A. figure 8.2 represents the case in which the cost of providing deposit insurance (AB) falls short of the default-risk premium (AC), and thus a case in which deposits increased. The increase in deposits seems the most probable case, since individual depositors are likely to be more risk averse than the deposit insurer.

Consider the extreme example of a banking system in which banks holding 2 percent of total deposits failed each year and in which the deposit insurer raised only half the value of those deposits from selling the remaining assets of the failed banks. This implies that the deposit insurer could operate by charging banks a yearly fee of (roughly) 1 percent of deposits. In figure 8.2, this would be represented by a cost (and a premium) per unit of deposits of gi_D ($=$ AB) and total costs of $gnDi_D$ when the level of deposits is D_D. In contrast, it is highly likely that depositors would demand significantly more than a 1 percent default-risk premium for accepting a 2 percent chance of losing half of their deposits (or for a 1 percent chance of losing all their deposits). Thus, if the compensation that depositors demand against losses exceeds the cost of covering those losses, one would expect that the development of a risk-sharing mechanism would benefit the involved parties.

Figure 2 confirms the a priori notion that risk-sharing mechanisms benefit both banks and depositors. Banks benefit because their per-unit cost of funds (including both interest and premiums) fall from i_A to g ($= i_D + gi_D$), while deposits increased from D_A to D_D. Thus, the benefit to banks from the existence of a fairly priced deposit insurance system is represented by the increase in banks' consumer surplus (i_AAng). Again, since banks would be covering the costs of the deposit insurer, there would not be a subsidy, but simply a benefit equivalent (in kind if not in volume) to that provided by a private provider of any safety net-related financial service.

Next, we consider how depositors would be affected. The triangle i_AAh would represent the amount of producer surplus retained by depositors prior to the introduction of deposit insurance. In turn, the parallelogram ACmh would represent the compensation received by depositors for default risk. Alternatively, compensation for default risk could be represented by the rectangle i_AACi_C and producer surplus could be represented (relative to a supply curve that is free from default-risk) by the triangle i_CCm. Thus, the introduction of fairly priced deposit insurance would benefit depositors, since the (default-risk free) interest rate that they receive would increase from i_C to i_D, while deposits increased from D_A to D_D. The size of this benefit would be represented by the associated increase in depositors' producer surplus (i_DDCi_C).[8]

Underpriced Deposit Insurance

Suppose, instead, that the government levies no deposit insurance premiums. Shifting the entire cost of deposit insurance from banks to the government implies that banks can acquire insured deposits below their cost of production (by the amount of the fair premium). At the initial deposit level D_D, the total size of the subsidy received by banks would equal the size of the government outlays ($gnDi_D$) and imply a subsidy to banks of gi_D per dollar of deposits. When the cost of deposits falls short of the price that banks are willing to pay, banks will add deposits. To attract more deposits, as shown by the upward-sloped supply curve, banks will have to offer higher deposit interest rates. To attract deposits banks are likely to increase interest and noninterest costs, such as marketing, operational expenses, and so on. The downward-sloped demand for deposits reflects the declining marginal profitability of banks' lending opportunities. As deposits increase, the gap between the price that banks are willing to pay and the total costs for each additional deposit head toward zero. At equilibrium point E, the higher level of deposits is associated with a higher deposit interest rate (i_E) than with fairly priced deposit insurance (i_D), but lower than without deposit insurance (i_A).

At point E, some of the deposit insurance subsidy does accrue to depositors and some resources are wasted. As deposits increase from D_D to D_E, the expected costs of the deposit insurance system, which are being entirely borne by the government, would increase by nqsD from $gnDi_D$ to $gqsi_D$. The subsidy that banks retain equals the (consumer surplus) trapezoid $gnEi_E$. The subsidy that depositors retain equals the (producer surplus) trapezoid of EDi_Di_E.

Benefits are the gains to trade when the prices paid for financial services (whether privately or publicly provided) cover total production costs. Subsidies arise when prices paid do not cover total production costs, with the difference picked up by the government. In figure 8.2, the trapezoids i_AAng and DCi_Ci_D measure the benefits from deposit insurance. The cost to government of the subsidies is represented by the rectangle $gqsi_D$.

Figure 8.2 also shows how the cost to government of subsidies exceeds the sum of the subsidies that accrue to banks and their customers. When the government charges no deposit insurance premium, it incurs costs equal to $gqsi_D$. Banks gained $gnEi_E$ and depositors gained EDi_Di_E. The triangles nqE and EsD measure waste, in that they are the costs incurred by the government that do not benefit banks or their customers.

EXAMPLES AND ESTIMATES OF BANKING SAFETY NET SUBSIDIES

The previous section analyzed safety net benefits and subsidies qualitatively. In this section, we discuss how policies and implementation of four categories of federal government programs generate safety net subsidies for banking: deposit insurance, the discount window, the payments system, and the FHLBs.[9] Conventional wisdom holds that underpricing of the services of the first three of these programs, the traditional triad, has long provided subsidies to banking.[10] Because of the recent growth of their size and activities, we also analyze how FHLBs increasingly contribute to banking safety net subsidies.

Deposit Insurance[11]

Historically, neither individual banks nor banks in the aggregate paid fully risk-based deposit insurance premiums. Until the early 1990s, the FDIC levied flat-rate insurance premiums on banks as a function of deposits, but not banks' risks. From 1935 to 1988, banks paid flat rate insurance premiums that never exceeded 8.3 basis points.[12] As a result of the depletion of the FDIC reserves due to the thrift and banking crises, premiums were then raised to as high as 31 basis points. The enactment of FDICIA in 1991 required that the FDIC introduce risk-based premiums. To date, however, the range of the premiums remains much narrower than the range of risk exposures of the FDIC to individual bank failures. Under the terms of the Deposit Insurance Funding Act of 1996, when the FDIC reserve fund exceeds 1.25 percent of deposits, the safest of banks pay no deposit insurance premium. Recently, that meant that more than 90 percent of banks, which held well over 90 percent of total bank assets, paid no premiums.

Figure 8.2 assumed that the cost of providing deposit insurance per dollar of deposits was constant across individual banks and across time. As the FDIC's expected losses vary across banks and across time, fair deposit insurance premiums should vary, too. If they do not vary sufficiently or if they reflect factors other than ex ante risks, then both aggregate and cross-subsidies are almost inevitable.

Often, governments underwrite the expenses of deposit insurance programs. Typically, they do not make explicit the expected costs that they incur by doing so. So long as a banking crisis does not occur, the expected costs are largely hidden in the form of contingent costs. To the extent that banks will not be required to cover all the actual costs of the deposit insurer, a government's commitment to make depositors whole during future crises means that the government incurs that implicit liability. In the United States, the government's provision of this "catastrophe insurance" as well as a no-fee line of credit, to the FDIC confers benefits and subsidies on banking. Thus, to a first approximation, deposit insurance premiums are underpriced to the extent that the government underprices the services that it provides to the FDIC.

The fair price for deposit insurance can be estimated in different ways. Option-pricing models have often been used to obtain estimates of fair deposit insurance premiums. When a bank becomes insolvent, insured depositors effectively have the option to sell (or "put") their deposits to the FDIC at par. The value of this put option is a measure of the fair premium for the deposit insurance. Calculating the option value of deposit insurance is not trivial. First, the most commonly used models for pricing options assume a finite time horizon. Thus, calculating the option value for any fixed short horizon will understate the fair value of the insurance, since the deposit insurance provided by the FDIC is ongoing. Second, the current health of a bank is a key determinant of the option's value. Third, bank regulations are important, such as minimum capital requirements, limitations on the types and amounts of assets that can be held or activities that can be undertaken, and the frequency of exams. Fourth, the value of the option is affected by supervisory practices, that is, the enforcement of the regulations.

Not surprisingly, options-based estimates of fairly priced deposit insurance premiums vary with the sample period, moving inversely with the overall health of the banking system. Jones and Kolatch (1999) reported that studies based on 1980s data estimated that premiums were underpriced only for the weakest banks, with most banks paying more than the fair premium. Both Jones and Kolatch (1999) and Whalen (1997) concluded that premiums were more generally underpriced in more recent periods. Whalen provided evidence based on the application of the option-pricing methodology to June 1996 data for the 50 largest BHCs. Based on a range of assumptions, Whalen reported the median put option value to be four basis points, if banks were closed when the market value of their assets declined to 90 percent of the market value of their liabilities.[13]

These estimates of the fair premiums exceed the costs of deposit insurance to the government by the amount of the expected, average contributions of banks to the FDIC. Further, the expected total costs of deposit insurance to the government exceed the subsidy received by banks. As shown in figure 8.2, an amount equal to the total costs incurred by the government is split among banks, depositors, and waste associated with resource misallocation.

Greenspan (1997) proposed an alternative to the option-based approach. His alternative is based on the assumption that safety nets provide funding advantages to a lead bank but not to its parent holding company. He advocated using the yield spread between the bonds of a bank holding company and those of its lead bank to measure the effect of safety nets on the bank proper. By this measure, the subsidy was in the range of 10 to 15 basis points in 1990, but only about half that value after 1994.

It seems unlikely that the relative impact of the safety net on a bank and its parent BHC is the sole reason for the yield differential. Jones and Kolatch (1999) cite *Moody's* and *Standard and Poor's* credit rating manuals for evidence that the priority of bank debt over BHC debt is the primary reason for bank debt having a higher rating. Bank supervisors can limit or prohibit dividend payments from a bank to its parent when the bank's financial health weakens. In addition, a BHC may be required to provide resources to its subsidiary banks to prevent their insolvency. Further, safety nets may reduce funding costs for both the bank and its holding company (which may consist of little more than a lead bank), implying that the yield spread underestimates the funding advantages conferred by safety nets.

Since its founding in 1934, the FDIC has collected premiums (and earned income on its accumulated reserves) that approximately equal its bank-failure and administration expenses. So far, the government has not ever explicitly injected funds into the FDIC. Nonetheless, the government has subsidized the FDIC by providing two valuable financial services at no cost to the FDIC and thereby to banks: a line of credit and catastrophe insurance.

The cost to the government of the FDIC's line of credit consists of any expected losses plus any interest rate subsidy. If credit were extended to the FDIC at interest rates below the (fully) risk-based level, the FDIC would receive a subsidy from government.[14] The underpricing of services to the FDIC enables it to levy lower premiums on banks.[15] Measuring the fair fee and interest rates for the FDIC's line of credit is problematic. Walter (1998) cites five basis points as the lower limit of the range of fees that private-sector, nonbank corporations pay to banks for their lines of credit. If an annual fee of five basis points were the fair fee for the FDIC's $30 billion line of credit, the FDIC has been paying $15 million less than the fair fee.

Although the FDIC has never received any explicit infusions of funds from the government, its backing by the full faith and credit of the U.S. Treasury introduces a subsidy in the form of a no-fee catastrophe insurance policy. There seems to be little doubt that, in practice, the full faith and credit of the United States stands behind the FDIC. Indeed, without objection from the Treasury, FDIC chairs have publicly stated that the full faith and credit of the United States does back up the FDIC (beyond the simple $30 billion line of credit). Regardless of whether that pledge is codified in the letter of the law, the government, the banking industry, and financial markets each do act as if such a pledge is in force.

In the event of bank failures, the insurance fund reserves presumably would be the first line of defense against FDIC losses. Next, the FDIC would turn to banks for premiums and special assessments to bolster the insurance fund and would next turn to the Treasury for liquidity by drawing upon its (repayable) line of credit.

FIRREA, FDICIA, and other legislative and regulatory changes may well have reduced the value of the backstop that the Treasury provides to the FDIC. In fact, some contend that the Treasury is no longer at risk from the FDIC because FDICIA, in effect, gives to the FDIC a call option on the aggregate stock of equity capital in banks to make good on the FDIC's deposit insurance obligations. They argue that that stock is much larger than any plausible loss that the FDIC could incur, and therefore that the Treasury bears no risk.[16]

At some point, the losses to the FDIC could indeed become so great that the interests of national welfare would argue for the Treasury to extend funds to the FDIC that would not be repaid by surviving banks. That point would presumably come long before the entire capital of the banking industry had been lost by banks or had been siphoned out of the remaining banks by the FDIC. If costs of bank failures are large (as in the savings and loans crisis or those implied by estimates of Japanese nonperforming loans), the fees to be imposed on banks could outweigh their capacity to generate revenues and to meet capital requirements. If FDIC fees sought to recoup the costs of bank losses quickly, they could exhaust the capital of surviving banks and lead to their closure. If FDIC fees were targeted such that capital requirements were met, extended periods of zero earnings could follow. Experience supports our contention that there is a catastrophe insurance policy in place. During the thrift crisis and its aftermath, some capital was indeed extracted from the remaining healthy banks, as well as thrifts, to help cover the obligations of the thrift deposit insurance program. But long before all of the capital of the remaining, solvent thrifts had been called, the Treasury agreed to cover the remaining losses without reimbursement.

Thus, estimates of the banking safety net subsidies also need to allow for fairly priced premiums of such catastrophe insurance policies. If one were to regard a fee of one basis point on domestic deposits of about $3 trillion as a reasonable estimate of the annual fee for both financial services, the FDIC would pay to the Treasury about $300 million annually. As our discussion of figure 8.2 noted, in general and these services are unlikely to be an exception, the total costs to the government of supplying underpriced services are likely to exceed their value to banks.

Discount Window

The Federal Reserve may provide collateralized loans to solvent banks (and to other solvent nonbank institutions) through its discount window. In this analysis, we regard the Fed's discount window as following the dictate that it make only fully collateralized loans. In that light, the window makes risk-free loans.[17] To the extent that the discount rate approximates the interest rate on risk-free borrowing, borrowing through the discount window would provide no or only very small subsidies. However, Ely (1999) notes that if the discount rate is slightly below the market risk-free rate, perennial borrowing from the discount window would subsidize the (small set of mostly small) banks that engage in this practice. The recent Fed decision to peg the discount rate slightly above the Fed funds rate beginning on January 9 (Lagomarsino 2002) would appear to further reduce, if not eliminate, this subsidy.

However, the discount window does provide banks with other benefits and subsidies. The discount window effectively offers the possibility that the Fed will extend credit to a bank that has a liquidity problem. To the extent that the window provides banks with access to loans when the private sector would not, the benefit of the discount window is that liquidity can be obtained at all. In that sense, the window has features of a line of credit. Also, to the extent that access to this source of credit reduces the risk that banks' liquidity problems would be converted into solvency problems, the discount window reduces the default risk faced by the bank's deposit and non-deposit creditors, and thus reduces the bank's cost of funds. Since this service could be provided in a manner that imposed its full, expected costs on banks, the existence of this line of credit and the better terms that it entails for banks on their other borrowing may be considered benefits to banks, and not subsidies. However, banks currently pay no fee to the Fed for this line of credit feature. Thus, the underpricing of the discount window services confers a safety net subsidy on banks.

There are few, if any, estimates of the value of access to the discount window. Along with Ely (1999), we regard the interest rate subsidy in discount window borrowing to be minor because, as noted above, such borrowing is collateralized and the discount rate typically is not very far from risk-free rates. However, a more sizeable subsidy emanates from the Fed's providing access to liquidity when banks are least likely to be able to obtain liquidity from the private sector. Walter (1998) notes that banks charge their nonbank customers annual fees in the range of five to 20 basis points of the dollar amount of the loan commitment. Lines of credit supplied by private-sector banks typically include clauses that allow banks to deny credit in the event of "material adverse conditions." By contrast, the discount window would be expected to be available to a bank so long as the bank is solvent at the time of borrowing, which would make the discount window more valuable than a private-sector bank line of credit. Another difficulty in estimating the value of this financial service, unlike a private line of credit, is that the ceiling of the line of credit is not explicitly specified. If the size of the line were taken to be as large, say, as the volume of assets that the Fed would accept as collateral to be pledged for the discount window loan, then it might be regarded as being as large as a substantial fraction of a bank's total assets.

Fedwire

The Federal Reserve operates a real-time gross settlement electronic payments system, commonly referred to as Fedwire. Via Fedwire, banks are able to transfer funds to other institutions' reserve accounts at the Fed. The Fed processes payment instructions as they are received in real time, even if the sender does not have sufficient funds in its reserve account to cover the transfer at the time of the payment instruction. The Fed guarantees payment finality: Once the Fed notifies a bank that the Fed has credited the bank's reserve account at the Fed, the funds cannot be recalled, even if the bank that sent the payment instruction is unable later to deliver the funds.

Historically, the Fed has underpriced the credit that it extends during the course of the business day by guaranteeing payments made via Fedwire. Until April 1994, the fee was zero; since April 1995, the effective rate has been 27 basis points at an annual rate. Compared with even the risk-free rate, not to mention the risky rate that would be most relevant for this unsecured borrowing, the fees charged for daylight overdrafts on Fedwire have been and remain extremely low.

The benefit to banks arises because they are extended a line of credit that permits them to have daylight overdrafts (i.e., negative balances in its reserve account prior to the close of Fedwire that day) as a result of transfers to other banks. Essentially, the Fed makes an intraday loan to a bank so that its transactions can clear without having to wait until its reserve account has a sufficient balance. The Fed absorbs the credit risk, which stems from the possibility that the sending bank will not be able to cover the daylight overdraft. The benefit to the bank includes the reduced need to hold reserves. The subsidy arises because banks are extended a line of credit for which they pay no fee and because the loan rate on daylight overdrafts is well below 1 percent annually, a rate charged on a risky daylight overdraft that is far below the average over time of the risk-free rate.

As with the subsidy associated with discount window access, there are few estimates of the value of the subsidy associated with below-market pricing of Fedwire daylight overdraft credit. Mengle, Humphrey, and Summers (1987) estimated that the market rate during the 1980s could have been in the neighborhood of 100–124 basis points. Increases in banks' capital ratios and various financial sector reforms may have reduced considerably the fair market interest rate for daylight overdrafts since the 1980s. We have no independent estimate of the current market rate for credit extended via daylight overdrafts. Suppose, however, that the midpoint of the estimated current range was one-half (56 basis points) of the midpoint (112 basis points) of the range cited above. Then, given average, aggregate, outstanding daylight overdrafts of about $30 billion, the current fee undercharges borrowers by over $40 million annually.[18]

Advances and MPF Programs at FHLBs

FHLBs are arguably part of the banking safety net because they share with the Federal Reserve a scaled-down version of the function of lender of last resort. FHLBs routinely extend credit in the form of advances to qualifying thrifts and commercial banks. In addition, FHLBs can be expected to continue to extend credit to banks and thrifts when other sources of funds dry up. In that manner, FHLBs provide banks and thrifts with implicit, and hence underpriced, lines of credit. Moreover, the rates that FHLBs charge on advances to thrifts and commercial banks are directly affected by the rates at which the FHLBs themselves can borrow. The rates at which FHLBs borrow are reduced by the full faith and credit of the U.S. government that is presumed to undergird their debts. These reductions in borrowing costs are then passed along to thrifts and commercial banks either directly or indirectly. The direct route is through reduced rates charged for advances or through above-market compensation for services provided to the FHLBs. The indirect route is by passing along higher FHLB earnings via dividends to the thrifts and commercial banks that constitute the FHLBs' shareholders.

In addition, the Mortgage Partnership Finance Program (MPF) run by the FHLBs also passes along some of the reduced borrowing and capital costs available to FHLBs. Under MPF, thrifts and commercial banks essentially act as mortgage loan origination agents for the FHLBs. They originate mortgages on behalf of the FHLBs without actually taking these mortgages onto their balance sheets. Instead, the FHLBs use their funding advantage to fund these mortgages. The thrifts and commercial banks also typically retain servicing rights. Thrifts and commercial banks thus earn fee income for originating and servicing mortgages.

As with other services that government provides to banking, it is important to distinguish benefits from subsidies. FHLB lines of credit provide banks a benefit but not a subsidy if banks paid the FHLBs the full cost of operating that service. However, since they are, again, provided at no cost to banks, subsidies are therefore present. The lower interest rates that banks receive from participation in FHLB activities consist of both benefit and subsidy components. The gains to banks arise from FHLBs' reduced financing costs, which stem from their diversification and securitization of assets and from their funding being implicitly guaranteed by the government.

GROSS vs. NET SUBSIDIES

Above, we showed examples and estimates of banking safety net subsidies. Participation in safety net programs may also impose costs on banks. Subsidies considered in absence of those costs might be termed gross subsidies. Subtracting the associated (but not the unassociated) costs of safety nets from the gross subsidies generates measures of net subsidies. The next section discusses some of the costs associated with safety nets and some estimates of their sizes. Afterward, we caution that the limitations associated with netting costs from gross subsidies are considerable.

Estimates of Costs to Banks of Safety Nets

While banking may benefit from some safety net subsidies, public policies also impose some safety net-specific costs that may partially offset subsidies. Indeed, some important aspects of bank supervision and regulation arose precisely to restrain banks from taking the excessive risks that the implementation of safety net–related policies may encourage. Other aspects of supervision and regulation have evolved for myriad other reasons. Whether they are reasonably netted from measures of safety net subsidies is open to question.

Among the supervisory and regulatory costs imposed on banking that have been attributed to safety nets are (1) examinations and reporting requirements, (2) activity restrictions, (3) balance sheet restrictions, and (4) the required reserve tax. Banks devote considerable time, material, and space resources to cooperate with bank examinations. For example, the largest national banks have bank supervisors on site continually. Banks are restricted from conducting certain financial activities from which they might profit. They are also constrained by bank supervision and regulations to either hold or not hold certain assets and liabilities on their balance sheets. For example, banks might prefer to have less equity capital and more debt on the liability side of their balance sheets; they might also prefer to hold assets that are more like equity and less like debt on the asset side of their balance sheets. Finally, banks are required to hold non-interest-bearing reserves against their transactions deposits. The opportunity cost associated with the reserves that are held in excess of the amount that a bank would hold in the absence of reserve requirements constitutes a regulatory cost to banks.

One may produce an estimate of the reserve tax associated with the requirement that banks hold reserves. Required reserves are based on a bank's transactions accounts and pay no interest. This calculation requires making an assumption about the opportunity cost of those reserves. Using an opportunity cost of 5 percent, Jones and Kolatch (1999) calculate a marginal cost of 15 to 50 basis points, depending on the size of the bank's transactions deposit balances. However, such an estimate seems too high. The opportunity cost should be calculated only on the binding portion of required reserves. That is, only on the amount by which required reserves exceed the amount of reserves a bank would hold in the absence of the reserve requirement.

The costs of supervisory and regulatory burdens are much more difficult to estimate. Both Jones and Kolatch (1999) and Whalen (1997) rely on estimates by the Federal Financial Institutions Examination Council (1992), though Jones and Kolatch (1999) observe, "good estimates . . . do not exist. . . ." The FFIEC study calculated banks' costs imposed by regulation and supervision of 6 to 14 percent of a bank's noninterest operating expenses, not including the opportunity cost of non-interest-bearing reserves. Using the lower bound of 6 percent, this amounts to about 35 basis points as a share of total deposits in 1995 (Whalen 1997) and 29 basis points in 1996 (Jones and Kolatch 1999). Since the FFIEC estimate is for the period prior to FDI-CIA, the costs do not incorporate any increased supervisory and regulatory costs associated with regulatory changes in the 1990s. Nor do they include higher regulatory costs associated with revisions to the Community Reinvestment Act or stricter enforcement of fair lending regulations.

Limitations in Netting Costs from Subsidies

We have pointed out some of the challenges involved in estimating the sizes of various safety net subsidies. The magnitudes of many subsidies vary with expected conditions in the macroeconomy and in the banking industry. They sometimes depend on the sizes of lines of credit, whose limits are unknown. Even when gross safety net subsidies and costs can be measured, if they apply to different margins, it may be misleading to merely subtract costs and interpret the result as the net subsidy. For example, the effects of a gross subsidy of $1 billion that was linked linearly to deposits would likely not be completely offset by a regulatory cost to banks of $1 billion linked to bank supervision or activity restrictions. While the direct effects on bank net worth might largely cancel, prices and quantities would still differ from their non-subsidized levels.

In addition, the myriad regulatory burdens cannot simply be assumed to be attributable to the existence of banking safety nets. Bank supervision and regulation predates both the existence of federal deposit insurance and even of the Fed by over half a century. Although some costs are imposed on banks as byproducts of attempts to limit the costs to government of providing banking safety nets, some are not. That view is supported to the extent that the elimination of all safety nets or safety net subsidies would be accompanied by the dismantling of banking regulation and supervision. For instance, neither the Community Reinvestment Act nor fair lending laws are linked to the provision of bank safety nets or subsidies.

THE FALL AND RECENT RISE OF SAFETY NET SUBSIDIES

Over time, both safety net subsidies and the offsetting costs associated with safety nets have changed by large amounts, both relative to the size of the banking industry and relative to each other. They have changed as a result of changes in public policies, of changes in the conditions of banks that arise from managerial choices and the economy more broadly, and of changes in financial technologies. The safety net subsidies and offsetting costs may well continue to change by considerable amounts in the future.

The Fall

Conventional wisdom holds that safety net subsidies began to decline in the late 1980s as a result of the following public policy changes: higher minimum required bank capital, more rigorous bank supervision, introduction of prompt corrective action (PCA), introduction of least-cost resolution of failed banks, higher deposit insurance premiums, introduction of national depositor preference, discount window reforms, and introduction of caps and fees on Fedwire daylight overdrafts. (See Walter [1998], Ely [1999], and Kaufman [2001].) This list of public policy changes consist of some lowering of safety net subsidies and some raising of the costs attributable to the safety net, both of which reduce the net safety net subsidy. Jones and Kolatch (1999) conclude that any resulting net marginal safety net subsidy is "very small."

Examples of higher costs in the 1990s that reduce safety net subsidies are the increases in fees for Fedwire daylight overdrafts. Average overdrafts rose to about $70 billion in the early 1990s and peaked at over $150 million. The Federal Reserve began charging fees for daylight overdrafts in 1994. The initial fee of 10 basis points (at an annual rate) rose to 15 basis points in 1995 and 27 basis points in 2000. In parallel, average overdrafts have fallen to about $40 billion.[19]

Some changes in banking regulations have also reduced banks' regulatory costs. The accumulation of regulations over the years, as well as rapid technological changes had no doubt rendered some regulations suboptimal. As a result, by the early 1990s the scale and scope for reducing banking regulations so that banks could reduce their explicit costs and foregone opportunities seemed quite large. Regulatory reforms like these would raise the net safety net subsidy to banking. A wide-ranging review in the early 1990s of banking regulations by a federal government interagency task force led to a concerted attempt to identify inefficient regulations that could be removed or reduced.

Overall, from the late 1980s through the middle of the 1990s, changes in public policies probably did reduce the safety net subsidy. The improvement in the overall health of the banking system is also likely to have reduced it. Public policies toward deposit insurance, the discount window, and Fedwire meant that the stronger the banking sector was, and therefore the less likely it was to fall into the safety net, the lower the magnitude and value of the subsidy.

The Recent Rise

What has been much less recognized has been the recent rebound in the value of safety net subsidies. Since about the middle of the 1990s, the subsidies to banks may well have risen significantly. Here we list several factors that have tended to raise, and perhaps raise substantially, safety net subsidies in recent years.

First, the required reserve tax has fallen sharply. Starting in the middle of the 1980s, required reserves rose from about $40 billion to about $60 billion. Required reserves then hovered around $60 billion until the middle of the 1990s. From the middle of the 1990s through the end of 2000, required reserves fell dramatically—to about $40 billion, their lowest level since the 1970s. (By the middle of 2002, required reserves were $37 billion.) Reductions in required reserve ratios and the increasing "sweeping" of households' reservable accounts at banks contributed importantly to the $20 billion decline in required reserves. As a result, banks could hold $20 billion more of interest-bearing assets instead of zero-interest required reserves. For the sake of example, suppose that banks earn a risk-free rate of 5 percent on the $20 billion of redeployed assets. That redeployment would reduce the costs to banks of the safety net subsidy and raise annual, before-tax income by $1 billion. Thus, the change in offsetting costs would have raised the net subsidy by over $1 billion annually.

Second, the Deposit Insurance Funding Act (DIFA) of 1996 prevents the FDIC from charging fully risk-based premiums. In effect, DIFA requires that nearly all banks now pay no explicit deposit insurance premium whatsoever. Making deposit insurance premiums lower and less risk-sensitive (again) probably reinforces some of the subsidy that stemmed from deposit insurance. Also, to the extent that insured deposits grow faster than the FDIC reserve fund (which currently grows roughly at the rate of return of its invested assets), the reserve fund would underfund potentially larger claims due to failed banks. Thus, the value of the two unpriced services provided by the Treasury to the FDIC would also increase. In essence, by lowering the premiums and reducing their risk sensitivity, DIFA has raised safety net subsidies.

Third, bank regulators noted that in the late 1990s banking had become noticeably riskier. Bank risks are likely to have risen then for several reasons. Lending practices had become more liberal. Continuing "capital arbitrage" effectively removed safer bank assets from bank balance sheets and thereby raised the average riskiness of retained assets relative to bank capital. Surveys also indicated that banks' commercial lending standards eased after the middle of the 1990s. The aggregate U.S. Tier 1 and total capital ratios drifted down after the middle of the 1990s. Thus, equity and options price-based calculations of bank risk would have indicated that banks generally had higher insolvency probabilities at the end of the decade than they did in the middle of the 1990s. Expected losses in the event of failure might have also increased. Taken together, these developments are likely to have increased the safety net subsidy that accrued to banks via the deposit insurance system.

Fourth, public policy responses to potential and actual financial crises during the 1990s (e.g., those in Mexico, Korea, Thailand, Indonesia, and Russia) may have raised financial markets' estimates of how far the financial safety nets provided by the U.S. government and international institutions extend. The Fed's involvement in the LTCM affair also may have raised the expected value of the safety net to banks proper and even more so to the parts of bank and financial holding companies beyond commercial banks.

Fifth, public policy recently further increased access of banks to the FHLB system at the same time that FHLBs increased their offerings of services to their member thrifts and banks. FIRREA in 1989 and GLBA in 1999 had already eased the access of commercial banks to FHLB advances. Increased access by commercial banks to FHLB advances and increased offerings of other services such as those associated with the MPS programs have contributed to the very rapid growth of FHLBs. From 1992 through 1999, the number of member institutions more than doubled to over 7,000, with more than 500 commercial banks that had more than $500 million in assets counted as members. By 1993, less than $6 billion in FHLB advances were outstanding to commercial banks. By 2000, nearly $150 billion were outstanding to commercial banks, comprising more than one-third of all FHLB advances. Thus, the safety net subsidy to banking that flows through the FHLB System may have grown substantially in recent years.

The Shadow Financial Regulatory Committee noted, "in the long run, the new powers granted to the FHLBs may be among the most significant elements of the [GLBA] legislation." GLBA permitted advances backed by agricultural and small business loans, thereby making additional FHLB subsidies available to small banks, and perhaps ultimately to large segments of the agricultural and small business lending market. The Shadow Committee concluded that GLBA allows for a major expansion of FHLB activities. Given their GSE status, that expansion offers the possibility of a major increase in this avenue for safety net subsidies to banking.

The Future

Will the net subsidy continue to rise? Here are some reasons that it might. First, the Federal Reserve has proposed that it be allowed to pay a market-related interest rate, rather than the long-standing rate of zero, on reserves held at its banks. Raising the rate paid on reserves would reduce offsetting costs and increase the net safety net subsidy. If 5 percent interest were paid on $7 billion held in reserve accounts at the Federal Reserve Banks, $350 million would be added to banks' pretax income.

Second, rules for sweep accounts may also be liberalized. Liberalization, for example to include all business and government accounts, would enable banks to reduce further their required reserves. At a 5 percent interest rate, reducing required reserves by another $20 billion, for example, would generate for banks another $1 billion in pretax income.

Third, potential Basel capital reform may enable many banks to hold less capital per unit of risk. Absent the prospect for aggregate reductions in capital per unit of risk, banks' support for reforms may be tepid and reforms unlikely. If the likely outcomes for reform are either none with continuing success at capital arbitrage or for lower aggregate capital requirements, the expected direction of "reformed" bank capital rules is a tilt toward liberalization.

Fourth, FHLBs' activities may continue to expand. Their activities have been growing very rapidly in recent years. FHLBs are unlikely to have completely penetrated the markets that have opened to them. As their activities grow, so will the subsidies that they confer on banks.

Fifth, the effective repeal of Glass-Steagall and provisions of GLBA may lead banks to extend their current reach into more activities. So far, relatively little has changed as a result of GLBA. If banks and their holding companies were to avail themselves of the opportunities opened up by GLBA, the safety net subsidy might increase noticeably.

Thus, perhaps the two most striking aspects of the current situation are how much the safety net subsidies to banking have risen and how they may rise in the future.

SUMMARY AND IMPLICATIONS

We have sought to distinguish the benefits from the subsidies attributable to financial safety nets. We highlighted that benefits arise when prices cover the full cost of (publicly or privately) producing financial services. Subsidies arise when prices do not completely cover the costs associated with producing financial services. Absent positive externalities, underpricing safety net-related financial services misallocates resources.

We applied our framework to the actual structure of deposit insurance in the United States. We argued that the provision of financial services to the FDIC, and thereby to banks, by the government at a cost of zero leads to a web of cross-subsidies among banks and to aggregate subsidies from government to banks. Safety net subsidies were likely reduced by improvements in the conditions of banks and changes in public policies after the 1980s. On the other hand, safety net subsidies appear now to have risen noticeably since the middle of the 1990s. Conditions and public policies may also be paving the way for banking safety net subsidies to rise further in the first decade of the new millennium.

We draw two implications from our research on these issues. First, the framework introduced here is likely to provide a useful guide for estimating banking safety net subsidies. By more concretely delineating the full costs of production and the subsidies. Second, the framework directs attention toward reforms of banking safety nets system that would improve allocational efficiency. For instance, more fully adjusting deposit insurance premiums for ex ante risks will likely reduce aggregate and cross-subsidies in banking.

By more concretely delineating the full costs of production incurred by government in its provision of banking safety nets and the division of those expenses into the subsidies to banks, the subsidies to their customers, and to waste, a foundation has been laid for constructing estimates of their magnitudes.

NOTES

1. For simplicity, we refer to any safety net subsidy that accrues to banks or any part of their holding companies as a safety net subsidy to banks or banking. We also ignore the distinctions associated with thrifts and their insurance fund. Much of this analysis would apply to them in the same way that it applies to banks.

2. The breadth of the coverage of safety nets in practice and the dollar value of the aggregate safety net subsidy to banking were debated fiercely during the legislative attempts at financial modernization that culminated in November 1999 in the passage of the Gramm-Leach-Bliley Act. Barth, Brumbaugh, and Wilcox (2000) discuss the impetus to the Gramm-Leach-Bliley Act and some of its implementation issues and important implications.

3. See Stojanovic, et al. (2000) for discussion of the expanded roles of the FHLBs.

4. See Passmore (1992) and Ely (1999).

5. In terms of the distribution of taxes and subsidies among producers and consumers, economic analysis generally holds that whether the legal recipient of the tax or subsidy is the producer or the consumer is largely irrelevant. Thus, whereas FDIC insurance is technically targeted at depositors and not banks, the analysis below shows both banks and depositors to receive subsidies from mispriced deposit insurance premiums.

6. When financial services are provided at a price of zero, the equilibrium quantity occurs where the demand curve intersects the horizontal axis.

7. The assumption of constant costs for government deposit insurance (across banks and across aggregate volumes of deposits) also implies that, if government costs are lower than private costs, there would be no private provision of deposit insurance. Lifting these assumptions would permit the coexistence of public and, as is the case, some (admittedly small amount of) private provision. Also, justification of caps on insured deposits may rest on such increasing costs of insurance.

8. For the case in which the cost of the deposit insurance system (AB) exceeds the default-risk premium (AC), the introduction of a fairly priced system would not benefit the average bank or depositor. Rather, the system would involve transfers from both surviving banks and depositors at surviving banks to the depositors of failed institutions.

9. In addition, Lehnert and Passmore (1999) broadened the conceptual range of the sources of the safety net with their theoretical framework in which the conduct of monetary policy can produce a safety net for banking.

10. See Carnell (1999). Among others, Jones and Kolatch (1999), Ely (1999), Kwast and Passmore (1999), and Walter (1998) have also pointed to these areas as the sources of subsidies.

11. For a complete discussion of the public subsidy that flows through deposit insurance and for a specific proposal that addresses it, see Wilcox (2001).

12. See Jones and Kolatch (1999).

13. The average ratio of market values of assets to liabilities at failed institutions during the thrift crisis was considerably below 0.90, and perhaps well under 0.70. After that period, FDICIA imposed prompt corrective action on regulators. To the extent that PCA is enforced, the average ratio might be in the neighborhood of 0.90.

14. That subsidization may arise through this mechanism is clear. For instance, subsidization would take place if the Treasury lent at 1 percent and had a cost of funds of 3 percent. Also, if the government were assumed to be a risk neutral borrower, non-subsidized government lending would have to charge interest rates that are high enough to cover the government's costs of funding, the administrative costs of a lending program, and expected defaults. In this light, government lending programs that charged an interest rate equivalent to only the government cost of funds would involve a subsidy if administrative costs and defaults were nonzero.

15. Of course, if the FDIC administration involved internal mismanagement and waste such that its lower costs were not passed on to banks as lower premiums, there would not be a subsidy passed to banks, but simply social waste equal to the total size of the cost of the subsidy.

16. See, for example, Kaufman (2001) and Ely (1999).

17. When a bank fails that has discount window loans outstanding, their collateralization pits the interests of two safety nets at loggerheads. If the Fed claims the collateral, it effectively subtracts it from the assets left for the FDIC, thereby imposing more costs on either on other banks or on taxpayers, or both.

18. This calculation omits charging a market-like premium for the consistent availability of such credit that the private sector is unlikely to provide.

19. Hancock and Wilcox (1996) estimated the price elasticity of banks' demand for

Fedwire daylight overdrafts implied by those fee increases and the concomitant declines in overdrafts.

REFERENCES

Barth, James R., R. Dan Brumbaugh, Jr., and James A. Wilcox. 2000. "The Repeal of Glass-Steagall and the Advent of Broad Banking." *Journal of Economic Perspectives* Vol. 14 (2), pp. 191–204.

Carnell, Richard S. 1999. "Straining Out Gnats and Swallowing Camels: The Question of Subsidy to Subsidiaries of Banks." *FRB Chicago 35th Annual Conference on Bank Structure and Competition*, Chicago, Ill., May.

Curry, Timothy, and Lynn Shibut. 2000. "The Cost of the Savings and Loan Crisis: Truth and Consequences." *FDIC Banking Review*, Vol. 13 (2), pp. 26–35.

Ely, Bert. 1999. "Banks Do *Not* Receive a Federal Safety Net Subsidy." Paper prepared for the Financial Services Roundtable, Washington, D.C., May.

Federal Financial Institutions Examination Council. 1992. *Study on Regulatory Burden.* Washington, D.C.

Greenspan, Alan. 1997. Testimony before the U.S. House Committee on Banking and Financial Services, Subcommittee on Financial Institutions and Consumer Credit. 105th Cong., 1st Sess., 13 February.

Hancock, Diana, and James A. Wilcox. 1996. "Intraday Management of Bank Reserves: The Effects of Caps and Fees on Daylight Overdrafts." *Journal of Money, Credit, and Banking*, November 1996, Vol. 28 (4), pp. 870–908.

Jones, Kenneth, and Barry Kolatch. 1999. "The Federal Safety Net, Banking Subsidies, and Implications for Financial Modernization." *FDIC Banking Review*, Vol. 12 (1), pp. 1–17.

Kaufman, George G. 2001. "The Current Status of Deposit Insurance in the United States and Proposals for Reform." Draft manuscript, 14 March.

Kwast, Myron L., and S. Wayne Passmore. 1999. "The Subsidy Provided by the Federal Safety Net: Theory and Measurement." *Journal of Financial Services Research*, Vol. 16 (2/3), September/December, pp. 35–55.

Lagomarsino, Deborah. 2002. "Fed Moves to Make Discount Window Rate More Useful Tool in Banking System." *Wall Street Journal*, 1 November, A6.

Lehnert, Andreas, and Wayne Passmore. 1999. "The Banking Industry and the Safety Net Subsidy." Working Paper, Board of Governors of the Federal Reserve System, August.

Mengle, David L., David B. Humphrey, and Bruce J. Summers. 1987. "Intraday Credit: Risk, Value, and Pricing." Federal Reserve Bank of Richmond. *Economic Review*, January/February, pp. 3–14.

Passmore, Wayne. 1992. "Can Retail Depositories Fund Mortgages Profitably?" *Journal of Housing Research*, Vol. 3 (2), pp. 305–340.

Shadow Financial Regulatory Committee, Statement #159, 13 December 1999.

Stojanovic, Dusan, Mark D. Vaughan, and Timothy J. Yeager. 2000. "Is Federal Home Loan Bank Funding a Risky Business for the FDIC?" Federal Reserve Bank of St. Louis. *Regional Economist*, October, pp. 4–9.

Walter, John R. 1998. "Can a Safety Net Subsidy Be Contained?" Federal Reserve Bank of Richmond. *Economic Quarterly*, Vol. 84 (1), Winter, pp. 1–20.

Whalen, Gary. 1997. "The Competitive Implications of Safety Net-Related Subsidies." Office of the Comptroller of the Currency Economics Working Paper 97–9, May.

Wilcox, James A. 2001. "MIMIC: A Proposal for Deposit Insurance Reform." *Journal of Financial Regulation and Compliance* Vol. 9 (4), November 2001, pp. 338–349.

PART II

International Perspectives

CHAPTER 9

Too Big to Fail: The Australian Perspective

Chris Terry and Rowan Trayler

INTRODUCTION

This chapter examines the relevance of firms in Australia being too big to be allowed to fail. The chapter also considers the alternative interpretation that financial (and other) conglomerates are too big to fail (TBTF) by virtue of their size and diversification. Observing the recent experience leads us to the conclusion that the insolvency of some firms is too important to ignore.

Australia, as an economy, is comparable in size (measured in terms of population and GDP) with, say, Texas or California and is a little smaller than Canada. Consequently our concept of bigness is not comparable to that of U.S. firms.

Australia is geographically isolated, with many highly concentrated industries that mainly serve the domestic economy. Most of the firms in these industries are not "big" and the insolvency of any one would not inflict serious injury either on the economy or the sector in which it operated. While insolvency is an unwelcome event for the stakeholders involved, most result in a stronger economy because they release resources for more efficient use by other firms. This has been the main reason that the Australian government has been reluctant to bailout insolvent firms.

Australia is a major producer of agricultural and mineral commodities and these products represent more than half of the country's exports. As a consequence these industries are TBTF and governments (both federal and state) have a record of periodically supporting them when they face insolvency. In the case of agriculture, the usual cause is drought conditions and financial assistance is provided to help sustain the industry until the drought breaks.

The financial sector is dominated by five financial institutions that are big. They are among the 10 largest listed companies judged in terms of their market capitalization. In our view, they are firms that could be regarded as being TBTF. Australia has a small number of other firms that are big and represent a dominant position in their industry (such as BHP Billiton and Telstra) and given that their industries are important to the economy they could also be TBTF.

Fortunately, though, Australia's recent history does not include any examples of financial (or non-financial) companies being bailed out because they were judged to be TBTF. Large corporate insolvencies have occurred, some with a high degree of notoriety, that attracted government intervention, but this was not because they were thought to be TBTF.

The TBTF question has arisen in the United States in part because of bailouts of major financial institutions, the emergence of financial conglomerates, and its government's response to some of the consequences of September 11, 2001.

The passage of the Gramm-Leach-Bliley Act (GBL Act) in November 1999 has stimulated the debate in the United States about financial conglomerates and the TBTF hypothesis. The basic concern is that " . . . the federal 'safety net' for banks could be wrapped around entire financial holding companies, thereby undermining the ability of regulators and investors to control the risks of those entities" (Wilmarth, 2001, 9).

The situation in Australia concerning financial conglomerates differs in two important respects. First, financial conglomerates have evolved more gradually over the past 20 years (although a government-commissioned inquiry in 1996–97 and subsequent policy decisions added impetus to the trend), and second, the approach to prudential supervision in Australia is less paternal than that portrayed in the above quotation from Wilmarth. In 1996 the Australian government established the Financial System Inquiry (FSI) to examine and make recommendations on (among other things) new prudential supervision arrangements and it argued that the emergence of financial conglomerates should *not* be restrained because of the TBTF hypothesis. The inquiry's recommendations relied on two beliefs. The first is that a financial conglomerate can be expected to be financially stronger than the sum of its constituent entities, and the second is that other prudential arrangements are available and capable of dealing with a financial institution that is suffering financial distress (and so there will not be a need to bail out a financial institution).

The recent Australian experience with insolvency includes only one case of a government bail out. This arose when United Medical Protection (UMP), a relatively small mutual organization that provides medical indemnity insurance, filed for voluntary liquidation in April 2002. The federal government decided to bail out the organization because, had it not, medical practitioners would not have had access to indemnity insurance and would have ceased to provide medical services. In other words, the bailout occurred not because UMP was TBTF, but because it was "too important to ignore." We discuss this case later in the chapter.

Governments (federal and state) have responded to several other recent insolvencies but in each case the aim was to assist stakeholders for whom the liquidation process would unfairly penalize, the most obvious example being the collapse of Ansett, Australia's second major airline, where the government agreed to fund the payment of employee benefits. Trade union agitation was a factor in this case, but the employee benefits arose in part through government-sanctioned processes, such as enterprise bargaining between the companies and their employees and through government-required employer contributions to employee superannuation schemes.

The other major example is the response of governments (federal and state) to the collapse of Australia's second largest general insurer, CE Heath International Holdings, better known as HIH. We examine this case in a later section because of the support provided to clients of HIH, and unlike UMP, the government did not bail out the enterprise.

Corporate importance within a regional community has also been a factor in several smaller insolvencies. In these cases the impact on the region contributed to the importance the government attached to the insolvency.

While Australia does not provide recent examples of government bailouts because the companies were thought to be TBTF, this does not mean the problem could not arise in Australia. As noted above, the major institutions in the financial sector probably are TBTF. For example, the National Australia Bank (known as NAB) has the largest market capitalization on the Australian Stock Exchange, at over $A 50 billion (approximately U.S. $27.5 billion) at the end of September 2002. The other major banks are the Commonwealth Banking Corporation (popularly known, because of a lengthy advertising campaign, as "which" bank), the Australia and New Zealand Banking Group (known as ANZ), Westpac Banking Corporation (known as Westpac) and St. George (the fifth largest bank). Given that collectively they represent about 70 percent of the financial system, the financial collapse of any one would pose great stress on the system's stability.

The remainder of this chapter is divided into three parts. The first deals with financial conglomerates and the approach of prudential regulation to their development. This part commences with a review of the approach of FSI to the future role of financial conglomerates in Australia and the approach of the prudential regulator, the Australian Prudential Regulation Authority (APRA), to the TBTF risk they pose and how this risk should be supervised. The second part of the chapter discusses the main examples of corporate collapses in Australia that resulted in some form of bailout or compensation by the Australian Government, and several collapses that did not attract a governmental response. The final part contains the conclusions.

FINANCIAL CONGLOMERATES AND THEIR TBTF RISK

Financial conglomerates, defined as financial institutions that provide at least two of the three major types of financial services (banking, insurance, and fund management products and services), emerged in Australia over the past 20 years or so, as financial institutions adjusted to the changing needs of their customers and to increasing regulatory tolerance to their formation. The two major inquiries into Australia's financial system over the past 20 years were important milestones in their emergence and the latter (i.e., the FSI) argued that their formation should not be restricted because of the TBTF risk.

The Emergence of Financial Conglomerates

Prior to the early 1980s, Australia's banks operated under a system of banking regulations where they were principally as deposit-taking institutions. Fund managers and insurance companies operated under separate legislation and regulatory agencies. Following a major inquiry into the financial system by the Australian Financial System Inquiry (AFSI), known also as the Campbell Committee, the banks and other institutions in the financial system were deregulated. Thus, competitive pressures were released within the financial sector that led banks to compete more aggressively with each other and with potential new entrants, including foreign banks.

One of the initial consequences of deregulation was the decline in the use of non-bank financial institutions (NBFIs) that had developed from the establishment of banking regulations in the 1940s. While many NBFIs have survived (such as credit unions, finance companies and merchant banks) their overall role in the provision of banking products has considerably diminished, due mainly to many of them being incorporated into banks.

Another consequence of deregulation was the introduction of prudential supervision of banks in accordance with the Basel accord. In essence, it was recognized that the more competitive environment and the increased volatility resulting from deregulated financial markets would intensify the risks faced by banks. Accordingly, the authorities moved (in the mid 1980s) to establish a framework of prudential supervision of banks.

One of the more fundamental consequences of deregulation, and the competitive forces it released, was the emergence of financial conglomerates. According to the FSI report (154)

The increase in competition, both from domestic markets and from abroad, has significant implications for the configuration of financial operations in Australia. For existing institutions, attention is focused on achieving more efficient conglomerate structures, outsourcing and alliance, to gain advantage through operational and marketing strategies' synergies. . . .

The FSI described a vision for the future as a basis for its recommendations. Regarding financial conglomerates, the FSI argued that they would develop further as providers of financial services mainly because of the economies of scale and scope they can exploit, and the FSI approached the issue of their regulation on the basis that the conglomerates are here to stay (13).

One of the basic reasons for the larger banks to evolve as financial conglomerates has been the market growth for fund management products and services relative to the market for banking products and services. This trend is shown in figure 9.1 by the data on funds under management and bank deposits. The main driving force has been the greater demand for retirement-income products as a consequence of the aging population and rising incomes.

The growth in demand for superannuation services has attracted banks into this area of financial services, in terms of redesigned banking products (such as Retirement Savings Accounts) and in the provision of fund management products and services. The major banks have built their funds management capabilities mainly through the acquisition of fund managers, such as the Commonwealth Bank's takeover of Colonial State (a regional bank that had been taken over by the life insurance and funds management firm, Colonial Mutual Life Assurance Society). The emergence of the Commonwealth Bank

Figure 9.1
Bank Deposits vs. Managed Funds, 1991 and 2001

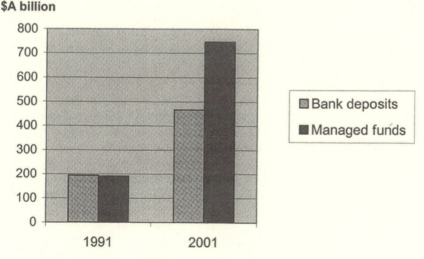

Source: RBA, *Bulletin*, BI and D3, various editions.

as a financial conglomerate is described below as a case study to illustrate how most Australian banks have evolved over the years.

Case Study: Evolution of the Commonwealth Bank

The Australian government founded the Commonwealth Bank of Australia in 1911 as both a savings and trading (i.e., commercial) bank, with the benefit of a government guarantee. Prior to the establishment of the Reserve Bank of Australia in 1959, it had responsibility for a number of central banking functions.

The bank amalgamated with the State Savings Banks of both Western Australia and New South Wales in 1931, having previously merged with similar institutions in Tasmania (1912) and Queensland (1920).

During the 1970s, the bank entered the fields of home insurance and travel, and formed its own finance company. In 1989 the bank acquired the New Zealand based ASB Bank Ltd.

In 1991, the Australian government floated the company, retaining just over 50 percent of the stock. Earlier that year it had acquired the Commonwealth Development Bank and the State Bank of Victoria (which had become insolvent due to the losses of its wholly-owned merchant bank). In mid-1996 the government sold its remaining shares in the bank.

In January 1993, all of the assets of the Commonwealth Savings Bank of Australia were vested in, and all of its liabilities were assumed by, the Commonwealth Bank of Australia. The Commonwealth Savings Bank ceased operations as of that date.

In 2000, the Commonwealth Bank merged with Colonial Limited, which had been formed through the take-over of the State Bank (of New South Wales) by Colonial Mutual Life. As a result the Commonwealth Bank had become a financial conglomerate that is a major bank, insurance company, and fund manager.

According to the bank's Web page (http://www.cba.com.au)

From its humble beginnings in 1912 with one office and staff of 12 the Commonwealth Bank Group as at June 2001, has 34,960 staff and over 1,066 branches throughout Australia, with additional access to banking facilities provided nationwide by 3,928 agencies, including Australia Post, and through 122,074 EFTPOS terminals and 3,910 ATMs. During this period the Bank's annual profit has risen from its first recorded profit of £2,222 for the half year ended 30 June 1915 to an operating profit after tax of $2,262 million, an increase of 9% over the previous year of 1999/2000.

The Bank is also Australia's leading on-line stockbroker as well as being a dealer in Australia's OTC [over the counter] markets. In 2001, its balance sheet assets totalled $A 230 billion and the Bank has $A 18 billion in shareholders' funds.

The Financial System Inquiry

The FSI report described its vision of the role of financial conglomerates in the following terms:

The emergence of new players will be matched by the continued evolution of large financial conglomerates, using their brand and other strengths to provide a wide range of financial services. (13)

The Reserve Bank of Australia (RBA), when it was the relevant authority, required the parent entity to be a bank (since the mid-1980s this could be a domestic or a foreign-owned bank provided it was subject to prudential supervision in accordance with the Basel accord). It also required a bank to have a wide spread of ownership (15% being the largest proportion of shares that a single shareholder could possess). It made an exception to these principles when it allowed a holding company to be the parent entity when Colonial Mutual took over the State Bank of New South Wales.

The RBA, when it was responsible for the prudential supervision of banks, was concerned about quarantining the activities of conglomerates, because of brand association and conflicts of interest within such groups. The FSI, though, argued that these concerns should not restrict the development of financial conglomerates. The FSI identified three prudential issues posed by financial conglomerates (Financial System Inquiry 346).

First, the assets and liabilities of the operating entities should be separated legally, which has a long history in the insurance industry, where statutory funds are separate from benefit funds. This would ensure that creditors of one operating entity did not gain priority over the creditors (e.g., depositors, in the case of a bank) of another.

Second, a financial conglomerate should be able to sustain the economic separation of their operating entities. The basic issue is whether the reputation and viability of the group is threatened by a loss by one of its entities.

Third, a financial conglomerate must be able to convince the market for each of its operating entities that they are, in fact, separate. For instance, a bank that has become a financial conglomerate must ensure that the market for its fund management products does not associate the risks of these products to those of its deposit-taking institution entity.

The FSI report argued " . . . that these concerns are not sufficient to stand against the general acceptance of conglomerate structures . . . " (346). It recommended that the (proposed single) prudential regulator accept the use of the non-operating holding company (NOHC) structure subject to standards relating to capital adequacy, management, firewalls, reporting of intra-group activities, and corporate governance (recommendation 49).

The FSI recommended that a single prudential regulator be established (recommendation 31) and that it adopt a functional approach rather than the (then) prevailing financial institutions' approach to supervision. The federal government anticipated this recommendation (based on comments at the time by the treasurer) and it established APRA (in July 1998) as the sole prudential regulator.

The FSI also examined the six pillars policy that was enunciated in 1990 by the then federal government to indicate its desire to prevent mergers between the four major banks and the two major insurance companies. While the policy had several underpinnings, one was the government's power under banking and insurance legislation to authorize banks and insurance companies and to approve their ownership. While these pieces of legislation did not prevent financial institutions being authorized under each, they allowed the federal government to enforce its six pillars policy.

It was not surprising that the FSI recommended the six pillars policy be removed (428) and that responsibility for dealing with the various possible consequences (such as anti-competitive behavior and the TBTF problem) be assigned to specified regulatory agencies.

The FSI report cited concerns expressed in the RBA's submission that TBTF concerns would apply should the number of major banks be halved through mergers. The FSI though did not share these concerns:

The Inquiry does not consider these arguments are persuasive from a prudential perspective. It is unlikely that the management of failure task would differ appreciably from that which would already confront a regulator if one of the existing majors failed. This is because the majors are already of a size which would limit the options for organised takeovers within Australia. If a large domestic institution fails, the options for resolution include joint ventures, foreign acquisition, partial acquisition by non-financial institutions, management by the regulator, recapitalization or break-up prior to sale. (427)

The FSI also addressed the question of how the failure of a financial institution should be handled. This is an important aspect of the TBTF hypothesis.

The FSI argued that distressed financial institutions should be identified by the prudential regulator well before its capital has been depleted, and that it should manage the exit of the institution through merger or sale before depositors' funds (or the claims of policyholders) are at risk. In Australia there is no guarantee of depositors' funds. Depositor protection is provided through the process of priority of claims on a deposit-taking institution's assets in the event of insolvency. The FSI argued that the "depositor preference" arrangements are superior to deposit insurance as the method for protecting depositors' funds, mainly on moral hazard grounds, especially for large deposit-taking institutions that have substantial liabilities in addition to its deposits.

The FSI proposed that the existing policyholder preferences continue for statutory funds of life companies and recommended that industry-wide fidelity funds be used to protect superannuation benefits from fraud by fund managers.

In summary, the FSI's position is that arrangements (largely those that were currently in force) would cope with the problems that would arise should a large financial institution suffer financial distress and consequently would greatly reduce the likelihood that TBTF situations would arise.

Prudential Responses to Financial Conglomerates

In 1999 APRA commenced the process of extending its prudential supervision framework to accommodate financial conglomerates that comprise a range of controlled entities (including non-financial entities). We will consider only those groups that include a deposit-taking institution and are controlled by either a non-operation holding company or a deposit-taking institution.

Deposit-taking institutions, of course, have been subject to prudential supervision since the mid-1980s and the capital adequacy requirement since the late 1980s. Hence the supervision of financial conglomerates that include a deposit-taking institution must ensure that the financial integrity of the deposit-taking institution is not compromised by it being part of a group.

The prudential framework requires NOHCs and their ownership structure to be authorized and that the structure of these groups "should be sufficiently transparent for APRA to be able to ascertain:

- where the various business lines are controlled;
- the risk profile of the group and its individual parts;
- the way in which internal risk management is organized and conducted; and
- what corporate, financial and other linkages exist between group members." (Australian Prudential Regulation Authority [APRA], April 2001, 5)

APRA's framework requires that the operations of a deposit-taking institution (as well as its earnings, assets, liabilities, and risks) be distinct within each group and that the differences in the risks and returns for the products in each entity must be made clear to consumers of these products. It also requires deposit-taking institutions to have independent directors and an audit committee and provides APRA with the right to veto the appointment of directors and senior managers whom it regards as not being "fit and proper."

APRA's framework accepts the FSI presumption that groups may be a source of financial strength, but it also presumes that groups can increase contagion risk for their controlled entities. Consequently the framework requires the board of a holding company to establish and apply a comprehensive risk monitoring and management system for the group, as well as for the risk posed by related entities to a constituent deposit-taking institution, which is reported to APRA.

The framework includes, for example, the requirement that when

determining limits on acceptable levels of exposure to related entities, the Board of a deposit-taking institution should have regard to the impact on the deposit-taking institution's stand-alone capital and liquidity positions, and on the ability of deposit-taking institution to continue operating, in the event of a failure of any related-entity to which the deposit-taking institution is exposed." (APRA, April 2001, 10)

In a later section we consider the collapse in March 2001 of the general insurer, HIH. Its losses were estimated by its liquidator to approach $A 5.3 billion Had HIH been a component of a financial conglomerate that included a deposit-taking institution, the above requirement would have imposed the responsibility on the deposit-taking institution's board to limit its exposure to HIH's loss. Given that APRA was not able to intervene in time to save HIH, this requirement would appear to pose a serious challenge for the board of the deposit-taking institution.

The framework also covers the economic risks posed by the related entities in a group to its deposit-taking institution. "These range from reputational risk arising from the use of common badging, common services, or cross selling of products, to the risks arising from confusion over the support provided by a deposit-taking institution to related entities and vice versa" (APRA, April 2001, 11). The principal supervision issue is the risk faced by the deposit-taking institution, rather than the risk of confusion to consumers of the group's non-banking products that the deposit-taking institution supports them.

Finally, the framework requires that separate external auditors be appointed for the group and for its controlled entities. That is, each entity must have an external auditor, even if it is the same auditor as for the group.

GOVERNMENTAL RESPONSES TO CORPORATE COLLAPSES

Corporate collapses are almost inevitable in market economies. Recessions, industry restructuring, changing consumer preferences, and bad management occur in market economies and cause companies to collapse. We examine in detail two cases of corporate insolvency to assess the relevancy of TBTF in Australia in recent years. The main corporate failures in Australia in 2001–2002 were HIH (in March 2001), One.Tel (in May 2001), Ansett (in September 2001) and United Medical Insurance (in May 2002). We discuss the HIH and UMP in following sections.

One.Tel

This was a telecommunications company that was established in 1995 to enter the telephone and mobile markets, initially as a reseller. It began as a private company and given the boom period for telecommunications and dot.com stocks its share price, once it was listed on the stock exchange in November 1997, rose strongly. The fact that only 0.5 percent of its stock was issued in the IPO (initial public offering) and that the Packer family (Australia's wealthiest) was associated with the company contributed to the demand for the stock.

The company decided to develop its own network and was able to attract the financial backing of Lachlan Murdoch (News Corporation) together with additional financial support from James Packer. This initiative contributed further upward momentum for the company's stock price, even though One.Tel needed to purchase spectrum to operate its network. Governments sold spectrum at auction and in Australia One.Tel paid well above the price it expected to pay (in January 2000) and in the U.K. (in April 2000) it was an under-bidder. In essence, there was a bubble in the price for spectrum, and this seriously weakened the ability of One.Tel to develop into a global telecommunications company.

Over the next year the company's financial performance fell short of expectations and was unable to finance its losses. In May 2001 James Packer and Lachlan Murdock decided to put the company into insolvency rather than invest more funds to cover its operating losses. In this case the federal government simply ignored the collapse since it had very little impact on Australia's telecommunications industry.

Ansett Australia

Over recent decades, with federal government agreement, the domestic airline industry comprised two carriers, Ansett and TAA. The latter was taken over by Qantas, whereas the former was taken over (in 1979) by TNT (a major road transport group in Australia) and News Ltd. Over the next two decades Qantas modernized its fleet, whereas the average age of the Ansett fleet increased and its mix of aircraft was expensive to maintain.

In 1996 Air New Zealand acquired TNT's 50 percent stake in the airline, which it took to 100 percent in April 2000 as a counter move to Singapore Airlines bid for a strategic stake in Ansett. Following the grounding of a number of its aircraft due to cracks in their engine mountings (in April 2000), Ansett simply could not generate sufficient revenue to continue to operate and was placed into voluntary liquidation in September 2001.

The company was unable to pay its 16,000 workers their entitlements and the government decided to meet this obligation, in part through finance raised from its introduction of a $10 levy on air tickets. Qantas and Virgin (which had entered the market as the third carrier on major air routes) were able to ensure the continuance of the domestic airline industry and so the government was not under pressure to bail out the company.

HIH

The collapse of one of Australia's largest general insurers, HIH, in March 2001, and the scale of its impact on policyholders provides an important test case of the TBTF hypothesis in Australia. The losses inflicted by HIH on its policyholders (one estimate is that the company had 78,000) are much greater than they would experience if their deposit-taking institution collapsed and they lost their deposits.

HIH was the leading Australian general insurance group in cover for professional indemnity, public liability, product insurance and builders' indemnities. It was a major force in household, motor vehicle and third party accident insurance and workers' compensation. (Jay 2001, 10)

The policyholders most affected by the collapse were those who were in the process of making a claim or would make claims in the future under the HIH policies, or who require insurance to conduct their business and (initially) were not able to secure a replacement policy. Parts of HIH business were sold prior to its collapse and some of its remaining business was taken over by other insurers following its collapse, although in the process insurance premiums increased as a result of the demise of HIH.

Both state and federal governments introduced schemes to assist policyholders who lost coverage due to the collapse of HIH. The federal government appointed a Royal Commission to examine the causes of the company's collapse and this commission was underway at the time of writing.

Brief History

Michael Payne and Ray Williams established the business in 1968 as an insurance broker specializing in workers' compensation. It was acquired in 1971 by CE Heath Pty Ltd., and was floated in 1992 as CE Heath International Holdings (hence, HIH). In 1995, Winterthur (a Swiss insurance company) bought 51 percent of the company, which then operated as HIH Winterthur. The Swiss insurance company, after commissioning reports into the operations of the company, decided to sell its interest in early 1998, following its merger in 1997 with the Credit Suisse Group. This represented a turning point for the company.

HIH specialized in the *long tail* segment of the general insurance industry:

Professional indemnity, product claims, workers' compensation, third party accident insurance and product liability are all classic long tail business. Someone may put in a claim for a bad back some years after the employment activities alleged to have caused it. (Jay 2001, 14)

The capacity to be successful in these segments of the insurance industry requires the insurer to possess "large capital reserves, a willingness to acknowledge good actuarial estimates of potential long-term liability and sufficient premiums to generate substantial, continuing investment income to build up reserves. HIH had none of the three" (Jay 2001, 15).

Moreover, during the 1990s the risks faced by the insurance industry increased dramatically through the growth in litigation (such as professional negligence claims against obstetricians) and the propensity of the courts to award large payouts (especially in the United States). Despite these adverse trends in the industry's operating environment, HIH decided in 1998 to expand into the U.K. and U.S. markets and acquire a general insurer in Australia. Its overseas expansion took it into risky insurance markets in the U.K. (where it entered the reinsurance market for aircraft and shipping) and the United States (where it entered the workers' compensation market in California).

In early 1999 HIH acquired FAI, a general insurer in the Australian market for $300 million in stocks and shares that possessed substantial premium income, but it did not undertake a due diligence review of FAI's financial position. While the takeover provided HIH with additional cash flow, within a year it was widely reported in the financial press that the true value of FAI to HIH was negative $A 105 million (Westfield, January 2000).

It is ironic that HIH rejected several takeover offers (in 1998 by Liberty Mutual and in 2000 by Suncorp-Metway) that were well above its market value ($A 550 million at the time of the second offer), allegedly because the bids were subject to due diligence conditions (Westfield, May 2000).

Each of its major acquisitions resulted in substantial losses for HIH, contributing to the fall in its share price from its high of $3.50 in late 1997 to $0.50 cents in September 2000 when the company announced the sale of its retail business to other insurers. This business had been acquired through its takeover of FAI because of the premium income it generated. Its sale, which was at a substantial loss, was the prelude to the subsequent resignations of Ray Williams (the original founder) and other directors (Westfield, August 2000).

During this period, APRA had circulated its proposed capital requirements for general insurers stating that it expected that they would have "a substantial impact on many players in the industry." However APRA, the prudential regulator, only took formal action to investigate HIH at the beginning of March 2001.

In mid-March 2001 the company applied for voluntary liquidation with a declared interim loss of $A 800 million, the day before APRA's investigation would have commenced. The day after the announcement many industries indicated that without the certainty of insurance protection work would stop, such as the building, legal and medical industries. The consequences of the latter are explained later in the chapter. The company subsequently (in August 2001) went into liquidation and the liquidator estimated its losses to be of the order of $A 5.3 billion.

TBTF Implications

Obviously, since HIH was not bailed out, it was not a company that was TBTF. The company's failure, though, is an interesting case study for a discussion of the TBTF hypothesis. We consider two groups of related questions and issues. First, should prudential supervision fail to protect policyholders, bailouts would become an option, so why did prudential supervision fail in this case and can it be expected to succeed more generally? Second, while HIH was not TBTF, governments (state and federal) did introduce arrangements to assist a range of policyholders. This means that HIH is an example of a collapse that was too important to ignore.

Prudential Regulation

Prudential regulation did not prevent the company's financial collapse. The main reasons were that the prudential regulator, APRA, which was only formed in July 1998, was still in the process of developing its prudential framework for general insurers and that the long-standing legislative requirements on insurance companies were inadequate. Related reasons are that its management's assurances about its risk management practices were not reliable and that the data provided by HIH appear to have been engineered to disguise the company's financial plight. (Clarke and Dean 2001, 75)

APRA was aware of the serious concerns about the company's financial position that were presented by two of its actuaries at an Institute of Actuaries conference held in 1999 (at which the Chairman of APRA was a participant). They referred in particular to HIH's under-pricing of policies, understatement of projected liabilities and inadequate reserves.

APRA would also have observed the fall in the company's share price, from its high of almost $3.50 in late 1997, to just under $2.50 in early 1999 (when it took over FAI) to $1.80 a few months later, and the halving of the share price in September 2000 (to 50 cents) and its subsequent fall to less than 20 cents prior to the suspension of trading by the Australian Stock Exchange. It would also have been aware of Standard & Poor's downgrading of the company's rating during 2000, the final downgrading being to BBB- in late February 2001. Its downgrades would have had an adverse effect on the company's underwriting capacity, because they would have discouraged insurance brokers from placing new business with HIH.

Financial journalists had written many articles over this period about the company's approach to pricing and its under-provisioning for abnormal claims (when the value of the industry's liabilities were rising). HIH (as well as FAI) priced its policies aggressively and did not set prudential margins when determining their provisions. (Both companies relied on reinsurance arrangements to cover abnormal losses.) Several journalists in particular were sceptical of the attempts by HIH directors to talk up the share price and gave regular and extensive coverage of the company's journey to oblivion. See especially the articles of Mark Westfield in *The Australian* (several are listed in the references) and also the discussion in Sykes (2001).

It would appear that APRA was not ready to take action (i.e., it did not have its act together) to protect the company's policyholders prior to mid-2000, when it advised HIH that it was concerned about the company's credit quality and capital levels. It is evident that APRA was reluctant to initiate an investigation into HIH because of the belief that this could trigger a collapse. Following the failure of HIH to file its December 2000 financial report, APRA, in March 2001, gave the company two weeks to respond to its intention to investigate its affairs, but the company sought voluntary liquidation rather than face this investigation.

APRA has since introduced its prudential framework and its chairman has suggested that had the requirements been in place in the mid-1990s, they would have triggered an investigation into HIH because the company would not have met the capital requirement. This of course presumes that APRA would have taken such action! It also presumes that the financial data provided by the company were reliable.

While the HIH experience does not prove that prudential regulation is incapable of protecting policyholders through a prudential supervision regime, it does not support the contra view. HIH simply occurred too soon to provide a test for APRA and its prudential regime, which was introduced in July 2002 following extensive public discussions. APRA, moreover, announced in September 2002 its future policy directions for the prudential supervision of general insurers in its submission to the HIH Royal Commission.

APRA's Prudential Framework for General Insurance

APRA emphasized in its submission that the new framework substantially enhances the regime that applied when HIH collapsed. The aim of the framework is to ensure that general insurers minimize the risks they pose to policyholders. That is, consistent with its approach to the supervision of other financial institutions, the framework does not seek to eliminate risk to policyholders.

The major features of the new regime are represented by four prudential standards that cover:

- The valuation of liabilities valuation by an APRA-approved actuary to a 75 percent sufficiency level that are discounted by the risk-free interest rate for balance sheet purposes
- The determination of capital adequacy for general insurers that is based on the risks to their financial soundness
- The establishment of effective corporate governance requirements relating to board composition, audit committees, fit and proper tests for board members and senior managers (whose appointment is subject to APRA veto) and actuaries
- The specification of risk-management strategies that are approved by boards of directors who are required to attest to their adherence to the regulatory requirements and to their implementation by the company.

The future directions identified in its Royal Commission submission include the

- Establishment of a group-wide basis for supervision and capital adequacy
- Enhancement of disclosure processes on insurance companies to ensure that markets, through their valuation of securities, can complement the regulator in signalling the financial soundness (or otherwise) of insurance companies
- Strengthening of APRA's enforcement powers, such as wider whistle-blowing protection and additional reporting requirements
- Establishment of compensation mechanisms for policyholders, given that the regulator cannot expect to prevent all general insurers from becoming insolvent

It is clear that the new regime and its proposed further extensions represent a strengthening of prudential supervision and is thus much more likely to ensure that self-induced collapses (such as HIH's) do not occur. But, as noted by APRA, the regime cannot prevent corporate failure. Does this mean that the general insurance industry can pose TBTF problems? The short answer is probably not, mainly because general insurance is a relatively small part of the financial services sector. The data in table 9.1 show that the expected value of future claims for the four largest classes of business, as at December 31, 2001, are relatively small amounts.

While the losses that appear to have been incurred by HIH exceeded the amount expected, the estimated loss would not have posed solvency problems had HIH been part of a financial conglomerate that included a major deposit taking institution. Moreover, there are mechanisms for other insurers to take over the policies of a failed insurance company and this diminishes the pressure on governments to determine that such companies are TBTF.

Corporate Disclosure

Prudential supervision relies on reliable corporate disclosure and HIH is one of many cases where disclosure was less than ideal. The company's balance sheet for June 2000 reflected the use of a number of questionable assets:

Table 9.1
Expected Future Payments on Outstanding Claims, as of 31 December 2001

Class of business	$ thousand
Compulsory third party motor vehicle	5,094,504
Public & product liability	2,342,944
Employers' liability	1,570,195
Professional indemnity	1,101,190
All other	2,349,287
Total	12,458,120

Source: APRA, Selected Statistics on the General Insurance Industry, December 2001.

HIH's 30 June 2000 balance sheet disclosed capitalised deferred *acquisition costs* of $304 million and *deferred costs* (including future income tax benefits) of $244 million. (Clarke and Dean 2001, 75)

The company also showed as an asset, goodwill of $475 million that represented the excess of the amount HIH paid for acquired insurance business lines (such as those of FAI) over the fair value of what HIH received when it sold them.

The important issue for the TBTF hypothesis is whether corporate disclosure, especially when a company's financial position is deteriorating, can be relied upon by prudential regulators that have power to act to protect depositors and policyholders. In a review of corporate losses and collapses over the past 30 years in Australia, Clarke and Dean (82–98) presented the view that there has been very little improvement in the quality of corporate disclosure over the period. They suggest this reflects the ineffectiveness of the various reforms in corporate regulations and accounting standards, rather than inaction. This is a disconcerting view since it implies that a prudential regulator, such as APRA, will always face the possibility of unreliable corporate disclosure.

Clarke and Dean emphasize two areas where accounting data may systematically not reflect the substantive position of a company. The first is the accounting of corporate groups and the second is the change in accounting and auditing standards.

Financial data for a group are fundamentally flawed, according to Clarke and Dean, because of the ambiguity in representing the financial position of the group and its controlled entities. The group's accounts can be used to disguise the financial position of individual subsidiaries. Alternatively, since each of the controlled entities is a separate legal entity, the assets and/or liabilities of the group can be quarantined in a subsidiary to protect the financial position of the group. It is noteworthy that APRA has identified this as one of the areas for further extension to its prudential framework for general insurers.

The quality of accounting data is fundamental to their ability to reflect a company's financial position. The capitalization of expenses and future income tax benefits by HIH complied with the new accounting standards even though in this case their inclusion in the company's balance sheet eroded the quality of the company's accounts. Moreover, auditors merely have to judge whether a company's accounts comply with these standards. Auditors are not required to certify that the accounts provide a true and fair picture of the company's financial position. Clarke and Dean argue, as a consequence, that reforms such as requiring firms to establish audit committees are unlikely to systemically improve the quality of financial data.

According to Clarke and Dean, the accounting standards should focus not on the standardization of accounting processes, but on ensuring the quality of accounting data so that they can be reliably used for assessing a company's financial position (92). Given the possibility that failed companies have traded while insolvent, it is difficult to answer this important legal question with unreliable accounting data.

The Impact of the Collapse on Policyholders

HIH was Australia's second largest general insurance company (refer to the asset and premium data as at June 30, 2000, in table 2) and thus its collapse

Table 9.2
Top Five General Insurance Companies, 30 June 2000.

Group	Total assets ($m)	Premium revenue ($m)
NRMA Insurance Limited	10,422	3,511
HIH	5,547	1,650
AMP General Insurance	4,382	1,040
Royal and Sun Alliance	4,141	1,947
CGU Insurance Limited	3,591	1,312

Source: APRA, Selected Statistics on the General Insurance Industry, December 2001.

placed many policyholders at great risk. Having specialized in long-tail business meant that the impact could be felt for many years. Its collapse also had an impact on the industry as a whole because of the effects on premiums (they increased following the demise of HIH) and the response of state governments to fund their assistance from levies on the industry.

The collapse of HIH meant that claims pending under existing policies were not paid and policyholders that required insurance cover were unable to remain in business. The main groups involved were lawyers and doctors who held professional indemnity policies, builders that required insurance to cover claims against their warranties, businesses that held a range of property, workers' compensation and liability insurance as well as individuals who held income protection and third-party property insurance policies.

Governmental Response

State and federal governments introduced arrangements to assist policyholders, depending on the type of policy. These arrangements included the payment of benefits in hardship cases, facilitating the transfer of policies to other insurers and the continuation of insurance policies. The funding arrangements included taxes and levies on the industry (for example as a levy on premiums) as well as taxpayer-funded payments. The total value of these arrangements was estimated to be $A 1.8 billion (White 2001, 53–54).

Where the government has taken over the liabilities of HIH to ensure that claims by policyholders are paid, it has become a creditor of the company and along with HIH's other creditors will seek to participate in the distribution of the assets of HIH by the liquidator.

United Medical Protection

In Australia medical indemnity insurance has been arranged by medical defense organizations (MDOs). These are quasi-insurance organizations that act as an intermediary between doctors and the actual insurance companies.

MDOs are mutual aid schemes in which members pool resources to provide coverage to the membership on a "discretionary" basis. They are not licensed or regulated under the Insurance Act because there are no contractual terms and conditions governing the payment of a claim. Claims are paid at the discretion of the organisation and only if there is sufficient capital. (APRA, August 2002)

In early 2002 this very small industry comprised just six MDOs, of which United Medical Protection (UMP) was the largest. The financial position of its subsidiary, Australasian Medical Insurance Ltd. (AMIL), deteriorated and was required by APRA in February 2002 to increase its capital by June that year.

In April 2002 AMIL announced that it would be unable to continue to provide indemnity coverage because it was unable to meet the cost of claims against it and thus the company applied for voluntary liquidation. The impact of this event would be that the majority (60 percent) of medical practitioners in Australia (90 percent of the medical practitioners in New South Wales, NSW) would be uninsured for patient claims of negligence. The doctor's medical association recommended that its members stop performing their duties, which would close down the nation's health care system. To ensure on-going medical services the federal government negotiated a rescue plan with the medical associations that included an emergency loan to the liquidator of UMP to allow AMIL to continue its provision of indemnity insurance. This assistance merely delayed the inevitable, since without substantial changes in the determinants of UMP's financial position the company would remain insolvent.

Sources of Financial Distress

AMIL's financial difficulties arose in part because of the increases in the size of court-awarded payments. They required substantial increases in premiums, which probably exceeded the capacity of the medical profession to pay.

A number of external events triggered AMIL's financial predicament:

- changes to NSW health care legislation in 2001, causing a significant spike in claims in 2001;
- investment losses and rising reinsurance costs in the aftermath of September 11, 2001;
- the failure of one of its reinsurers (HIH); and
- a withdrawal of reinsurance capacity in global markets. (APRA, February 2002)

Moreover, UMP was seriously under-capitalized and it had embarked on a growth plan that involved the use of low premiums to attract new members. In addition it followed the practice of MDOs of not treating incurred but not reported claims as liabilities and this disguised its exposure to liabilities of over $400 million. This practice is followed by MDOs because they decide whether to accept each claim depending on their available capital.

The Federal Government's Response

Australia has a national health system and thus the prospect of the withdrawal of medical services posed a serious political problem for the federal government. In general the present federal government favors a users pay approach to insurance, and thus it expects the medical profession to pay for its medical indemnity insurance.

It decided to bailout UMP with a loan on the conditions that it strengthened its balance sheet and adopted improved financial reporting as recommended by APRA and that the policyholders eventually meet the cost of the unreported liabilities through a levy on the doctors covered by UMP. The government also agreed to examine all of the determinants of the problem of medical indemnity insurance and announced plans to subsidize premiums for high-risk medical services and implement law reforms to limit compensation payouts. For its part, MDOs engaged in discussions with APRA for the purpose of complying with APRA's prudential regime for general insurers. These processes were still underway at the time of writing.

The bailout of a medical indemnity insurance provider was undertaken because of the importance of such insurance to the provision of medical services within a national health system. The bailout is not really an example of TBTF, since UMP is not a large enterprise but it was too important to fail, as a reduction in medical services is unacceptable. This story cannot be completed because the recovery scheme was still being defined and implemented when this chapter was completed.

CONCLUSIONS

The TBTF hypothesis arises in Australia mainly in relation to financial conglomerates, which dominate Australia's financial sector. Following a major inquiry and lengthy public discussion the prudential regulator has determined its approach to the risk of TBTF posed by financial conglomerates. In essence, the regulator is relying on its prudential framework to ensure that financial conglomerates manage their financial position over time to avoid the scale of loss that would cause their insolvency and so trigger a TBTF event.

Our consideration of the HIH collapse indicates that the prudential supervision regime for general insurance that was in place in early 2000 was not adequate because the company collapsed before any official intervention occurred. Our review of the new regime suggest that it is much stronger and its future extensions are appropriate but may not overcome difficulties posed by current accounting and auditing standards.

Unlike the UMP case, the government did not bailout HIH. Federal and state governments intervened in the insolvency process to protect community interests. As in the Ansett case, the response required the industry to contribute to the funding of the assistance arrangements. This is, in effect, a retrospective fidelity fund arrangement. It appears to the authors that bailouts are unlikely to arise in the general insurance industry because of the relatively small size of general insurance firms and the industry's capacity to absorb the policies of a failed company. It is more likely that insolvency by a general insurance company will be too big to ignore (rather than TBTF).

The only example of a bailout in Australia in recent years arose through the insolvency of UMP. Given its small size and the critical importance of medical services to the community we view this as an example of a collapse that was too important to ignore. In this case the rescue arrangements were unfolding at the time this chapter was written and so we cannot present a conclusion. Indications are that the government's bailout of UMP will be recouped by a levy on doctors who were insured with UMP over five years and by changes to the law on compensation payouts.

REFERENCES

APRA, Prudential Supervision of General Insurance. Policy Discussion Paper, Sydney, March 2001.

Australian Financial System Inquiry, Australian Financial System; Final Report of the Committee of Inquiry into the Australian Financial System, Campbell, J.K. Chairman, AGPS, Canberra, 1981.

Australian Prudential Regulation Authority. *Future Policy Directions for the Regulation and Prudential Supervision of the General Insurance Industry.* Submission to the HIH Royal Commission, September, 2002.

Australian Prudential Regulation Authority. "APRA Presses Forward on Medical Indemnity Reform." Press Release, 29 August 2002.

Australian Prudential Regulation Authority. "Australasian Medical Insurance Ltd. (AMIL)." Press Release, 27 February 2002.

Australian Prudential Regulation Authority. *Capital Adequacy and Exposure Limits for Conglomerate Groups Including ADIs.* Discussion Paper, October 2001.

Australian Prudential Regulation Authority. *Policy Framework for the Prudential Supervision of Conglomerate Groups Containing Authorized Deposit-taking Institutions.* Policy Information Paper, April, 2001.

Breusch, John. "HIH collapse: why insurance regular took no action," *The Australian Financial Review,* March 22, 2001.

Clarke, Frank and Graeme Dean, "Corporate collapses analysed," in CCH, *Collapse Incorporated,* CCH Australia, North Sydney, 2001, pages 71–98.

Financial System Inquiry, *Final Report,* AGPS, Canberra (known also as the Wallis Report), March 1997.

House of Representatives Standing Committee on Economics, Finance and Public Administration, *Review of the Australian Prudential Regulation Authority,* Commonwealth of Australia, Canberra, 2000.

Jay, Christopher (2001). "The Day of Reckoning," in CCH, *Collapse Incorporated,* CCH Australia, North Sydney, 2001, pages 9–40.

Ryan, Colleen. "Mounting Medical Bill Long Overdue," *Australian Financial Review.* April 23, 2002.

Sykes, T. *The Numbers Game,* Allen and Unwin, Sydney, 2001.

Westfield, Mark. "Friendless HIH between a rock and a vicious circle," *The Australian,* 22 January 2000.

Westfield, Mark, "No one buys HIH bid silence," *The Australian,* 30 May 2000.

Westfield, Mark, "Share price rise a brief respite for HIH," *The Australian,* January 28, 2000.

White, Andrew, "Flow on effects of recent collapses," in CCH, *Collapse Incorporated,* CCH Australia, North Sydney, 2001, pages 41–70.

Wilmarth, Arthur E. "How Should We Respond to the Growing Risks of Financial Conglomerates." Public Law and Legal Theory Working Paper No. 034, George Washington University Law School, 2001.

www.cba.com.au, (Commonwealth Bank of Australia webpage).

www.apra.gov.au, (Australian Prudential Regulation Authority webpage).

CHAPTER 10

Too Big to Fail: A Taxonomic Analysis

Steven A. Seelig[1]

Too big to fail (TBTF) is a frequently used term in the banking literature. It is used to refer to banks that are of a size that the government will not impose those losses on the creditors of an insolvent bank that would be imposed if the bank were smaller. In the nonfinancial sector, TBTF has been used to refer to government policies that bailed out large manufacturing firms.

The use of the term TBTF has taken on a bit of the flavor of the use of the word pornography—namely, that one knows what it means when one sees it. However, the terms contained within TBTF are not clearly spelled out in the literature. This paper explores the meaning of the term too big to fail and identifies various public policy meanings that the phrase has had in different countries. Examples from the banking and industrial sectors are highlighted to illustrate that "bigness" and "failure" can have various meanings.

INTRODUCTION

Henry Kaufman, in accepting the Adam Smith Award from the National Association of Business Economists, noted that our system does not "tolerate well the harshest of competitive outcomes—business failure—especially when it comes to the largest corporations, banks, and other enterprises."[2] In his analysis of financial regulation in the European Monetary Union, Vives (2001) notes that most merger and acquisition (M&A) activity has been domestic and has resulted in firms that he characterizes as "national champions that may be deemed too big to fail."[3] The banking literature that focuses on banking in the United States is replete with references to TBTF. Recently, Bongini, Claessens, and Ferri (2001) found evidence of too big to fail policies in the handling of financial institution distress during the economic crisis in East Asia. Kaufman and Seelig (2002) examine the limitation on the access to depositor funds as a possible cause for TBTF policies for banks in many countries to banks.

While the term too big to fail is commonly used in the banking literature, its literal meaning is usually not made explicit. Literally, one could interpret the term as meaning that a firm is so large that it cannot fail. A more common usage of the term is, because a firm is so big, *government intervention is necessary to prevent its failure.* Alternatively, the expression could mean that because a firm is so big the government *must prevent its failure.* However, these usages beg the question of what is meant by "too big" and "failure." Typically, one thinks of TBTF applying to large firms where the creditors and/or shareholders are protected when the firm becomes insolvent. The protection comes, not from the law, but from government policy. Henry Kaufman (2001, p. 9) noted that "Historically, when they [the largest corporations] have fallen into serious trouble, the government—weighing the immediate social and economic costs—has shown a propensity to step in to shore up the faltering giants with loan guarantees, tax breaks and other subsidies."

In the United States, frequently cited examples of firms that were too big to fail have included Chrysler Corporation, Lockheed, and Continental Illinois National Bank. A frequently cited example in Europe has been Crédit Lyonnais. All of these were large firms, both in a relative sense and in absolute terms. However, international experience has shown that smaller firms have also not been allowed to "fail" and, in fact, the term "failure" has a very different meaning in many countries. In much of the world, failure implies that a business closes its doors and the employees lose their jobs. This contrasts with the notion of failure meaning that shareholders lose their ownership rights but is independent of the subsequent operating status of the firm.

This paper examines the taxonomy of the term too big to fail and highlights the issues and differences in international practice in applying the concept. It first focuses on various definitions of "too big" and explores different measures of bigness and then examines the meaning of the term "failure" within the TBTF context. Finally, the paper explores international experiences and introduces the concept of too public to fail (TPTF).

TOO BIG

The expression "too big" is an ambiguous one. It could mean that an institution is too big relative to some objective standard. Alternatively, it could be large relative to other firms in the country. Or it could be that it is too important to let fail. Size can be an absolute or a relative concept but under either standard there is a need to quantify size. In some situations it can be measured by assets but in other circumstances employment may be a more relevant benchmark. Determining what is meant by the term "too big" is a first step in understanding what is meant by TBTF.

Bigness implies size and the term "too big" implies either absolute or relative size. However, in practice the term may not necessarily be size related. Rather it may relate to the systemic importance of a firm or its role in the economy. In the context of banking, traditionally size was the important factor but in recent years systemic importance has replaced size. In some countries the fact that a firm is state owned makes it "important" enough to warrant special treatment when it encounters financial difficulties. This section explores some of the various measures of "bigness" that have been used internationally and identifies the meaning of the term "too big" in the context of TBTF.

Absolute Size

For many years, the term TBTF was applied to the banking sector in the United States and had the meaning that banks over a certain absolute size were too big for the FDIC to impose losses on uninsured depositors through a payoff. Thus the FDIC would be forced to do a purchase and assumption resolution that protected all creditors of a large failed bank. Prior to 1982 the conventional wisdom, based on the experience to date, was that the maximum size limit for a payoff was $100 million. After the failure of Penn Square National Bank in July 1982 the figure rose dramatically. Penn Square had deposits of about $500 million and was the largest payoff ever done by the FDIC up to that time. The decision to payoff insured depositors was controversial. The Federal Reserve feared that there would be adverse consequences in financial markets that would impair the ability of large banks to borrow funds if a purchase and assumption transaction was not used. However, once the dust settled, market perceptions shifted to reflect the action of the FDIC. It was no longer clear that a fixed absolute size provided uninsured creditors with protection against loss in the event of a bank insolvency in the United States. This perception remained until 1984 and the resolution of Continental Illinois National Bank.

Relative Size

In the post–Penn Square period, there appeared to be a shift in perception of TBTF to relative size. The perception was that creditors of the ten largest banks were protected. The concept of relative size appears to influence the thinking in many countries as well. Relative importance of an institution, as measured by size, seems to influence the thinking of government officials and the market. In some countries, where banks are not very large and where there is no deposit insurance, the authorities have been unwilling to close the largest banks, even when they have closed many others. There appears to be a mystique surrounding the failure of the "largest" or "third largest" institution. This preoccupation with relative size may be the result of a political principal-agent issue in that the failure of a relatively large regulated firm would be perceived as a failure of the regulators to do their job properly. In other cases, there is a fear that foreign investors will assume that the failure of the largest financial institution is a reflection of underlying weakness in the domestic economy. For whatever the reason, relative size becomes the determining factor in the TBTF decision.

Observers have noted that TBTF concerns have also influenced policy in Europe. Vives (2001) puts forth the notion that domestic mergers create firms that he characterizes as "national champions." These firms then reach a size relative to the rest of the domestic industry that TBTF influences government policy decisions when these financial institutions become insolvent. He cites two specific examples, Banesto in Spain and Crédit Lyonnais in France.[4]

In the mid-1990s, Crédit Lyonnaise was the largest bank in France, and one of the largest banks internationally, with total assets of about $340 billion.[5] It was wholly owned by the government. Nevertheless, it pursued a strategy of rapid growth between 1987 and 1993, accompanied by imprudent lending. The bank began to hemorrhage in 1993, and losses and provisions increased in 1994. The government of France chose to rescue the bank. Clearly given its size, both in absolute and relative terms, and its government ownership, it was viewed as TBTF. Given Crédit Lyonnais' size, however, it is unclear whether bigness was absolute or relative in this application of TBTF. It is equally unclear whether the government's decision to protect creditors resulted from its ownership of the bank.

Relative size also seems to have been an important consideration in the government's decision to protect certain non-financial firms from failure. In these instances, size does not appear to have been determined by assets but by employment or relative importance based on subjective factors. For example, Chrysler Corporation was the third largest automobile manufacturer in the United States. Nevertheless, the United States government determined to "bail out" Chrysler when it fell on hard times in 1979. The choice was a clear one, either Chrysler would go into bankruptcy or the government had to bail it out.

Notwithstanding the fact that Chrysler had total assets in excess of $1.7 billion, it appears that size, in terms of assets, was not the critical factor. Rather, as Maryann Keller, an auto industry analyst observed, "My gut feeling is Chrysler is too big, too important, has too many employees, and pays taxes in too many states for the government not to consider seriously the possibility of the company going out of business."[6] In terms of relative size, its employment, both primary and secondary (employment of vendors who were dependent on Chrysler), played a key role. Relative to other industries, automobile manufacturers employed very large work forces. In 1979 Chrysler employed about 125,000 employees. A study undertaken by the Department of Transportation estimated that 85–90 thousand production workers would lose their jobs if the company failed and the secondary effects would result in the loss of 292,000 additional related jobs with suppliers, dealers, and shipping and other service providers.[7] Even higher estimates of unemployment were made by Data Resources Incorporated (DRI) in a study prepared for the Congressional Budget Office.[8] The available evidence clearly supports the view that one of the key factors that led the government to provide financial assistance to Chrysler was its relative size as measured by its direct and indirect employment. While the loss of jobs of this magnitude would be very significant in many countries, DRI estimated that by the end of 1981 the cumulative effect would be to raise the unemployment rate by only one tenth of a percentage point to "6.9 percent instead of the 6.8 percent it would otherwise be."[9]

Systemic Importance

While the term "big" implies size, within the context of TBTF it can also relate to the systemic importance of a firm. Systemic importance implies that the failure of a firm would result in significant externalities affecting the smooth functioning of the economy. Within the context of the financial sector, a bank's role in the payment system may make it systemically important. This notion has long been widely accepted as the basis for justifying central bank lender of last resort assistance to an insolvent bank.[10] Roth (1994, p. 43) points out that the main rationale for TBTF "is the avoidance of systemic risk, i.e., the danger that a run on a failing bank might lead to a run on the whole banking system, to a paralysis of the payment system, and to short-term credit availability problems."

Similarly systemic importance has also been used to justify government financial assistance to protect certain private firms in industries deemed vital to the welfare of the country. These can include a significant defense contractor (one deemed critical for a country's national defense). An example would be the U.S. government's bailout of Lockheed. The Lockheed Corporation had been one of the United States' most important suppliers of weapon systems during the 1960s. It troubles resulted from cost over-runs on defense contracts, the slowing of demand with the winding down of the Vietnam War, and the collapse, in 1971 of Rolls-Royce. The British government conditioned its rescue of Rolls-Royce on a U.S. government guarantee of $250 million in new loans to facilitate Lockheed purchases from Rolls-Royce. In comparison to the Chrysler situation, the failure of Lockheed would have resulted in a loss of 63,000 jobs.[11] The justification for the bailout of private creditors and shareholders was the broadly defined public interest, or put another way, the systemic importance of the firm.

The concept of systemic importance rests upon the notion that the failure of a specific firm would be disruptive not only to the typical stakeholders of the firm but to the economy at large. This disruption may take the form of triggering macroeconomic shocks, disrupting the smooth operations of markets, or harm the national welfare.

TO FAIL

The term "failure" potentially has different meanings within the context of TBTF. Business failure has meant that a firm was unsuccessful as an economic venture and ceased to exist. Following the practices contained in bankruptcy laws, this involves common shareholders suffering the first loss, followed by preferred shareholders, subordinated creditors, and general creditors. Typically, senior management pays the price for its lack of success through the loss of employment. The process of business failure should result in the exit of a firm (at least in its old form) from the market. However, as Henry Kaufman noted, government TBTF policies do not always mirror these results. Protecting critical stakeholders from the consequences of the insolvency of a firm may dramatically increase moral hazard for management and shareholders.

An examination of some TBTF cases may help identify the different meanings of failure. In the case of Continental Illinois National Bank, the FDIC recapitalized the bank and took an ownership position. The structure of the transaction had the effect of effectively wiping out the old shareholders while protecting the interests of all of the creditors of the bank, including uninsured depositors. Senior management was removed and the members of the Board of Directors were replaced. Clearly, here TBTF meant that Continental was too big *for creditors to suffer losses*.

An example of a smaller bank, but one that likely was relatively important in its country was the Bank of Crete. It was a privately owned bank and was the tenth largest in Greece. In 1988, the bank's owner diverted its funds fraudulently. The central bank guaranteed all depositors against loss and recapitalized the bank, assuming ownership control. A number of years later the bank was privatized through a merger with another bank. Here again, failure would have involved imposing losses on creditors, but the resolution strategy protected them but not the owners.

The Chrysler bailout involved a loan guarantee by the government with the government receiving warrants convertible into Chrysler common stock. The result was that while the shareholders were not wiped out, as they would have been in a bankruptcy, they were diluted. Creditors had to accept lower interest rates on their loans but were protected against loss. Hence, one can conclude that, despite the government having negotiated a relatively good deal for itself, its financial assistance package clearly protected claimants who would have suffered losses in a bankruptcy. The Lockheed assistance package did not result in any upside potential for the government, so shareholders benefited significantly more than in the Chrysler assistance program. In both the Chrysler and Lockheed resolutions the definition of failure, in the TBTF context, was broad enough so that no one suffered total loss. This contrasts with the TBTF treatment of banks where shareholders have taken the first loss.

When examining TBTF policies it is important to understand the implications of failure and whether the assistance package, or resolution, achieves results that are similar to those that would occur in a failure. If by failure one means that the firm ceases to exist, its doors are closed, and its workers are no longer employed, then all of the firms that have been assisted because they were TBTF avoided failure. However, if failure means that shareholders suffer the first loss and the consequences are the same as they would have been in a chapter 11 bankruptcy had the government not intervened, one has a different definition of TBTF that views the firm as being of a size, or systemic importance, to justify government intervention to protect some, but not all of the claimants who would be adversely affected in a bankruptcy.

The concern with failure implying more than just a financial loss for shareholders has influenced the thinking in many countries. The notion of closing a bank conjures up images of employees losing their job and banking services not being available to the public. This has frequently led the authorities to recapitalize an insolvent bank; often without imposing any penalties on any of the claimants.

TOO PUBLIC TO FAIL

An informal survey of financial sector professionals within the IMF indicated that many countries had used TBTF policies. However, many of the banks that had been recapitalized by the government were state-owned banks. In some cases these were the largest banks in the system, in others countries they were considerably smaller. Recently, Indonesia recapitalized a bank, in which the government owned a majority interest, rather than declaring the bank insolvent and resolving it using normal resolution techniques. The question then becomes whether these institutions are not being allowed to fail because of their public ownership or because of their size, including systemic importance.

State-owned, or public, firms frequently are very large. In part this may be the result of these firms being natural monopolies. In a number of countries governments own the public utilities and other vital service providers. During the period when the Commonwealth of Independent States (CIS) countries were under the Soviet Union the number of banks that existed was relatively limited and their relative size was large. With the break-up of the Soviet Union some of these banks remained state owned while others became the dominant banks in their countries.

In all instances, where a government faces the issue of declaring a state-owned firm insolvent and imposing losses on shareholders and creditors, it faces two other issues that are unique to these firms. First, is the obvious one, the government is the shareholder and will bear the losses. Second, in many countries there is an implicit guarantee on the liabilities of state-owned enterprises. The public does not believe that the government will default on its obligations, even when these are indirect obligations. The combination of these two factors imposes significant reputational risk for the authorities in dealing with an insolvent state-owned firm. The loss of reputation, or the political consequences, results in a desire not to "close" the bank or firm, or even officially declare it insolvent.

It is difficult to determine what role size plays in decisions as compared to governmental reputation. Nevertheless, in many countries it appears that there is a clear policy of a firm being too public to fail (TPTF). While information on nonfinancial firms is less readily available, it is likely that this policy also applies to other state owned enterprises, which often are among the largest firms in a country.

Some of the former communist countries faced problems in their financial sectors shortly after introducing democratic governments and market-based economic policies. Both newly licensed private banks and state banks that survived from the communist era experienced difficulties.

In the early 1992–93 many banks in Poland experienced difficulties. These problems accompanied the transition to a market-based economy and resulted from fraud, imprudent lending, and a recession. The problems affected some of the newly licensed banks as well as the large state banks that had been created during the communist period. In dealing with these problems, the government "protected the fate of state banks and eventually decided to recapitalize them."[12]

The Czech Republic was another transition economy that experienced similar difficulties in its banking sector.[13] As part of its economic liberalization program new licenses were granted to banks and the number of banks increased from 5 (four of which were the old state banks) on January 1, 1990, to 13 by the end of the year. Within a short period of time the banking sector began to experience difficulties. The government dealt with the small private banks by placing them into conservatorship and either closing them or merging them with other banks. The large state banks were dealt with differently. Here TPTF policies were applied and the banks were recapitalized. Eventually they were consolidated and privatized, allowing the government to recover much of its investment in these banks.

Other examples of TPTF can also be found in the developed Western countries. In 1990 the State Bank of Victoria, owned by the government of the Australian State of Victoria, experienced severe financial difficulties. The Australian authorities resolved this bank by merging it with one of the four largest banks in the country and the State government provided financial assistance to assure that no creditors or depositors lost any funds.[14] In contrast, in 1979 when the Bank of Adelaide, a private bank, collapsed as a result of losses experienced by its finance company subsidiary, the other major banks provided a subordinated loan facility and the bank was merged with a larger bank. In this instance, as compared with the handling of the State Bank of Victoria, no government funds were used to facilitate the resolution.[15]

Other countries, in the early stages of a systemic banking crisis, protected their larger private banks and their state-owned banks. Examples of these countries include Norway and Indonesia. In Uruguay, creditors of a "state bank" (one that was chartered as a state institution) enjoy total protection in the event of the failure of the bank. As a result, the government does not benefit from letting the bank fail. Once a country is hit with a systemic banking crisis the decision to protect all creditors through the use of a blanket guarantee is made for broad systemic and macroeconomic reasons. Hence, it is inappropriate to view such a guarantee, when applied to all banks, as being a TBTF or TPTF policy.

CONCLUSION

A TBTF policy has traditionally implied that, because of its size, a firm will not be allowed to fail in a manner that would impose losses on a stakeholder group that normally would lose. The term too big to fail is an ambiguous one and the policy has been applied in various ways in different contexts. One of the key issues relates to the meaning of the phrase "too big" in TBTF. As shown above, it can refer to absolute size or relative size. It appears that most applications of TBTF have focused on relative size. In part this may result from an altogether different measurement of size—systemic importance.

As one looks beyond the financial sector, systemic importance seems to become the clear factor that influences government policy and determines whether the government will intervene and protect a firm from failure. Similarly, in the financial sector, it may be difficult on first blush to separate relative size from systemic importance. In some cases, a large bank is critical to the smooth operations of the payment system; in other instances the bank may be critical to availability of banking services in a region of a country. In the nonfinancial sector, the size of a firm's labor force or the importance of its output to the national interest may make a firm TBTF.

"Failure" within the context of TBTF also can have a range of meanings and types of stakeholders who will suffer loss. These stakeholders include employees, creditors, managers, and shareholders. In a pure sense, the benchmark failure is analogous to the outcome in a chapter 7 bankruptcy where the business ceases to exist and the assets are liquidated to satisfy creditor claims. Typically, creditors suffer some loss of principle and shareholders are wiped out. Managers and employees lose their employment. A more common use of the term failure in the TBTF context has been that a firm is too large to impose losses on creditors. This has been the result in the handling of most TBTF bank insolvencies in the United States. However, in the case of nonfinancial firms creditors and shareholders have been protected, at least partially, compared to the outcome that would have occurred had the government not intervened.

Many countries have state-owned enterprises and clearly these have been treated differently from private firms. While the literature uses the expression TBTF in describing policy actions relating to some of these firms, an alternative that may be more appropriate is TPTF (too public to fail).

TBTF has become a common term in the policy literature. However, there is a need to clearly define what it means with greater precision. Terms such as bigness and failure should have specific meanings if there is to be a clear understanding of the policy options and implications of government resolution actions.

NOTES

1. International Monetary Fund. The views expressed are solely those of the author and do not reflect those of the IMF or its executive board.

2. Kaufman (2001, p. 9).

3. Vives (2001, p. 57).

4. Vives (2001, p. 67).

5. *Bankers' Almanac* (1997).

6. Reich and Donahue (1985, p. 102).

7. Reich and Donahue (1985, pp. 315–316).

8. Reich and Donahue (1985, pp. 313–315).

9. Reich and Donahue (1985, p. 314).

10. See He (2000) for a discussion of international practices regarding the use of lender of last resort facilities.

11. Reich and Donahue (1985, p. 65).

12. Gronkiewicz-Waltz (1997, p. 321).

13. See Tošovský (1997) for a discussion of the restructuring of banking in the Czech Republic.

14. Goodhart (1995, p. 372).

15. Ibid.

REFERENCES

Bankers, Almanac. Various years. West Sussex, England: Reed Business Information.

Bongini, Paola, Stijn Claessens, and Giovani Ferri. 2001. "The Political Economy of Distress in East Asian Financial Institutions." *Journal of Financial Services Research* 19 (1), 5–25.

Goodhart, C.A.E. 1995. *The Central Bank and the Financial System.* Cambridge, Massachusetts: The MIT Press.

Gronkiewicz-Waltz, Hanna. 1997. "The Banking Sector in a Transition Economy: The Case of Poland." In *Banking Soundness and Monetary Policy,* edited by Charles Enoch and John H. Green. Washington D.C.: International Monetary Fund.

He, Dong. 2000. "Emergency Liquidity Support Facilities." IMF Working Paper No. 00/79.

Kaufman, George G., and Steven A. Seelig. 2002. "Post Resolution Treatment of Depositors at Failed Banks: Implications for the Severity of Banking Crises, Systemic Risk, and Too Big to Fail." Federal Reserve Bank of Chicago. *Economic Perspectives*, 2nd quarter, 27–41.

Kaufman, Henry. 2001. "What Would Adam Smith Say Now?" *Business Economics* 36 (4), 7–12.

Reich, Robert B., and John D. Donahue. 1985. *New Deals, The Chrysler Revival, and the American System*. New York: Times Books.

Roth, Michael. 1994. " 'Too-big-to fail' and the stability of the banking system: Some insights from foreign countries." *Business Economics* 29 (4),43–49.

Tošovský, Josef. 1997. "Restructuring the Banking Sector: The Case of the Czech Republic." In *Banking Soundness and Monetary Policy*, edited by Charles Enoch and John H. Green. Washington D.C.: International Monetary Fund.

Vives, Xavier. 2001. "Restructuring Financial Regulation in the European Monetary Union." *Journal of Financial Services Research* 19 (1), 57–82.

CHAPTER 11

Avoiding a Permanent Banking Crisis: The Hungarian Banking Sector in the 1990s

By Júlia Király and Éva Várhegyi

INTRODUCTION

This paper examines the transition from the monobank system of a centrally planned economy to the two-tier banking system of a market economy in the Central and Eastern European banking systems. The primary focus here is on the Hungarian banking sector. The transition from the monobank system to the two-tier system is distinguishing five stages of development:

- Stage 1: monobank system of the late socialist economy
- Stage 2: the creation of a two-tier banking system
- Stage 3: period of reconstruction and consolidation
- Stage 4: financial systems at the crossroads
- Stage 5: a successfully reorganized banking sector

A detailed description of stage 1 can be found in the vast literature on the Centrally Planned Economies (e.g., Nuti 1992; Kessides et al. 1989). Under the centralized monobank system, funds were centrally allocated either according to the economic plan, or as a result of a bargain between the enterprises and the state. In this planning/bargaining economy, the state was involved directly in the allocation of funds, and funds were allocated without the full consideration of the possibility of repayment.

Economies in stage 1 were usually demonetized, and specialized banks were created under the control of the Central bank. These specialized arms of the Central bank—Savings Bank, Investment Bank, Foreign Trade Bank—

functioned as bureaucratic entities. Money was primarily an accounting instrument of aggregation and control.[1]

In this stage, no loans were classified as nonperforming, since the central bank had the exclusive right of debiting the firm's account or revolving the credit. "Credit is mostly short term and is automatically available to enterprises to finance their working capital needs, it is granted by the Central Bank at an almost symbolic interest rate to cover banks' administrative cost" (Nuti 1992). Thus, bankers were state bureaucrats whose "king" was the central plan for allocating funds.

The onset of stage 2 was the introduction of a two-tier banking system. The specialized banks and the lending directorates of the Central bank were converted into associated but separate commercial banks. Though the transition from a one-tier to a two-tier system was usually accomplished overnight, the transformation of the banks and banking rules took much longer, since the "overnight banking reform" could not sweep out the old standards and practices.

In most countries in the region, the transition was accompanied by the collapse of the former East European markets and a deep recession. Prior to and during the early years of the recession, the banking sector had expanded and was profitable. However, as the recession deepened and during the recovery phase, loan portfolios deteriorated, profits shrank, and the banking sector was becoming insolvent. Bank performance lagged the economy during the early post-socialist period. These problems are detailed in the second section.

Diminishing profits and the technical insolvency of banks called for state intervention, application of the too big to fail policy, and reconstruction and consolidation of the banking sector. The various attempts and failures of this solution are analyzed in the third section.

In the fourth section, the intermediate financial sectors are described with regard to privatization, state control, universal banking and deregulation.

The fifth section describes the reorganization and privatization of the Hungarian banking sector.

Finally, the sixth section outlines possible further developments in Hungary, which no longer includes state intervention.

Each Central and Eastern European (CEE) banking sector underwent these stages of evolution. However, their evolution differed, as they entered the individual stages at different points of time. At the beginning of the 1990s, all of the countries were shaken by the collapse of the Eastern market (referred to as the Big Shock), which was accompanied by collapsing demand, rocketing inflation, severe balance of payment problems, and a deep economic recession. Each country attempted to find different solutions to the emerging problems. Despite the parallel development of CEE banking sectors, the paths are far from being identical. The Hungarian case is used here to illustrate the development in the banking sector.

DIMINISHING PROFITS AND DETERIORATING LOAN PORTFOLIOS

The birth of the two-tier banking system was the beginning of stage 2. Central banks were deprived of their omnipotence and the right of corporate and household finance was delegated to independent commercial banks that were mainly derived from the Central banks. Those commercial banks and bankers who entered stage 2 before the Big Shock experienced a euphoric period. East European banks were the leaders of the *Bankers Top 1000* with respect to profitability. ROAs fluctuated around 3–5 percent and ROEs were in some cases over 80 percent. In the 1987–90 period in Hungary, the average ROE for commercial banks was over 50 percent. These figures are overstated because profits included accrued but unpaid interest, there were no provisions for bad loans, and the capital stake was low.

Banks grew rapidly during the "euphoric era," and their total assets compared to the GDP increased at a significant rate. In Hungary, the bank assets were 65.8 percent of GDP in 1988 and 84.6 percent in 1991. Although it was still much lower than the Western European average (150–200%), it indicated more active financial intermediation compared with the previous period. This boom was partly due to increased household savings that soared from a single digit to 13–15 percent.

Due to easy entry, low capital requirements, and high profitability, private newcomers and foreign banks entered the market, thereby creating competition. However, the competition was mitigated by the significant differences in market size. The largest new banks had less than 5 percent of market shares, while the original big banks dominated the markets. Strict segmentation and concentration of the banking sector had not been significantly modified in stage 2 (see e.g., Várhegyi 1995). The dominance of big SOBs (state-owned banks) had been mitigated during stage 2, but had not disappeared.

Consider the retail market and the corporate market. In retail market, the former saving banks and, in some cases, the cooperatives had close to a monopoly position in household savings (Ábel and Székely 1994). These banks began to shift toward the corporate market as their household loans declined. They provided funds to the emerging interbank market, which was augmented by the cheap funds of joint ventures and foreign banks. The borrowers in the money markets were the big state banks. The domestic newcomers, who lacked a low cost deposit base, were highly exposed to "hot money." Consequently, restrictive monetary policy had a different impact on banks with a strong deposit base than on banks exposed to money market borrowing. The former group was unaffected, while the latter group faced serious liquidity problems.

The corporate market was segmented too. The big SOBs that were spun off from the Central bank inherited the giant SOEs (state-owned enterprises). In contrast, the new domestic banks financed medium-sized state-owned corporations, especially in the agriculture, and the new small- or medium-sized private entrepreneurs. Foreign banks provided services and financed emerging joint ventures (Piper et al. 1994; Várhegyi 1994).

In the early years of stage 2, bank profits were high. However, deteriorating loan portfolios, a brutal decline in profitability and growth, and a diminishing capital base followed the bright period of banking. The crisis, and especially its depth, was unexpected. As an example take the Hungarian banking sector (see table 11.1).

The deterioration of bank loan portfolios began in 1990, but the biggest decline took place in 1992–93 (Spéder and Várhegyi 1992). The increase in nonperforming loans in 1992 did not follow from the new advances. In 1992 banks did not throw "good money after bad." The crisis was not a problem of flows, but of stocks (Bonin and Schaffer 1995). In 1992, nonperforming loans were 20 percent of the balance sheet total and were 35 percent of corporate loans. These loans also were on the balance sheet in 1991. New accounting principles excluded unpaid accrued interest from income. The new bankruptcy law, which forced corporations to go bankrupt if they were insolvent, and the new banking act, which prescribed strict rules for loan qualification, all contributed to make the problems transparent.

The extreme deterioration of the loan portfolios was partially concealed by a remarkable shift in the share of investments: the dynamic growth of nonfinancial investments based on bad debt—equity swaps (Spéder 1991). This shift of qualified loans into investments later became a frozen stock with zero yield and especially high risk.

Table 11.1
Doubtful Debts in the Banking System, 1990–93

	1990	1991	1992	1993
Doubtful debts (HUF bn)	43.3	87.5	273.1	536.0
% of balance sheet total	2.7	4.1	12.0	20.4
% of corporate loans	6.8	11.4	35.4	70.4

Source: NBH [1992], State Banking Supervision Annual Report 1992, 1993 (estimate).
Note: The rules of portfolio qualification were only set down in the 1991 act on Financial Institutions, and then by the regulations of the Banking Supervision. In the table, the term "doubtful debt" is used to include all qualified credits. In 1991 several banks, probably because they misinterpreted the rules, indicated a smaller volume of doubtful debts than they actually had. The 1992 figures reflect the situation before the credit consolidation.

As far as profits are concerned, in 1993 only 5 of 42 banks increased profits substantially, while most financial institutions had large losses. In some cases, the size of the losses exceeded the bank's equity. The banks losing money accounted for 40 percent total assets of the entire banking sector (and an even larger share in corporate lending), and produced a combined HUF 179 billion in losses in 1992 and 1993. The profitable banks in the same period generated profits of merely HUF 23.8 billion (Várhegyi 1995). The losers can be divided into two large groups: the three big SOBs, and the medium-sized domestic banks with little or no foreign participation.

In 1993, the ROE of the Hungarian banking sector was –102.7 percent. The banking sector had lost its entire equity. Of course, not all banks lost their capital (e.g., the majority of the joint-venture banks were profitable in the period), while some banks had losses several times the size of their equity base. The big losers were those banks that dominated the corporate lending market. The quickly vaporizing capital revealed the fact that banks had been undercapitalized—the minimum capital requirement proved to be insufficient in the risky environment.

All of the symptoms of a typical banking crisis—increasing cost of intermediation, declining income, deteriorating loan portfolios, and diminishing capital—were observable except for one—there was no bank panic. In standard theory, the propagation of the crisis should include a banking panic, with bank runs and a spectacular drop in bank deposits. Hungary and most Central and East European countries, maybe with the only exception of the former Soviet Union (FSU) (Pohl 1995), experienced a banking crisis without a panic. The loss of confidence in banks had not taken the usual form. One of the most typical signs of a banking panic is the dramatic increase in the cash/deposit ratio. The Hungarian bank crisis happened together with the spreading of cashless methods of payment. Consequently, the cash/deposit ratio did not increase. Instead, it went down from 35–36 percent to 26–27 percent during this period. The confidence in the banking sector was not shaken. Accounts closed at one bank went to another. Foreign deposits in one Hungarian bank fled into foreign-currency deposits in another Hungarian bank. The vast majority of depositors believed in implicit deposit insurance—the state would never let small depositors lose.

To sum up the development of stage 2: a seemingly flourishing banking sector appeared to have serious problems. The crisis revealed that the high reported profits were not real, growth was unsustainable, and the banks were undercapitalized.

The real picture had been disguised because it was in the common interest of all of the actors. If the banking sector seemed to be healthy and nonperforming credits seemed to be performing, there was no reason to cut back credit lines. The beneficiaries of this belief were the SOE giants whose economic power had been significantly shaken during the years of transition. The government was also a winner. If the banking sector produced profits, the government's budget benefited from corporate taxes and dividends as the state was the largest shareholder.

The accounting practices supported the sham. Accrued but uncollected interest appeared as earned income. Banks were not forced to make provisions on nonperforming loans, and there were no write offs. In Hungary, where the Banking Act was introduced in 1992, a long "period of adjustment" had been declared. That is, banks had the right to adjust to the rules during five years.

The effect of implicit taxation should not be forgotten when analyzing the income streams of the banks. In Hungary, as in most of the East European countries, required reserve rates were around 15–18 percent. As a consequence only 80–85 percent of collected deposits could be transformed to income generating assets, and 20–25 percent of the nominal interest margins were lost. In addition, the realized interest margin included much lower risk premiums than is expected on risky loans, and they did not cover expected losses.

A recurring question is whether the worsening macroeconomic conditions (particularly the recession, the Big Shock) or the serious faults in bank management were mostly to blame for the increasing losses. We may assume that the "holy trinity" of reasons: bad luck (external, exogenous reasons), bad policy (lack of well-suited monetary policy and regulation), and bad banking (lack of prudent management) all contributed to the crisis.

The bad luck can be identified with the Big Shock, that is, with the collapse of the Eastern market and its consequences including the decline of exports, declining industrial output, inflation, internal and external imbalances as shown for Hungary in table 11.2.

The corporate sector was shaken by the shock. Profitability declined. The ROA of the companies that accounted for almost 90 percent of GDP plunged from 3.88 percent in 1989 to 0.69 percent in 1991. It was negative in the majority of domestic, mostly state-owned companies by 1991 (Abel and Pander 1995). Former SOEs lost half of their net worth during the crisis.

The corporate crisis affected the banking sector. Companies whose capital base eroded due to losses were or became overindebted to banks. Their financing problems as well as their capital shortage became even more burning issues. For the banks, this implied that borrowers' ability to repay loans diminished and the collateral behind the loans lost its value. Overindebted giant SOEs played the main role in the banks' capital loss. The bank portfolios deteriorated both because of the losses on the loans inherited and from the continuing losses of the clientele they inherited. In Minsky-terms, the speculative units became Ponzi-units and the situation led to systematic financial fragility.

Big state-owned banks, which inherited the SOEs as customers from the central bank, had no real possibility of ending their financing of these over indebted giants. To reduce the credit lines of the SOEs, which produced a large share of GDP, seemed to be impossible in the first years of banking

Table 11.2
Macroeconomic Indicators for Hungary 1989–93

Growth rates	1989	1990	1991	1992	1993	1994
Real GDP (percent)	+0.74	-3.50	-11.90	-3.00	-0.80	+2.00
Industrial output (percent)	-2.1	-10.2	-16.6	-9.8	+4.0	+9.2
Export (in real terms, percent)	0.3	-4.1	-4.9	1.0	-13.1	+16.6
Export for former socialist countries (percent)	**-6.1**	**-20.7**	**-44.4**	**-1.4**	**-6.2**	**+4.0**
Consumer Price index (percent)	17.0	28.9	35.0	23.0	22.5%	18.8
Corporate bank loans / GDP (percent)	26.6	28.3	30.8	26.3	21.5	20.3
Current balance of payments (million USD)	-1437	+127	+267	+324	-3455	-3911

Source: National Bank of Hungary, Annual Report 1994.

reform (Várhegyi 1994). Too big to fail was the basic principle of large banks in bailing out large companies. The SOEs problem was coupled with that of small- and medium-sized new enterprises, the clients of the medium-sized domestic banks, which became indebted. Both banks and clients were highly geared toward producing a kind of junk-bond phenomenon.

Nevertheless, the impact of bad luck was not universal. Most of the joint venture and 100 percent of foreign-owned banks avoided the bad portfolio problem. They were profitable and their market share was increasing. The pattern demonstrates that good banking may help to overcome bad luck.

How much bad policy contributed to banking crisis is debatable. During stage 2 in most countries, restrictive monetary policy was declared in order to curb the inflation and/or restore external and internal equilibrium. The later the measures were taken, the more abrupt the steps were. As a side effect, however, both higher interest rates and inadequate financing aggravated the problems of indebted enterprises (Ábel and Prander, 1995), and the resulting disintermediation forced enterprises to chose higher cost alternative channels of finance.

There is also a debate about the necessity of strict regulation of banks. Some argue that the application of Western standards aggravated the situation. That is, the new laws introduced in Hungary in 1991–92, namely, the Bankruptcy Act and the Banking Act, may have caused the banking crisis. In their view, the weak corporate and banking sectors, shaken by the Big Shock, could not adopt Western standards, which were devised for a healthy and mature market economy. The Banking Act was strictly built on the principles of the first Basel Capital Accord and the EC guidelines on prudent banking. In practice, strict bank regulation was not applied, more and more exemptions were made, which undermined the effectiveness of the rules.

Other experts stress that lack of strict control gave rise to moral hazard. Banks were not interested in revealing their problems, and anticipated that state help would be available in case of technical insolvency. In this view, the capital loss through the reduced market value of the portfolios had happened before the passage of these two acts. Thus, "institutional changes, for the most part, did nothing more than reveal the earlier dramatic drop in the economic value of the loan portfolios" (Szalkai 1995, 194).

The third reason, bad banking, had its own role in the story. Bad banking included at least three factors: lack of prudential internal controls, lack of risk management, and lack of managerial skills. Lack of prudential internal controls resulted in credits being granted without regard to credit ratings, or in some cases without any documentation. Lack of lending manuals, controlling systems and internal audit, contradictory incentive schemes, untrained credit officers, decentralized decision-making, and the unlimited right of the CEO all contributed to the later losses. Lack of managerial skills and lack of commercial banking experience resulted in badly-organized banking firms without appropriate incentives, controls, and MIS systems.

The prerequisite of effective risk management is the measurement of risks. In stage 2, banks were not aware of the different types of risks involved in bank operations. They were not identified, measured, or controlled. Lack of credit risk management resulted in overconcentrated loan portfolios with bad loan quality. Lack of liquidity and interest rate risk management contributed to the quick decline in income.

Bad banking, bad luck, and bad policy all contributed to a severe bank crisis. Thus, stage 2 ended with a cry for state intervention.

STATE INTERVENTION: RECONSTRUCTION AND CONSOLIDATION OF THE BANKS

Stage 3 is the beginning of the crisis of the banking sector and the recognition of the need for state intervention. Nevertheless, there was an option to conceal the size of the crisis, and to play a kind of Ponzi-game. The other possibility to avoid massive state intervention was to put the burden on depositors—to inflate away bad debt and deposits as well. Elements of both solutions were applied in all countries. Sgard (1995) argues that the Czech banking sector is typically a Ponzi-country, while Pohl (1995) and Long-Rutkowska (1995) point out the impact of inflation on loans and deposits in the former Soviet Union. Hungary is one of the countries where the real value of debt was not reduced by inflation. Strict regulation had been introduced early, and the banking crisis was revealed with a relatively short time lag.

Before comparing the possible forms of intervention, we should not forget the three elements of the crisis emphasized in the previous section: deteriorating portfolios, declining cash income, and declining capital. State intervention aimed at solving all three problems at the same time had dubious results. In Hungary, there were three waves of bank consolidation, each having a different approach towards solving the problems, but gradually proceeding towards a solution (Balassa 1996; Várhegyi 2001).

The first wave, called the "loan consolidation program," was aimed at cleaning up the banks' loan portfolios. The banks had to make an inventory of the qualified nonperforming loans at a given moment of time according to prescribed qualification principles. Long-term government bonds replaced the bad loans. Previously the bad loans were bought by a special state-owned institution (Hungarian Investment and Development Bank) at an average 80 percent of the face value. Since this institution proved woefully unprepared for the task, banks were asked to manage the loans under a special contract. This first wave proved to be a failure, not only because of the inconsistent details that were worked out in a hurried fashion during a few weeks, but also because of the built-in pitfalls.

First, bargaining was an inevitable side effect of this process. Banks wanted to get rid of as many of the nonperforming loans as possible, while the authorities, who were afraid of free riding, attempted to cut back the amount proposed by the banks. Fiscal considerations were a driving force in the process. The formal qualification principles resulted in shifting out of the portfolio temporarily nonperforming but otherwise "good" loans, while a significant part of the unmoved portfolio soon proved to be nonperforming (see table 11.1).

Second, many of the enterprises responsible for nonperforming loans remained bank clients after the consolidation process. Consequently, while banks formally got rid of bad loans, actually they had to continue to sacrifice human and financial resources to manage those loans.

Third, this one-time cut presumed that it was a crisis in the nonfinancial sector. It ignored the fact that the bad debt problem was the problem of bad banking and bad luck as well, and these factors had not yet diminished.

Fourth, the solution ignored the income and capital problems of the banks. Long-term state bonds generated permanent cash inflows. However, these bonds were not marketable, and they paralyzed the banks' ability to make new loans. On the other hand, as the banks' capital had not been increased, there was no buffer to cover the possible future losses.

Fifth, the future of the bad loans was unclear. Special agents with long experience in working out bad debts were missing. The official agent of the state, the Investment and Development Bank, lacked the necessary experience, professionalism, and partners to carry the delegated task.

The first wave of consolidation was followed by a second wave, the so-called "bank consolidation scheme," with a much wider scope. This was a general enterprise and bank recapitalization program. 12 enterprises (the "dirty dozen"), accounting for 60 percent of all bad loans, were selected, and their bank debt purchased at 90 percent of the loans' face value. Banks were recapitalized with long-term government bonds to produce the required 8 percent capital adequacy (4% in the case of medium-sized banks). A so-called "consolidation contract" was set up between the banks and the Ministry of Finance, prescribing a detailed reorganization procedure between banks and indebted enterprises.

The second wave of consolidation did not achieve its original goals, but provided useful lessons:

First, the measures taken as part of the second wave penalized past responsible behavior on the part of the banks. Banks that took steps to improve profitability and aggressively provisioned against bad debt lost ground to those who were engaged in imprudent lending, paying lavish salaries, gaining market share, and forgetting provisions. The carefully selected dirty dozen were recapitalized, and their portfolios were partly cleaned up: "the worse you are, the more you get." If bank consolidation becomes a reward for bad banking and not a compensation for bad luck, then moral hazard emerges. Moral hazard did emerge in Hungary, because of the actions taken and the failure to replace bank management.

The second problem concerns corporate governance. Neither the state agencies representing the major shareholder, nor the banks representing the major financing bodies were successful in improving corporate governance of the reorganized enterprises. The question was, whether the banks should play the central role in the work out process. If the answer was yes, as was intended by the measures of the second wave, then banks would be left with less financial and human resources to finance and govern the good enterprises. The segmentation of the banking market would be marked by a new line: healthy, unconsolidated banks would finance a healthy, unconsolidated clientele, while weak recapitalized banks should devote energies to reconstruction of weak, badly organized firms without experience in corporate governance (Long and Rutkowska 1995). The results, so far, have been ambiguous. Enterprise reorganization programs have shown little success, while consolidated banks have lost significant parts of their markets.

A third problem was the cash income of the banks; 25–60 percent of the portfolio of consolidated banks is permanently frozen in low income, non-marketable, long-term government bonds. The banks' future activity is dependent on the future of these bonds. Unfortunately, no final solution about restructuring these bonds has yet emerged. The outcome was that the banking sector outgrew the illiquid assets/consolidated bonds that were 12.5 percent of total assets in 2000, and 3 percent in 2002.

Fourth, recapitalization standards were quite formal. The magic 8 percent capital adequacy ratio was considered as a universal sign of fitness, forgetting that the 8 percent is typically a rule of thumb for well-functioning, healthy banks. Instead of taking the risk of closing some of the small- and medium-sized state-owned banks, all the institutions have been recapitalized at an insufficient level. The general problem of undercapitalization has remained unsolved.

The third wave of consolidation includes mergers and acquisition of banks with state support in the form of guarantees, aiming at privatization of banks with fresh cash capital from foreign professional and/or institutional investors. These measures were part of the crucial choice lying before Hungarian policymakers and the banking sector in 1995, to be discussed in detail in the next section.

FINANCIAL SECTORS AT THE CROSSROADS IN 1995

The success of the third wave of bank reconstruction depended on lowering the risk level and increasing both the profitability and the capital base of the consolidated banks. The relationship between the government and the market was crucial in this process. Authorities had to give up the illusion that financial markets and market actors will emerge from nothing and are able to reduce tensions in the short term. As a consequence, the government had to

- intervene actively in areas where market mechanisms were lacking or inappropriate and behave as a market-maker in emerging financial markets;
- modify regulatory and operational conditions to enforce prudent banking behavior; and
- promote the privatization of state-owned banks.

The first issue concerns the active intervention of government in the markets. Naturally, fears of government intervention were deep-rooted. Nobody could guarantee that the government would find a middle-of-the-road policy where it intervened only on account of the missing market mechanisms and then built the market. There were two special areas where government intervention seemed to be beneficial. Given the history of bad loans and the banks' limited ability to judge risk, banks had become risk averse. Loans were falling and funds were extremely scarce. Recovery and reconstruction were hampered by a shortage of funds in the region. The question was, should governments intervene by providing credit guarantees? On the one hand, government guarantees could increase the danger of moral hazard, but, on the other, they might speed economic recovery and reduce the need of direct intervention into the banking sector. The solution was that the issue of guarantees was delegated to independent bodies (Credit Guarantee Ltd., Export Credit Guarantee Ltd.), which mitigated the discretionary power of the government.

The other possibility for government intervention was market development. At the beginning of the two-tier banking system, the central bank took the responsibility for creating an interbank market, and it behaved as an intermediary in this market. Without this market-making function, the Hungarian interbank market could not have developed. The emerging derivative markets were unlikely to develop without the government acting as an intermediary to increase liquidity. These markets are crucial for banks and corporations to cover their interest rate and foreign exchange risks. However, the government did not provide liquidity to these markets, and derivatives markets are less deep now than they were in 1997, before the Russian crisis of August 1998. The OTC markets are shallow as well. Nevertheless, this did not prove to be as much of an obstacle to the banking system as it was in 1995.

The second aspect of government's role relates to regulations. Deregulation has been a worldwide trend following innovations that have destroyed the foundations of the old rules. In many countries regulations are being revised to remove the fire wall between the banking sector and capital markets. The banks in CEE countries have consistently followed the trend toward universal banking, with existing managers and bank regulators gradually preparing themselves to deal with complex problems raised by universal, as compared with commercial, banking. Hungarian banks, for example, now act as full-service universal banks, and some of the unsolved problems of corporate governance mentioned in the previous section have not yet emerged.

Regulation contributed to prudent banking. Nevertheless, decision makers had to be careful in determining the frontiers of prudent banking. Hence regulations could not be excessively restrictive. Risks should be held at a reasonable level without restricting the sector from profitable activity. After the first waves of consolidation partly due to more prudent banking, corporate lending by banks declined in both real and absolute terms. Excessive credit rationing and a credit crunch was the problem. Restrictive monetary policy and restrictive bank regulation could have crowded out good corporations from the bank loan market, as well. Banks could have lost their leading role in intermediation, and a direct form of financing would replace them (Király 1995). The successful operation of the banking system significantly depends on the role of bank as channel for corporate finance. East European economies are bank-oriented economies, and the capital markets play a secondary role. Nevertheless, banks' corporate loans expressed as a percentage of GDP (10–30% except of the Czech Republic) has been very low when compared to market economies. The EU legal harmonization process, however, brought on tolerable and legal changes that contributed to convergence towards optimal level of risk taking.

The third aspect is the ownership of the banks and the role of government in the privatization process. In the mid-1990s, it was agreed that banks should be privatized because they need new products and techniques, clear profit incentives, and fresh capital, which the government was not able to provide.

It was argued that before privatization occurred, some banks should shrink by selling their consolidation bonds and removing their bad loans. Others should stabilize their market share, but cut operation costs by closing unprofitable branches and reducing staff. In both cases, government was seen as the key agent supporting both processes.

The government, being the largest shareholder, may promote institutional development based on mergers and acquisition prior to privatization. The reasoning behind this was that Hungarian and most East European banks were not competitive in international markets. A mid-sized Swiss bank is as big as the whole Hungarian banking sector. The relative size of the banking sector in 1993 and 1994 was and still is less than 70 percent of GDP, while in many Western European countries the average size is 200 percent.

Nevertheless, a drastic organizational reconstruction initiated by the government could have been harmful, and the Hungarian experience showed the pitfalls of such an initiative. Some recapitalized banks with heavy losses were merged into the Hungarian Investment and Development Bank, a special government agency, which already played an active role in the first wave of the bank consolidation process. Two other recapitalized banks were merged, without regard to the advantages of the merger. The merger was not successful, and the merged bank was not suitable for privatization.

Three approaches to privatization have been applied in Eastern European countries (Bonin 1995). The Czech experience is based on mass (voucher) privatization. The major banks set up investments funds and collected the majority of the vouchers. Consequently, significant cross-ownership evolved which strengthened further the nonmarket relationships between banks and their company clients. In Poland, an initial private offering was used, and it was applied in four successful cases. This process of privatization was quick and efficient. However, the capitalization of the Warsaw Stock Exchange may not absorb new issues. The small size of the capital market is a problem. Hungary selected a slower privatization strategy. It was a private placement with strategic foreign financial investors. This process resulted in successful privatization.

A SUCCESSFULLY PRIVATIZED BANKING SECTOR—THE CASE OF HUNGARY

The Privatization Process in Hungary

Privatization raised two crucial policy issues: (1) whether Hungarian banks must be sold to strategic or portfolio investors, and (2) whether to develop concentrated or diversified banking structures. The privatization of banks having taken part in the restructuring program by the state generally followed the same pattern: participants were selected on the basis of the price offered and promised capital injections. The strategic investors acquired majority stakes or they were granted an option for future purchase, provided that they made large capital injections.

The Hungarian bank privatization includes two exceptions—OTP and Postabank—based on strategic investors and producing concentrated holdings. OTP and Postabank are the two largest retail banks. OTP was given in a private placement to foreign institutions, Hungarian institutions, private investors, employees, and the management. In the case of Postabank, government policy produced a diversified, but not transparent ownership structure. The bank suffered large serious losses, and required a state bail-out by 1998.

The Hungarian bank privatization created clear and transparent ownership in most of the banks. Hungary's policy of favoring international strategic investors was beneficial not only because the Hungarian banks were taken over by capital-rich and experienced owners, but also because it prevented the emergence of cross-ownership holdings, the hotbed of conflicting interests. The Banking Act, which prescribed that no nonfinancial institution may hold an interest over 15 percent, already restricted this opportunity.

Prior to the Government's privatization program in 1994, foreign and joint banks had been growing mainly through green-field investments. The majority of the state-owned banks were privatized between 1994 and 1997, which means that the share of public ownership dropped to 20 percent. The massive presence of the foreign banks is a consequence of the large number of new entries and the method of privatization, according to which most of the state-owned banks were sold to foreign institutions (Várhegyi 1999 and 2001). At the end of 2000, of a total of 42 credit institutions, 33 were operating with majority foreign shareholders, and one with minority stake of foreigners. They hold two-thirds of the total registered capital and control 91 percent of the assets in the market.

The ownership structure in the Hungarian banking sector differs from most Eastern countries. The high share of foreigner ownership is the result of a lack of capital-rich domestic institutional investors at the time of privatization, and the liberal licensing practice concerning green-field (i.e., New, *de novo*) investments. Because the weak state-owned banks required strategic investors that were able to increase capital, the majority of them were put under the control of foreign banks.

Many EU-based banks own Hungarian credit institutions. The organizations that have a strong presence in Hungary include BLB, IntesaBci, KCB, ABN Amro, HVB and BA, Commerzbank, SanPaolo-IMI, DG and BNP Paribas. Their subsidiaries own 55 percent of the Hungarian banks' assets (Várhegyi 2002).

Non-EU-owned banks also have a significant market share. Foreign inves-

Table 11.3
Ownership Structure of the Hungarian Banking Sector (by Registered Capital)

Type of owner	1995	1996	1997	1998	1999	2000
Hungarian owners	63.9	50.5	37.2	36.4	32.4	30.8
State and social securities	*41.8*	*35.6*	*20.3*	*21.1*	*17.1*	*19.3*
Other domestic institutions	*17.8*	*11.6*	*14.4*	*12.5*	*12.7*	*9.5*
Private persons	*4.2*	*3.2*	*2.5*	*2.8*	*2.6*	*2.0*
Foreign owners	35.7	45.8	61.1	60.9	65.0	66.6
Credit institutions	*26.8*	*38.9*	*52.8*	*46.5*	*49.9*	*50.8*
Other foreign institutions	*8.8*	*10.1*	*8.6*	*14.4*	*15.1*	*15.8*
Preferential and own shares	0.4	3,7	1,6	2.7	2.6	2.6
Total	**100.0**	**100.0**	**100.0**	**100.0**	**100.0**	**100.0**

Source: National Bank of Hungary.

tors own 35 percent of OTP. GE and Citigroup own Budapest Bank and Citibank. And Russia's Gazprombank owns Postabank.

Commercial banks are the principal owners in the Hungarian financial sector. They own 19 of the 21 investment companies, three-quarters of the fund managers, and almost half of the 18 leasing companies, and the 38 brokerage firms.

MEASURABLE IMPROVEMENTS IN THE BANKING SECTOR

The entry of foreign banks accelerated the restructuring process. The majority of the foreign banks are among the top one hundred on *The Banker's* "Top World 1,000" list. The parent banks provided substantial capital to promote the growth of their Hungarian subsidiaries, and the high earnings were retained for investment. Between 1995 and 2000 the foreign owners provided total capital of U.S. $800 billion, which is more than half of the current subscribed capital in the sector. Their foreign bank subsidiaries had a 60 percent market share in 2000. OTP, with control over almost one-quarter of the market, has been a blue-chip stock on the Hungarian and it is listed on some foreign stock markets. It has no difficulty in raising funds.

Stability of the banking system has been enhanced by the prudent operation of most foreign banks, and improved risk management, which is reflected in the low level of bad debts. In other CEE countries, only Estonia has a lower

Table 11.4
Share of Foreign-Owned Banks in Total Assets*

	1995	1996	1997	1998	1999	2000
1. Banks with majority stake of foreigners	41.8	46.2	53.0	64.0	66.4	68.1
2. Banks with minority stake of foreigners	37.5	36.8	40.3	25.0	24.2	22.9
Banks with foreign ownership (1+2)	79.3	83.0	93.3	89.0	90.6	91.0

*Without savings and credit co-operatives, and building societies.

level of nonperforming loans to total assets. It is somewhat higher in Slovenia, and much higher in Poland and the Czech Republic (RZB 2001). The average capital adequacy ratio of 15 percent in recent years is a further indicator of stability.

Although the efficiency of the Hungarian banking sector improved in the second half of the 1990s, it is inadequate in a number of respects. It generates a handsome return for its owners, but it does not do enough to serve its customers. The Hungarian banking system lends to relatively few companies and households. The loans to GDP ratio is low, but growing to 35 percent by the end of 2001. The reasons for the low figure include the poor credit-worthiness of small businesses, weak demand by households for credits, as well as the banks' high interest margin (Várhegyi and Spéder 1996). In the past three years, most banks abandoned the "redlining" policy, and they are making increased efforts to acquire creditworthy SMEs (Király and Várhegyi 1998).

The efficiency of the banking sector improved in the second half of the 1990s, but many indicators are still below the corresponding EU figures. The net interest margin dropped from 5.4 percent 1995 to 4.0 percent in 2000, while the NIM for Hungarian banks fell from 5.0 percent to 3.7 percent in the same period. Subsequently, there has been a slight improvement in the NIM as banks shift toward the retail business as opposed to corporate business. Compared to the other CEE countries, the spread was much lower already in 1996, and similar figures were only reached in 2000 (RZB 2001).

Hungarian banks were not as efficient as banks in the European Union. In 2000, operating costs accounted for 3.5 percent of the total assets, double the EU average. Some of the costs were used to modernize the banks (IT, infra-structure investments), so it should be considered a positive, rather than a negative phenomenon.

Table 11.5
Progress of Efficiency and Stability of the Hungarian Banking Sector*

	1995	1996	1997	1998	1999	2000	2001
Balance sheet total as percentage of GDP	66.4	67.2	67.2	68.2	64.4	65.3	65,2
Loan to customers, percent of assets	33.4	32.5	35.0	34.2	36.3	41.3	44.1
Customers' deposits, percent of liabilities	47.4	47.7	49.7	49.3	53.4	53.0	51.9
Bad and doubtful loans, percent of assets	7.4	4.0	3.2	1.8	2.6	2.0	1.5
Capital adequacy ratio	18.3	18.9	17.3	9.9	15.0	15.2	14.2
ROA (according to pre-tax profit), percent	1.5	1.7	1.3	-2.1 (0.9)**	0.6	1.3	1.7
ROE (according to pre-tax profit), percent	18.2	20.6	14.3	-25.4 (10.7)* *	6.3	15.1	16.8
Operating costs, percent of assets	3.7	3.6	3.8	4.0	3.7	3.5	4.2
Net interest margin, percent of assets	5.4	4.9	4.5	4.5	4.1	4.0	4.7
Spread, percent***	4.9	4.7	4.3	4.2	3.7	3.7	n.a.

Source: National Bank of Hungary and State Supervision of Financial Institutions.
* Without savings and credit co-operatives.
**Without losses of two banks which had produced losses as a consequence of bad loan policies of several years, and resulted in liquidation of one and state bail-out of the other in 1998.
*** Difference between the interest income on interest-earning assets and the interest payments on interest-bearing funds.

The cost of provisioning for bad loans does not put a larger strain on the margin than in most EU banks. In 2000, it was 0.6 percent of total assets. It is remarkable that the provisions fell when loan operations were gaining in intensity. In the period after portfolio cleansing and privatization, the average profitability of the Hungarian banks was satisfactory. Average ROA, calculated with pretax profits, was typically 1–2 percent. Average ROE is more varied, and it can be evaluated in relation to the inflation. In 1996–97 it was 2–3 percentage points below the inflation rate, then in 2000 it crept up to 5 percentage points, in the first half of 2001 10 percentage points above the inflation rate.

Improved efficiency is due primarily to increased competition. The positive effects were first felt in corporate banking. Initially, the banks vied for the large corporations only, but recently several of them targeted the more reliable SMEs. The powers are fairly balanced on the corporate credit market: the four largest players have 10–12 percent each, while the next three control 6–7 percent. Today, falling real lending rates are a good sign of the competition. However, the situation is less balanced on the retail credit market, although the share of the market leader has been falling year by year, and newcomers gradually strengthen their positions. Nowadays, competition is intense for both consumer and home loans, with the real rates of the latter plunging. The specialized foreign banks made a great contribution to the growing popularity of consumer loans, but foreign-owned credit institutions are also becoming more active on the home loan market.

Most of the foreign banks that arrived early in the Hungarian market have been more efficient from the outset than the ones that were privatized under the burden of an appalling legacy (bad debts, inefficient branch network, poor IT). The former operated with lower cost ratios, lower net interest margins, and a higher degree of profitability than the privatized banks. Some privatized banks could improve their efficiency if they are spurred by the owners' expectations and by the competition. However, not all the new owners can galvanize their Hungarian subsidiaries, even if they made major investments and hired foreign managers.

Despite the mixed results, one can state that the radical shift in the ownership structure has been a key factor in raising efficiency in the banking sector. In addition to increasing competition, the foreign banks have fundamentally changed attitudes. The owners establish strict efficiency requirements for the management, while contributing capital, technology, and products to the creation of economies of scale.

LIKELY FUTURE TENDENCIES IN THE DEVELOPMENT OF THE FINANCIAL SECTOR IN HUNGARY

Financial intermediation underwent considerable progress in Hungary in the 1990s. The institutional framework that a market economy requires has been put in place, the operation and the ownership of the financial organizations have become transparent, and the regulatory and the supervisory conditions for safe operation have been, by and large, created. The amendments to the financial legislation aim to achieve full compliance with EU norms and standards, and to increase market transparency and supervisory effectiveness. The new laws on banking, securities, and insurance, coming into force in

2001, gave a larger weight to market risk assessment, the underlying capital, and the internal risk management practices of financial service providers.

The current trend of consolidation and the cleaner market are likely to raise the risk-taking ability of the financial institutions, hence the security of the industry. This phenomenon is particularly conspicuous among brokerage firms: the Russian crisis of 1998 caused several of them to exit the market, and most of the survivors are in the hands of banks. The introduction of the trading book regulation (which is also due in the near future) will allow the integration of securities trading into banks, which, in turn, may enhance the competitiveness of banks and universal financial service providers.

The majority of the Hungarian banks are owned by major international financial institutions (ABN AMRO, KBC, Citicorp, GEC, Commerzbank, HypoVereinsbank, BLB, WestLB, BA-CA, RZB, Erste Bank, DG Bank, Banca Commerciale, Sao Paolo di Torino, etc.), and run as quasi-branches. There is a single bank in Hungary (OTP) with a diverse ownership structure, that is, one without a strategic investor. On the other hand, OTP controls roughly a quarter of the whole market, with an almost 50 percent share in the retail market.

Almost all the banks have brokerage firms, investment banking arms, leasing companies, mutual fund management companies, mutual insurance funds, or property management companies. Some of them incorporate building society type businesses, one owns an insurance company, and insurance companies have gained interests in some of the banks. By the way, the great majority of the Hungarian insurance companies also belong to large international insurers (Allianz, Aegon, NN, etc.), operated as quasi-branches too. Most of the investment banks and brokerage firms are linked to international financial institutions through their owner banks.

This should lead us to conclude that the future of financial institutions in Hungary depends not only on the domestic market but also on the position and intentions of their foreign owners. Experience shows that the major international banks are willing to shoulder loss-making operations for a couple of years in order to gain a hold on the Hungarian (East European) market. During 1999–2000, ABN AMRO, KBC, and Sao Paolo di Torino, for instance, provided capital injections to compensate the losses of their banks and brokerage firms in Hungary. So far, Hungarian subsidiary banks have only been sold as part of mergers between the parent banks. The situation of brokerage firms without a banking background is different: several have failed or been taken over in recent years.

The future may, of course, hold further take-overs and consolidations. However, the large foreign owners are unlikely to leave the Hungarian market in the short term, as the demand for financial services will certainly expand. The expected growth of the Hungarian economy, the diversification of financial transactions, and the rising propensity to save will all contribute to the expansion of demand for financial services. Nevertheless, the institutions, which at present are bound to incur high unit costs, will be increasingly concerned about efficiency. Unless the current banking investments are recovered in a few years, the owners will probably consider the sale of their Hungarian subsidiaries.

Some of the foreign owners may respond to inefficiency by changing corporate governance. It appears that the banks in which operative management is performed by Hungarians with adequate knowledge of the local market, extensive contacts, and a high degree of expertise, are more efficient than those without such resources. The banks that are operated as quasi-branches by foreign bankers with limited authority have had fewer successes than the organizations managed by more independent, highly professional locals. The explanation is that a troupe of competitive and qualified Hungarian bank managers had evolved by the late 1990s that is less corruptible because of the competitive compensation packages they receive, and possesses the local knowledge and contacts that are indispensable for efficient banking operation.

The integration of financial markets, the expansion of cross-border transactions, and the changing nature of financial services (e-banking) will gradually diminish the importance of local presence, which, in the long run, should lead to a modified structure of the financial institutions and the services they provide. The competitiveness of the service providers that are present in Hungary will not primarily depend on their local profitability but on the extent to which they are profitable on a global scale, and the local services make a very small contribution to the latter.

Investment services make up the bulk of financial globalization, where country borders are indeed crumbling these days. The most protected field is insurance, where the foreign investment of premium reserves is restricted in many countries, including Hungary. However, such restrictions will have to be abolished once Hungary has become a member of the European Union. Banking is in an intermediate position: branches will continue to be indispensable in the retail and the small business sectors for quite a while, but they are losing importance in corporate banking.

NOTE

1. The economies at that time were characterized by "money circles" or "loops." This terminology, used in the earlier socialist literature, attempts to describe the situation when different "money" is used by corporations and by households in spite of the fact that there is one central bank and one legal tender. Money within the economy is not homogeneous, which is a rather curious phenomenon.

REFERENCES

Ábel, I.—Prander, K. (1995): "Impediments to Financial Restructuring of Hungarian Enterprises" in *Company Management and Capital Market Development in the Transition*, ed. M. Jackson and V. Bilsen. LICOS Studies on the Transitions in Central and Eastern Europe, Vol. 2, 8, 10.

Ábel, I—Siklós, p.l. (1994): "Constraints on Enterprise Liquidity and Its Impact . . . " *Comparative Economic Studies* Vol. 36 No. 1 Spring 1994.

Ábel, I., and P. I. Székely. (1994): "Market Structure and Competition in the Hungarian Banking System." In *The Development and Reforms of Financial Systems in Central and Eastern Europe*, edited by J. P. Bonin and I. P. Székely. Cheltenham, U.K., Edward Elgar.

Ábel, I., and P. I Székely. (1995): "Financial Intermediation and Industrial Restructuring in Central and Eastern Europe" in Landesmann, M. A.—Székely, P. I. (1995): "Industrial Restructuring and Trade Reorientation in Eastern Europe," Cambridge Univ Press, 337–362.

Annual Reports of the National Bank of Hungary 1987–1995.

Annual Reports of the State Supervising Agency 1991–1993.

Balassa, Ákos. (1996): "Consolidation of the Hungarian Banking System and Its Present Situation" (in Hungarian). *Külgazdaság* no. 4 and 5.

Begg, D.—Portes, R. (1993): "Enterprise Debt and Financial Restructuring in Central and *Eastern* Europe" *European Economic Review* Vol. 37 pp. 396–407.

Bonin, J. P. (1995): "Banking in Transition: Privatizing Banks in Hungary, Poland, and Czech Republic." Mimeographed.

Bonin, J. P., and M. E. Schaffer. (1995): "Bank, Firms, Bad Debts and Bankruptcy in Hungary 1991–1994." Mimeographed.

Bonin, J. P.—Székely, P. I. (1994): The Development and Reforms of Financial Systems in Central and Eastern Europe, Edward Elgar.

Claessens, Stijn. (1998): How does Foreign Entry Affect the Domestic Banking Market? The World Bank. *Policy Research Working Paper* 1918. June.

Estrin, S.—Hare, P.—Surányi, M. (1992): "Banking in Transition" *Soviet Studies*, Vol 44, 1992/5, 785–808.

Fries, S. et al. (1994): "Transitions: private sector development and the role of financial institutions" EBRD Working Paper No. 13, 1994 July.

Gedeon, S. (1985): "The Post Keynesian Theory of Money: a Summary and an Eastern European example" *Journal of Post Keynesian Economics*, Winter, 1985–86, Vol. 8, No. 2, 208–221.

Honohan P. -Vittas, D. (1995): "Ownership and Control in Banking: Policy Issues for Developing and Transitions Economies" Paper to be presented at the Eleventh World Congress of the IEA, Tunis, 18–22 December 1995.

Institute for Small Business Development. (1998): State of Small and Medium Sized Business in Hungary. Annual Report.

Kessides, C., T. King, M. Nuti, and C. Sokil., eds. (1989): "Financial Reform in Socialist Economies." The World Bank, Washington, D.C.

Király, J. (1993): "Development of the Financial Sector 1993–2005" *Mimeo*.

Király, J. (1995): "The Hungarian Fisher-Cycle." *Acta Oeconomica* 47 (3–4): 323–42.

Király, J., and É. Várhegyi. (1998): "SME Finance—an SME bank? Possibilities and Constraints of Setting Up a Specialised Financial Agency Supporting SMEs." In *The Hungarian SME Sector Development in Comparative Perspective*, edited by L. Csaba. Budapest: KOPINT-DATORG Foundation–Center for International Private Enterprise, 1998.

Király, Júlia et al. (2000): Experience with internationalisation of Financial Sector Providers. Case study: Hungary. In: Claessens, S. and Jansen, M. (eds) (2000): The Internalization of Financial Services. *Kluwer Law Interational*.

Laky, Teréz. (1994): Small enterprises benefitting from Start Credit, Budapest: *HFEP*, *SME Research Booklet*, No. 1.

Landesmann, M.—Ábel, I. (1995): "Industrial Policy in Transition" in Landesmann, M. A.—Székely, P. I. (1995): "Industrial Restructuring and Trade Reorientation in Eastern Europe," Cambridge, Univ Press, 313–336.

Landesmann, M. A.—Székely, P.I. (1995): "Industrial Restructuring and Trade Reorientation in Eastern Europe," Cambridge, Univ Press, 1995.

Long, M., and I. Rutkowska. (1995): "The Role of Commercial Banks in Enterprise Restructuring in Central and Eastern Europe." World Bank Policy research working paper, WPS 1423.

Nuti, D. M. (1992): "Socialist Banking." In *The New Palgrave Dictionary of Money and Finance*, edited by P. Newman, et al. London, Macmillan Press Limited.

Piper, R., et al. (1994): "Transformation at Crossroads: Financial Sector Reform and Enterprise Restructuring in Hungary." Blue Ribbon Commission Policy Study No. 5. Budapest.

Pohl, G. (1995): "Banking Reforms in Russia and Eastern Europe." Mimeograph.

RZB. (2001): EU-Convergence. Banking Systems. RZB Group, March.

Sgard, J. (1995): "Finance la transition dans six pays d'Europe centrale et balkanique: une macroéconomie orthodoxe á la merci d'une microéconomie faible?" Mimeograph.

Spéder, Z. (1991): "The Charasteristic Behaviour of Hungarian Commercial Banks." *Acta Oeconomica* 43 (1–2), pp. 131–148.

Spéder, Z., and É. Várhegyi. (1992): "On the Eve of the Second Banking Reform." *Acta Oeconomica* 44 (1–2).

Székely, I. P.—Newberry, N.M.G. (ed) (1993): "Hungary: An Economy in Transition" Cambridge University Press 1993.

Vajda, Ágnes (1997): Small enterpreneurs and the Micro Credit Programme 1992–1995, Budapest: *HFEP, SME Research Booklet*, No. 6.

Várhegyi, É. (1995): "Banks in Competition" *8th Conference of Group of Banking Supervisors from Central and Eastern European countries*, April 26–28, 1995, Budapest.

Várhegyi, É. (1994): "The 'Second' Reform of the Hungarian Banking System." In *The Development and Reforms of Financial Systems in Central and Eastern Europe*, edited by J. P. Bonin and I. P. Székely. Edward Elgar.

Várhegyi, É., and Z. Spéder. (1996): "Money Market and Crediting Situation of SMEs." Budapest: HFEP, SME Research Booklet, No. 5.

Várhegyi, Éva. (1999): "Hungarian Banking Sector after Privatization." *Central European Banker*, February.

Várhegyi, Éva. (2002): "Hungary's Banking Sector: Achievements and Challenges." In *The Financial Integration of an Enlarged EU: Banking and Capital Markets*. EIB Papers 7 (1).

Várhegyi, Éva. (2001): "Reforms and Development of the Banking Systems in the Transition Economies." In *Central Europe towards Monetary Union: Macroeconomic Underpinnings and Financial Reputation*, edited by R. Macdonald and R. Cross. Kluwer Academic Publishers, Boston/Doerdrecht/London.

CHAPTER 12

Banking in Japan: Will Too Big to Fail Prevail?

Adrian van Rixtel, Yupana Wiwattanakantang, Toshiyuki Souma, and Kazunori Suzuki

INTRODUCTION

Since the beginning of the nineties, the Japanese economic success story has lost a lot of its appeal. As a result of the collapse of the "bubble" economy, Japanese banks became saddled with huge amounts of nonperforming loans, and a significant number of them failed. In addition, the stability of the financial system was further jeopardized by many scandals, which often implicated the monetary authorities themselves and resulted in major administrative and financial reforms. Increasingly, international monetary authorities and economic organizations showed their concern about the situation in Japan, in particular regarding the banking crisis and deflationary spiral (see, for example, Ahearne et al. 2002).

The purpose of this contribution is to review the evolution of the Japanese banking sector and the development of the banking crisis in Japan in the context of too big to fail (TBTF), which we characterize as "supervisory ad hoc pragmatism." It describes the deterioration of the Japanese financial sector caused by the bad loan problems, and the failure of policymakers to get a grip on the underlying problems. The latter aspect of the banking crisis in Japan is reflected in the policy shifts of the supervisory authorities, who at times seemed to be willing to end too big to fail, but at other times seemed unwilling to let problem banks fail and instead tried to bail them out by injecting public funds in the major banks only. In general, the ruling political parties, which were concerned about possible negative economic consequences emanating from bank failures and often also maintained close connections with the banking industry, preferred a policy of "muddling through" instead of taking swift and decisive action. All in all, also at the start of the new century, Japanese policymakers continue to struggle to find the right policy response to tackle the banking problems and how to avoid moral hazard behavior intertwined with too big to fail concerns. In any case, the increasing concentration in the Japanese banking industry, which is now dominated by five huge financial conglomerates, should make it more difficult to definitely end too big to fail in Japanese prudential policy. In this respect, we believe that it can be argued that too big to fail in Japan will prevail.

The issue of too big to fail has been widely discussed in the literature, in particular after the debacle with Continental Illinois National Bank in Chicago in the United States (see Roth 1994; Federal Deposit Insurance Corporation [FDIC] 1997; Stern 1997; Gup 1998; Kaufman 2002; for an earlier analysis see Hetzel 1991). As regards a definition of too big to fail, we agree with Kaufman (2002) that it is often a much misunderstood term, and that in practice—at least in the United States—it implies that a bank is "too-big-to-liquidate" (Kaufman and Seelig 2000, p. 1). In this contribution, we speak of too big to fail if supervisory authorities provide financial support, for example in the form of capital injections, or take other action that prevents a problem bank actually going bankrupt. This is in line with Gup (1998), p. 69, who states that " . . . the TBTF doctrine means that the organization may continue to exist, and insured depositors will be protected; but stockholders, subordinated debt holders, managers, and some general creditors may suffer losses." If a bank is actually allowed to fail and goes bankrupt, we believe this is a clear case of ending too big to fail, or an example of "let fail." Finally, when the government is nationalizing problem banks, we interpret this as "too-big-to-liquidate," as the banks have actually failed but are continued under the same charter and a different name.

The outline of this contribution is as follows. The second section describes the evolution of the Japanese banking system, from the post-war situation to the current banking sector, and pays attention to the process of financial reform. The third section reflects on the banking crisis, analyzes its causes and discusses the policy response to this crisis. The fourth section addresses the issue of too big to fail in Japan and defines our interpretation of "supervisory ad hoc pragmatism." It also presents a case study of "let fail," showing the consequences of the failure of the Hokkaido Takushoku Bank. Finally, the final section is the conclusion.

THE EVOLUTION OF JAPANESE BANKING

The Pre-Reform Japanese Financial System and the Regulation of Banking

The financial system during the post-war period until around the middle of the 1980s is well known as a bank-based system. The stock and bond markets were deliberately suppressed by various regulations. The banking system was heavily regulated as well, and the status quo was protected under the so-called "convoy system" (Patrick 1999; Spiegel 1999). Under the "convoy system," banks were ensured that de facto there would be no competition, and they would grow roughly at the same rate. This was achieved via regulatory measures of controlling interest rates, fees, and financial products, dividing business lines and branch restrictions (Hoshi 2002; Van Rixtel 2002). So-called administrative guidance, or "moral suasion," by the Ministry of Finance (MoF) was often used to make sure that all the banks would move together. Most importantly, until 1995 when the Hyogo Bank was liquidated, no bank would be allowed to fail (Cargill et al. 1997; Hoshi 2002). The Ministry of Finance encouraged bank mergers that prevented bank failures—by allowing strong banks to take over weaker banks. The maintenance of the convoy system was logical from the perspective of Japanese regulators, given that the main source of corporate finance was lending through banks. This predominance of indirect finance (intermediation) resulted mainly from the underdevelopment of the capital markets, which was caused by the low level of issuance of government bonds, the use of interest rate and foreign capital controls, and the reduced level of asset accumulation after the Second World War. Additionally, the preference for indirect finance can be explained partly by the domination of transactions based on customer relationships rather than on funding through the capital markets (Cargill and Royama 1988, p. 44).

The evolving structure of the post-war financial system was expected to fulfill three important requirements (Teranishi 1990, pp. 5–6; Teranishi 1993). First and most importantly, the system had to supply sufficient long-term funds to realize economies of scale for developing industries, using borrowed technology (the "catch-up" process). The second role assigned to the financial system was enhancing the availability of funds in low productivity and traditional areas. Third, the financial system was required to be safe and stable.

The post-war financial system was segmented according to functions and types of clients. Competition was restricted between various business areas, as each financial institution was not permitted to enter the business areas of other financial institutions. As a result, a functional segmentation of financial institutions was established, for example, between securities and banking business. Furthermore, by formal regulation and informal guidance, banking and trust business were separated and financial intermediaries established a specialization of lending. Some financial institutions specialized in long-term finance, while others became occupied with short-term lending activities. Moreover, specialization of lending areas could be found in special financial institutions for small- and medium-sized firms and agricultural business. This system of functional segmentation of various kinds of financial institutions was strengthened further by various interest rate regulations.

As a result, this heavily regulated financial system became categorized into banks, *shinkin* banks, credit unions and associations, cooperatives, securities firms, life and non–life insurance companies, the postal savings system, and government financial institutions for specific functions. The banking industry was divided into three groups: commercial banks, trust banks, and long-term credit banks. Commercial banks were segregated by location and client size into city banks and regional banks. Their focus used to be on short-term lending, but in practice this orientation was blurred into long-term lending as well. City banks (*toshi ginkō*) have been headquartered in the major cities, with nationwide operations, and became the main financiers of "Japan, Inc." Regional banks (*chihō ginkō*) have their headquarters in smaller cities and, as their name suggests, have a largely regional function. Regional banks are classified into regional banks and second tier regional banks. The latter were former *sogo* or mutual savings banks, and reclassified in 1989 into commercial banks, which became members of the so-called Second Association of Regional Banks (*Dai-ni Chihō Ginkō Kyōkai*). Traditionally, regional banks have been experiencing problems in competing with other regional banks, as well with city banks, since their branch network (number and places) has been restrained by administrative guidance.

Furthermore, during the post-war period, long-term financing was provided by trust banks (*shintaku ginkō*) and long-term credit banks (*chōki shinyō ginkō*). As regards the former, besides operating in the trust business, they have been conducting banking activities, which include accepting deposits and make long-term loans. As regards the latter, originally three of these banks (Industrial Bank of Japan, Long-Term Credit Bank of Japan, and Nippon Credit Bank) were set up in 1952 to provide long-term funds to large manufacturing firms, but, as will be discussed later, two of them failed in 1998— their activities were continued in two new banks. The long-term credit banks raised funds through specific deposits and the issuance of bank debentures. As of 1991, there were 12 city banks, 64 regional banks, 68 second-tier regional banks, seven trust banks, and three long-term credit banks (see table 12.1). These major banks held 61.9 percent of the total deposits of all financial institutions.

In addition to the commercial banks and banks for longer-term finance, smaller financial institutions were created to provide financing services for special groups of customers. Financial institutions for small businesses comprise three groups: credit associations (*shinyō kinko*) or *shinkin* banks, credit cooperatives (*shinyō kumiai*), and the Central Cooperative Bank for Commerce and Industry (*Shōkō Kumiai Chūō Kinko*) or *Shōkō Chūkin* Bank. Financial institutions for agriculture (*nōgyō*), forestry (*ringyō*), and fishery (*gyogyō*) are organized on national, prefectoral, and municipal levels, and provide financial services to farmers, foresters, and fishermen on a mutual base.

The Process of Financial Reform: Financial Innovations, Liberalization, and Globalization

Most of the restrictions regarding the business activities of Japanese financial institutions, however, were gradually liberalized during the latter half of

Table 12.1
Financial Institutions in Japan in 1991 and 2002

Category	1991 Number	1991 Share in total deposits (%)	1991 Total assets (in yen trillion)	2002 Number	2002 Share in total deposits (%)	2002 Total assets (in yen trillion)
City banks	12	31.1	376.6	7	23.9	363.1
Long-term credit banks	3	1.4	76.6	3[1]	1.0	53.1
Trust banks	7	2.8	59.3	8	3.4	64.5
Regional banks	64	19.5	187.9	64	18.8	205.7
Second tier regional banks	68	7.1	68.8	53	5.8	61.9
Shinkin banks	451	10.3	96.0	349	10.7	112.1
Credit cooperatives	407	2.8	24.1	247	1.6	18.3
Labor cooperatives	47	0.9	7.5	39	1.3	13.4
Agricultural co-operatives	3,600	7.0	58.4	1,264	7.6	75.2
Securities companies[3]	272		27.0	290		19.4
Life insurance companies	26		130.3	42		184.4
Non-life insurance companies	24		26.2	35[2]		33.5
Postal life and annuity			51.8	24,778[2]		124.8
Postal savings		17.1		24,778[2]	25.9	
Government institutions	11		92.9	11		159.4

Sources: Bank of Japan, *Economic Statistics Annual* and *Financial and Economic Statistics Monthly*; Federation of Bankers Associations of Japan; Ministry of Finance, *Statistics Monthly*; Economic Planning Agency of Japan, *Economic White Paper,* 1995; Japan Securities Dealers Association, *Annual Report,* 2002; Postal Services Agency, *Statistics of Postal Service Agency.* The numbers of financial institutions for each category in 2002 are from the Web site of their respective associations.

Note: Figures are as of March 1991 and March 2002 (the end of the fiscal year).

[1]Long-term credit banks include the Industrial Bank of Japan, Shinsei Bank, and Aozora Bank.

[2]The number is as of March 2001.

[3]These numbers include 52 and 49 foreign securities companies as of March 1991 and March 2002, respectively.

the 1990s. By 2000, the barriers to entering each other's line of business had almost completely disappeared. The process of financial reform in Japan started around the late 1970s, when Japan began to deregulate its financial system mainly due to the pressure from macroeconomic factors, in particular the shift to lower economic growth, higher levels of public debt, the increasing accumulation of financial assets, and internal reserves by individuals and companies, respectively.[1] The reform process was very gradual during the 1980s until the mid of the 1990s in order to maintain the convoy system and avoid disruption of the status quo in market shares and business territories between financial institutions.

Financial reforms consisted mainly of three interrelated processes: financial innovations, financial liberalization, and financial globalization. As part of financial innovations, a number of new financial instruments and markets were introduced and developed. Examples are certificates of deposits (1979), investments in medium-term government bonds (1980), and money market certificates (1985). New markets that were developed are, for example, the markets for banker's acceptances (1985), treasury bills (1986), a financial "offshore" market (1986), and commercial paper (1987). The second reform process, that is financial liberalization, included reforms that eased and abolished existing financial regulations. This process changed the regulatory structure of the Japanese financial system drastically. For example, bond issuance restrictions were first eased around 1975 when issuance of unsecured bonds was allowed for the first time. In 1990, all accounting criteria related to debt securities issuance were abolished, and firms were able to issue rated bonds. Bond issuance was fully liberalized in 1996. Furthermore, interest rate regulations for large bank deposits were lifted in October 1985. By the end of 1980s, all interest rates were fully liberalized except deposit rates. Deposit rate controls were completely abolished in 1993. The third process related to financial reform that has been identified here, financial globalization, can be described as the process that exposed Japan (firms as well as individuals) to the international financial markets and vice versa. There were at least two important reforms in this respect. The first was the removal of the so-called yen conversion limits, which restricted the amount of foreign currency to be converted into yen by financial institutions. The second was the abolition of the so-called real demand doctrine, which allowed forward exchange transaction only for trade (or real) finance. This reform gave firms the opportunity to get away from some of the restrictions imposed in the domestic market. Larger firms started to issue bonds in the international financial markets, where the issuance rules were much more relaxed.

In sum, the process of financial reform increased the competition not only between banks in the same banking category but also between various banking categories. The traditional segmentation of the activities of financial institutions became increasingly blurred, as banks and securities companies started to operate more and more on each other's business territories. Furthermore, the city and major regional banks diverted their operations towards smaller- and medium-sized companies, forcing the smaller banks and credit cooperatives to look for new business opportunities. Also the traditional segmentation between short- and long-term lending by respectively commercial banks and long-term financial institutions was in practice not followed anymore. All in all, the Japanese financial system started to move slowly but steadily towards a universal banking system.

The process of financial reform also turned out to be one of the major causes of the creation of the bubble and subsequently the banking crisis (see the third section). It undermined the convoy system, as it eliminated regulatory rewards that the Ministry of Finance used to give to banks as incentives to rescue troubled banks. The process of financial reform, in parallel with the evolving banking crisis, resulted also in a major change in the structure of the banking sector. The situation of this sector at the turn of the century will be discussed in the next section.

The Present Japanese Financial System: Importance of Indirect Finance, Increased Concentration, and Universal Banking

To conclude the overview of the Japanese financial system and banking sector, this section presents a statistical overview of their main characteristics at the start of the 21st century. In sum, these are the importance of indirect finance, particularly through banks, the increased concentration of financial institutions, and the trend towards a universal banking system.

As was previously discussed in the previous section, the Japanese corporate sector depended heavily on bank lending as source of finance. Table 12.2, which compares bank borrowing patterns of firms in Japan and the United States and Japan by firm size in 1990, 1995, and 2000, shows the importance of bank debt as of total assets of Japanese manufacturing firms compared with those in the United States. The figures show that indeed these Japanese firms have been much more reliant on bank financing than their U.S. counterparts. While the average ratio of bank debt to total assets for all manufacturing firms in the United States was about 10 percent during the 1990s, the similar average ratio for all Japanese manufacturing firms was between 21–24 percent during the same period. The table also shows the impact of the process of

Table 12.2
Bank Debt as a Percentage of Total Assets of Manufacturing Firms

Year	All firms		Small firms		Large firms	
	US	Japan	US	Japan	US	Japan
1990	0.103	0.237	0.201	0.361	0.098	0.152
1995	0.086	0.260	0.193	0.403	0.081	0.161
2000	0.096	0.216	0.208	0.334	0.092	0.140

Sources: The U.S. data are from the Bureau of Census, *Quarterly Financial Report for Manufacturing, Mining and Trade Corporation (QFR)*. The Japanese data are from Ministry of Finance, *Hojin Kigyo Tokei*.

Note: U.S. large firms are defined as firms with total assets of more than USD 10 million, whereas Japanese large firms are defined as firms with a book value of more than yen 1 billion.

financial reform and the banking crisis, as in percentage terms the reliance of Japanese manufacturing firms—both small and large firms—on bank debt decreased from 1990 to 2000. However, it is clear that Japanese firms are still not using the capital markets, through the issuance of equity and debt securities, for financing purposes to the same extent are similar American firms.

The lesser dependence on securities in Japan compared with the United States can also be found in the composition of the assets of households. As is shown in table 12.3, which presents an overview of the allocation of household financial assets as of March 2001 for Japan, Germany, and the United States, the financial assets of Japanese households consisted for more than 54 percent of deposits and cash, whereas holdings of bonds, shares, and equities remained rather limited at almost 11 percent. Even in a country with a universal banking system like Germany, households held only 34.5 percent of their financial assets in cash and deposits, and almost 23 percent in bonds, shares, and equities. The exception here is the United States, where only 11.9 percent of household financial assets were held in the form of cash and bank deposits, whereas 42.5 percent of their financial assets consisted of bonds, shares, and equities. The importance of bank deposits in Japanese households' financial assets becomes even clearer if one takes into account that cash holdings con-

Table 12.3
Financial Assets Held by Households: An International Comparison

Assets	Japan	Germany	US
Cash and deposits	54.3	34.5	11.9
Bonds	3.7	9.8	8.4
Investment trusts	2.3	11.9	12.9
Shares and equities	7.2	13.0	34.1
Insurance and pension reserves	28.7	30.8	29.9
Other	3.9	0.0	2.8
Financial assets (in trillion Yen, Euro, and USD)	1,420	3.6	32.1
Financial assets as a percentage of the GDP	282.1	176.4	318.4

Sources: The data for the United States and Japan are from Bank of Japan, *Flow of Funds.* The data for Germany are from Deutsche Bundesbank, *Monthly Report.*
Note: For December 2001; figures are percentage of total assets, except as otherwise indicated.

stitute only a very limited part of these assets. For example, as of end-March 2002, 54.5 percent of the financial assets of Japanese households were held in cash and deposits, of which only 2.7 percent were in cash. Thus, as of end-March 2002, more than a half of household financial assets in Japan were held in deposits.

The second characteristic of the present Japanese financial system and banking sector is the increased concentration, which has resulted in a significant reduction in the number of financial institutions during the last 10 years. This was mainly the result of the consolidation process among financial institutions and the relatively large number of bank failures resulting from the banking crisis. The consolidation in the banking sector was in response to both the increased competition resulting from the process of financial reform, as well as to the mounting bad loan problems. Often, it crossed the traditional lines of business, namely involving short- and long-term banking, trust banking, securities business and life and non–life insurance activities. In fact, this consolidation process was made possible by the financial reform program that eliminated the traditional functional segmentation between various financial institutions.

Table 12.4 shows that the increased concentration affected in particular the city and second tier regional banks among the major banks, and smaller financial institutions such as *shinkin* banks, and credit, agriculture, and forestry cooperatives. For example, the number of city banks decreased from twelve in 1991 to seven in March 2002, which was mainly the result of mergers, as only one city bank actually failed during this period (the Hokkaido Takushoku Bank in 1997). The most significant merger was the one between the Fuji Bank, the Industrial Bank of Japan, and the Dai-Ichi Kangyo Bank in September 2000, to form a mega bank group called Mizuho Financial Group. Three other mega mergers involving its main competitors in April 2001 followed this. The Bank of Tokyo-Mitsubishi, the Mitsubishi Trust, and the Nippon Trust merged to form the Mitsubishi-Tokyo Financial Group. The second merger was between the Sakura Bank and the Sumitomo Bank, which established the Sumitomo Mitsui Banking Corporation (SMBC). The third merger involved the Sanwa Bank, the Tokai Bank, and the Toyo Trust to set up the United Financial of Japan (UFJ) group. The most recent consolidation was in December 2001 when the Daiwa Bank, the Kinki Osaka Bank, and the Nara Bank merged. In March 2002, the Asahi Bank joined them to form another financial group that was tentatively named Resona in October 2002. Table 12.5 shows that, as of end-March 2002, the Mizuho Financial Group was the largest banking conglomerate in Japan with total assets of about Yen 151.3 trillion (30.2 percent of GDP), deposits of Yen 74.1 trillion (14.8 percent of GDP), and loans of Yen 84.6 trillion (16.9 percent of GDP). At that time, the Mizuho Financial Group was also the largest banking group in the world. The second largest group was the Sumitomo Mitsui Financial Group with total assets amounting to Yen 108 trillion (21.6 percent of GDP).

Table 12.4
Number of Financial Institutions in Japan

	1991	1995	1999	2002	Change since 1991
City banks	12	11	9	7	-5
Long-term credit banks	3	3	3[1]	3[1]	0
Trust banks	7	7	7	8	1
Regional banks	64	64	64	64	0
Second tier regional banks	68	65	60	53	-15
All major banks	154	150	143	135	-19
Shinkin banks	451	416	392	349	-102
Credit cooperatives	407	368	298	247	-160
Agriculture and forestry cooperatives	3,634	2,461	1,606	1,303	-2,331
Insurance companies	50	55	80	77	27
Securities companies	272	285	288	290	18

Sources: Group of Ten (2001); Bank of Japan, *Economic Statistics Annual;* Federation of Bankers Associations of Japan, *Analysis of Financial Statements of All Banks.* The data for *shinkin* banks, credit cooperatives, agriculture and forestry cooperatives, insurance companies, and securities companies are obtained from the respective association's Web site.
Note: The data are as of the end of the year except for 2002, which is as of March (i.e., the end of fiscal year 2001).
[1]Long-term credit banks include for 1999 and 2002 Shinsei Bank and Aozora Bank, which are the successor banks of the two long-term credit banks that failed in 1999.

Finally, the process of financial concentration in general and the mega mergers described above in particular have led de facto to the emergence of a universal banking system in Japan, where financial conglomerates operate in various financial activities, including traditional banking, securities business, asset management, and insurance. As of October 2002, there are five banking conglomerates in Japan, which have the character of universal banks, including six commercial banks (see also table 12.5).[2] The combined total assets, loans, and deposits of these mega banks in terms of GDP are truly impressive. Their total assets account for almost 97 percent of GDP; their deposits and loans combined are almost 57 percent and 55 percent of GDP, respectively. It is important to note that these figures were estimated by summing up the figures of the individual banks before the mergers. Whether they will shrink after the process of consolidation and restructuring is finished, however, remains to be seen. The importance of the five banking giants in Japan is even more striking when one makes a comparison with the United States: these five banks combined are much larger than all commercial banks taken together in the United States. It also suggests that if one of these bank-

Table 12.5
Universal Banking: Financial Groups in 2002

Group name	Date of establishment	Major financial institutions in the group	Assets	Deposits	Loans
Mizuho Financial Group	September 29, 2000	Mizuho Bank, Mizuho Corporate Bank, Mizuho Securities, Mizuho Trust & Banking	151.3 (30.2%)	74.1 (14.8%)	84.6 (16.9%)
Sumitomo Mitsui Financial Group[1]	December 2, 2002	Sumitomo Mitsui Bank	108.0 (21.6%)	65.0 (13.0%)	63.6 (12.7%)
Mitsubishi Tokyo Financial Group	April 2, 2001	The Bank of Tokyo – Mitsubishi, Mitsubishi Trust and Banking Corporation	99.5 (19.9%)	59.9 (12.0%)	49.1 (9.8%)
UFJ Group	April 2, 2001	UFJ Bank, UFJ Trust Bank, UFJ Tsubasa Securities	79.8 (15.9%)	50.8 (10.1%)	46.0 (9.2%)
Resona Group[2]	December 12, 2001	Daiwa Bank, Kinki Osaka Bank, Nara Bank, Asahi Bank, Resona Trust & Banking	45.0 (9.0%)	33.8 (6.8%)	30.0 (6.0%)

Source: Each group's financial statements for the fiscal year 2001.

Note: Ranked by total assets; as of March 2002; unit = yen trillion. Assets and deposits are based on consolidated accounts as of March 2002 for each holding company. The data for the Sumitomo Mitsui Financial Group are those of Sumitomo Mitsui Bank's consolidated accounts, because this group does not have a holding company yet. Figures in parentheses are percentages of the GDP.

[1]This establishment is scheduled on December 2, 2002.

[2]The current name of this financial holding company was renamed from Daiwa Bank Holdings, Inc. on October 1, 2002.

ing groups would fail, the repercussions and implications for the Japanese financial system and economy would be enormous, most likely to a much greater extent than in other countries. Thus, as the big banks in Japan have become even bigger, too big to fail concerns may have become even more important. This aspect will be investigated in more detail in the next sections.

THE JAPANESE BANKING CRISIS AND THE POLICY REACTION

The Causes of the Banking Crisis

Japan experienced a strong surge in asset prices during the eighties, in particular in the second half. This situation of excessive asset price inflation gave rise to the terminology of the bubble economy. To a large extent, this development was caused by the process of financial reform, which was described in the previous section (Ministry of Finance 1993; Nakajima and Taguchi 1995; Okina et al. 2000). This process increased the competition not only between the banks in the same banking category but also between banks and other private financial institutions. The increased competition put heavy pressure on the banks' profit margins. As a result, banks started to look for more profitable, less traditional, but riskier projects: they expanded their lending to real estate and construction companies and non-bank financial institutions such as consumer credit institutions and leasing companies. Furthermore, Japanese banks extended considerable amounts of credit to the corporate sector for investment in stocks and other financial assets. In the end, Japan experienced a rather classic credit-induced real estate boom and financial assets' bubble, fuelled by a vicious spiral of rising asset prices, higher collateral value, and increasing bank credit. However, as inflationary pressures started to mount, the Bank of Japan changed its policy stance, and started to tighten its policy in May 1989. This change would mark the start of the collapse of the bubble.

Unfortunately, the burst of the bubble in the early 1990s caused severe problems to banks (Takeda and Turner 1992; Hamada 1995). First, a significant number of real estate companies and other non-banks found it increasingly difficult to service loans. Furthermore, the decline of asset prices diminished the value of the collateral of extended loans, in many cases below those of the loans they secured. Consequently, banks became saddled with nonperforming loans. Second, the collapse of the bubble and the subsequent deflation of asset prices caused problems for Japanese banks in meeting the Bank for International Settlements (BIS) solvency requirements, as the unrealized profits on their securities holdings, 45 percent of which could be counted as Tier II capital, eroded. All in all, the situation in the banking sector deteriorated, and slowly but steadily the problems of Japanese banks started to take the dimension of a real banking crisis. This will be described in the next section.

The Banking Crisis

The development of the banking crisis can be shown on the basis of three indicators: the increasing amount of bad loans, the "Japan premium," and the number of failed institutions. Table 12.6 provides the amount of nonperforming loans (NPLs) of Japanese depository institutions according to two definitions: first, projections by the supervisory authorities—from 1998 based on the so-called self-assessment results of banks—and second, "risk management loans," which are published by individual banks on their financial statements.

The amount of bad loans using the self-assessment definition increased from Yen 7–8 trillion (1.5–1.7 percent of GDP) at end-March 1992 to Yen

Table 12.6
Bad Loans of All Deposit-taking Financial Institutions in Japan

	Amount of bad loans (self-assessment)	Amount of bad loans (risk management loans)
End March 1992	7 ~ 8 (1.5% ~ 1.7%)	——
End March 1993	8.4 (1.7%)	12.8 (2.6%)
End March 1994	10.5 (2.2%)	13.6 (2.8%)
End March 1995	11.6 (2.4%)	12.5 (2.5%)
End March 1996	34.8 (6.9%)	28.5 (5.7%)
End March 1997	27.9 (5.4%)	21.8 (4.2%)
End March 1998	87.1 (16.7%)	38.0 (7.3%)
End March 1999	80.6 (15.7%)	38.7 (7.5%)
End March 2000	81.7 (15.9%)	41.4 (8.0%)
End March 2001	82.7 (16.1%)	43.4 (8.5%)
End March 2002	87.5 (17.5%)	53.0 (10.6%)

Sources: Ministry of Finance; Financial Supervisory Agency/Financial Services Agency; Hall (1998).
Note: Amounts in yen trillion; Figures in parentheses are as a percentage of GDP.

87.1 trillion (16.75 percent of GDP) at end-March 1998, which was around 11 percent of total private lending. The big jump in the figures for 1998 is to a large extent caused by the shift to the definition of bad loans based on self-assessment results. The amount of bad loans then dropped to Yen 80.6 trillion (15.7 percent of GDP) in the next year—basically due to bankruptcies of some large banks—but rose steadily to a record of Yen 87.5 trillion (17.5 percent of GDP) as of end-March 2002. In terms of risk management loans, the maximum amount of bad loans was Yen 53.0 trillion (10.6 percent of GDP), also at end-March 2002. It is worth noting that the nonperforming loans figures estimated by independent international organizations and private sector institutions were higher than the figures based on both definitions. For example, the estimation of the IMF on the amount of nonperforming loans in the Japanese financial industry in 1998 was almost Yen 60 trillion higher (12 percent of GDP) than the official government figures.

An alternative way to investigate the development of the Japanese banking crisis is by analyzing the trend in the so-called Japan premium. This premium is the difference between the interest rates quoted by major Japanese banks for their interbank Eurodollar and Euroyen borrowing and those quoted by large American and European banks (in figure 12.1 it is the difference between the interest rate quoted by the Bank of Tokyo-Mitsubishi and the interest rate quoted by the Barclays Bank in the three-month Eurodollar market concentrated in London) (Peek and Rosengren 1998, p. 1; Saito and Shiratsuka 2000, p. 3).

As shown in figure 12.1, the Japan premium peaked during the last months of 1997, when a number of large Japanese financial institutions collapsed. Subsequently, it came down but increased again sharply towards the end of 1998 when two long-term credit banks failed. Thus, the emergence and increase of the Japan premium were a clear indication of the severe nature and magnitude of the Japanese banking crisis, and showed the damaged confidence of the international financial community in the Japanese banking sector. A closer look at the movement of this premium over the past few years reveals two things. First, it is interesting to see that the Japan premium has been close to zero since the beginning of 1999, which is a clear indication that the fi-

Figure 12.1
The Japan Premium. The Japan premium is the interest rate quoted by the Bank of Tokyo-Misubishi less the interest rate quoted by the Barclays Bank in the three-month Eurodollar market (London).

Percentage Points

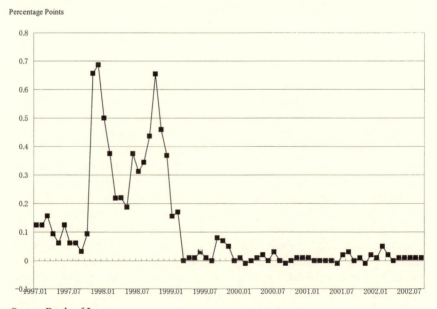

Source: Bank of Japan.

nancial markets believed that Japanese financial institutions would be bailed out in times of financial trouble. Thus, there has been a strong belief in the markets that at least some elements of too big to fail have been in place in Japan during this period. Second, the premium came back from time to time, reflecting continued bad economic news and uncertainty concerning a possible public bailout of Japanese problem banks (Spiegel 2001, p. 3); however, it always stayed below 0.1 percent.

Finally, the yearly number of failed depository institutions since 1990 can show the development of the banking crisis in Japan. This is shown in table 12.7 (see Hanazaki and Horiuchi 2002).

The seriousness of the banking crisis is reflected in a total number of 176 depository institutions that collapsed over a period of 12 years. The figures indicate that the failures of banks—the most important group of financial institutions in the table—were concentrated in the period 1997–1999, when eight of them went bankrupt. Thus, during these years, it seems that too big to fail concerns in prudential policy were at least temporarily lifted, allowing some of the largest financial institutions to fail. It is also clear that since 1999 mostly small depository institutions went bankrupt, suggesting that either the

Table 12.7
Number of Failed Depository Institutions

	Banks[1]	*Shinkin* banks	Credit cooperatives	Total
1990	0	0	0	0
1991	1	0	0	1
1992	0	1	0	1
1993	0	1	1	2
1994	1	0	4	5
1995	1	0	5	6
1996	2	3	3	8
1997	5	0	7	12
1998	3	1	31	35
1999	5	6	15	26
2000	1	5	27	33
2001[2]	1	9	37	47
Total	20	26	130	176

Source: Hanazaki and Horiuchi (2002), p. 23.

Note: This table contains not only the cases of bank failure dealt with by the government but also those privately disposed of. For example, in October 1994, Mitsubishi Bank rescued Nippon Trust Bank at the brink of bankruptcy; the government did not provide any financial support in this case. This case is included in this table.

[1]This column includes city banks, regional banks, second tier regional banks, trust banks, and long-term credit banks.

[2]Until November 2001.

problems among the banks—the largest institutions—had become less severe or that the government re-adopted certain elements of too big to fail in its policy response. This aspect of the banking crisis will be discussed in the next section.

The Policy Response

The collapse of the bubble and the resulting problems in the Japanese banking industry prompted the Japanese supervisory authorities to take action, which, however, was often "too little, too late." Their response can be typified as a combination of regulatory forbearance and financial reform, often hoping that the problems would disappear by themselves (see, for example: Hoshi and Kashyap 1999; Kanaya and Woo 2000; Van Rixtel 2002). The policy response also included sequences of the use of too big to fail elements and then followed by abandoning these elements, at least temporarily.

The policy response to the banking crisis can be separated in seven phases. During the first phase, which started after the collapse of the bubble economy until the enactment of the financial reform laws in June 1996, the monetary authorities often denied that there were significant problems in the banking sector and maintained a general policy of nondisclosure, but implemented some measures to solve the bad loan situation and related collateral problems, while maintaining a general policy of too big to fail. In addition, some smaller financial institutions were allowed to go bankrupt, such as credit cooperatives and second tier regional banks.

The second phase that ended around the end of 1996 was characterized by the implementation of reform legislation, which aimed in particular at the bail-out of the collapsed housing loan companies (*jūsen* resolution package) and strengthening of the Deposit Insurance Corporation (*Yokin Hoken Kikō*), and the related establishment of public institutions such as the Resolution and Collection Bank (*Seiri Kaishū Ginkō*). The *Diet* passed legislation, which aimed at improving the transparency of bank supervision through the introduction of so-called prompt corrective actions (PCA), following similar initiatives by the U.S. supervisory authorities in the early nineties. All in all, the policy of too big to fail was basically kept unchanged.

The third phase started after the administrative reform proposals adopted by the Hashimoto Administration in December 1996 that formed the start of the process to break up the Ministry of Finance. The magnitude of banking crisis was revealed to the general public and international financial community in "Black" November 1997, when two banks and two securities houses collapsed. It was clearly the most important erosion of the convoy system such as maintained in the post-war Japanese financial system. That is, it became clear that the era of unrestricted too big to fail had ended. However, this did not imply an immediate and definite end to the convoy system as well. Finance Minister Mitsuzuka publicly stated that the government did not intend to consider the implementation of a new framework for using public funds to restore the stability of the financial system. In other words, it was clear that the government was not ready for massive injections of public money yet.

During the fourth phase—from January until June 1998—initially developments in the Japanese financial system were dominated by major scandals. In March, public funds were injected in the banking sector and later on major financial reforms such as the "Big Bang" financial reform package were implemented. The injections of public money in March were the first in this kind and aimed only at the major bank categories such as commercial banks, long-term credit banks, and trust banks. Thus, this clearly involved elements of too big to fail, as the measures were basically aimed at avoiding collapses among the biggest banks. Funds in total of Yen 30 trillion (6 percent GDP) were to be distributed through the Deposit Insurance Corporation.

The fifth phase (June–October 1998) was characterized by the establishment of a new supervisory authority, the Financial Supervisory Agency (*Kinyū Kantoku Chō*) (FSA). However, this phase also showed embarrassing signs of political impotence to adopt adequate measures, which resulted in a near collapse of national and international confidence in the Japanese banking sector. Clearly, to many observers, too big to fail seemed to be as important as ever. In the meanwhile, it became clear that the Long-Term Credit Bank of Japan (LTCB), the second largest long-term credit bank, needed substantial financial assistance. Merger talks with the Sumitomo Trust & Banking, one of the largest trust banks, were started, with full support from the government. Finance Minister Kiichi Miyazawa declared that public funds should be used; however, the opposition opposed a government plan involving substantial capital injections into the LTCB in August.

In the next phase (October 1998–June 2000), important legislation aimed at solving the banking problems was implemented, including the establishment of the Financial Reconstruction Commission (*Kinyū Saisei Iinkai*) (FRC), and at least some degree of stabilization and control of the crisis was achieved. The new legislation made it possible to use the method of temporary nationalization, which was used for the first time in October in the case of the failed LTCB (see the next section for a detailed discussion). It was followed by the insolvency and subsequent temporary nationalization of the Nippon Credit Bank (NCB), another long-term credit bank, in December. However, both banks continued their business under different names and the same bank charter. Thus, paradoxically both elements of too big to fail (i.e., de facto the two banks were kept alive under new names) and an end to too big to fail (i.e., the banks did actually fail) were adopted. All in all, it seemed a clear case of "too-big-to-liquidate," or the interpretation of too big to fail followed in practice by the U.S. supervisory authorities (see first section; Kaufman and Seelig 2000, p. 1). A general sense of careful optimism started to emerge in the first months of 1999, which was strengthened by the injection of around Yen 7.5 trillion in 15 of the largest banks in March, which seemed a clear case of too big to fail. The positive developments in the Japanese financial system were reflected in a decrease of the Japan premium (see figure 12.1). After having stabilized the situation at the largest banks, the supervisory authorities turned to the regional and second tier regional banks and other smaller financial institutions, followed by the insurance industry.

Finally, in the seventh and final phase (July 2000–), further consolidation of bank supervision was achieved. At the same time, it seemed that a flexible policy of too big to fail was followed regarding the banking sector, whereas other financial institutions such as certain insurance companies were allowed to go bankrupt. However, this phase saw a gradual deterioration of the renewed optimism that had characterized the start of 1999. Evidence mounted again that the real amounts of bad loans in the banking sector were substantially larger than the official figures showed and that they were still not fully recognized and provisioned, that the government was increasingly reluctant to pursue further financial reform and that the problems in the banking and insurance industries could exacerbate each other in the years to come. Furthermore, as stock prices continued to decline and the outlook for the Japanese economy deteriorated further at the beginning of 2001, the Japan premium slightly increased with about five basis-points in the course of January (see figure 12.1), which received considerable attention in the Japanese media in particular, despite being considerably lower than in both 1997 and 1998 when major banks failed. All in all, a number of developments underlined a renewed sense of concern about the situation in the Japanese financial system and banking sector, which continued to dominate the economic headlines about Japan in the course of 2002 as well.

From this summarized overview of the policy response to the banking crisis it is clear that the Japanese supervisory authorities followed a rather flexible and pragmatic interpretation of too big to fail, which we will typify as supervisory ad hoc pragmatism. This will be discussed in depth in the next section.

TOO BIG TO FAIL IN JAPAN: SUPERVISORY AD-HOC PRAGMATISM

The Banking Crisis and Too Big to Fail

We believe that the policy of too big to fail in Japan can most aptly be described as supervisory ad-hoc pragmatism. By this we mean that the policy response to the banking crisis included sequences of the use of too big to fail elements, followed by a temporary halt to this policy, and then a re-introduction of too big to fail elements. It seemed that the Japanese supervisory authorities were sometimes convinced that in order to restore confidence in the Japanese banking system, some large banks had to fail. It is also clear that the injection of public funds in the major banks, which can be interpreted as too big to fail—a better description most likely would be "too big to liquidate"—was often delayed because policymakers in general and politicians in particular were concerned about an electoral backlash, as this financial support was (and is) not very popular among the Japanese people. On the other hand, it can equally be argued that indeed, at other times, public support was given, because of international pressure, fear for the economic consequences of bank failures, political considerations, or the existence of close links between certain banks and policymakers. This ad hoc pragmatic element, that is, the switching back and forward in the use of too big to fail elements in the policy response to the banking crisis, which was also due to a lack in expertise on the side of policymakers and in transparency and public disclosure, is in our view a notable characteristic of too big to fail in Japanese supervisory policies over the past decade (see also Nakaso 2001).

The evolution of too big to fail in Japan or supervisory ad-hoc pragmatism can be summarized as follows. Until 1995, a policy of "no bank failures" was pursued under the convoy system, under which the MoF intervened by merging a troubled bank with a larger or healthier one. This policy was publicly ended when Hyogo Bank was allowed to collapse in August 1995. It was the first collapse of a Japanese bank in post-war Japan, which, however, was not interpreted as a definite end to too big to fail, as at the same time some much larger problem banks were allowed to continue their business, mainly by disguising and understating the size of their actual problems (lack of transparency and disclosure). A new framework to resolve bank failures, established under legislation that passed parliament in June 1996, was adopted for the first time with the failure of the Hanwa Bank in November. Contrary to the past, the MoF did not attempt to arrange a "rescue merger" with a healthier organization but simply ordered Hanwa to close. However, this bank was not one of the largest commercial banks, thus its closure should not be interpreted as a clear end of too big to fail as well. But it is clear that since the failure of the Hanwa Bank, the government appeared to have allowed some banks to fail as far as their collapse would not affect overall financial stability (Choy 1999).

When the banking crisis reached its peak at the end of 1997, as can be seen from the development of the Japan premium in figure 12.1, and the situation became almost uncontrollable, the Japanese government terminated its traditional policy of too big to fail and used a "hard-landing" or "let fail" approach, in order to restore confidence and trust in the Japanese banking sector. As a result, several "big" financial institutions such as the Hokkaido Takushoku Bank and Yamaichi Securities were allowed to go bankrupt in November 1997. The Hokkaido Takushoku Bank, which despite restructuring attempts earlier in the year, announced its failure on November 17, the first city bank to shut its doors since the end of the Second World War. This announcement was widely interpreted as the end of the unrestricted too big to fail policy of the Japanese supervisory authorities, which in previous years had allowed only the smaller financial institutions to close down.

After the series of failures of financial institutions at the end of 1997, the pubic opinion quickly turned against Prime Minister Hashimoto.[3] People started complaining that the series of financial failures and the subsequent turmoil in the financial system were more than what they were willing to bear, and demanded that the government had to take action. To reverse the let fail policy, which the Hashimoto Administration had initiated with the collapse of the major financial institutions in November 1997, and to go back to the old too big to fail policy would have been political suicide. The Administration tried to soften the adverse economic effects emanating from even more bank failures by widening the financial safety net. In February 1998, it introduced another package of emergency measures for stabilizing the financial system that included substantial injections of public money into the major banks for the first time in the history. Obviously, Japan still was within the general framework of the convoy system that did not allow for a failure of major financial institutions. The measures clearly included the elements of too big to fail as it appears that the aim of the measures was basically to avoid collapses of the biggest banks. The amount of Yen 30 trillion (6 percent of GDP) was distributed through the Deposit Insurance Corporation (DIC).

The public fund was to be used for the following purposes. First, Yen 13 trillion was for the establishment of an "Account for Financial Crisis Management," which aimed to strengthen the capital base of viable banks and broadening of the financial basis of the DIC. Second, Yen 17 trillion was for the establishment of one unified "Special Account," which would have to ensure the full protection of deposits and could be used to finance the consolidation of the banking industry. By March 1998, however, only Yen 1.8 trillion of the Yen 13 trillion had been distributed to 18 major and 3 regional banks, mainly because of the strict restructuring conditions attached and the stigma of taking public support. It was clear that the major banks preferred to abstain from public capital injections out of fear of losing their independence and having to accept some form of government control. All in all, it can be concluded that this recapitalization attempt failed. In the middle of 1998, the situation at the LTCB deteriorated. It was placed on credit watch by some credit rating agencies and its share price started to plummet. The ruling Liberal Democratic Party (LDP) came up with additional schemes (the so-called Total Plan) to resolve the banking crisis, which consisted of building "bridge banks" that would assume the credit lines of failed banks while the banks were being reorganized. This plan, however, never materialized.

Since the government could not solve the banking and economic problems, the LDP lost badly against the Democratic Party in the Upper House election that took place in July 1998. Hashimoto had to resign. He was succeeded by Keizo Obuchi.[4] The new government had to come up with more decisive measures to end the banking crisis, since the opposition (i.e., the Democratic Party) offered a nationalization plan to counter the LDP's bridge bank plan.

In the meantime, the crisis in the banking sector worsened when in September, Japan Leasing, the largest of three leasing companies affiliated with

LTCB, applied for court protection. National and international confidence in Japan's financial system dropped significantly, as reflected in the rise of the Japan premium to almost 70 basis points (see figure 12.1).

In October, the government and opposition party finally reached an agreement on the injection of substantial amounts of public money in the banking industry and the establishments of several new institutions to solve the banking problems. Among them, the Financial Reconstruction Commission (*Kinyū Saisei Iinkai*) (FRC) was the single most important (Milhaupt 1999; Kanaya and Woo 2000; Nakaso 2001; Van Rixtel 2002). This FRC was established on October 12, 1998, when the Financial Reconstruction Law was passed. This law sets the framework on how to deal with failed or insolvent financial institutions. This law also contained some elements of the bridge bank scheme.

Furthermore, on October 16, the Financial Function Early Strengthening Law was enacted, which developed measures to rescue weak but in principle healthy financial institutions. This law provides a framework for the recapitalization of weak banks through stock purchasing by the government using funds provided by the DIC. To facilitate this measure, a new "Financial Function Early Strengthening Account" with Yen 25 trillion (5 percent of GDP) was established at the DIC. To finance successor banks, public bridge banks and nationalized banks, the *Diet* approved the establishment of a "Financial Revitalization Account" with Yen 18 trillion (3.6 percent of GDP) at the DIC. In combination with the Yen 17 trillion "Special Account" established in February 1998, the DIC had at the moment a total amount of Yen 60 trillion (12 percent of GDP) of public money in its accounts to solve the bad loan problems.

In fact, the enactment of the Financial Reconstruction Law was immediately followed by the LTCB's application to be nationalized in October 1998. In December 1998, another long-term credit bank, the Nippon Credit Bank (NCB), was also nationalized. The NCB failed even though it was given substantial bailout packages including management dispatching from the Bank of Japan and capital injections of Yen 290 billion (in July 1997). The DIC became a shareholder of these two failed banks and was involved in the management and resolution of these banks. These two banks were eventually sold to new investors. A group of investors led by the American investment fund Ripplewood purchased the LTCB in March 2000, and a consortium of Softbank, Orix, and Tokio Marine and Fire Insurance bought the NCB in September 2000. One could argue that the nationalization of the LTCB and NCB included elements of both the re-enactment of "too big to liquidate" (i.e., capital injections and practical continuation of the banks under different names but the same bank charter) and an end to too big to fail (i.e., the banks were allowed to go bankrupt and actually failed). The emphasis was on the former element, however. Practically, it is clear that the public takeover of these banks with continuation of most of their business was an example of "too big to liquidate."

Regarding other financial institutions than banks, in particular the insurance sector, several large life insurance companies—although not among the top five—went bankrupt in the course of 2000. It appeared that the government ended too big to fail in the insurance sector, although one may possibly argue that these failures involved less important insurance companies and that the government could reinstate the too big to fail policy once a "big" insurance firm would threaten to collapse.

In conclusion, the Japanese government adopted a rather flexible approach to too big to fail, a policy stance that we have defined as "supervisory ad hoc pragmatism." When it deemed necessary to restore confidence, the government sent clear signals to financial markets by allowing specific "big" financial institutions to fail, thus ending its policy of unrestricted too big to fail and basically adopting a "let fail" policy. At other times, however, it provided public support, often because of political considerations or instigated by demands from specific interest groups, in the form of purchasing preferred stocks and subordinated bonds from specific problem financial institutions, thus de facto re-instating elements of too big to fail. As examples the capital injections in the biggest banks in 1998 and 1999 could be mentioned. The total amount of public funds injected for the banks belonging to the five financial groups in Japan are shown in table 12.8.

Further to too big to fail in Japan, there have been also clear cases of "too big to liquidate," as the nationalization of the Long-Term Credit Bank of Japan and Nippon Credit Bank demonstrated. In any case, the absolute guarantee of the Japanese government, in place since the end of World War II, that no bank would be allowed to go bankrupt is at present clearly no longer valid in Japan, after the collapse of some of the largest financial institutions in the second half of the nineties. In this respect, the strong version of too big to fail, that is the unrestricted guarantee that large banks and other financial institutions cannot fail, does no longer exist in Japan. One could argue that a more softer and flexible approach of too big to fail exists as of today in Japan, at least some elements of it, given the ongoing discussions of public bailouts of banks and the continuing sense of crisis that overshadows the Japanese banking industry. It can only be regretted that because of this pragmatic and ad hoc too big to fail approach, the government stopped implementing serious measures to solve the underlying causes of the banking crisis. For example, the government should have improved the quality of public disclosure of the major banks, particularly concerning the quality of bank assets and the amount of bad loans, which could have minimized the future contagion effects of a bank failure through lower costs resulting from information asymmetries. That is, unless market participants can trust the quality of bank disclosure and distinguish between "good" and "bad" banks, once a bank fails, no bank will be trusted to be of good quality: a typical adverse selection problem. This could spread contagion fears and undermine financial stability. Thus, one may argue that the Japanese version of too big to fail,

Table 12.8
Amount of Public Funds Received by the Five Major Financial Groups

Group name	Banks that received funds	Total equity of the group	Total amount of public funds received by each group	
			Preferred stocks	Subordinated bonds
Mizuho Financial Group	Dai-Ichi Kangyo Bank, Fuji Bank, Industrial Bank of Japan	4.73	1.95 (41.2%)	0.85 (18.0%)
Sumitomo Mitsui Financial Group	Sakura Bank, Sumitomo Bank	2.91	1.30 (44.7%)	0.20 (6.9%)
Mitsubishi Tokyo Financial Group	Bank of Tokyo Mitsubishi, Mitsubishi Trust and Banking Corporation	3.32	0.00 (0.0%)	0.00 (0.0%)
UFJ Group	Sanwa Bank, Tokai Bank, Toyo Trust and Banking Corporation	2.60	1.40 (53.9%)	0.35 (13.5%)
Resona Group	Daiwa Bank, Asahi Bank, Kinki-Osaka Bank	1.29	0.87 (67.3%)	0.30 (23.3%)

Sources: Own calculations based on the data obtained from the Deposit Insurance Corporation of Japan, *Annual Report*, 2001.

Note: Unit = yen trillion. Figures in the parentheses represent the percentage of the respective public funds of each group's total equity. Public funds were injected into the banks under provisions in the Financial Function Stabilization Law and Financial Function Early Strengthening Law in 1998, 1999, and 2001. Total equity is based on consolidated accounts of each holding company as of March 2002. The data of the Sumitomo Mitsui Financial Group, however, is from the Sumitomo Mitsui Bank's consolidated accounts, as this group does not yet have a holding company. The current portion of the public funds held by the Mitsubishi Tokyo Financial Group is zero because it repurchased all stocks bought by the government and paid back the bonds on 28 February 2000, 22 December 2000, 22 December 2001, and 24 January 2001.

which we have interpreted as supervisory ad hoc pragmatism, and its ongoing continuation in the new century, have undermined the stability of the Japanese financial system and banking sector.

The Costs of Ending Too Big to Fail: A Case Study

To have a balanced approach, we present in this section what actually happens if supervisory authorities do end a policy of too big to fail. The bankruptcy of the Hokkaido Takushoku Bank (HTB) provides the natural research laboratory for investigating the impact of a bank failure on its corporate clients. It is the first and only failure of a city bank since the end of World War II. Among some other reasons, it is widely thought that the lessons from the bankruptcy of HTB made the government reaffirm the importance of too big to fail in the late 1990s and convinced it to maintain the policy of supervisory ad hoc pragmatism. Also, the collapse of HTB is a more relevant case study than the failures of the two long-term credit banks (LTCB and NCB), as HTB's clients included all sizes of firms, while the LTCB and NCB specialized on providing long-term finance to large firms.

The Hokkaido Takushoku Bank tried to outgrow its competitors by focusing on loans to ventures in the Hokkaido area. In the 1980s, synchronizing itself with the lending spree to real estate sectors spread all over Japan, the bank extended its credit actively to local real estate firms. After the collapse of land and share prices in Japan, HTB was left with a large amount of nonperforming loans. As of end-March 1997, its ratio of nonperforming assets to total loans was around 13.4 percent, the worst among the major city banks. In fact, this ratio was substantially larger than those of the other two major bank failures, LTCB and NCB, with ratios of 6.1 percent and 13.9 percent, respectively.

On November 17, 1997, the bank declared insolvency. In the aftermath of the bankruptcy, many borrowers of HTB rushed to find new lenders. The Hokuyo Bank, the second largest regional bank in the (same) Hokkaido area, agreed with the Ministry of Finance to take over only high quality clients of HTB that were classified as Category I grade. However, following an outcry of the local community to request a more "generous" succession of loans, the Hokuyo Bank was encouraged by the government to succeed loans to lower quality companies that were classified as Category II grade.

According to the *Nikkei Kinyuu Shimbun*, which published the results of a survey conducted by Tokyo Shoko Research in 1998, interviewing former client firms of HTB that survived after the bank's failure, 84.5 percent of these firms switched to the Hokuyo Bank, while 14.4 percent of them switched to other banks where they also had borrowed form along with HTB. Only 1.1 percent of the firms were able to obtain loans from new lenders.

Not surprisingly, the adverse effects of the failure of the Hokkaido Takushoku Bank on the performance of its client firms appear to have been significant. To date, quantitative analyses of the impact of bank failures are still limited in Japan as bank failures are only recent experiences. To our knowledge, there are three empirical studies that address this issue. The first study is the 2000 "White Paper on Small and Medium Enterprises" (*Chusho Kigyo Hakusho*) that reports the results of a survey conducted by the "Regional Bureaus of International Trade and Industry of Hokkaido" (*Tsusho Sangyo Kyoku*) (Small and Medium 2000). In the survey, the Bureau asked small- and medium-sized firms in the Hokkaido area several questions regarding their perception of the impact of the HTB bank's collapse on their business and the Hokkaido economy. One of the main questions was whether the firms felt that they were "affected" by the HTB failure. It is important to note here that the definition of being affected is not clearly defined anywhere in the survey. Hence it is not clear if the answers can be objectively compared. Regarding the sample firms, 19 percent of the firms had HTB as their main bank, 23 percent of the firms had some business relations with HTB, and the other 48 percent of the firms had no transaction with HTB (10 percent did not respond).

Not surprisingly, firms having strong ties with HTB appear to be affected most severely. Specifically, about 57 percent of the firms that had HTB as their main bank reported that they were affected moderately to strongly, whereas only 27 percent of overall firms felt the same degrees of the impact. The adverse effects were mainly due to tougher credit assessments in particular poor quality firms. Out of the companies that reported losses, 50 percent of them indicated that they felt a negative impact. Nineteen percent of the firms that had HTB as their main bank revealed that they faced tough credit line assessments from new lenders. In 11 percent of these firms, the maturity of their loans was indeed shortened.

The survey also reported the total number of corporate bankruptcies that occurred in the Hokkaido area between November 1997 and December 1998, one year after the failure of HTB. The results are in line with the other survey that a significant number of firms that had HTB as their main bank were negatively affected and became insolvent following the collapse of the bank. Statistically, 78 firms that had HTB as their main bank went bankrupt within one year after the bank failed. These firms accounted for about 7 percent of the overall bankrupt firms in Hokkaido. Further, out of the defaulted debt in Hokkaido, 25 percent belonged to HTB former client firms, and 80 percent belonged to HTB affiliated firms. We think that the failure of HTB might even have had a stronger impact on its client firms, in particular those who had the bank as their main bank, if some of the firms could not have switched to the Hokuyo Bank as discussed earlier. In addition, special loans were made available from public financial institutions and/or through government guarantees to (private) financial institutions, as well as emergency liquidity support from the Bank of Japan to help ease their liquidity problems. In fact, the "White Paper" reveals that these measures did help the firms survive and mitigated the negative consequences of HTB's failure.

The findings of an event study by Yamori and Murakami in 1999 are also consistent with the survey results that firms that had HTB as their main bank were hurt the most strongly when the bank failed. They find that companies that had HTB as their main bank showed significant negative abnormal returns (5–6 percent depending on the definition of main bank) after it failed. Another study, Hori and Takahashi (2001) examined the same issue. They used accounting data of both publicly listed companies and private companies and found similar results. Consistent with the survey by the "Regional Bureaus of International Trade and Industry," they find that low quality firms with a poor credit rating suffered the most from the HTB failure. Otherwise, there is no significant difference between the performance (according to accounting standards) of companies whose main bank was HTB and other companies. As argued earlier, we suspect that the alternative sources of financing might have eased the impact of HTB's failure.

As has been shown, Japanese firms, particularly smaller firms, have been heavily dependent on bank borrowing. In such a bank-based economy, the government had good reasons to worry that a negative impact similar to the negative consequences of HTB's collapse would occur in the event of a failure of other major banks. Political reasons also appear to have been more important. In Japan, traditionally owners of small firms have been one of the most important constituencies of the LDP. They might have put pressure on the LDP to continue to bail out banks.

In addition to the empirical evidence, it is also believed, at least in Japan, that the collapse of HTB reinforced the economic slowdown in Japan. In fact, certain macroeconomic data, such as the manufacturing index (*kokogyo seisan shisuu*) presented in table 12.9, seem to support this argument. The nationwide manufacturing index (1995 = 100) plummeted from 106.0 in 1997 to 98.4 in 1998, while that for the Hokkaido area dropped from 103.1 in 1997 to 96.5 in 1998.

CONCLUSIONS

In this chapter, we have presented an overview of too big to fail in Japan, which in our view can be described most aptly as "supervisory ad-hoc prag-

Table 12.9
Industrial Production Index during 1996–2001 (1995 = 100)

	Nationwide		Hokkaido Area	
Year	Index	Change	Index	Change
1995	100.0	—	100.0	—
1996	102.3	2.3	103.8	3.8
1997	106.0	3.6	103.1	-0.7
1998	98.4	-7.2	96.5	-6.4
1999	99.2	0.8	98.0	1.6
2000	105.0	5.8	100.9	3.0
2001	96.8	-7.8	94.6	-6.2

Source: Hokkaido Local Finance Bureau, *Hokkaido Syuyo Keizai Sihyo* (Main Economic Indicators in Hokkaido).
Note: All figures are after seasonal adjustment.

matism." This can be summarized as follows. First, at certain times, the problems at specific banks had become so severe and outrageous that the Japanese public demanded action. In some cases, which however were (and are) still rather exceptional, the ruling parties complied with these demands and let certain "big" banks fail. The most famous cases are the Hokkaido Takushoku Bank, the Long-term Credit Bank of Japan, and the Nippon Credit Bank. We have typified the latter two cases as "too big to liquidate."

Second, at other times, the supervisory authorities decided to provide public financial support to specific banks, for example, through capital injections. This was typical too big to fail behavior; as the money was pumped into the big banks, that is, the commercial (city and regional) banks, trust banks, and long-term credit banks.[5] However, these cases were also rather exceptional, due to lack of political support (these bailouts were not popular with the general electorate) and resistance by banks, as the capital injections would imply some degree of government control of their business and possibly some bank executives would even lose their jobs.

Third, most of the time, however, the policy stance of the Japanese supervisory authorities was characterized by inaction and regulatory forbearance. In other words, a "wait and see" attitude, which could be a rational approach for supervisory authorities who are confronted with a situation of political paralysis, and can do no better than react pragmatically on a case by case basis. We believe that this attitude of supervisory ad hoc pragmatism can only be changed by political reform, which, however, will be difficult to materialize relatively soon. Longer delays in solving the banking problems could turn out to be costly: for example, the savings and loan crisis in the United States cost taxpayers approximately USD 124 billion and the thrift industry another USD 29 billion, totaling USD 153 billion (Curry and Shibut 2000, p. 33). The Japanese regulators could learn from the experiences of addressing other banking crises and existing know-how in this field (see for example: Stern 1997; Dziobek and Pazarbaşıoğlu 1998; Woo 2000; Bennett 2001; Chicago Fed Letter 2001; Enoch et al. 2001).

In the autumn of 2002, it seemed that Japanese supervisory authorities were finally getting serious in solving the banking problems when Heizo Takenaka was appointed to the joint posts of State Minister for Financial Services and for Economic and Fiscal Policy on September 30, 2002. In an interview with *Newsweek* magazine, he declared that banks should no longer be considered to be too big to fail, implicitly admitting that up to then Japan was indeed following this policy line, and set up a task force charged with the task to devise recommendations to solve the bad loans situation (Standard & Poor's Ratings Services 2002). The proposals included stricter accounting methods to assess banks' assets and the converting of preferred shares held by the government into common shares, which would have given the state voting rights in the banks. With the benefit of hindsight, we can conclude that Takenaka had been too ambitious. The measures that he proposed were rather drastic—too drastic for both the political and banking communities—and some believed that they, if implemented, would have led to acute financial difficulties at certain banks, requiring further injections of public funds. Most likely, some problem banks would have collapsed and possibly nationalized, and hence incumbent management would have been removed. Consequently, this plan was opposed strongly by not only the management of the five "big" financial groups but also by members of the ruling Liberal Democratic Party, who were afraid that this plan would damage their political support among owners of firms in the construction, retailing, and real estate industries. All in all, Takenaka had to water down his plan substantially, and the end result was deemed ineffective by many observers.

Finally, it is clear that the high and increasing concentration in the Japanese banking industry had made "big" banks even bigger, which makes it quite likely that too big to fail in Japan is now for Japanese regulators actual and relevant like never before. As discussed in the chapter, five financial groups now dominate the Japanese financial system. To bail out these mega banks would require enormous amounts of funds. For example, to stop a bank run when the failure of a bank is announced, an injection of additional capital of at least 30 percent of total deposits might be necessary. This figure is based on the experience with the failure of the Hokkaido Takushoku Bank. Statistically, 15 percent of its total deposits were withdrawn in the first week after the announcement of its collapse, and by the first month after the failure 28 percent of all deposits were withdrawn (Nakaso 2001). Based on this experience, a failure of the biggest financial group, the Mizuho Group, might need at least Yen 22.23 trillion of liquidity support from the Bank of Japan.

NOTES

1. For a more elaborate analysis of the process of financial reform see Feldman (1986); Suzuki (1986, 1987; Cargill and Royama (1988); Eijffinger and Van Rixtel (1992).

2. The Mizuho Financial Group has two commercial banks, namely, the Mizuho Bank and Mizuho Corporate Bank, which each focus on different types of clients.

3. The December 1997 opinion poll of the *Nihon Keizai Shimbun* showed that only 35 percent of those questioned supported Hashimoto, versus 45 percent who disapproved of him.

4. The Prime Minister is practically elected by the majority vote of the Lower House, so that the LDP continued to be in power, since it maintained its majority in this House.

5. As Fukao (2001) has observed, it could be very costly to keep these—in his terminology—"zombie" banks alive.

REFERENCES

Ahearne, A., J. Gagnon, J. Haltmaier, and S. Kamin. 2002. "Preventing Deflation: Lessons from Japan's Experience in the 1990s." Board of Governors of the

Federal Reserve System, International Finance Discussion Papers, No. 729, June.

Bennett, Rosalind L. 2001. "Failure Resolution and Asset Liquidation: Results of an International Survey of Deposit Insurers." *FDIC Banking Review* 14, 1–28.

Cargill, Thomas F., and Shoichi Royama. 1988. *The Transition of Finance in Japan and the United States: A Comparative Perspective.* Stanford: Hoover Institution Press.

Cargill, Thomas F., Michael M. Hutchison, and Takatoshi Ito. 1997. *The Political Economy of Japanese Monetary Policy.* Cambridge, Mass.: The MIT Press.

Chicago Fed Letter. 2001. "The Financial Safety Net: Costs, Benefits, and Implications." No. 171a, November.

Choy, Jon. 1999. "Japan's Banking Industry: The Convoy Disperses in Stormy Seas." *JEI Report* No. 10A, 12 March, Washington: Japan Economic Institute.

Curry, Timothy, and Lynn Shibut. 2000. "The Cost of the Savings and Loan Crisis: Truth and Consequences." *FDIC Banking Review* 13, 26–35.

Dziobek, Claudia, and Pazarbaşıoğlu. 1998. "Lessons from Systemic Bank Restructuring." International Monetary Fund, Economic Issues, no. 14, April.

Eijffinger, Sylvester C. W., and Adrian Van Rixtel. 1992. "The Japanese Financial System and Monetary Policy: A Descriptive Review." *Japan and the World Economy* 4, 291–309.

Enoch, Charles, Gillian Garcia, and V. Sundararajan. 2001. "Recapitalizing Banks with Public Funds." International Monetary Fund, Staff Papers, 48 (1), p. 58–110.

Federal Deposit Insurance Corporation. 1997. "Continental Illinois and 'Too-big-to-fail.' " In "History of the Eighties—Lessons for the Future," Volume 1: "An Examination of the Banking Crises of the 1980s and Early 1990s," Symposium Proceedings, 16 January.

Feldman, Robert Alan. 1986. *Japanese Financial Markets: Deficits, Dilemmas, and Deregulation.* Cambridge, Mass.: MIT Press.

Fukao, Mitsuhiro. 2001. "Financial Deregulations, Weakness of Market Discipline, and Market Development: Japan's Experience and Lessons for Developing Countries." Paper presented at IDB-JCIF Workshop, 11–12 June, organized by the Japan Bank for International Cooperation.

Group of Ten. 2001. Report on Consolidation in the Financial Sector, Bank for International Settlements.

Gup, Benton E. 1998. "Too-Big-to-Fail: An International Perspective." In *Bank Failures in the Major Trading Countries of the World: Causes and Remedies.* Westport, Conn.: Quorum Books, 69–88.

Hall, Maximilian J. B. 1998. *Financial Reform in Japan—Causes and Consequences.* Cheltenham, UK: Edward Elgar.

Hamada, Koichi. 1995. "Bubbles, Bursts and Bailouts: A Comparison of Three Episodes of Financial Crises in Japan." In *The Structure of the Japanese Economy: Changes on the Domestic and International Fronts,* edited by Mitsuaki Okabe. Houndmills, Basingstoke: Macmillan Press, 263–286.

Hanazaki, Masaharu, and Akiyoshi Horiuchi. 2002. "A Review of Japan's Bank Crisis from the Governance Perspective." Paper presented at the 2002 FMA Annual Meeting, San Antonio, 16–19 October 2002.

Hetzel, Robert L. 1991. "Too-Big-to-Fail: Origins, Consequences, and Outlook."

Federal Reserve Bank of Richmond, Economic Review, November/December, 3–15.

Hori, Masahiro, and Tomoyuki Takahashi. 2001. "The Value of Bank Relationship: A Study on the Hokkaido Takushoku Bank's Failure." ESRI Discussion Paper Series No. 4, Economic and Social Research Institute, Cabinet Office (in Japanese).

Horiuchi, Akiyoshi. 2000. "The Big Bang: Idea and Reality." In *Crisis and Change in the Japanese Financial System*, edited by Takeo Hoshi and Hugh Patrick. Boston, Mass.: Kluwer Academic Publishers, 109–136.

Hoshi, Takeo. 2002. "The Convoy System for Insolvent Banks: How it Originally Worked and Why it Failed in the 1990s." *Japan and the World Economy* 14, 115–180.

Hoshi, Takeo, and Hugh Patrick. 1999. "The Japanese Financial System: An Introductory Review." In *Crisis and Change in the Japanese Financial System*, edited by Takeo Hoshi and Hugh Patrick. Boston, Mass.: Kluwer Academic Publishers, 1–33.

Hoshi, Takeo, and Anil K. Kashyap. 1999. "The Japanese Banking Crisis: Where Did It Come from and How Will It End?" NBER Working Paper No. 7250.

Hoshi, Takeo, and Anil K. Kashyap. 2001. *Corporate Financing and Governance in Japan*. Cambridge, Mass.: The MIT Press.

Kanaya, Akihiro, and David Woo. 2000. "The Japanese Banking Crisis of the 1990s: Sources and Lessons." IMF, Working Paper, WP/00/7.

Kaufman, George G. 2002. "Too-Big-to-Fail in U.S. Banking: Quo Vadis?" Mimeograph, 21 October.

Kaufman, George G., and Steven A. Seelig. 2000. "Post-resolution Treatment of Depositors at Failed Banks: Implications for the Severity of Banking Crises, Systemic Risk, and Too-Big-to-Fail." Mimeograph, 27 November.

Milhaupt, C. J. 1999. "Japan's Experience with Deposit Insurance and Failing Banks: Implications for Financial Regulatory Design?" Bank of Japan, Monetary and Economic Studies, August, 21–46.

Ministry of Finance. 1993. *The Mechanism and Economic Effects of Asset Price Fluctuations: A Report of the Research Committee*. Tokyo: The Institute of Fiscal and Monetary Policy, Ministry of Finance.

Nakajima, Zenta, and Hitoo Taguchi. 1995. "Toward a More Stable Financial Framework: Long-term Alternatives—An Overview of Recent Bank Disruption Worldwide." In *Financial Stability in a Changing Environment*, edited by Sawamoto Kuniho, Zenta Nakajima, and Hiroo Taguchi. Houndmills, Basingstoke: Macmillan Press, 41–98.

Nakaso, Hiroshi. 2001. "The Financial Crisis in Japan during the 1990s: How the Bank of Japan Responded and the Lessons Learnt." Bank for International Settlements, BIS Papers, No. 6, October.

Okina, Kunio, Masaaki Shirakawa, and Shigenori Shiratsuka. 2000. "The Asset Price Bubble and Monetary Policy: Japan's Experience in the Late 1980s and the Lessons." Bank of Japan, Institute for Monetary and Economic Studies, Discussion Paper Series, No. 2000-E-12.

Patrick, Hugh. 1999. "The Causes of Japan's Financial Crisis." Pacific Economic Paper No. 288, Canberra: Australia-Japan Research Center.

Peek, Joe, and Eric S. Rosengren. 1998. "Determinants of the Japan Premium: Actions

Speak Louder Than Words." Federal Research Bank of Boston, Working Paper No. 98–9.

Roth, Michael. 1994. " 'Too-Big-to-Fail' and the Stability of the Banking System: Some Insights from Foreign Countries." *Business Economics*, October, 43–49.

Saito, Makoto, and Shigenori Shiratsuka. 2000. "Financial Crises as the Failure of Arbitrage and Monetary Policy: Evidence from the 'Japan Premium' Phenomenon." Paper prepared for the Ninth International Conference on 3–4 July 2000, sponsored by the Institute for Monetary and Economic Studies, Bank of Japan.

Small and Medium Enterprise Agency. 2000. "White Paper on Small and Medium Enterprises in Japan."

Spiegel, Mark M. 1999. "Moral Hazard under the Japanese Convoy Banking System." *FRBSF Economic Review* 3, 1–13.

Spiegel, Mark M. 2001. "The Return of the 'Japan Premium': Trouble Ahead for Japanese Banks?" Federal Reserve Bank of San Francisco, Economic Letter 2001–06, 9 March.

Spiegel, Mark M., and Nobuyoshi Yamori. 2000. "The Evolution of 'Too-Big-to-Fail' Policy in Japan: Evidence from Market Equity Values." Center for Pacific Basin Monetary and Economic Studies, Economic Research Department, Federal Reserve Bank of San Francisco, Pacific Basin Working Paper Series No. PB00–01, April.

Standard & Poor's Ratings Services. 2002. "Recapitalizing Japan's Banks: Impact on Bank and Sovereign Ratings." 7 October 2002.

Stern, Gary H. 1997. "The Too-Big-to-Fail Problem." Federal Reserve Bank of Minneapolis, *The Region*, September.

Suzuki, Yoshio. 1986. *Money, Finance, and Macroeconomic Performance in Japan*. New Haven: Yale University Press.

Suzuki, Yoshio. 1987. *The Japanese Financial System*. Oxford: Clarendon Press.

Takeda, Masahiko, and Phillip Turner. 1992. "The Liberalization of Japan's Financial Markets: Some Major Themes." Bank for International Settlements, Economic Papers 34.

Teranishi, Juro. 1990. "Finance and Economic Development in Post-war Japan." Paper presented at the Conference on Financial Development in Japan, Korea, and Taiwan, Institute of Academia Sinica, Taipei, August.

Teranishi, Juro. 1993. "Financial Sector Reform after the War." In *The Japanese Experience of Economic Reforms*, edited by Juro Teranishi and Yutaka Kosai. Houndmills, Basingstoke: Macmillan Press, 153–177.

Van Rixtel, Adrian. 2002. *Informality and Monetary Policy in Japan: The Political Economy of Bank Performance*. Cambridge: Cambridge University Press.

Woo, David. 2000. "Two Approaches to Resolving Nonperforming Assets during Financial Crises." International Monetary Fund, IMF Working Paper, WP/00/33, March.

Yamori, Nobuyoshi, and Akinobu Murakami. 1999. "Does Bank Relationship Have an Economic Value? The Effect of Main Bank Failure on Client Firms." *Economic Letters* 65, 115–120.

PART III

Too Big, or Not Too Big to Fail: Fannie Mae, Freddie Mac, and Enron

CHAPTER 13

Are Fannie Mae and Freddie Mac Too Big to Fail?

Benton E. Gup[1]

INTRODUCTION

We cannot directly observe the conditional or unconditional probability that a large financial institution may fail. Therefore, we must rely on other measures to monitor risk taking of the regulated entities. A decade after the Savings and Loan (S&L) Crisis, theories of how firms take excessive risks and ultimately become insolvent are still poorly developed. Empirical evidence is weak because we don't know precisely when a large financial institution actually becomes insolvent even after the fact; we only know that they do. Arguments still persist in academic circles as to when many U.S. Banks and Savings and Loan institutions that failed in the late 1980s actually became insolvent—when the loans were made or when they actually became nonperforming, and ultimately led to insolvency.

Some would argue that Too Big To Fail (TBTF) is the only prominent policy option for very large financial firms. After all, who could seriously consider resolving a trillion dollar entity? In a sense TBTF has become the theory that affects what we observe. Large financial institutions can't be allowed to fail, the reasoning goes. Many consider TBTF to be an essential tool in the regulator's arsenal for maintaining financial stability. Fear plays a role, but all economists worry that TBTF plays havoc with risk assessments. Some believe that TBTF is merely a political and regulatory rationalization, rather than a policy option with economic justification.

TBTF does not mean large institutions literally can't fail. Since the mid-1990s, large firm failures have become a fact of life. Enron, Worldcom, Global Crossing, and LTCM have left the public uneasy about insolvency, how to monitor it, and what to do about it.[2] Although the isolation and containment of the failure is entirely appropriate, once economic failure has occurred, maintaining any insolvent institution in its existing form and protecting its shareholders has little economic justification. When government acts to protect investments gone awry and limit losses to those who have taken improper risks, it distorts risk signals.

When a large, regulated, financial institution failure becomes reality, and risks taken over extended periods suddenly materialize as losses, the regulator must not only deal with the current insolvency, but external criticisms about monitoring failures. Why were those risks not deemed excessive? Did the regulator's safety and soundness procedures fail? Almost as much as to deflect blame as to ensure financial stability, regulators out of frustration and desperation choose TBTF as tempting socially justified absolution for regulatory failure.[3] The specters of Henry Thornton (1802) and Walther Bagehot (1873), promise to haunt any regulator who seeks to favorably compare the short-term benefits of a politically expedient TBTF policy with the long-term economic costs of such a policy.

Let us have no illusions. Any firm, regardless of size or government affiliation, may fail economically. Firms that many considered to be TBTF have "failed" in the past and will certainly continue to do so in the future. What looms as a greater uncertainty, however, is how the government plans to treat such failures after the 1990s wave of consolidations and mergers. The set of potential TBTF candidates has expanded notably, because size does matter.

HISTORICAL PERSPECTIVE OF TBTF

TBTF traces its roots in the United States to the banking system and the creation of the central bank in 1913. When Congress created the Federal Reserve System, it authorized the central bank to take those actions necessary to ensure a sound money supply and a safe banking system. The jump to TBTF was relatively easy. Safety and soundness are hard to define and easily extend to the preservation of institutions rather than markets.

At its discretion, the Federal Reserve interpreted its mandate to keep very large banks, despite their financial condition, open to ensure confidence and the flow of funds in the economy. Although not formally codified into law until the 1950 amendment to the Federal Deposit Insurance Act of 1934, the "essentiality doctrine" also known as "too big to fail" states that government may rescue any failed bank when "continued operation of the such bank is essential to provide adequate banking service to the community."[4] In 1984, Todd Conover, comptroller of the currency and regulator of national banks, actually announced that the top 11 banks in the United States (based on assets) would not be permitted to fail. In the intervening 20 years, no bank or thrift with more than $20 billion in assets has been resolved. TBTF was actually codified into law for depository institutions with the explicit insertion of the systemic risk exception clause to Prompt Corrective Action provisions in FDI-CIA in 1991. Most recently the Federal Reserve endorsed TBTF when it interceded with banks to keep Long Term Capital Management (LTCM) afloat after it had become effectively insolvent.

Bank stockholders and creditors were not the only investors protected by TBTF. In the 1974 Lockheed and 1979 Chrysler bailouts, for example, the government chose to breathe new life into these firms and prevent their failures.[5] During 2002, Congress considered TBTF as a policy option after the events of September 11 when it deliberated an $18 billion bailout of firms in the airlines industry.

MOTIVATIONS FOR TBTF

Three primary considerations motivate TBTF: a fear of systemic events[6], an inability of government regulators to reasonably and efficiently conduct a resolution of multi-billion dollar enterprises, and political concerns associated with the first two considerations. Ironically, none of these three considerations provides sufficient *economic* justification of TBTF.[7] Governments permitted WorldCom, Enron, Drexel, Barings, and other large complex financial and nonfinancial firms to fail. Why were these firms not TBTF? After the fact, we can conclude that TBTF was ruled out as a public policy alternative in these cases but not in the cases of LTCM, Lockheed, Continental Illinois, Penn Central, or Chrysler.[8]

Ultimately, the political appeal of TBTF is undeniable. TBTF appears to save jobs, avert financial disaster, and ensure financial stability. Although it may actually accomplish none of these goals, it is simply what many want to hear and believe. Perhaps, it is comforting to know that some institutions will always be with us. Even so, such comfort comes at a price. TBTF actually costs jobs, contributes to financial disaster, and de-stabilizes. It has, however, become the politically correct policy of choice. It seems to provide an orderly transition for a difficult problem, and reduces regulatory agency criticisms. The TBTF policy plays to a deceptive regulatory self-image that the regulator is truly managing systemic risk by using TBTF effectively, prudently, and justifiably.

Regulators fashion themselves to be doctors who supply medicine for sick and terminally ill patents. The medicine in this case is the TBTF pill that infuses an insolvent financial institution/patient with positive cash flow or capital. With luck, it becomes the miracle cure effectively resurrecting a dead or insolvent institution. The TBTF pill has such potency, one critic asks, "How can there even be systemic risk, if an institution is too big to fail?"[9] If we refuse to recognize failure, then there can be no systemic risk in this line of reasoning. The result is tautological.

Unfortunately no firm is really too big to fail in an economic or financial sense. Failures occur whether the regulator sees it coming or not. Even institutions with hundreds of billions of dollars in assets can succumb to failure. The TBTF pill, although tempting to administer if only to buy time, has insidious side effects. It erodes market discipline, destroys competition, and encourages moral hazard. It distorts risk estimation, risk-based pricing and valuation, and serves to stimulate inefficient mergers and growth. Much, although not all, of the cost of failure may have already been incurred by the time failure is recognized.

In 1873, Walter Bagehot suggested that the government was generally incapable of discerning the difference between a liquidity problem and an insolvency problem.[10] This remains true, particularly for regulated enterprises. No government agency can distinguish unequivocally between liquidity and solvency problems. Why is this so?

Consider a competitive unregulated firm and the sequence of events leading to its insolvency. An external or internal event precipitates diminishing cash flow indicating a liquidity problem. Profitability drops. Stock prices fall and the cost of capital rises. If cash flow problems remain sufficiently persistent and severe, unpaid creditors begin to clamor for payment of services rendered. Creditors ultimately force an unprofitable firm into bankruptcy if it cannot remedy its cash flow problems or attract additional capital. Creditors seeking legal recourse call attention to the fact that the failure of the firm is imminent. Market discipline exerted by investors in both equity and bond markets continue to extract a toll as falling stock prices and rising costs of debt continue to signal a firm's potential demise. The signals are clear and unambiguous. WorldCom and Enron are but two of many recent and prominent examples. Thus, demise of competitive unregulated firms is heralded by a recognizable series of events making its ultimate failure reasonably well anticipated. The legal system handles the failure regardless of the size of the firm.

Banks, thrifts, brokerage firms, and government sponsored enterprises (GSEs), do not provide such clear and unambiguous signals when regulators, investors, or creditors embrace TBTF. Market discipline is least effective when market participants discount the possibility of losses and firm failure. Consequently without the signals of stock market price declines, increasing bond yields, and a growing disparity between book and market valuations, regulators are ill-prepared to monitor these firms as well as they could within a normal market valuation.

In regulated industries, the regulators must assess whether the expected market value assets less the market value of liabilities is greater than zero. This requires that regulators have reasonably precise estimates of both the market value of assets and liabilities *before* they decide to initiate resolution proceedings. In virtually all instances, regulators do not have this information and must use informed judgments. This means that the value of capital is stochastic, not simply an univariate book-valued regulatory measure.

Failure is appropriately viewed from the perspective of the regulator as a conditional random variable—a firm is "failed" when the expected discounted cash flows under the assumption of normal business conditions become negative. Is failure then just subjective assessment, made in the eye of the beholder?

The answer is yes. Failure is a condition in which the expected discounted future cash flow *appears* to be negative—it is a condition in which the firm faces at least a 50% chance of generating a negative cash flow into the foreseeable future. And from that perspective, every effort must be made to assure that that subjective assessment also reflects market data and financial condition. Regulators therefore should view failure in probabilistic terms—as a conditional random variable: any firm that exhibits a positive likelihood of failure under reasonable assumptions over a finite time period.

One particularly important reason for approaching failure in this manner is that government regulators never know whether a firm has truly failed. Their decision about TBTF is always made when the institution is still functioning, even if it is exhibiting a negative cash flow. Doubt inevitably persists that a failure has occurred. Economic circumstances can always change and a firm may well ultimately survive. Consequently the notion of economic or financial failure is unlike biological death where there is no question that life has ceased.

SYSTEMIC RISK: A REAL CONCERN OR MUCH ADO ABOUT NOTHING?

> In contrast to most professional economists, policy officials and leaders of the private business sector worry a great deal about the risk of major breakdowns in the function of the economy. Many of the conditions and the events of the 1980s—the failure of most of the less developed debtor countries to service their debts, the deterioration of capital among money-center banks, the large numbers of bankruptcies of the thrift institutions, the wide swings of currency exchange rates, the increase of corporate debt, and the stock market crash of 1987—have contributed to the fear of an impending major economic crisis. Rapid changes in financial markets and a dramatic increase in the complexity of financial instruments have heightened those fears.
>
> Martin Feldstein, (1991), "Introduction," The Risk of Economic Crisis: An NBER Conference Report, p. 1.

One of the simpler definitions is that systemic risk is the probability that some minimal predetermined level of macroeconomic losses will occur as the result of the decisions made by regulated financial institutions.[11] Analysts who accept this definition or a similar definition tend to be optimistic. They conclude that rational governments, better early warning systems, and prudent policies can mitigate the potential macroeconomic losses associated with a financial crisis and perhaps even avert a systemic event.[12]

Regulators, including the Federal Reserve, reveal their preference to treat systemic risk seriously by demanding and funding systemic risk research and sponsoring systemic risk conferences on an international scale.[13] Accordingly, the systemic risk literature expanded dramatically during the last decade with a plethora of technical and nontechnical papers, reports, and studies in regulatory sponsored publications and conferences.[14]

COMPELLING EVIDENCE OF SYSTEMIC RISK

> The use of the more- sophisticated techniques . . . especially the various forms of derivatives, are, by construction, highly leveraged. They are thus prone to induce speculative excesses, not only in the U.S. financial system, but also through out the rest of the world. The greater potential for systemic risk can be contained by improvements in effective risk management in the private sector, including market discipline based on better public disclosure, and by improvements in bank supervision and regulation in the public sector.
>
> Alan Greenspan, Address to ABA, October 7, 2002.

Surveys indicate that many regard systemic events as increasingly common global phenomena. The Group of Thirty released the report *Global Institutions, National Supervision, and Systemic Risk* (1997) that asked representatives of global financial institutions (not regulators!) how concerned they were about systemic risk. The survey results indicated that the *majority* of respondents considered a "serious systemic disruption" arising from financial turmoil a distinct possibility. Approximately 75 percent of those initially contacted, "generally agreed that a serious disruption of the international financial system could occur, rating the likelihood at one in five over the next five years."[15] According to our definition, however, a financial system disruption, by itself, may not qualify for a systemic event unless it is accompanied by macro-economic losses.

History supports the view that such losses do indeed occur. During the last two decades, serious financial crises with accompanying macroeconomic losses have occurred with sufficient frequency that financial regulation has itself come under increasing scrutiny for its failure to contain systemic events.

Minsky (1975, 1982, 1986, and 1991) draws a critical connection between financial crises and economic crisis.[16] No longer viewed as remote and unlikely, systemic events are more often viewed by many as infrequent but on average *regularly occurring events*. For example, 130 of the 180+ member countries of the International Monetary Fund (IMF) reported severe banking problems between 1980 and 1995. Severe banking problems in this context ipso facto become systemic losses.

Such events naturally give rise to speculations like "If these crises were better anticipated, could they somehow be avoided or could the economic losses have been limited through prudent regulatory policies?" This IMF survey defined serious banking problems as "bank runs, collapses of financial firms, or massive government intervention as well as less damaging but extensive unsoundness of financial institutions."[17] With few exceptions, virtually all countries with sophisticated financial systems suffered at least one financial crisis during this period (1980–1995) that had negative spillover effects on the macro-economy. The IMF estimated that these spillovers resulted in cumulative losses that reduced trend GDP by 4.3 percent, distributed over one and a half years. Applying this same average loss rate to an $11 trillion dollar U.S. economy produces a $400 + billion loss in real GDP, roughly twice the taxpayer exposure and resolution costs associated with the entire S&L Crisis.[18]

In October 1997, Chairman Greenspan of the Federal Reserve Board (FRB)suggested that global financial efficiency had a downside—it created mechanisms that could generate "losses at an inconceivable rate." He follows this statement with a conclusion that this has increased the potential for systemic risk:

> . . . Not only has the productivity of global finance increased markedly, but so, obviously, has the ability to generate losses at a previously inconceivable rate. Moreover, increasing global financial efficiency, by creating the mechanisms for mistakes to ricochet throughout the global financial system, has patently increased the potential for systemic risk.[19]

Even systemic risk skeptics note that the Federal Reserve hosted or cohosted four systemic risk conferences since 1995 that support the chairman's view. The Bank of Japan, the Board of Governors of the Federal Reserve System, and the European Central Bank hosted three Joint Central Bank Research Conferences entitled *Risk Measurement and Systemic Risk* (New York City, United States [1995]; Tokyo, Japan [1998]; and Basel, Switzerland [2002]). The FRB, with the U.S. Comptroller of the Currency and the Bank of England, also hosted another conference entitled *Banks and Systemic Risk* in London England (2001).

Papers presented at these conferences argue that systemic risk has become both more likely and more important in recent years. They attribute this to

1. economic development that increases the importance and interdependence of banking and the global financial interdependencies between countries (the more important financial institutions become, the greater the likelihood that problems or failures get transmitted to the overall system);

2. advances in computer and telecommunications technologies that permit funds to be transferred more easily, quickly, and cheaply across large distances and national boundaries (the faster the telecommunications, the faster increases in the speed of shock transmissions);

3. the failure of regulatory early warning systems to keep pace with financial institu-

tions (regulatory early-warning systems tend to lag behind financial-sector early-warning systems);

4. prevailing trends in the concentration and size of financial institutions (institutions have become more concentrated and much larger).

One surprise that emerges from these conferences is that not one paper actually offers a way to measure or monitor systemic risk, thereby leaving the question of the immediacy of a systemic event and the potential losses associated with it open to question. Measurement remains critical; it is difficult to monitor and manage that which cannot be measured.[20]

SYSTEMIC RISK: TO WHOM, OF WHAT, AND FOR HOW LONG?

Few analysts struggle with the "systemic" part of the definition. It is the "risk" part that tends to be elusive. We must define risk before we measure it. Risk is the potential for someone or something to bear *future* losses. Potential might be measured as a probability, possibility, likelihood, or indication of a degree of uncertainty. We cannot directly measure risk so we use advances in mathematical finance, statistics, and economics to estimate, derive, or impute risk estimates using a variety of procedures, the most prominent being the implied conditional probability distributions of future returns or losses. Such distributions are convenient statistical and empirical constructs that permit us to define systemic risk and estimate it as a conditional probability of system wide losses that exceed some dollar denominated level.[21]

An example may help. Let us say that we estimate that there is a one percent chance that systemic losses may exceed $500 billion—GDP may be $500 billion lower than it would be without the occurrence of a systemic event. The estimate of one percent, the conditional probability of large losses (greater than $.5 trillion), is an estimate for the potential for loss measured over some time period. It is conditional upon many things including monetary and fiscal policies, technological changes, and periodicity of the business cycle.

We complete this definition by asking and answering three additional questions.

1. *The Risk To Whom?* Systemic Risk is the probability of losses to society at large and to tax payers in particular that result from financial institutions' failures or financial institutions' ability to inflict losses throughout the system as a whole. Note that this is not the risk to investors, to the Enterprises, or to creditors.

2. *The Risk of What?* Systemic risk is risk of an economy-wide slowdown or decline in real economic activity where losses are measured by reductions in real GDP, productivity, and economic growth relative to what real GDP, productivity, and economic growth would be without such losses. Tabulated in the national income and

product accounts and discerned through changes in the flow of funds, systemic risk is the probability of negative economic impacts on a system-wide scale.

3. *The Risk over Time?* Systemic risk is time dimensional. In many cases, even systemic losses will only result in temporary market disruptions. When other financial firms can take up the slack in the event of a financial firm failure, the losses dissipate, eventually restoring a market equilibrium, albeit possibly one with a lower growth rate.

ARE FANNIE MAE AND FREDDIE MAC TOO BIG TO FAIL?

This paper focuses on Fannie Mae (FNM) and Freddie Mac (FRE) and asks whether they are in fact TBTF. In late 2002 when this chapter was written, neither government-sponsored enterprise (GSE) appeared in imminent danger of failure, and TBTF might be considered a moot point that needs to be addressed only when the need arises. This paper argues that the need arises now. Neither firm should ever be declared TBTF and market discipline should be encouraged.

Over the last 10 years, FNM and FRE have significantly outperformed the Dow Jones, S&P500, and NASDAQ. Fannie Mae is the 2nd largest corporation in America. Freddie Mac is roughly three-fourths the size of Fannie Mae and the 5th largest corporation in America. Together they boast revenues that exceeded $90 billion during 2002. Their respective successes and abilities to achieve both housing goals set by Housing and Urban Development (HUD) and profits generated for their shareholders, as government-sponsored enterprises, are well known and to some extent a matter of national pride. Ironically, their successes and growth raise a basic question: Have these Enterprises grown so large as to become too big to fail?

The quick answer is "no." Explaining the answer requires the rest of this chapter.

Many plausible scenarios can be contemplated in which the Enterprises would fail or become sufficiently financially compromised to create serious cash flow and credit problems in the housing sector. Neither Enterprise is perfectly hedged. Both are highly leveraged, and the market values of their assets are tied to real estate values and interest rates that exhibit volatility. They are vulnerable to housing price bubbles, economic downturns, and radical changes in interest rates. Consequently, they exhibit a nonzero likelihood of failure, although preliminary indications suggest that this likelihood is a small number.

The current regulator of the Enterprises, Office of Federal Housing Enterprise Oversight (OFHEO), through its on-site and off-site supervision and examinations, attempts to ensure that the Enterprises pursue business practices and activities commensurate with their mandated charters and appropriate levels of risk management, but neither it nor any other regulator can provide systemic risk guarantees. So the first question with which we must deal is do the Enterprises pose systemic risk?

ENTERPRISE AND SYSTEMIC RISK

Current literature provides only a limited perspective of systemic risk because it focuses on banks. The prevailing academic and conference literature focuses on a divergence of opinion as to whether banks, as financial intermediaries have real output effects in the macroeconomy. This argument centers on whether banks can contribute to real output effects—macroeconomic losses. No such divergence exists with respect to Fannie Mae and Freddie Mac. These GSEs were chartered explicitly to affect real output through the secondary mortgage markets. These Enterprises exist to channel real investment into housing. One possible excuse for lack of attention to systemic risk posed by the Enterprises is that neither institution was sufficiently large to pose a serious systemic threat as little as a decade ago. Their relatively recent growth in relation to their current size, measured as book value assets, mortgage guarantees, or liabilities elevates them to obvious systemic risk candidates.[22]

ENTERPRISE OVERVIEW

Congress chartered Fannie Mae and Freddie Mac to overcome historical limitations in the nation's decentralized banking system that led to sporadic credit crunches in local and regional mortgage markets over the last century. Lack of mortgage credit appeared to hurt the housing sector and otherwise reduce real output. By providing implicit and explicit government subsidies, Congress encouraged Fannie Mae and Freddie Mac (the Enterprises) to channel the funds to the United States housing sector through the secondary mortgage market.[23] To fulfill their obligations, the Enterprises buy mortgages from lenders, who retain a portion of the monthly mortgage payments as compensation for servicing the loans in the pool. The Enterprises finance those purchases through the issuance of debt securities and creating and selling guaranteed securities backed by pools of loans, or by guaranteeing mortgage backed securities (MBS) issued by lenders. The Enterprises retain guarantee fees and pass the balances of the monthly payments to the holders of the MBS for each loan pool.

ENTERPRISE SUBSIDIES

The charters of Fannie Mae and Freddie Mac and other provisions of federal law convey substantial benefits as compensation for pursuing their congressionally stipulated goals. For example, explicit benefits include the following:

- A $2.25 billion conditional line of credit at the Treasury
- Eligibility for Federal Reserve open-market purchases
- Eligibility for their securities to serve as collateral for most state and local deposits and as collateral for loans from Federal Reserve and Federal Home Loan Banks
- Unlimited investment potential by depository institutions—banks and thrifts may invest in the Enterprises' securities in unlimited amounts, stimulating the demand for Enterprise issued mortgage backed securities and debt instruments
- Access of the Fedwire, the Federal Reserve's electronic system for transferring funds and issuing and transferring securities[24]
- The market's perception that the government implicitly guarantees the Enterprises' obligations—the most important source of savings. This perception arises from the cumulative benefits Fannie Mae and Freddie Mac enjoy as GSEs, their ability to borrow in the GSE credit market, and strong Congressional support for their public purposes[25]
- Limited competition—only two similar GSEs hold such charters, although the Federal Home Loan Banks enjoys a similar charter
- Mortgage backed securities (MBS) issued by banks and thrifts must be protected by subordinated tranches, overcollateralization, reserve funds, or with external credit enhancements like bond insurance. These requirements provide the Enterprises a distinct advantage over potential creditors

Freddie Mac and Fannie Mae claim these benefits are not subsidies, but reflections of their efficiency of operations. The Congressional Budget Office (CBO) (2001) differs and released a study that estimated the cumulative implicit and explicit Enterprise subsidies reached 40 percent of their current net earnings, or $13 billion, in 2000.[26] In 2001, the returns on equity for Fannie Mae and Freddie Mac exceeded 25 percent. A perfectly hedged firm would have had returns more in the neighborhood of 5 to 8 percent. Neither Enterprise claims to hedge perfectly, but the discrepancy is noteworthy and the basis for the CBO calculation. The CBO contends that most of the differential is subsidies. Others support CBO's contention that the subsidies are formidable.[27]

Both Enterprises contend that the subsidies are substantially less, and the differential between actual returns and risk free returns can be explained by good business practices and market sagacity. Freddie Mac issued a study by Miller and Pearce who estimated subsidies to be less than $4 billion, but the study did not address the differential between actual returns and that of a perfectly hedged firm. Curiously neither the CBO nor the Enterprises examined what the magnitude of the subsidies would be if an Enterprise suffered a serious financial set back. Economic theory suggests debate over levels of subsidies may be moot because subsidies rise and fall with the financial health of the Enterprises. For example, the values of the subsidies must rise asymptotically as financial institutions get closer to insolvency and decline as the financial health of institutions improves.

A TWO-EDGED SWORD: THE POTENTIAL FOR
REDUCING OR INCREASING SYSTEMIC RISK

Both Fannie Mae and Freddie Mac contend that they have not and will not contribute in any way to systemic risk.[28] Their intentions are laudable and denial understandable. They point to their continued excellent financial performance and deny that they pose systemic risk.

Both institutions have outperformed the major stock indicators over the past decade. Fannie Mae is the 2nd largest corporation in America and Freddie Mac the 5th largest. It is probably true that their excellent financial performance helped to mitigate the severity of the 2001 recession. They demonstrated a unique ability to bring liquidity to the housing sector even in the midst of financial turmoil, such as the Asian Crisis 2000–2001. Unfortunately their ability to provide such a positive and powerful economic force in our economy also raises the potential that they could easily become a negative force. The same abilities that allow the Enterprises to reduce systemic risk—their dominance in the secondary market, their enormous debt issuances, and their ability to supply credit through the secondary mortgage markets make them candidates for precipitating a systemic event. The sword cuts both ways.

One edge cuts a path paved with meaningful contributions to economic growth, productivity, mortgage securitization, and their housing goals. The other edge cuts a path into the debt, equity, and credit markets where pricing has been distorted by implicit government guarantees and the market perception that the enterprises are too big to fail. There is general agreement that the Enterprises have become *the* dominant players in a housing market that contributes more than more than $1 trillion yearly to the nation's economic output and accounts for over 11 percent of Gross Domestic Product (GDP). They directly or indirectly affect a complex, concentrated network of housing finance and credit interdependencies.

Fannie Mae and Freddie Mac have cultivated extensive business relationships with a wide range of other financial institutions and nonfinancial firms throughout the financial and housing sectors. Structurally, these cultivated interdependencies contribute to their success and growth but such interdependencies also provide a list of potentially vulnerable institutions to a financial crisis brought on by the Enterprises.

Direct interdependencies include the following:

- Seller/Servicers. Firms that originate mortgages, sell them to the Enterprises, service the loans, and may provide credit enhancements of pools of loans supply the Enterprises with mortgage pools and services for those pools. Those seller/servicers include mortgage banks, commercial banks, savings associations, credit unions, and other types of lenders.

- Mortgage Insurers (MIs). MIs assume some of the risk of loss on many loans owned or securitized by Fannie Mae and Freddie Mac and provide additional coverage on some pools.

- Counter-parties. Global securities firms and commercial banks serve as counter-parties to the financial derivatives contracts that the Enterprises use to hedge their exposures to interest rate and other forms of market risk.

- Financial Intermediaries that Sell Debt. Fannie Mae and Freddie Mac also rely on securities firms to sell their debt and MBS.

- Software Firms and Underwriters. Finally, the Enterprises have relationships with software providers, partly as a result of the development of automated underwriting and the increased use of the Internet in the mortgage lending process.

ENTERPRISE GROWTH: UNFETTERED, SUBSIDIZED, AND SCARY!

Over the decade prior to 2001, the combined mortgage asset portfolios of Fannie Mae and Freddie Mac rose to over $1.3 trillion. This represents an eight-fold increase in size. The combined outstanding MBSs held by other investors amounts to over $1.5 trillion. Size does matter. Perceptions matter.

Fannie Mae and Freddie Mac's holdings exceeded 43 percent of outstanding residential mortgage debt at the end of 2001. During the last decade, the share of all residential mortgages outstanding in the Enterprises' retained portfolios rose from less than 5 percent to over 19 percent. The combined debt outstanding of the Enterprises rose from $154 billion at the end of 1990 to $1.33 trillion of callable debt at year-end 2001. Fannie Mae and Freddie Mac are the largest purchasers of conventional single-family mortgages in the secondary market and represent nearly 45 percent of originations of those mortgages. The Enterprises together purchased roughly $1 trillion of such loans in 2001, roughly 50 percent of the nearly $1.9 trillion in conventional single-family mortgages originated in that year.

The Enterprises' combined total book of business—mortgages securitized and held on the balance sheet—now represent 26 percent of outstanding residential mortgage debt. To manage the interest rate and credit risks associated with this debt, the Enterprises have developed and expanded the market for interest rate swaps and other over-the-counter (OTC) derivative instruments used to hedge risks, so much so that by end of the 2001, the Enterprises had become major end users of those instruments. The notional amount of the Enterprise derivatives outstanding increased from $72 billion at the end of 1993, the first year for which comparable data were reported, to $1.6 trillion at year-end 2001. The change in notional amount of derivatives, however, is only an imperfect indicator of the extent to which the variance of the discounted net-earnings stream of either Enterprise may or may not be reduced. Regulators and market analysts find it difficult to distinguish between hedging and speculation. Both enterprises engage in extensive risk management procedures but the risks tend to be managed on a financial instrument-by-instrument basis, raising questions about the nature of the risk management at the Enterprise-wide level.

Fannie Mae and Freddie Mac funded the growth in their asset portfolios and off-balance sheet activities in the 1990s by issuing debt. The Enterprises issue debt with a wide range of maturities, from discount notes with maturities as short as overnight, to bonds with maturities as long as 30 years. Many of these are intermediate and long-term debt securities with embedded call features. In 1998, as the volume of U.S. Treasury debt declined, with a shrinking U.S. Budget Deficit, market participants looked for other securities that could provide a large liquid market of debt with low credit risk. Fannie Mae and Freddie Mac complied and introduced debt issuance programs that now rival the dollar volume of Treasury issues outstanding. Today the Enterprises auction short-term discount notes (Fannie Mae's Benchmark Bills and Freddie Mac's Reference Bills) and medium- and long-term noncallable securities (Fannie Mae's Benchmark and Freddie Mac's Reference Notes and Bonds) in such significant volumes and with sufficient regularity that they are welcomed by banks, thrifts, and comparable investors, as close substitutes for U.S. Treasury securities, although they offer a slightly higher yield.

Fannie Mae and Freddie Mac each provide corporate guarantees of MBS collateralized by residential mortgages originated by approved sellers. Each Enterprise's outstanding MBS (excluding securities held in the Enterprise's own portfolio) continue to grow but at slower rates in recent years than in the 1980s and early 1990s.[29] Fannie Mae's outstanding MBSs rose at an annual rate of 8 percent between 1992 and 2001 after increasing at 28 percent per year between 1986 and 1992. Similarly, Freddie Mac's outstanding MBS grew 4 percent in the recent period after rising at 16 percent a year between 1986 and 1992.

An analysis of their on and off balance sheet performance and income statements over the last half decade leads to several conclusions. The Enterprises appear to be well managed and operate efficiently. They enjoy AAA ratings and are frequently recommended by many stock analysts and portfolio managers as excellent/superior investments. But, can they fail? Certainly they can. Is it likely that they will fail in the immediate future? No. Could circumstances change putting them at immediate risk? Yes.

WHO REALLY MANAGES THE ENTERPRISES' SYSTEMIC RISK?

Neither Enterprise has direct responsibility or motivation to manage systemic risk. The Enterprises manage interest rate, credit, market, and operations risk but they have little incentive to manage systemic risk, except to avert failure. The Enterprises have invested tremendous resources in the development of new analytical procedures and better ways to quantify many types of risk. Although each uses advances in telecommunications, computers, financial products, and so forth. to create opportunities for profit by measuring and managing its own risks (probabilities of potential losses), neither Enterprise endeavors to measure or monitor systemic risk (probabilities of potential macroeconomic losses). Of course other financial institutions such as banks and thrifts also have little incentive to monitor systemic risk.

The responsibility for managing systemic risk belongs to multiple government agencies. Agencies like the U.S. Department of Treasury, the Department of Housing and Urban Development, OFHEO, and federal and state financial bank and thrift regulators all share the responsibility to measure, monitor, and manage systemic risk. The U.S. Congress mandates that financial regulators monitor and maintain the safety and soundness of the U.S. financial system and the economy, but no agency really measures or monitors the U.S. economy's exposure to the Enterprises.

MEASURING, MONITORING, AND MANAGING ENTERPRISE SYSTEMIC RISK: AVOIDING TBTF

Financial regulators committed to an effective and efficient risk-based examination and oversight process focus their attention on the individual Enterprises.[30] OFHEO solicits Enterprise feedback to adjust its risk-based examination practices and to improve the efficiency and effectiveness of supervision activities. However, the risk-based supervision process applies primarily to Enterprise business activities and the assessments of interest rate risk, credit risk, and operations risk—the same risks estimated by the best practices at every good financial institution. Because there are no best practices when it comes to systemic risk measures, it falls to the regulators to develop such practices.[31]

OFHEO, like the FDIC, OCC, OTS, and other regulators, demands that complex financial institutions, like the Enterprises, routinely measure and quantify their earnings at risk. OFHEO, like other regulators, appropriately reviews decisions by the Enterprises in terms of how such decisions will, on the margin, affect their discounted future earnings streams, cash flows, and the volatilities of those streams and flows. From that information, estimates of systemic risk may be constructed.

POTENTIAL POLICY OPTIONS

If size and growth have indeed propelled the Enterprises to the level of systemically suspicious entities then the most prominent policy option is to observe whether the existing financial and housing markets will limit their growth and size as a normal market function. Subsidies interfere with this process, however, by muting market signals and limiting competition. Barring a market solution, OFHEO's options for Enterprise-related systemic risk fall into three general categories: (1) limit growth; (2) fragmentation; and (3) greater market discipline.

Limit Growth

Few would disagree that the Enterprises' exponential growth has propelled them into a position where they now yield an enormous concentration of political and economic power.[32] Therefore, one of the most prominent policy options for limiting systemic risk is having regulators limit unconstrained Enterprise growth.

Regulators ideally would allow those long run market forces like demographic changes, more attractive investment alternatives, and even recessions in regional housing sectors to naturally limit Enterprise growth where possible. The current level of subsidies, however, does not appear to discourage growth.

As required by the Federal Housing Enterprises Safety and Soundness Act of 1992, OFHEO has established minimum and risk-based capital standards for Fannie Mae and Freddie Mac based on conventional best practices and firm-specific financial health.[33] But these standards have not contained growth; on the contrary, they may have stimulated it. Until capital constraints become binding and OFHEO finds that one of the Enterprises is "critically undercapitalized," it is unlikely that the Enterprises' costs of capital would increase sufficiently and/or their earnings would subsequently tail off to limit growth in the current economic climate.[34]

The Enterprises' limited asset diversification, minimal core capital standards, highly leveraged derivative portfolios, and the current inability of regulators to measure the extent of systemic risk requires OFHEO to take a cautious approach to the continued growth of the Enterprises. OFHEO must begin to consider policies that would at least constrain growth until a time when empirical evidence supporting such growth was justified by market conditions.

If regulators were to consider limiting growth, they could do so by restricting debt issuance or asset growth or by stimulating Enterprise competition through elimination of some or all of their subsidies. The Treasury, for example, could refuse to permit additional debt issuance. OFHEO could require downsizing as a legitimate way to raise capital ratios. Raising capital standards by requiring the Enterprises to maintain core capital equal to 4 percent of on balance sheet assets (in contrast to the current 2.5 percent standard) would be consistent with the 4 percent minimum capital requirement for federally insured commercial banks and might also slow down Enterprise growth.

Alternatively, rather than directly trying to slow down Enterprise growth, regulators could encourage more competition in the secondary mortgage markets. Commercial banks and thrifts may now legally securitize mortgages and offer competition in the secondary mortgage markets, but have done so sparingly. Higher core capital targets for the Enterprises could eliminate the GSE advantages and increase non-GSE competition, market discipline, and more indirectly limit Enterprise growth. The Federal Home Loan Banks, another GSE, have also begun to offer the Enterprises competition in purchasing mortgages, although the extent of their inroads into the secondary mortgage market is extremely limited.

Fragmentation

A market without government intervention could have produced a system with 1,000 entities, each with $3–4 billion in assets rather than only two Enterprises with $3–4 trillion in assets, The economic failure of a few institutions out of a population of 1,000 certainly appears less onerous than the failure of a single multi-trillion dollar institution. The fact that Congress has not seen fit to fragment or break up the Enterprises heretofore does not mean that it could not or should not consider some type of fragmentation in the future.

Any policy that attempts to break up the Enterprises must deal with the fact that fragmentation could destroy economies of scale, scope, size, and so forth; threaten property rights; and result in monumental litigation. Fragmentation in the near term would likely raise the average costs of secondary mortgage market participation and might even increase the likelihood of a systemic event in the aftermath of fragmentation. Consequently, fragmentation is not necessarily the first choice among all policy options, but any policy intent on reining in systemic risk must consider the benefits and costs associated with atomizing, or fragmenting, the existing system.

Greater Market Discipline

Market discipline refers to the ability of investors to track and comprehend the changing financial condition and risk of firms and securities, to price securities accordingly, and to reward or punish the actions of management. For market discipline to exist, three conditions must be met: institutions must make appropriate public disclosures, investors must believe they are at risk for loss (the government will not absorb any losses they incur), and legal clarity exists about the conditions under which investors will incur losses and the procedures for determining their magnitude.

Regulators must insist that enterprises disclose appropriate and useful information on their financial condition and risks that allow investors to make more informed decisions than they currently make. The following comments by Federal Reserve Governor Laurence Meyer in a speech in January 2000 applies to Fannie Mae and Freddie Mac:

As large . . . institutions become increasingly complex—and fund themselves more from non-insured sources—market discipline and its prerequisite, public disclosure, must play a greater role. Indeed, increased transparency and market discipline can also help substantially to address concerns about increased systemic risk associated with ever-larger institutions and to avoid the potentially greater moral hazard associated with more intrusive supervision and regulation.[35]

Fannie Mae and Freddie Mac were exempt from the registration requirements of the Securities Act of 1933 until July 2002 when they announced that they would voluntarily comply with Securities and Exchange Commission (SEC) regulations. The original statute required all corporations issuing stock or debt securities with maturities of more than nine months to register such offerings with the SEC, disclose uniform information about the securities, and pay registration fees. They will now do so.

OFHEO could urge Congress to adopt stochastic capital standards. Neither OFHEO, nor any other regulator, can assure Congress with 100 percent certainty that capital is adequate or inadequate. OFHEO could view and report capital adequacy in a probabilistic framework. For example, OFHEO might conclude in the current quarter for example that it is 95 percent certain that capital is adequate. If OFHEO estimates of capital adequacy slips, say from 95 percent assurance in the previous quarter to say 75 percent assurance in the following quarter, then systemic risk may have increased. Markets, the Enterprises, and Congress may take note. Such a slippage might raise costs of capital and lower stock prices. The Enterprises would become subject to market discipline and have sufficient incentive to regain the 95 percent assurance level. In its current determination of capital adequacy, OFHEO makes no such distinctions and declares capital is adequate in both cases.

Imposing a mandatory subordinated debt requirement on Fannie Mae and Freddie Mac has been proposed as a way to enhance market discipline for the Enterprises.[36] The greater the perception that investors in an Enterprise's subordinated debt are at risk and the larger the outstanding volume of such obligations, the greater the potential for increased market discipline. This argument, however, is specious if the regulator has advanced a TBTF policy. If such a policy exists, the signals from subordinated debt pricing are of limited use. Only if the holders of subordinated debt believe they are at risk does the spread between the yields on those obligations and an Enterprise's senior debt include a credit risk premium that will vary with perceptions of the Enterprise's risk. The idea that fluctuations in that spread would enhance market discipline indirectly by providing signals to the government and other investors about changes in the perceived risk has no merit in the presence of TBTF. Fannie Mae and Freddie Mac began issuing a new type of subordinated debt in 2001.

Other options for improving market discipline of Fannie Mae and Freddie Mac focus on the direct interdependencies among the Enterprises and depository institutions. At mid-2001, more than 30 percent of commercial banks with assets above $1 billion had credit exposures to Fannie Mae or Freddie

Mac by virtue of their investment in either Enterprise's debt that exceeded 10 percent of the bank's equity.

Some of the largest banks also have potentially large credit exposures to Fannie Mae and Freddie Mac because they are counter parties to Enterprise financial derivatives contracts. One option would be for the OCC to make sure that any commercial bank functioning as a dealer in financial derivatives that enters into derivatives transactions with Fannie Mae or Freddie Mac establishes netting arrangements with the Enterprise and requires it to post collateral to cover any increases in the uncollateralized net positive market value of the dealer's net position. Netting arrangements between Fannie Mae and Freddie Mac and present derivatives are common; the Enterprises, however, do not post collateral to cover dealers' credit exposures. Such requirements would reduce the potential for the insolvency or illiquidity of an Enterprise to impose credits losses on a derivatives' counter party. Alternatively, Congress could authorize OFHEO to require that Enterprise OTC derivatives contracts include provisions requiring the Enterprises to post collateral when their positions have negative mark-to-market value.

Another option would be to phase out gradually the current exemption of the debt of Fannie Mae and Freddie Mac from the statutory limitation on commercial banks' investment in the investment securities of individual firms. This limitation generally limits a bank's investment in the debt obligations of any one issuer to 10 percent of the bank's unimpaired capital and surplus. Phasing the exemption out over a sufficient period of time would minimize the likelihood of any disruptions in the markets for the Enterprises' debt.

All of these options for enhancing market discipline of Fannie Mae and Freddie Mac would likely increase the Enterprises' operating costs. A mandatory subordinated debt requirement, minimum loss-sharing by investors in senior or subordinated Enterprise debt, and a gradual phase-out of the exemption of Fannie Mae and Freddie Mac from the limitation on a bank's investments in their debt would increase each Enterprise's borrowing costs, perhaps substantially. Requiring the Enterprises to post collateral to cover the credit exposures of their derivatives' counter parties would increase their cost of using financial derivatives. Both those effects would lower the profitability of the asset portfolios of Fannie Mae and Freddie Mac. The Enterprises could respond by raising the guarantee fees they charge, which could raise the interest rates on conforming fixed-rate mortgages.

Legal certainty about what will happen when financial institutions fail, however, may also help to mitigate systemic risk. Studies of systemic risk in the banking system emphasize how clear specification in advance of the postresolution treatment of depositors at failed banks can limit both the cost to taxpayers of such failures and their potential to worsen financial crises and systemic events.[37] FDIC increases certainty and limits losses to the bank insurance fund when a bank fails by promptly advancing funds to depositors before the agency, acting as a receiver, sells all of the institution's assets. As a result, insured depositors receive nearly immediate payment of their deposits at par value, and uninsured depositors receive nearly immediate payment of the present value of their pro-rata share of the estimated recovery value of the bank's assets.

Those procedures reduce the cost of funds of and lower the risk that depositors will run from financially weak banks and limit pressure by uninsured depositors for FDIC bailouts. In general, market discipline by uninsured bank depositors increases if policymakers commit to a baseline pattern of regulatory response to bank insolvency that curtails officials' discretion to protect depositors from losses.[38]

In the recent stock market repricing of dot coms, several trillion dollars changed hands without any systemic losses. One reason for the ability of the system to absorb such market corrections is that stock holders were legally certain that they did not have guarantees and that they had little choice but to absorb the ensuing losses. The ability of the financial system to absorb such losses is encouraging and the importance of legal certainty cannot be overemphasized.

Congress could revise the 1992 Act to allow OFHEO to close and appoint a receiver to manage the affairs of an insolvent Enterprise. The revised statute could specify the conditions under which Enterprise securities holders would incur losses and how those losses would be allocated. For example, policymakers could require the regulator to close an Enterprise that was critically undercapitalized and deemed insolvent. A regulator could specify that the claims of investors in an Enterprise's equity would be extinguished if the Enterprise were closed.

Congress could authorize OFHEO to impose losses on investors in the Enterprise's subordinated debt and provide that claims of investors in the Enterprise's MBS would have priority over those of investors in the Enterprise's senior debt.

Congress could direct OFHEO to administer a requirement that investors in a closed Enterprise's debt incur losses if the federal government provided financial assistance to the Enterprise. By making explicit the degree to which investors in Fannie Mae and Freddie Mac equity and debt securities are at risk, those changes in law would enhance market discipline of Fannie Mae and Freddie Mac and reduce the potential for an Enterprise insolvency to increase systemic risk. Like other options for enhancing market discipline of the Enterprises, the changes would increase their borrowing costs and could lead them to raise their guarantee fees.

CONCLUSION

This study recommends that OFHEO, the financial regulator of the Enterprises: (1) announce that neither enterprise is TBTF, embrace regulatory transparency, and refute any constructive ambiguity policy; (2) indicate that stockholders and subordinated debt holders should and will incur their share of the full resolution costs in the unlikely event of Enterprise failure; (3) explain how it intends to use its position as conservator to immediately remove the Board of Directors of a failed Enterprise and notify Congress that the Enterprise has failed; (4) encourage sufficient market discipline to provide more effective signals of systemic risk; (5) initiate a formal process of monitoring and managing systemic risk.

In an unprecedented policy option, the U.S. Department of Treasury, the Federal Reserve, and OFHEO should make a joint policy statement that the Enterprises are not too big to fail and provide a strategy for dealing with them that clearly establishes who is at risk, the nature of the risks in terms of time and magnitude, and what a coordinated group of federal regulators intends to do. This approach at regulatory disclosure simply tells the public what the regulators intend to do if either Enterprise becomes insolvent and does not contradict the implicit guarantee accorded under federal charter. Such a statement, however, is likely to elicit a healthy dose of market discipline that is likely to result in the repricing of debt and securities with some implicit constraints imposed on continued growth.

Why is now the appropriate time to consider these policy options for imposing market discipline and limiting systemic risk? The answers are simple. The Enterprises appear to be in good financial health and capable of withstanding any announcement effect that they are not too big to fail. Limits to Enterprise growth are necessary and prudent. It is far better to permit the markets to limit growth than to impose an arbitrary regulatory strategy, but existing subsidies may preclude this from occurring. Finally, regulators have learned difficult lessons during the 1980s and 1990s. They know that forbearance and too big to fail approaches have resulted in astronomical real losses emanating from financial institution failures.

NOTES

1. The names of the principal authors are withheld.

2. In September 1998, the Federal Reserve organized a rescue of Long-Term Capital Management, a very large and prominent hedge fund on the brink of failure. The Fed intervened with a TBTF policy because it was concerned about possible dire consequences for financial markets if it allowed so large a hedge fund to fail. To some, it suggested that a TBTF doctrine that the Fed should prevent the failure of large financial firms. It encourages irresponsible risk taking; and it undermines the moral authority of Fed policymakers in their efforts to encourage their counterparts in other countries to persevere with the difficult process of economic liberalization. In short, some observers believe that LTCM was yet another TBTF mistake that raises the following question: Why LTCM and not Enron, Global Crossing, and Worldcom? Enron is considered in the next chapter of this book.

3. A government TBTF policy does exist (Goodhart and Schoenmaker [1993], Santomero and Hoffman [1999]), even if it is applied anecdotally. It is characterized,

first, by the fact that certain firms are rescued while others are not (see Hughes and Mester [1993]); second, by the fact that the bailout policy is never announced ex ante. Regulators prefer to use "constructive ambiguity" rather than clear delineation of policy. The justification of the constructive ambiguity stems from an argument that the government will permit the first firm to fail but stands ready to keep the system from failing. This approach is based on the argument that free riders will be limited if uncertainty exists about who will benefit from the TBTF policy and implies that a TBTF policy may not erode all market discipline because no firm wants to be the first to fail. Unfortunately, too many bailouts have occurred historically. Although there has been a general trend toward limiting the rescue packages, rescue packages will invariably be offered to insolvent banks whose bankruptcy would have large negative externalities. Freixas (1999) examined the cost-benefit analysis of bailouts and emphasizes the need to take the social cost of bailouts into consideration. Even then, he concludes that it may be worth rescuing TBTF institutions and using a mixed strategy to decide on the smaller institutions that have complied with regulatory requirements. The regulators motives however are suspect whenever such bailouts are considered. Discrepancy between the regulators' objectives and the efficient decisions has been discussed at length, but a clear illustration is provided by Kane (1990), who contends the bailout policy followed in the savings and loan crisis was excessive and unjustified. For a similar view see Boot and Thakor (1993). The authors show regulators will always tend to implement an excessively lenient bank closure policy. Mailath and Mester (1994) emphasize the fact that the regulator's objective function may be a restriction to regulation policy. This is indeed the case as a regulator's threats have to be credible and therefore a bank will never be penalized for its past breaches of regulation if the penalty worsens the regulator's outcome. Repullo (2000) has illustrated the second point, regarding the limits set by enacted banking regulation, by examining how the delegation of the rights to close or rescue a bank could be made more efficient by making different parties responsible for the decision in different circumstances. We are, at the end, left in a world of second best, where perfect regulation is infeasible and spillover from necessary regulatory tools has deleterious effects on the equilibrium characteristics of the system.

4. Paul A. Samuelson and Herman E. Krooss, *Documentary History of Banking and Currency in the United States*, Vol. IV (New York: Chelsea House Publishers, 1983), p. 354.

5. When Alan Greenspan first reacted to the Chrysler bailout over two decades ago he said that what he feared "was not that it would fail, but that it would succeed," according to John Gordon, "History Repeats in Finance Company Bailouts," *Wall Street Journal*, October 7, 1998. Greenspan was alluding to the fact that fear and greed are two compelling forces present in markets. Each keeps the other in check. Remove the fear of failure and the greed can run amok. Yet in 1998, Mr. Greenspan arranged the bailout of Long-Term Capital Management, a $200 billion hedge fund with only $4.5 billion in assets. This highly leveraged fund had seriously misgauged its risks. Greenspan apparently felt that the short-term consequences of not bailing LTCM out would very likely have been worse than the long-term ones of doing so. Roughly 5 years later, it is unclear as to whether Greenspan reversed himself again. In his keynote address to the Bank Structure Conference, May 2002, Greenspan castigated financial markets for displaying "excessive greed." Mr. Greenspan seems

to be of two minds on this particular subject. On June 7, 1995, Greenspan answered reporters' questions during a banking conference in Seattle. Two prominent newspapers reported conflicting headlines. *The New York Times* published the following headline: "Greenspan Sees Chance of Recession." *The Washington Post* published the headline: "Recession Is Unlikely, Greenspan Concludes." When asked about the discrepancy, Greenspan laughed and called his answers at the press conference "constructive ambiguity." He clearly treats TBTF the same way, thereby preserving regulatory flexibility, avoiding the admission of regulatory failure, and appealing to every politician receiving political donations from the prospective failed entity.

6. That is, that there is a likelihood of enormous collateral economic and financial damage associated with the failure of a large financial institution.

7. The failure of any firm, however painful to its stockholders, employees, and creditors, ultimately entails the passing of its assets into other more efficient hands, even if the local, regional, or even national economy were to suffer. TBTF does not, by definition, pass assets into more efficient hands.

8. Alan Greenspan, May 2000, Keynote Address, Federal Reserve Bank of Chicago Bank Structure Conference: "There are many that hold the *misperception* [author's italics] that some American financial institutions are too big to fail. I can certainly envision that in times of crisis the financial implosion of a large intermediary could exacerbate the situation. Accordingly, the monetary and supervisory authorities would doubtless endeavor to manage an orderly liquidation of the failed entity, including the unwinding of its positions. But shareholders would not be protected and I would anticipate appropriate discounts or haircuts for other than federally guaranteed liabilities."

9. Bert Ely, 2002.

10. Walter Bagehot, *Lombard Street: A Description of the Money Market* (London: Kegan, Paul & Co., 1873).

11. As former president of the Federal Reserve Bank of New York, Gerald Corrigan (1991, p. 3), has noted: "More than anything else, it is the systemic risk phenomenon with banking and financial institutions that makes them different from gas stations and furniture stores. Indeed, there appears to be little fear of contagion and systemic risk in most other, nonfinancial sectors of more or less equal importance, such as automobiles, computers, transportation, and even agriculture (food)."

12. Kindleberger (1978); Minsky (1967, 1977); B. Friedman (1991); H. Kaufman (1986); Flood and Barber (1982); Blanchard and Watson (1982); Goodfriend and King (1988); Todd (1988); Meltzer (1982); Gutentag and Herring (1988); Calomiris and Gorton (1991); Miskin (1991); Glosten and Milgrom (1985); Davis (1992); and Krugman (1991) provide rationales for systemic risk that range from asset bubbles to asymmetric information. Irving Fisher (1933) first linked the financial institutions to real output losses in the height of the Great Depression. John Gurley and Edward Shaw (1955), tie financial intermediation to real economic growth. They insist that the role of money stock diminishes in importance as the flow of credit becomes more binding. They focus on "financial capacity" and linked credit demand and supply to real output. In the Gurley-Shaw (GS) world, "financial capacity" limits the supply of credit, which limits economic growth.

13. William Poole, President, Federal Reserve Bank of St. Louis, "Financial Stability," (The Council of State Governments, Southern Legislative Conference Annual Meeting New Orleans, Louisiana, Aug. 4, 2002), on three reasons why GSEs present

a systemic threat: "First, the GSEs are certainly large. In the United States today, GSE securities and government-related mortgage pool securities outstanding, excluding deposits, exceed the total outstanding securities issued by all—I repeat, all—other private financial sector firms taken together. Fannie Mae and Freddie Mac alone, as of last December 31, had securities outstanding of $1.3 trillion and had guaranteed another $1.8 trillion of mortgage-backed securities (MBS). Looked at another way, the total of GSE direct and guaranteed debt is 40 percent larger than the federal government's debt. That debt, which we loosely call the national debt, has, of course, been a matter of considerable discussion in recent years in the debates about federal deficits and surpluses. Second, although financial experts understand the vulnerability, my judgment is that too few in the markets and in government understand the issues. Consequently, if there is ever a problem, it will take many by surprise. Third, there is tremendous ambiguity about the status of the GSEs. The market prices GSE debt as if there is a federal guarantee, or a high probability of a guarantee, standing behind the debt. Yet, there is no explicit guarantee in the law."

14. Glenn Hoggarth, Ricardo Reiss, and Victoria Saporta (2001), "Costs of Banking System Instability: Some Empirical Evidence" (Bank of England Working Papers EC2R 8AH) estimate that banking crises over the last two decades in 21 countries produced economic losses that averaged 15–20% of GDP. Gerald Caprio and Dorothy Klingebiel (1999) document 100 episodes of systemic crises worldwide in recent history ("Bank Insolvencies: Cross Country Experience," World Bank Policy and Research Working Papers 1574). The IMF reports 130 financial crises among IMF members since 1985 in "Financial Crises: Characteristics and Indicators of Vulnerability" (May 1998, Chapter 4, World Economic Outlook). Olivier DeBandt and Phillip Hartmann (2000), "Systemic Risk: A Survey" (European Central Bank Working Paper Series No. 35) cite more than 300 journal articles and publications in their survey of recent systemic risk literature. Central Banks, the IMF, the World Bank, the Group of 30, and various financial regulatory institutions sponsored the majority of these citations. With few exceptions, the majority of papers expressed the view that systemic risk is a serious concern.

15. Borio (1995), for example, views payment systems as a major source of systemic risk. He suggests that payment systems' risks must have increased substantially with trillions of dollars flowing through payment systems daily. Any interruption of such a cash flow would have immediate consequences on the financial sectors. In the United States, firms have become more dependent on the Fedwire System, the Clearing House Interbank Payments system, and the Automated Clearing House, which have each become considerably more complex than in the past. Recall that the failure of Banhaus Herstatt in 1974 precipitated the costly gridlock of a European payments system that was so onerous that it actually led to the creation of the original Basel Committee on Banking! Eisenbies (1995) notes that when BCCI (Bank of Credit and Commerce International) failed in 1991, individual institutions lost millions of dollars because of payment system failures. In the early 1990s, a simple computer glitch required an overnight extension of loans to one national bank of $22.6 billion.

16. Minsky argues that events in financial markets affect real investment by affecting the subjective valuations placed on the assets constituting the investments. A rise in the subjective value of investment leads to a decline in the money price of capital and

financial assets, which are valued mainly for their ability to affect future income. A fall in these prices lowers the difference between the price of capital asset and the supply prices of investment output; which in turn lowers investment. A fall in the price of financial assets means that the investing units will have to pledge larger future payments in order to obtain a given amount of investment financing. Such a change in terms of financing will constrain investment. A financial crisis leads into an economic crisis when investment declines so that a decline in profits as well as output, employment, and wages takes place. The decline in profits leads to both a further fall in asset values and a further decline in the ability of units to meet their financial commitments. Further declines in employment, output, wage incomes, and profits follow where a sharp fall in commitments for financing of investment takes place.

17. Lindgren, Carl-Johan, Gillian Garcia, and Matthew Saal, *Bank Soundness and Macroeconomic Policy* (Washington, D.C., International Monetary Fund [IMF], 1996).

18. In one of the few studies available that attempted to quantify the effects of the S&L Crisis on the U.S. Economy, George Iden and Joyce Manchester, 1992, *The Economic Effects of the Savings and Loan Crisis, A CBO Study* (January 1992) estimates resolution costs and tax payer exposures. They also estimate a 3 multiplier associated with taxpayer losses. That is, the resolutions costs and taxpayer exposures amounted to roughly $150 billion, but they estimated that lost GDP losses attributable to the thrift crises exceed $500 billion (real) using the McKibbin-Saks Model of The Brooking Institution.

19. Alan Greenspan, "Technology Boosts Market Risk," 15th Annual Monetary Conference of the Cato Institute, 14 October 1997.

20. In his address before the Council of State Governments, William Poole (2002), President, Federal Reserve Bank of St. Louis, honestly noted "In the case of the GSEs, the massive scale of their liabilities could create a massive problem in the credit markets. If the market value of GSE debt were to fall sharply, because of ambiguity about the financial soundness of GSEs and about the willingness of the federal government to backstop the debt, what would happen? I do not know, and neither does anyone else."

21. Whalen and Bartholomew (1995) conclude: "Considering the extensive economic and financial literature on banking and related monetary topics, and the various public policy discussions that have followed the notable financial calamities of the past two centuries, it is rather incredible that few authors have offered an actual definition of the term 'systemic risk' and that there is little consensus on what comprises a 'systemic event.'" Common definitions of systemic risk include the following:

- Greenspan (1995), providing a keynote address in an OCC Conference on systemic risk, acknowledges, "its [systemic risk's] definition is still somewhat unsettled." He suggests that systemic risk "is . . . a propensity for some sort of significant financial system disruption."
- Bank of International Settlements Promisel Report (1992) defines systemic risk as "the risk that a disruption at a firm in a market segment, or to a settlement system, etc. will cause widespread difficulties at other firms, in other market segments or in the financial system as a whole."
- Davis (1992) defines systemic risk as "the probability of a financial crisis . . . a

major collapse of the financial system, entailing inability to provide payment services or to allocate capital; realization of systemic risk."

- Whalen and Bartholomew (1995) define systemic risk as the "likelihood of a sudden, usually unexpected, collapse of confidence in a significant portion of the
banking or financial system with potentially large real economic effects."

- Bentson (1994); Benston and Kaufman (1994); and Carnell (1994) emphasize that
the *size* of losses must be taken into account and contagion is a necessary element
in a systemic event. Technically, they all suggest that some threshold amount of
losses must be part of the definition that appears as "a collapse in confidence that
precedes a systemic event."

- Mishkin (1995) defines systemic risk as "the likelihood of a sudden, usually unexpected, event that disrupts information in financial markets, making them unable to effectively channel funds to those parties with the most productive
opportunities."

- Lacker (1998) defines systemic risk as "the risk that significant financial distress
occurs at a significant number of institutions at the same time and seems causally
related."

Reviewing these definitions we define systemic risk as the conditional probability
that the financial system could adversely and significantly affect real output. Kaufman
(1999) makes a distinction between rational or information-based systemic risk and
irrational, non-information-based, random, or "pure" contagious systemic risk (Kaufman, 1994; Kaminsky and Reinhart, 1998). He defines rational or informed contagion
as a phenomena in which investors (depositors) can rationally differentiate among
parties on the basis of their market fundamentals. Random contagion, based on actions
by uninformed agents, is viewed as more frightening and dangerous as it does not
differentiate among parties, impacting innocent as well as guilty parties, and is therefore likely to be both broader and more difficult to contain.

22. Richard Carnell, former Assistant Secretary of Treasury, "Reforming the Regulation of Fannie Mae and Freddie Mac," before the Subcommittee on Capital Markets,
Insurance, and Government Sponsored Enterprises Committee on Financial Services,
U.S. House of Representatives, July 11, 2001, testified before the Subcommittee on
HR 1409 that the Enterprises did indeed represent a systemic threat and supported a
strengthening of OFHEO's regulatory authority. Carnell examines the GSEs with
respect to systemic risk and notes "FNM and FRE are often characterized as too big
to fail . . . meaning that the government would be forced to rescue them lest their
failure unleash 'systemic risk' that would harm the nation's financial system and
economy. . . . If investors expect the government to rescue troubled GSEs, the investors
will tend to let GSEs take greater risks than they otherwise would have taken. This
weakening of market discipline on the GSEs will, in turn increase the risk that the
GSEs ultimately will get into trouble. . . . too big to fail and systemic risk . . . become
self-fulfilling prophecies" (p. iii).

23. The Federal Housing Enterprises Financial Safety and Soundness Act of 1992
("the 1992 Act") require the Enterprises to support several broad public policy purposes. Specifically, the charters authorize Fannie Mae and Freddie Mac to

1. Provide stability in the secondary market for residential mortgages
2. Respond appropriately to private capital markets

3. Provide ongoing assistance to the secondary market for residential mortgages (including activities relating to mortgages on housing for low- and moderate-income families involving a reasonable economic return that may be less than the return earned on other activities) by increasing mortgage investment liquidity and improving the distribution of capital available for residential mortgage financing

4. Promote access to mortgage credit nationwide by increasing mortgage invest-ment liquidity and improving the distribution of capital available for residential mortgage financing

Each Enterprise is privately owned, issues stock traded on the New York Stock Exchange, and operates as a unitary firm on a nationwide basis. In July 2002 they agreed to comply voluntarily with SEC disclosure requirements.

The 1992 Act gives the Secretary of Housing and Urban Development (HUD) general regulatory authority over the Enterprises, including the power to issue regu-lations necessary to ensure that they carry out their public mission. The Secretary also sets, monitors, and enforces affordable housing goals that require each Enterprise to devote a proportion of its mortgage purchases to loans that finance housing that is affordable to very low-, low-, and moderate-income households and geographically underserved areas. In addition, the Secretary has specific fair lending responsibilities with respect to the Enterprises.

The act also established Office of Federal Housing Enterprise Oversight (OFHEO) as the regulator of the Enterprises. OFHEO conducts examinations and provides reg-ulatory supervision and oversight for the two enterprises.

24. The principal payment and settlement systems used by Fannie Mae and Freddie Mac are the Fedwire Funds Transfer and Fedwire Securities Transfer Systems, elec-tronic transfer systems operated by the Federal Reserve System that enable financial institutions to transfer funds and book-entry securities. The Enterprises are among the major users of Fedwire. While the number of daily Fedwire transactions by Fannie Mae and Freddie Mac is relatively small, each Enterprise's daily dollar volume is substantial.

Fedwire links more than 9,000 institutions with the Federal Reserve Banks, allowing the movement of balances among correspondent banks and enabling those banks to transfer funds on behalf of their customers. In 2001, Fedwire made some 112.4 million fund transfers, with a total value of approximately $424 trillion and an average value per transfer of $3.77 million. Transfers on behalf of bank customers include funds used to make deposits and other large-scale, time-sensitive payments. All funds transfers are immediate, final, and irrevocable when processed. The Federal Reserve's extension of credit to make such payments is generally perceived to be part of the federal financial safety net.

The Federal Reserve has policies to reduce the risks to the Federal Reserve Banks, the banking system, and others posed by Fedwire and other payment systems. The Federal Reserve imposes limits on the size of Fedwire transactions and limits on neg-ative positions in an institution's Fedwire account at any time during a business day. Fannie Mae and Freddie Mac each maintain multiple accounts at the Federal Reserve. A "General" account is used for funds transfer and certain other Fedwire activities. A "Principal and Interest" account is used to process the regularly scheduled payment of principal and interest on securities and the original issue of Enterprise securities.

Each Enterprise is subject to a transactions on its General Account, and typically pays relatively modest amounts annually for daylight overdrafts on that account, but is not subject to such fees on its Principal and Interest (P&I) account. The Federal Reserve Board noted in 1994 that most Enterprise daylight overdrafts were related to the regular payment of principal and interest on securities issued by the Enterprises through the Federal Reserve. Reducing those overdrafts could require a delay until later in the day in the making of Enterprise principal and interest payments, which could have the effect of increasing the size and duration of daylight overdrafts of depository institutions that receive corresponding credits. To avoid that outcome, the Board instituted a policy, which remains in effect, that exempts Enterprise P&I accounts from daylight overdraft restrictions. Board of Governors of the Federal Reserve System, "Interpretation of the Payments System Risk Reduction policy: Daylight Overdrafts of Government Sponsored Enterprises," Federal Register, May 13, 1994.

25. The federal agency credit market is the market in which the debt of federal agencies, such as the Postal Service and the Tennessee Valley Authority and GSEs such as Fannie Mae and Freddie Mac, and MBS issued or guaranteed by the Government National Mortgage Association (Ginnie Mae) are issued and traded.

26. Carnell (2001) agrees with CBO and suggests that the government's perceived implicit backing of FNM and FRE "actually provide a greater net subsidy than FDIC insurance." He lists six structural reasons: (1) unlimited coverage of all GSE obligations; (2) no clear receivership mechanism (no regulatory authority to force a resolution in the event of failure; (3) no cross-guarantees to protect taxpayers (a $2 billion line of credit with the Treasury); (4) until July 2002, freedom from SEC regulation; (5) limited competition by virtue of charter; (6) not having to pay comparable insurance fees.

27. Economists have sought to quantify the net-subsidies that Fannie Mae and Freddie Mac enjoy by virtue of their government charters. A recent study compared the yields on general obligation, non-callable Enterprise debt issued in the 1995–1999 period to those on similar instruments issued by non-GSE financial institutions. B.W. Ambrose, and A. Warga, "An Update on Measuring GSE Funding Advantages," (unpublished paper prepared for the Congressional Budget Office, November 2000) found that the spreads between those yields ranged from 43 to 60 basis points, with an un-weighted average of 49 basis points. Those savings are attributable only to the perception of an implicit federal guarantee of the Enterprises' obligations, their liquidity, and the lower amount of capital that banks are required to maintain against the obligations. The Congressional Budget Office and the Department of the Treasury have concluded that the cost savings enjoyed by Fannie Mae and Freddie Mac constitutes federal subsidies. See U.S. Department of the Treasury, *Government Sponsorship of the Federal National Mortgage Association and the Federal Home Loan Mortgage Corporation* (Washington, D.C.: Government Printing Office, 1996); and U.S. Congressional Budget Office, *Assessing the Public Costs and Benefits of Fannie Mae and Freddie Mac* (Washington, D.C.: Government Printing Office, 1996), and *Federal Subsidies and the Housing GSEs* (Washington, D.C.: Government Printing Office, 2001). The Enterprises dispute that view, but independent economists generally concur. See, for example, E.J. Kane, "Housing Finance GSEs: Who Gets the Subsidy," *Journal of Financial Services Research* 15, no. 3 (2001): 197–209; and R. Feldman, "Estimating and Managing the Federal Subsidy of Fannie Mae and Freddie Mac: Is Either Task Pos-

sible? *Journal of Public Budgeting, Accounting and Financial Management* 11, 1 (2002): 81–116.

28. In their responses to an OFHEO inquiry for public comments with respect to systemic risk in 2001, Fannie Mae asserts "far from being a source of systemic risk, Fannie Mae operates to stabilize the financial markets in which it operates. . . . regardless of which definition [of systemic risk] is applied, Fannie Mae does not pose systemic risk." Freddie Mac states that "[it] is the least likely of large financial institutions to cause significant financial disruptions. . . . Our credit risk, interest-rate risk, capital management and disclosure practices make Freddie Mac strong and well managed." For a complete review of all the public comments solicited by OFHEO on systemic risk please refer to the OFHEO Web site http://www.ofheo.gov/.

29. Multi-class MBSs outstanding, primarily REMICs, are re-securitizations of single-class MBSs and, thus, are a subset of total MBSs outstanding.

30. Each quarter, the OFHEO examination staff updates conclusions relating to more than 150 separate components of financial safety and soundness. These conclusions pertain to such key risk management areas as credit risk, interest rate risk, liquidity management, information technology, internal controls, business process controls, internal and external audit, management information and process, and board of director governance and activities. OFHEO examiners meet frequently with management to discuss and assess business strategies and plans, financial performance results, risk management framework and practices, and each Enterprise's overall risk profile. These discussions include future trends and management's controls and practices to anticipate and prepare for potentially adverse trends in any risk area or combination of risk areas. Examination teams identify opportunities for improvements in existing Enterprise risk management practices and work directly with management to address identified opportunities to enhance financial safety and soundness. Through the risk-focused examination framework, OFHEO constantly evaluates such critical areas as:

1. The Enterprises' overall risk management strategies and practices;
2. The composition, risk profile, and significant trends in their retained, and guaranteed, mortgage portfolios;
3. The Enterprises' ability to effectively manage interest rate risk and other key financial exposures;
4. The Enterprises' ability to efficiently issue debt and hedge financial exposures, and effectively manage liquidity; and
5. The quality of financial performance and the quality of information on which the Enterprises' boards and management rely in reaching key business and risk management decisions

31. The monitoring and measurement process must be geared to measuring the likelihood of failure and Enterprise wide risk, estimating the extent of collateral damage to taxpayers, other financial and nonfinancial institutions and innocent parties in the unlikely event of financial duress or failure.

32. Michael Farrel, Annual Mortgage, "[the Enterprises] are about as central to the American Capital markets as the Treasury Department." *American Banker*, September 2, 2002, p. 8.

33. FHEO uses those standards to classify each Enterprise at least quarterly into

one of four capital classifications ("adequately capitalized," "undercapitalized," "significantly undercapitalized," and "critically undercapitalized") based on the level of capital maintained by that Enterprise. Estimates of capital adequacy are obtained using a discounted cash flow analysis of capital under stress. From this off-site analytical approach OFHEO developed its minimum and risk-based capital standards.

34. Peter Barta, *Wall Street Journal*, August 6, 2002. "Fannie and Freddie have already gotten all the low-hanging fruit," says James Bianco, president of Bianco Research in Chicago. Research firm Fulcrum Global Partners argued in a report earlier this year that Fannie and Freddie face "the mathematical inevitability of market saturation," in part because of the difficulty in finding new, untapped pockets of new homeowners nationwide. They face an eventual future of slower growth and decreasing profit margins, said the report, and "we believe the only quibble is over the exact timing." Not everyone agrees however. Barta reports that "Donald Gher, chief investment officer of money manager Coldstream Capital Management in Bellevue, Wash., calls the possibility of slower growth 'the critical issue for these companies' but believes it could be five to 10 years before their growth slows." Fannie Mae Chief Economist David Berson concurs and expects U.S. mortgage debt outstanding to grow even faster this decade than its 7%-a-year pace in the 1990s. According to Barta, Berson projects such debt at between $11.5 trillion and $14 trillion by 2010, compared with about $6 trillion now.

35. Lawrence Meyer, "Prudential Supervision: What Works and What Doesn't," *National Bureau of Economic Research Conference*, Islamorada, Florida, January 14, 2000, p. 2. Meyer believes that better market discipline could provide better signals so that large firms could avoid getting into trouble. This of course does not lower the probability of a systemic event and may even hasten it. Moreover, Meyer does not like intrusive regulations including artificial capital constraints and examiner directives based upon rules of thumb.

36. See E. L. Golding, "Regulating the Secondary Mortgage Market," *Secondary Mortgage Markets* (Freddie Mac, Fall 1990), 3–6; and U.S. Congressional Budget Office, *Controlling the Risks of Government-Sponsored Enterprises* (Washington, D.C.: Congressional Budget Office, April 1991), 55–58.

37. G. G. Kaufman and S. A. Seelig, "Post-Resolution Treatment of Depositors at Failed Banks: Implications for the Severity of Banking Crises, Systemic Risk, and Too-Big-to-Fail" (Chicago, IL: Federal Reserve Bank of Chicago, Working Paper 2000–16, November 2000).

38. E. J. Kane, "Using Disaster Planning to Optimize Expenditures on Financial Safety Nets," *Atlantic Economic Journal*, 29, no. 3 (September 2001), 1–11

REFERENCES

Acharya, V. 2001, January. "A Theory of Systemic Risk and Design of Prudential Bank Regulation." Working Paper, Department of Finance, Stern School of Business, New York University.

Ambrose, B. W., and Warga, A. 2001. "An Update on Measuring GSE Funding Advantages." Unpublished paper prepared for the U.S. Congressional Budget Office.

Avery, R. B., Belton, T. M., and Goldberg, M. A. 1988. "Market Discipline in Regulating Bank Risk: New Evidence from the Capital Markets." *Journal of Money, Credit, and Banking* 20: 597–610.

Baer, H., and Klingebiel, D. 1995. "Systemic Risk When Depositors Bear Losses." In *Research in Financial Services*, ed. G. Kaufman, 7:195–302. Greenwich, CT: JAI Press.

Bagehot, W. Lombard. 1873. *Street: A Description of the Money Market*. London: Kegan, Paul & Co.

Bank for International Settlements. 1994, September. "Public Disclosure of Market and Credit Risks by Financial Intermediaries." Basel, Switzerland.

Bank for International Settlements. 1994, June. *Annual Report, 1993–1994*. Basel, Switzerland.

Bank for International Settlements. 1997a. "G10 Report on Financial Stability in Emerging Market Economies." Basel, Switzerland.

Bank for International Settlements. 1997b. "Real-time Gross Settlement Systems: A Report Prepared by the Committee on Payment and Settlement Systems of the Central Banks of the G10 Countries." Basel, Switzerland.

Bank for International Settlements. 1998. "Report of the Working Group on Strengthening Financial Systems." Basel, Switzerland.

Barth, J., Brumbaugh, D., and Litan, R. 1990. "Banking Industry in Turmoil: A Report on the Condition of the U.S. Banking Industry and the Bank Insurance Fund," Testimony before the U.S. House of Representatives, Committee on Banking, Finance, and Urban Affairs. Washington, D.C.

Bartholomew, P. 1991. *Budgetary Treatment of Deposit Insurance a Framework for Reform: A CBO Study*. Washington, D.C.: Congressional Budget Office.

Bartholomew, P. 1998. "Banking Consolidation and Systemic Risk" *Brookings-Wharton Papers on Financial Services*. Washington, D.C.: The Brookings Institution Press.

Bartholomew, P., and Whalen, G. 1995. "Fundamentals of Systemic Risk." In *Research in Financial Services: Banking Financial Markets and Systemic Risk*, ed. G. Kaufman, 3–18. Greenwich, CT: JAI Press.

Benston, G. 1994. "International Harmonization of Banking Regulations." *Journal of Financial Services Research* 8: 205–25.

Benston, G., and Kaufman, G. 1988. *Risk and Solvency Regulation of Depository Institutions: Past Policies and Current Options*. New York: Salomon Brothers Center, Graduate School of Business, New York University.

Benston, G., and Kaufman, G. 1994a. "The Intellectual History of the Federal Deposit Insurance Corporation Improvement Act of 1991." In *Reforming Financial Institutions and Markets in the United States*, ed. G. Kaufman, 1–17. Boston: Kluwer Academic Publishers.

Benston, G., and Kaufman, G. 1994b. "Improving the FDIC Improvement Act." In *Reforming Financial Institutions and Markets in the United States*, ed. G. Kaufman, 99–120. Boston: Kluwer Academic Publishers.

Benston, G., and Kaufman, G. 1995. "Is the Banking and Payments System Fragile?" *Journal of Financial Services Research* 9: 209–40.

Benston, G., and Kaufman, G. 1996. "The Appropriate Role of Bank Regulation." *Economic Journal* 106: 688–97.

Benston, G., and Kaufman, G. 1998. "Deposit Insurance Reform in the FDIC Improvement Act: The Experience to Date." *Federal Reserve Bank of Chicago*, second quarter, vol. 22(2): 2–20.

Benston, G., Brumbaugh, Jr., D., Guttentag, J., Herring, R., Kaufman, G., Litan, R., and Scott, K. 1989. *Blueprint for Restructuring America's Financial Institutions.* Washington, D.C.: The Brookings Institution.

Benston, G., Eisenbeis, R., Horvitz, P., Kane, E., and Kaufman, G. 1986. *Perspectives on Safe and Sound Banking.* Cambridge: MIT Press.

Berger, A., and Davies, S. 1994. "The Information Content of Bank Examinations." *Proceedings, Conference on Bank Structure and Competition, Federal Reserve Bank of Chicago.* Chicago.

Berger, A., Davies, S., and Flannery, M. 1998, March. "Comparing Market and Regulatory Assessments of Bank Performance: Who Knows What When?" Working paper, Federal Reserve Board.

Bernanke, B., and Gertler, M. 1995. "Inside the Black Box: The Credit Channel of Monetary Policy Transmission." *Journal of Economic Perspectives*, 9 (Autumn): 27–48.

Black, F. 1995. "Hedging, Speculation, and Systemic Risk." *Journal of Derivatives* 2:6–8.

Blanchard, O., and Watson, M. 1982. "Bubbles, Rational Expectations and Financial Markets." In *Crises in Economic and Financial Structure*, ed. P. Wachtel, 295–315. Lexington, MA: Lexington Books.

Boot, A., and Thakor, A. 1993. "Self-Interested Bank Regulation." *The American Economic Review* 82 (2): 206–12.

Bordo, M. 1986. "Financial Crises, Banking Crises, Stock Market Crashes and the Money Supply: Some International Evidence, 1870–1933." In *Financial Crises and the World Banking System*, ed. F. Capie and G. E. Wood, 190–248. London: MacMillan.

Bordo, M. 1990, January/February. "The Lender of Last Resort: Alternative Views and Historical Experience." *Federal Reserve Bank of Richmond Economic Review*, 18–29.

Borio, C. 1995. "Payment and Settlement Systems: Trends and Risk Management." In *Research in Financial Services: Banking, financial Markets and Systemic Risk*, ed. G. Kaufman, 87–110. Greenwich, CT: JAI Press.

Brinkmann, E., Horvitz, P., and Huang, Y. 1996. "Forbearance: An Empirical Analysis." *Journal of Financial Services Research* 10: 27–42.

Calomiris, C., and Gorton, G. 1991. "The Origins of Banking Panics: Models, Facts and Bank Regulation." In *Financial Markets and Financial Crises*, ed. G. R. Hubbard, 107–73. Chicago: University of Chicago Press.

Calomiris, C., and Mason, J. R. 1997. "Contagion and Bank Failures During the Great Depression: The June 1932 Chicago Banking Panic." *American Economic Review*, 87: 863–83.

Caprio, Jr., G., and Klingebiel, D. 1995. "Dealing with Bank Insolvencies: Cross Country Experience." Working Paper, World Bank.

Caprio, Jr., G., and Klingebiel, D. 1999. "Bank Insolvencies: Cross Country Experience." Working Papers, World Bank Policy and Research: 1574.

Carnell, R. 1992. "A Partial Antidote to Perverse Incentives: Implementing the FDIC Improvement Act of 1991." In *Rebuilding Public Confidence Through Financial Reform*, 31–51. Columbus: College of Business, Ohio State University.

Carnell, R. 2001. "Reforming the Regulation of Fannie Mae and Freddie Mac." Before
   the Subcommittee on Capital Markets, Insurance, and Government Sponsored
   Enterprises Committee on Financial Services, U.S. House of Representatives
   on HR 1409.

Christian Science Monitor, 2002. "Reforming Fannie and Freddie." 29 April.

Conover, C. 1984. "Testimony." *Inquiry Into the Continental Illinois Corp. and Continental
   Illinois National Bank: Hearing Before the Subcommittee on Financial Institutions
   Supervision, Regulation, and Insurance of the Committee on Banking, Finance and
   Urban Affairs*, 98–111. U.S. House of Representatives, 98th Cong., 2nd Session,
   18–19 September and 4 October.

Corrigan, G. 1990. Statement Before U.S. Senate Committee on Banking, Housing
   and Urban Affairs, Washington, D.C.

Corrigan, G. 1991. "The Banking-Commerce Controversy Revisited." *Quarterly Review* (Federal Reserve Bank of New York) 16: 1–13.

Crenshaw, A. 1996. "CBO Faults Subsidies for 2 Finance Firms." *Washington Post* 30
   May: D9.

Crockett, A. 1996. "The Theory and Practice of Financial Stability." *Economist* 144
   (4): 531–68.

Davies, H. 1997. "Financial Regulation: Why, How and by Whom?" *Bank of England
   Quarterly Bulletin* February: 107–12.

Davies, H. 2001. "Capital Requirements and Crisis Prevention Policies." *Banks and
   Systemic Risk Conference*, Bank of England, 25 May.

Davis, E. 1992. *Debt, Financial Fragility and Systemic Risk*. Oxford: Oxford University
   Press.

DeAngelo, H., and DeAngelo, L. 1990. "Dividend Policy and Financial Distress."
   Journal of Finance 45: 1415–31.

DeBandt, O., and Hartmann, P. 1998, November. "What is Systemic Risk Today?"
   *Risk Measurement and Systemic Risk: Proceedings of the Second Joint Central Bank
   Research Conference*, Bank of Japan, 37–84.

Dickinson, A., Peterson, D., and Christiansen, W. 1991. "An Empirical Investigation
   into the Failure of the First Republic Bank: Is There a Contagion Effect?"
   Financial Review Summer: 303–18.

Dimson, E., and Marsh, P. 1995. "Capital Requirements for Securities Firms." *Journal
   of Finance* 50: 821–51.

Eisenbeis, R. 1995. "Private Sector Solutions to Payment System Fragility." *Journal of
   Financial Services Research* 9: 327–50.

Ely, B. 2002., Ely Associates Response to OFHEO inquiry on Systemic Risk. England,
   Issue 7, November.

Erdman, P. 1996. "The Day the Check Wasn't in the Mail." *Washington Post National
   Weekly Edition*: 24–35.

Federal Deposit Insurance Corporation. 1995. *1994 Annual Report*, Washington, D.C.

Federal Deposit Insurance Corporation. 1998a. *History of the Eighties: Lessons for the
   Future*. Vols. I and II. Washington, D.C.: FDIC.

Federal Deposit Insurance Corporation. 1998b. "Continental Illinois and TBTF." *History of the Eighties: Lessons for the Future*, Chap. 7. Washington, D.C.: FDIC.

Federal Deposit Insurance Corporation. 1998c. "Managing the Crisis: The FDIC and
   the RTC Experience." Washington, D.C.: FDIC.

Federal Deposit Insurance Corporation. 2000a. "A Brief History of Deposit Insurance." Washington, D.C.: FDIC.

Federal Deposit Insurance Corporation. 2000b. "Deposit Insurance: an Annotated Bibliography 1989–1999." Washington, D.C.: FDIC.

Federal Deposit Insurance Corporation. 2000c. "Deposit Insurance: Options Paper." Washington, D.C.: FDIC.

Federal Deposit Insurance Corporation. 2001. "Recommendations for Deposit Insurance Reform." Washington, D.C.: FDIC.

Feldman, R., 2002. "Estimating and Managing the Federal Subsidy of Fannie Mae and Freddie Mac: Is Either Task Possible?" *Journal of Public Budgeting, Accounting and Financial Management* 11 (1): 81–116.

Feldman, R., and Rolnick, A. 1997. "Fixing FDICIA: A Plan to Address the Too-Big-To-Fail Problem." *1997 Annual Report.* Minneapolis: Federal Reserve Bank of Minneapolis.

Flannery, M. 1988. "Payments System Risk and Public Policy." In *Restructuring Banking and Financial Services in America*, ed. W. S. Haraf and R. M. Kushmeider, 261–87. Washington, D.C.: American Enterprise Institute.

Flannery, M. 1995. "Prudential Regulation for Banks." In *Financial Stability in a Changing Environment*, ed. K. Sawamoto, Z. Nakajima, and H. Taguchi, 281–318. New York: St. Martin's Press.

Flannery, M. 1996. "Financial Crises, Payment System Problems and Discount Window Lending." *Journal of Money, Credit and Banking* 28: 804–24.

Flood, R., and Garber, P. 1985. "Bubbles, Runs and Gold Monetization." In *Crises in Economic and Financial Structure*, ed. P. Wachtel, 275–293. Lexington MA: Lexington Books.

FMwatch. 2000. "America's Second Mortgage: Skyrocketing Housing GSE Debt." *FMwatch*, 26 April.

Follet, K. 1994. *A Dangerous Fortune.* New York: Dell Publishing.

Fox, J. 1995. "Banks Say Too Much Capital Required by Market Risk Rules." *American Banker,* 22 September: 3.

Freixas, X. 1999. "LOLR Review of the Literature." *Financial Stability Review* 7:151–166.

Freixas, X. 1999. "Optimal Bail Out Policy, Conditionality and Creative Ambiguity." mimeo, Bank of England.

Freixas, X., Parigi, B., and Rochet, J. C. 1998a. "Systemic Risk, Interbank Relations and Liquidity Provision by the Central Bank." mimeo, IDEI.

Freixas, X., Parigi, B., and Rochet, J. C. 1998b. "The Lender of Last Resort: A Theoretical Foundation." mimeo, IDEI.

Friedman, B. 1991. *The Risk of Financial Crisis*, ed. M. Feldstein. Chicago: University of Chicago Press.

Friedman, M., and Schwartz, A. 1963. *A Monetary History of the United States, 1867–1960.* Princeton: Princeton University Press.

Garcia, G. 1995. "Comparing and Confronting Recent Banking Problems in Foreign Countries." Working Paper, International Monetary Fund.

Garcia, G., and Plautz, E. 1988. *The Federal Reserve: Lender of Last Resort.* Cambridge, MA: Ballinger.

Gawith, P. 1996. "Bankers Clash Clearing Plan Over Global." *Financial Times* 27 March: 5.

Gertler, M. 1988. "Financial Structure and Aggregate Economic Activity: and Overview." *Journal of Money Credit and Banking*, 20 (3).

Glosten, J., and Milgrom, P. 1985. "Bid, Ask, and Transaction Prices in Specialist Market with Heterogenously Informed Traders." *Journal of Financial Economics* March: 71–100.

Golding, E. 1990. "Regulating the Secondary Mortgage Market." *Secondary Mortgage Markets.* Freddie Mac, Fall: 3–6.

Goodfriend, M., and King, R. 1988."Financial Deregulation, Monetary Policy and Central Banking." *Federal Reserve Bank of Richmond Economic Review* 74 (3).

Goodfriend, M., and Lacker, J. M. 1999. "Limited Commitment and Central Bank Lending." Working paper, Federal Reserve Bank of Richmond: 99–102.

Goodhart, C. 1995. *The Central Bank* and *the Financial System.* Cambridge: MIT Press.

Goodhart, C. 1999. "Myths About the Lender of Last Resort." *International Finance* 2:3.

Goodhart, C., and Schoenmaker, D. 1993. "A Comment on Financial Services Regulation—Making the Two-Tier System Work." *FMG Special Papers Financial Markets Group and ESRC.* (RePEc:fmg:fmgsps:sp0056).

Gordon, J. 1998. "History Repeats in Finance Company Bailouts." *Wall Street Journal* 7 October.

Gorton, G. 1988. "Banking Panics and Business Cycles." *Oxford Economic Papers* 40: 751–81.

Gorton, G., and Santomero, A. 1990. "Market Discipline and Bank Subordinated Debt." *Journal of Money Credit and Banking* (Ohio State University Press) 1: 119–128.

Graham, F., and Horner, J. 1988. "Bank Failure: An Evaluation of the Factors Contributing to the Failure of National Banks." *Proceedings of a Conference on Bank Structure and Competition:* 406–35. Chicago: Federal Reserve Bank of Chicago.

Graham, G. 1996. "Timing System Set To Take Risk Out Of Settlement." *Financial Times*, 22 April: 6.

Greenspan, A. 1995. "Remarks at a Conference on Risk Measurement and Systemic Risk." Washington, D.C.: Board of Governors of the Federal Reserve System.

Greenspan, A. 1996. "Remarks on Evolving Payment System Issues." *Journal of Money Credit and Banking* 28: 689–95.

Greenspan, A. 1997. "Technology Boosts Market Risk." 15th Annual Monetary Conference of the Cato Institute, 14 October.

Greenspan, A. 1999. "Lessons from Global Crises" Remarks Before the World Bank Group and the International Monetary Fund, Program of Seminars, 27 September. Washington, D.C.

Greenspan, A. May, 2000. Keynote Address. *Federal Reserve Bank of Chicago Bank Structure Conference.*

Greenspan, A. 2001. "The Challenge of Measuring and Modelling a Dynamic Economy." Remarks Before Washington Economic Policy Conference for the National Association for Business Economics. 27 March. Washington, D.C.

Gurley, J., and Shaw, E. 1955. "Financial Aspects of Economic Development." *American Economic Review* 45 (September): 515–38.

Guttentag, J., and Herring, R. 1983, May. "The Lender of Last Resort Function in an International Context." *Princeton Essays in International Finance*, Number 151.

Hirsch, F. 1977, March. "The Bagehot Problem." *The Manchester School of Economic and Social Studies.*

Hoggarth, G., Reiss, R., and Saporta, V. 2001. "Costs of Banking System Instability: Some Empirical Evidence." *Bank of England Working Papers*, EC2R 8AH.

Hughes, J., and Mester, L. 1993. *Journal of Productivity Analysis* 4 (September).

Humphrey, D. B. 1986. "Payments Finality and Risk of Settlement Failure." In *Technology and Regulation of Financial Markets: Securities, Futures and Banking*, ed. A. S. Saunders and L. J. White, 97–120. Lexington, MA: Lexington Books.

Humphrey, D. 1987. "Payments System Risk, Market Failure, and Public Policy." In *Electronic Funds Transfers and Payments*, ed. E. Solomon, 83–110. Boston: Kluwer Academic Publishers.

Humphrey, T. 1989. "The Lender of Last Resort: The Concept in History." *Federal Reserve Bank of Richmond Economic Review*, March/April: 8–16.

Iden, G., and Manchester, J. 1992, January. *The Economic Effects of the Savings and Loan Crisis, A CBO Study*. Washington, D.C.: U.S. Congressional Budget Office.

International Monetary Fund. 1998. "Financial Crises: Characteristics and Indicators of Vulnerability." *World Economic Outlook*, Chapter 4. International Monetary Fund.

James, C. 1991. "The Losses Realized in Bank Failures." *Journal of Finance* September: 1223–42.

Juncker, G., Summers, B., and Young, F. 1991. "A Primer on the Settlement of Payments in the United States." *Federal Reserve Bulletin* 77: 847–58.

Kaminsky, G., and Reinhart, C. 1998. "The Twin Crises: the Causes of Banking and Balance-of-Payments Problems." *International Finance Working Papers*, Washington, D.C.: Federal Reserve Board.

Kane, E. 1985. *The Gathering Crises in Federal Deposit Insurance*. Cambridge: MIT Press.

Kane, E. 1989. *The S&L Mess*. Washington, D.C.: Urban Institute.

Kane, E. 1992. "How Incentive-Incompatible Deposit Insurance Plans Fail." In *Research in Financial Services*, ed. G. Kaufman. Greenwich, CT: JAI Press.

Kane, E. 1995a. "Three Paradigms for the Role of Capitalization Requirements in Insured Financial Institutions." *Journal of Banking and Finance* 19: 431–59.

Kane, E. 1995b. "Why and How Should Depository Institutions Be Regulated." Paper prepared for conference at Koc University (Turkey).

Kane, E. 2001a. "Housing Finance GSEs: Who Gets the Subsidy." *Journal of Financial Services Research* 15 (3): 197–209.

Kane, E. 2001b. "Using Disaster Planning to Optimize Expenditures on Financial Safety Nets." *Atlantic Economic Journal* 29 (3): 1–11.

Kaufman, G. 1988. "Bank Runs: Causes, Benefits and Costs." *Cato Journal* 7: 559–88.

Kaufman, G. 1991. "Lender of Last Resort: A Contemporary Perspective." *Journal of Financial Services Research*, 5: 95–110.

Kaufman, G. 1992. "Capital in Banking: Past, Present and Future." *Journal of Financial Services Research* 5: 385–402.

Kaufman, G. 1994. "Bank Contagion: A Review of the Theory and Evidence." *Journal of Financial Services Research* 8: 123–50.

Kaufman, G. 1994. "Bank Contagion: A Review of the Theory and Evidence." *Journal of Financial Services Research*, 123–150.

Kaufman, G. 1995a. "The U.S. Banking Debacle of the 1980s: An Overview and Lessons." *Financier* 2: 9–26.

Kaufman, G. 1995b. "Comment on Systemic Risk." In *Research in Financial Services*, ed. G. Kaufman, 47–52. Greenwich, CT: JAI Press.

Kaufman, G. 1996. "Bank Fragility: Perception and Historical Evidence." Working Paper No. 96–6, Chicago: Loyola University.

Kaufman, G. 1997, forthcoming. "Lessons for Traditional and Developing Economies from U.S. Deposit Insurance Reform." In *Standards and Politics: Banking and Finance Regulations in the NAFTA Countries*, ed. G. M. von Furstenberg. Boston: Kluwer Academic Publishers.

Kaufman, G., and Seelig, S. A., 2000, November. "Post-Resolution Treatment of Depositors at Failed Banks: Implications for the Severity of Banking Crises, Systemic Risk, and Too-Big-to-Fail." Working Paper 2000–16, Federal Reserve Bank of Chicago.

Kaufman, H. 1986. "Debt: The Threat to Economic and Financial Stability." *Proceedings*, Federal Reserve Bank of Kansas City.

Kindleberger, C. 1989. *Manias, Panics and Crashes: A History of Financial Crises.* New York: Basic Books.

Krugman, P. 1994. *Peddling Prosperity.* New York: W.W. Norton.

Krugman, P. 1999. "Balance Sheets, the Transfer Problem and Financial Crises." *Journal of Money, Credit, and Banking*, 11: 311–25.

Kuttner, R. 1991. "Deposit Insurance—Now More Than Ever." *Washington Post National Weekly Edition.* 29.

Lacker, J. 1999. "Limited Commitment and Central Bank Lending." *Risk Measurement and Systemic Risk: Proceedings of a Joint Central Bank Research Conference.* Federal Reserve Bank, Bank of England, Bank of Japan.

Lamy, R., and Thompson, G. 1986. "Penn Square, Problem Loans and Insolvency Risk." *Journal of Financial Research* Summer: 103–12.

Lang, L., and Stulz, R. 1992. "Contagion and Competitive Inter-Industry Effects of Bankruptcy Announcements." *Journal of Financial Economics* 32: 45–60.

Lang, W., and Robertson, D., 2000, March. *Analysis of Proposals for a Minimum Subordinated Debt Requirement.* Working Paper 2000–4, Office of Comptroller of the Currency, Economic and Policy Analysis.

Lavargna, C. 1993. "Government-Sponsored Enterprises Are 'Too-big-to-fail': Balancing Public and Private Interests." *Hastings Law Journal.*

LaWare, J. 1991. "Testimony." *Economic Implications of the "Too-big-to-fail" Policy: Hearing Before the Subcommittee on Economic Stabilization of the Committee on Banking, Finance and Urban Affairs.* U.S. House of Representatives, 102nd Cong., 1st Sess., 9 May.

LaWare, J. 1993. "Bank Failures in a Sound Economy." In *The Basic Elements of Bank Supervision*, ed. F. Shadrack and L. Korobon, 93–100. New York: Federal Reserve Bank of New York.

Lindgren, C., Garcia, G. and Saal, M. 1996. *Bank Soundness and Macroeconomic Policy.* Washington, D.C.: International Monetary Fund (IMF).

"LTCB Aftermath: Banks Thought Too-big-to-fail." 2002, January. *Profit and Loss* 3 (27). ISSN14672650.

Lutton, T., and Gordon, P. 1994. T*he Changing Business of Banking: A Study of Failed Banks from 1987 to 1992: A CBO Study.* Washington, D.C.: Congressional Budget Office.

Lutton, T., and Hanweck, G. 2002. "Causes and Measurement of Systemic Risk: Origins and Timing of a Systemic Event." *OFHEO Working Paper Series.* Washington, D.C.: Office of Federal Housing and Enterprise Oversight.

Mailath, G., and Mester, L. 1994. "A Positive Analysis of Bank Closure." *Journal of Financial Intermediation*, 3 (June): 272–99.

McDonough, W. J. 1998. "Statement Before the Committee on Banking and Financial Services, U.S. House of Representatives." Washington, D.C.

McMillin, W. D. 1993. "Bank Portfolio Composition and Macroeconomic Activity." *Journal of Economics and Business* (Temple University). 45: 111–127.

McNee, A. 2001. "The Great FM Debate." *Erisk*. Available at www.erisk.com/news/analysis/news_analysis2001–03–22_01.asp.

Meltzer, A. 1985. "Rational Expectations, Risk, Uncertainty and Market Responses." In *Crises in Economic and Financial Structure*, ed. P. Wachtel, 3–22. Lexington, MA: Lexington Books.

Mengle, D. 1995. "Regulatory "Solutions to Payment System Risk." *Journal of Financial Services Research* 9: 381–92.

Merton, R. 1995. "A Functional Perspective of Financial Intermediation." *Financial Management* 24: 23–41.

Merton, Robert C. 1996. "On Oversight and Management of Financial Risk." *Symposium on Financial Innovation and Risk Management*. Harvard University.

Meyer, L. 2000. "Prudential Supervision: What Works and What Doesn't." Presentation, *National Bureau of Economic Research Conference*, Islamorada, Florida.

Meyer, L. 2001, May. "Controlling the Safety Net." *37th Annual Conference on Bank Structure and Competition*, Federal Reserve Bank of Chicago.

Michael, I. 1998. "Financial Interlinkages and Systemic Risk." *Financial Stability Review* (Bank of England) 4 (Spring): 26–33.

Minsky, H. 1967. "Financial Stability Revised: The Economics of Disaster." *Reappraisal of the Federal Reserve Discount Mechanism*. Board of Governors of the Federal Reserve System 3: 95–136.

Minsky, H. 1977. "A Theory of Systemic Fragility." In *Financial Crises: Institutions and Markets in a Fragile Environment*, ed. E. Altman and A. Sametz. New York: John Wiley.

Minsky, H. 1995. "Longer Waves in Financial Relations: Financial Factors in the More Severe Depressions." *Journal of Economic Issues* (March).

Mishkin, F. 1991. "Asymmetric Information and Financial Crises." In *Financial Markets and Financial Crises*, ed. R. G. Hubbard, 69–108. Chicago: University of Chicago Press.

Mishkin, F. 1991. "Asymmetric Information and Financial Crises: A Historical Perspective." In *Financial Markets and Financial Crises*, ed. M. Feldstein, 69–108. University of Chicago Press, Chicago.

Mishkin, F. 1995. "Comments on Systemic Risk." In *Banking Financial Markets and Systemic Risk: Research in Financial Services, Private and Public Policy*, ed. G. Kaufman, 31–45. Greenwich, CT: JAI Press.

Mishkin, F. 1995. "Symposium on the Monetary Transmission Mechanism." *Journal of Economic Perspectives*, 9 (Autumn).

Mishkin, F. 1999. "Moral Hazard and Reform of the Government Safety Net." Paper prepared for FRB Chicago conference *Lessons from Recent Global Financial Crises*. Chicago, 30 September–2 October.

Nader, R. "Bailouts." *Nader 2000 Letters and Testimony*.

Nakajima, Z., and Taguchi, H. 1995. "Toward a More Stable Financial Framework: An Overview of Recent Bank Disruption Worldwide." In *Financial Stability in a Changing Environment*, ed. K. Sawamoto, Z. Nakajima, and H. Taguchi, 41–98. New York: St. Martin's Press.

O'Conner, J.F.T. 1938. *Banking Crisis and Recovery Under the Roosevelt Administration*. Chicago: Callaghan and Co.

Office of Federal Housing Enterprise Oversight Committee. 2001. "Comments on Proposed Systemic Risk Study." Available at http://www.ofheo.gov/.

Parry, R. 1996. "Global Payments in the 21st Century: A Central Banker's View." *FRBSF Economic Letter*, Federal Reserve Bank of San Francisco, 3 May.

Phaub, M. 1996. *Assessing the Public Costs and Benefits of Fannie Mae and Freddie Mac: A CBO Study*. Washington, D.C.: Government Printing Office.

Phaub, M. 2001. *Federal Subsidies and the Housing GSEs: A CBO Study*. Washington, D.C.: Congressional Budget Office.

Poole, W. 2002. "Financial Stability." The Council of State Governments, Southern Legislative Conference Annual Meeting. New Orleans, LA, 4 August.

Posner, Kenneth. 2002, February. "The American Dream Industry, 2002–2020." U.S. Mortgage Finance, Morgan Stanley Equity Research North America.

Promisel, L., et al. 1992. "Recent Developments in International Interbank Relations." Bank for International Settlements. Basel, Switzerland.

Rahl, L. 1999. *Measuring Financial Risk in the 21st Century*. Presentation at OCC Conference, Washington, D.C.

Repullo, R. 2000. "Bank Capital and Risk Taking," *Bank of England Working Papers*.

Richards, H. 1995. "Daylight Overdraft Fees and the Federal Reserve's Payment System Risk Policy." *Federal Reserve Bulletin* 81: 1065–77.

Roll, R. 2000, October. "Benefits to Homeowners from the Mortgage Portfolios Retained by Fannie Mae and Freddie Mac." Fannie Mae, Washington, D.C.

Sahel, B., and Vesala, J. 1999. "Financial Stability Analysis Using Aggregated Data." *BIS Papers* No. 1. Banking Supervision Committee, Economic Union, European Central Bank.

Salsman, R. 1983. "Banking Without the TBTF Doctrine." In *Documentary History of Banking and Currency in the United States*, Volume IV, ed. Paul A. Samuelson and Herman E. Krooss. New York: Chelsea House Publishers.

Samuelson, P. A., and Krooss, H. E. 1983. *Documentary History of Banking and Currency in the United States*, Vol. IV. New York: Chelsea House Publishers.

Samuelson, R. 1995. "Daiwa's Deeper Lesson." *Washington Post National Weekly Edition*: 5.

Santomero, A., and Hoffman, P. 1998. "Problem Bank Resolution: Evaluating the Options." *The Wharton School Financial Institutions Center* Discussion Paper: 98–105.

Santomero, A., and Hoffman, G. 1999. "Problem Bank Resolution: Evaluating the Options." In *International Banking Crises, Large Scale Failures, Massive Government Interventions*, ed. B. Gup. Westport, CT: Greenwood Publishing.

Saunders, A. 1987. "The Interbank Market, Contagion Effects and International Financial Crises," in *Threats to International Financial Stability*, ed. Portes and Swoboda, 196–232. CEPR.

Saunders, A., and Wilson, B. 1996. "Contagious Bank Runs: Evidence from the 1929–1933 Period." *Journal of Financial Intermediation* 5: 409–23.

Schoenmaker, D. 1996. "Contagion Risk in Banking." *LSE Financial Markets Group* Discussion Paper No. 239.

Schwartz, A. 1986. "Real and Pseudo-Financial Crises." In *Financial Crises and the World Banking System*, ed. F. Capie and G. Woods, 11–40. London: Macmillan.

Schwartz, A. 1988. "Financial Stability and the Federal Safety Net." In *Restructuring Banking and Financial Services in America*, ed. W. Haraf and R. M. Kushmeider, 19–30. Washington, D.C.: American Enterprise Institute.

Schwartz, A. 1995. "Systemic Risk and the Macroeconomy." In *Banking Financial Markets and Systemic Risk: Research in Financial Services, Private and Public Policy*, ed. G. Kaufman, 19–30. Greenwich, CT: JAI Press.

Seiler, R. 1991, April. *Controlling the Risks of Government-Sponsored Enterprises: A CBO Study*. Washington, D.C.: Congressional Budget Office. 55–8.

Seiler, R. 1999. "Fannie Mae and Freddie Mac as Investor-Owned Public Utilities." *Journal of Public Budgeting, Accounting & Financial Management* 11: 117–154.

Selgin, G. 1989. "Legal Restrictions, Financial Weakening, and the Lender of Last Resort." *Cato Journal* 9: 429–59.

Selgin, G. 1992. "Bank Lending 'Manias' in Theory and History." *Journal of Financial Services Research* 5: 169–86.

Shadow Financial Regulatory Committee. 1992. "Statement No. 41: An Outline of a Program for Deposit Insurance and Regulatory Reform." *Journal of Financial Services Research* (supplement) 6: S78-S82.

Sharpe, A. 1990. "Asymmetric Information, Bank Lending and Implicit Contracts—A Stylized Model of Customer Relationships." *Journal of Finance* 45: 1069–87.

Shull, B. 1984. "The Separation of Banking and Commerce: An Historical Perspective." *Proceedings Bank Structure and Competition*. Chicago: Federal Reserve Bank of Chicago.

Smith, F. 2000. "Fannie and Freddie: Fiscal Frauds." InPrint@CEI, Competitive Enterprise Institute August/September.

Stanton, T. 1991. *A State of Risk*. New York: Harper Collins.

Stanton, T. 2001. "Government Sponsored Enterprises (GSE): Why is Effective Government Supervision Hard to Achieve?" *37th Annual Conference on Bank Structure and Competition*. Chicago: Federal Reserve Bank of Chicago.

Stern, G. 2000. "Thoughts on Designing Credible Policies after Financial Modernization: Addressing the Too-Big-Too Fail and Moral Hazard." *The Region*. Minneapolis: Federal Reserve Bank of Minneapolis.

Stiglitz, J., Orszag, J., and Orszag, P. 2002, March. "Implications of the New Fannie Mae and Freddie Mac Risk Based Capital Standard." *FannieMae Papers*. Washington, D.C.

Summers, B. 1994. *The Payment System, Design, Management and Supervision*. Washington, D.C.: International Monetary Fund.

Thornton, H. 1802. "An Enquiry into the Nature and Effects of the Paper Credit of Great Britain."

Todd, W. 1988. "Lessons of the Past and Prospects for the Future in the Lender of Last Resort Theory." *Proceedings of the Conference on Bank Structure and Competition*. Chicago: Federal Reserve Bank of Chicago.

Todd, W., and Watts, A. 1991, January. "Current Intervention and Closure Options of Federal Banking Agencies." *Conference on Bank Structure and Competition*. Dallas: Federal Reserve Bank of Dallas.

U.S. Congress, House of Representatives, Subcommittee on Financial Institutions Supervision, Regulation and Insurance 1984. *Hearing: Inquiry Into Continental*

Illinois Corp. and Continental Illinois National Bank, 98–111. 98th Cong., 2nd Sess., 18–19 September and 4 October.

U.S. Congressional Budget Office. 1991, April. *Controlling the Risks of Government-Sponsored Enterprises.* Washington, D.C.: Congressional Budget Office. 55–58.

U.S. Congressional Budget Office. 1996. *Assessing the Public Costs and Benefits of Fannie Mae and Freddie Mac.* Washington, D.C.: Government Printing Office.

U.S. Congressional Budget Office. 2001. *Federal Subsidies and the Housing GSEs.* Washington, D.C.: Government Printing Office.

U.S. Department of Treasury. 1985. *Recommendations for Change in the Federal Deposit Insurance System.* Washington, D.C.

U.S. Department of Treasury. 1991. *Modernizing the Financial System: Recommendations for Safety, More Competitive Banks.* Washington, D.C.

U.S. Department of Treasury. 1996. *Government Sponsorship of the Federal National Mortgage Association and the Federal Home Loan Mortgage Corporation.* Washington, D.C.: Government Printing Office.

U.S. Government Accounting Office. 1991. *Deposit Insurance: A Strategy for Reform.* Washington, D.C.

U.S. Office of Management and Budget. 1991. *Budgeting for Federal Deposit Insurance.* Washington, D.C.

Wall, L., and Peterson, D. 1990. "The Effect of Continental Illinois Failure on the Performance of Other Banks." *Journal of Monetary Economics* August: 77–99.

Wattenberg, B. 1998. "The Too-Big-To-Fail Doctrine of Double Standards." AEI Articles. American Enterprise Institute for Public Policy Research.

Wicker, E. 1980. "A Reconsideration of the Causes of the Banking Panic of 1930." *Journal of Economic History* September: 571–83.

Williams, M. 1995. "The Efficacy of Accounting-Based Bank Regulation: The Case of the Basel Accord." Working Paper No. 95–5, Santa Monica, CA: Millken Institute.

CHAPTER 14

Enron: Not Too Big to Fail

Benton E. Gup

There are about 24 million business concerns in the United States of which 4.8 million are corporations. Most corporations, partnerships, and proprietorships are small privately held firms with receipts of under $1 million. Relatively few businesses go bankrupt. During the 1985–1999 period, between 37,000 to 67,000 business concerns per year filed for bankruptcy.[1] About 70 percent of the bankruptcies result in liquidation (Chapter 7 of the Bankruptcy Code), followed by reorganization (Chapter 11).

In 2001, there were 257 publicly held companies that filed for bankruptcy.[2] As shown in Table 14.1, Enron was the largest company, with assets of $63.3 billion. Enron was listed as Number 7 on the *Fortune* 500 list of the largest companies in the United States. It had over 18,000 employees located in more than 30 countries. For six years Enron was voted "most innovative" on the *Fortune* list of most admired companies.

Other well-known companies that failed that year include Bethlehem Steel Corporation and Sunbeam Corporation. Some large companies in financial trouble asked the government to bail them out, but few were successful. In 2000, ANC Rental Corp. (National and Alamo Rental cars) was in financial difficulty before the September 11 terrorist attacks, and it asked Congress for funds and was denied.[3]

Enron filed for bankruptcy in December 2001. Enron also asked for government aid, and it too was denied support. This article examines Enron's growth and collapse. In addition, it explains why Enron did not get a government bailout, and some of the outcomes from its failure.

The remainder of the article is divided into four parts. Part 1 examines Enron's history. Part 2 concerns the immediate spillover effects from the bankruptcy. Part 3 explains why no bailout was forthcoming, and Part 4 is about the outcomes from Enron's demise.

ENRON'S HISTORY

The Boom Period

In 1985, Kenneth L. Lay arranged the merger of his Houston Natural Gas Company with InterNorth of Nebraska to form Enron, a natural gas pipeline company.[4] The pipelines were used to transmit gas to public utility companies and businesses. However, because of its huge debt burden, Kenneth Lay decided to transform Enron from a company that transported and sold gas into an energy commodity-trading firm. In 1989 Enron began trading natural gas commodities, and by 1995 it controlled one-fifth of the market in North America—a market that it helped to create. Enron traded its first units of electricity in 1994. With the deregulation of the electric power markets, Enron executives recognized that because of fluctuations in wholesale energy prices, there were market opportunities for derivatives and options contracts to hedge price risks in electricity and natural gas. In 1997, Enron bought Portland General Corporation to gain their expertise in trading wholesale and retail electricity. It owns Portland General Electric, an Oregon electric utility company serving over 680,000 customers.[5]

Table 14.1
Five Largest Public Company Bankruptcies—2001

Company	Bankruptcy Date	Total Assets Pre-Bankruptcy ($ billion)
Enron Corp.	12/3/2001	$63.3
Pacific Gas and Electric Co.	4/6/2001	$21.5
FINOVA Group, Inc., (The)	3/7/2001	$14.1
Reliance Group Holdings, Inc.	6/12/2001	$12.6
Federal-Mogul Corp.	10/1/2001	$10.2

Source: www.BankruptcyData.com (visited 3/12/03).

In 1999, EnronOnline became the first global trading Web site. Enron became a marketer and trader of derivative and option contracts on electricity and natural gas. It also traded metals, wood products, weather derivatives, and broadband.[6] Enron invested $1.2 billion in fiber-optic capacity and trading facilities, but market for broadband capacity collapsed. Other poor investments included billions of dollars invested in the Dabhol Power Plan Company in India, and the Wessex Water (water and wastewater) services business in England and around the world with its Azurix subsidiary.

According to the Securities and Exchange Commission, between 1997 and 2002, Enron Corp. had changed its line of business, measured by the Standard Industrial Classification (SIC) code, from "Wholesale Petroleum Products (No Bulk Stations)" [SIC 5172] "Wholesale Petroleum" to "Security & Commodity Brokers, Dealers, Exchanges & Services" [SIC 6200].

During its growth phase, Enron created over 4,000 Special Purpose Entities (SPEs) called partnerships. They were used to keep debts off the balance sheet, to hide the true amount of Enron's debts, and to reduce taxes. SPEs do not have to be consolidated on the balance sheets as long as outside investors contribute 97 percent of the investment, most of which is non-recourse debt. Under accounting rules, at least 3 percent equity risk capital had to come from independent investors in order to keep the partnerships financial statements off their books. Enron recognized gains when assets were transferred to the partnerships. Their tax reduction strategies boosted their profits by almost $1 billion between 1995 and 2001.[7]

Some of the SPEs were complex. Consider the following simplification of Whitewing Associates LLP. Enron and Osprey Trust funded Whitewing. Enron contributed $1.7 billion in stock and notes.[8] Osprey Trust was funded by mutual funds, pension funds, and insurers who bought $1.5 billion in short-term notes that were to pay 8.31 percent and were due January 15, 2003. The $3.2 billion invested in Whitewing Associates LLP was used to invest $807 million in Enron projects, $139 million in Enron Notes, $165 million in other investments, and $2.1 billion in another entity, Condor, that held Enron Convertible Stock.[9] If the investments could not be sold to repay the Osprey notes, Condor could convert the Enron Convertible Shares to help pay Osprey's Investors or Enron could use cash to make up the difference. If Enron's debt was downgraded to junk status and its share prices remained low, the noteholder could try to force Enron to put up more stock or cash. Enron shareholders were not aware of this contingent claim that in November 2001 amounted to about $2 billion.

One SPE, Chewco Investments LLP (named after a character in *Star Wars*) was run and partly owned by Michael J. Kopper, a managing director of Enron, who profited from the deal and made about $10.5 million.[10] This partnership allowed Enron to keep about $600 million in debt off of its books.

Chief Financial Officer Andrew S. Fastow also bent the rules on conflict of interest. The outside investors in the RADR SPEs included Fastow's wife, some of her relatives, Kopper's domestic partner, and a Houston Real Estate Broker. It is estimated that Fastow made $30 million from managing various SPEs (e.g., LJM1 and LJM2). LJM are the initials of Fastow's wife and two children. Other insiders invested in SPEs, too.[11] More will be said about Fastow and Kopper at the end of the article.

Enron wanted to be "asset light" and keep the debt on its books low and its credit rating high. Jeffrey K. Skilling, Enron's CEO, held the philosophy that assets were bad and intellectual property was good.[12] By having SPEs borrow funds, debts were kept off Enron's balance sheet. Enron also used Monthly Income Preferred Shares (MIPS) to mask debt and cut taxes. The payments made on these securities were reported as tax-deductible debt to the Internal Revenue Service and as equity to the shareholders. This allowed Enron to have about $3 billion less debt appear on its tax books and slash its tax payments.[13]

In 1993, Enron established a subsidiary called Enron Capital LLC in the Turks Islands and Caicos Islands, tax havens. Enron Capital sold about $214 million MIPS through Goldman Sachs, promising to pay investors 8 percent annual dividends in monthly installments. Enron Capital then lent the funds to its parent company, Enron, to be paid back over 50 years or longer. Lea Fastow, Andrew Fastow's wife, who worked in corporate finance at Enron, told the *Institutional Investor* magazine in October 1994 that MIPS would reduce Enron's debt-to-equity ratio and increase its credit rating.[14] To further reduce taxes, Enron placed 692 of its subsidiaries in the Cayman Islands, 140 in Holland, 119 in the Turks and Caicos Islands, 43 in Mauritius, and 8 in Burmuda, all of which are tax havens.[15]

The SPEs and trust-preferred securities were part of the corporate culture of *earnings and cash flow management* that enabled Enron to provide minimal financial disclosure. This also concealed losses and gave the appearance of profitability. For example, SPEs could be used to facilitate the prepayment for 20 years worth of services from a customer and simultaneously recognize the full value of the earnings over time. In another earnings management deal, Enron swapped fiber-optic cable and services at exaggerated prices with Quest Communications to improve each other's financial reports.[16] Simply stated, Enron had a corporate culture of pushing the limits—a culture of arrogance.[17]

In February 1999, David Duncan, Arthur Anderson LLP's lead auditor, told Enron's board of directors' audit committee that Enron's high risk accounting practices were pushing the limits, and that other auditors might take a different view about accounting.[18] Nevertheless, Anderson was on board with them. The directors on the audit committee raised no objections to Enron's practices, and they claim that they had no inkling that Enron may have been in jeopardy.

Enron was growing. In mid-2000 it formed a joint venture with Blockbuster to use Enron's fiber-optic network to bring movies into millions of homes. But by March 2001, only 1,000 customers in four cities had signed up, and the deal fizzled.[19]

Enron's Peak Period

Everything looked good to uninformed outsiders in September 2001, and the stock was selling at a peak price of $90 per share. However, there were problems looming on the horizon. As early as 2000, Arthur Anderson accountants were debating various ways to avoid showing large losses in the Raptor SPEs.[20] A footnote in Enron's 2000 annual report states that judgment is required in interpreting market data and different assumptions and methodologies may affect the estimated values. They used poor judgment. Eventually Enron did recognize the losses that contributed to the $1.01 billion charge on October 16, 2001.

Some assets that were carried on Enron's books were overvalued. In 1998 Enron bought a 46 percent stake in Elektro-Electricdades e Servicos SA, a Brazilian utility, for $1.27 billion, which Enron carried on its books at $2 billion. Enron claims that it invested more than $3 billion in this project to build a 1,870-mile pipeline to bring natural gas from Bolivia to Brazil's industrial heartland. The project encountered delays, environmental problems, economic instability in the region, and other problems. By March 2002, the fair market value was estimated to range from $0 to $250 million.[21]

Another problem was that Enron allegedly manipulated the price of California's energy markets so that it could profit from trading electric power and natural gas. Their strategies involved maneuvers with code names like "Death Star," "Get Shorty," "Inc-ing," "Fat Boy," and "Ricochet." Ricochet involved sending power out of California and then reselling in California to avoid price caps that applied to in-state transactions. Another gimmick involved submitting false information to California's electric grid manager and conspiring with several other companies to take advantages of weaknesses in California's energy market. Their actions contributed to soaring energy costs in California in mid-2000–early 2001. California Governor Gray Davis and Senators Dianne Feinstein and Barbara Box asked U.S. Attorney General John Ashcroft to investigate Enron's practices and look into possible fraud charges.[22]

Political Influence Abounded

Enron was well connected politically. In 1992 Kenneth Lay backed Democrat Bob Kerry's run for President.[23] He donated to the 1994 campaign for Texas Democratic Governor Ann Richards, and he served on President Clinton's Council on Sustainable Development.

From 1997 to 2000, Enron donated $10.2 million to influence Washington politicians, and another $5.8 million in Texas where its headquarters were located.[24] When President George Bush was governor of Texas, he referred to Enron's Chairman, Kenneth Lay, as "Kenny Boy." Kenny Boy contributed $461,000 to Bush's two successful gubernatorial campaigns. In 2000, Lay contributed over $290,000 to George W. Bush's presidential election campaign.[25] Lay sat in the "Pioneers" box for the presidential inauguration, and the next day attended a private lunch at the White House.

The government contacts and political contributions paid off. As governor of Texas, Bush deregulated the electric utility markets, eased rules on corporate polluters, and supported laws protecting companies from lawsuits. Max Yzaguirre, who headed Enron's operations in Mexico, was named to the Texas Public Utility Commission.[26] It was good for politics, good for Enron.

When Bush won the presidency, he put Kenneth Lay on the presidential transition team. President Bush also appointed Enron backer and Texas Public Utility Commissioner Patrick H. Wood III as Chairman of the Federal Energy Regulatory Committee (FERC). Enron received $1.2 billion guarantees from the Overseas Private Investment Corporation (OPIC) and $650 million from the Ex-Im Bank to help finance their overseas investments.[27] Both the OPIC and Ex-Im Bank loans are backed by the full faith and credit of the U.S. Government. One OPIC loan guarantee for $200 million helped to finance a 390-mile pipeline from Bolivia to Brazil through the Chiquitano Dry Tropical Forest. This is one of the world's most endangered ecological regions.[28]

There was interaction between Enron executives and Bush's energy task force that involved Vice President Dick Cheney. The vice president spoke to the Indian government to help Enron recoup its stake and unpaid bills in the controversial $2.9 billion Dabhol power project near Bombay. Secretary of State Colin Powell also talked to Indian officials about Dabhol.[29] President's Clinton's ambassador to India, Richard Celeste, and President Bush's ambassador, Robert D. Blackwell, as well as other government officials in both administrations also pressured the Indian government.[30]

Bush appointed Karl Rove as his senior advisor. Rove owned more than $100,000 in Enron stock, but he did not divest the stock until June 2001. As senior advisor he helped shape the president's energy plan and legislation in May 2001. Other Enron connections in the Bush administration include but are not limited to Thomas White, Secretary of the Army (former Enron Vice President), Lawrence Lindsey, White House Economic Advisor (consultant to Enron), Robert Libby, aid to Cheney (Enron stock holder), Robert Zoellick, U.S. Trade Representative (former Enron advisory board member), and Marc Racicot, Chairman of the Republican National Committee (former Enron lobbyist).[31]

Finally, Wendy Gramm, wife of Senator Phil Gramm (R-TX), served on Enron's Audit Committee. She was the former Chairman of the Commodity Futures Trading Commission (CFTC) that regulated some of Enron's trading activities. While she was at the CFTC, she "shepherded a commission ruling that exempted a significant amount of Enron's trading from federal oversight . . . in 2000 . . . Senator Gramm sponsored the Commodity Futures Modernization Act, which made the exemption law."[32]

After Enron's financial troubles were revealed in 2001, Kenneth Lay and other Enron officials had telephone conversations with Treasury Secretary Paul H. O'Neill, Under Secretary of the Treasury for Domestic Finance Peter Fisher, Commerce Secretary Donald L. Evans, Federal Reserve Chairman Alan Greenspan, and other government officials. Enron did not get the help that it asked for.

In addition, many politicians from both parties, including Rep. Richard A. Gephard (D-MO), Sen. Tim Hutchison (R-AR), and others, rushed to return or get rid of their political contributions from Enron.[33] Every politician wanted to distance themselves from Enron and the criminal charges that followed its failure.

Pulling the Trigger and Going Bust

The beginning of the end was October 16, 2001, when Enron announced its third quarter results in a press release, stating that it would have nonrecurring charges of $1.01 billion after taxes. The losses were due to the consolidation of several SPEs (e.g., Chewco, JEDI, LJM1, and LJM2) into their financial statements and write-offs from failed investments in water companies, broadband trading, and retail electricity sales.[34] This charge resulted in a loss of $1.11 per share for the third quarter 2001.

Enron's stock price continued its downward spiral from a high of $90 per share in September 2000, to about $38 per share at the time of the October 2001 announcement, to $0.11 per share on January 29, 2002. At its best, Enron returns were 6–7 percent, well below its 11 percent estimated cost of capital.[35]

On November 1, 2002, Enron secured over $1 billion in credit lines from JP Morgan Chase and Citigroup's Salomon Smith Barney.[36]

On November 8, 2001, Enron filed its Form 8-K with the Securities and Exchange Commission (SEC) restating earnings and financial statements for 1997–2000 as shown in Table 14.2. On that same day, Enron began talks with Dynergy, Inc., a smaller competitor, that Enron hoped would rescue them.

On November 19, 2001, Enron filed the Form 10-Q with the SEC and refined the restated earnings and reduced its shareholder equity by $1.2 billion. As a result of the restated financial statements, Standard & Poor's downgraded Enron's senior unsecured debt rating to BBB on November 12, 2001. This was a "Trigger Event" that resulted in $690 million in debt becoming payable if Enron did not post additional collateral by November 27, 2001. On November 28, 2001, Moody's Investor Service and Fitch also downgraded

Table 14.2
Enron's Net Income and Equity

Years	Reported Net Income	Restated in Form 8-K (11/8/01)	Restated in Form 10-Q (11/19/01)
1997	$105	$9	$26
1998	$703	$590	$564
1999	$893	$643	$635
2000	$979	$847	$842
	Reported Equity		
1997	$5,618	$5,305	$5,309
1998	$7,048	$6,600	$6,600
1999	$9,570	$8,736	$8,724
2000	$11,470	$10,306	$10,289

Source: Enron Corp., Forms 8-K (11/8/01) and 10-Q (11/19/01), SEC Filings.
Note: All figures in millions.

Enron's debt to junk status. Then Dynergy terminated its plans to merge with Enron. The merger offer from Dynergy was about $23 billion.

Enron's stock price plays an important role in its demise. High stock prices were used in SPEs to help keep potential losses off its books. When the stock price declined, low stock prices were additional "Trigger Events" that required Enron to repay, refinance, or cash collateralize additional credit facilities amount to $3.9 billion in connection with certain SPE agreements.[37]

Enron was unable to meet the financial requirements triggered by the low stock prices and credit downgrading, and it declared Chapter 11 bankruptcy on December 2, 2001. Enron and its U.S. subsidiaries filed in the U.S. Bankruptcy Court for the Southern District of New York because that is where the majority of their largest customers and the attorneys representing them are located.[38] In addition, that court has considerable experience with large, complicated bankruptcies.

When it filed for bankruptcy, Enron had reported assets of $63.3 billion

(Table 14.1). Enron had on-balance sheet debts of $31.2 billion and off-balance sheet debts and contingent liabilities of $27 billion. In April 2002, Enron reported that a material portion of the assets at the time of bankruptcy was overstated by $14 billion due to accounting errors and irregularities.[39]

THE IMMEDIATE SPILLOVER EFFECTS

The immediate spillover effects of Enron's bankruptcy were relatively small and no major economic catastrophes are associated with it. Enron had over 21,000 employees worldwide. About 11,000 employees had their 401(k) retirement accounts invested in Enron stock that became worthless when it plunged from $90 per share to a few cents per share. Kenneth Lay and other Enron executives also sustained large losses on the stock. However, Lay had benefits that were unavailable to other employees, such as prepaid life insurance premiums on a $12 million life insurance policy.[40] Similarly, Jeffery Skilling had an $8 million life insurance policy.

About 4,000 out of 7,500 Enron employees in Houston lost their jobs in connection with the bankruptcy. An additional 1,100 employees in London were laid off.

Other stock market investors lost billions of dollars. Stock market analysts from Goldman Sachs, Lehman Brothers, Solomon Smith Barney, and UBS Warburg recommended Enron's stock to investors even after some of its problems became public.[41] Every mutual fund and pension plan that had a passive portfolio mimicking the S&P 500 lost money on Enron. Alliance Capital Management Holding LLP lost $282 million for Florida's state pension fund by investing in Enron stock weeks before the company collapsed.[42] Investment bank J P Morgan Chase may have lost about $1.1 billion by investing in Enron partnerships. Some of that loss may be covered by insurance.[43] CSFB had a loss of about $126 million related to Enron.[44] Bank of America wrote off $210 million in loans to Enron.[45] Northern Trust had $43.5 million in unsecured loans to Enron, and $24.5 million in secured loans.[46] Four of Australia's biggest banks, France's Credit Lyonnais, and Holland's ABN Amro all lost large sums.[47]

Loretta Lynch, president of the California Public Utilities Commission stated that Enron's sham transactions contributed to the energy crises in California in 2000–2001.[48] Enron's demise had a small effect on wholesale electricity in Germany and Scandinavia.

The greatest effect of the Enron scandal was that it increased investor's awareness that there might be other scandals to be discovered—and they were right. More will be said about that shortly.

NO BAILOUT WAS FORTHCOMING

An article in the *Economist* entitled "The Ship that Sank Quietly" (2002) said that "A hurricane in the Gulf of Mexico would have been more disruptive than the fall of Enron." It claimed that Enron was never as formidable as it claimed because of its accounting practice of booking the entire value of trades as revenues, rather than booking the profits earned on those trades. That is part of the story, but not all of it. Despite Enron's size and political clout before its failure, no government bailout following its demise was forthcoming for the following reasons. First, its failure did not result in large-scale economic distress that extended beyond the firm and its creditors and investors. Second, its failure was associated with accounting practices and financial behavior that at best were scandalous, and at worst, fraudulent. Third, politicians wanted to distance themselves from Enron, and cut their political losses of being associated with it. A skeptic might say that Enron did not control any electoral votes, so that there would be no gain to the politicians in bailing it out. Finally, Enron grew to be a major powerhouse as a market maker and trader, but it never declared itself as a bank or a broker, and therefore avoided being regulated.[49] In doing so, it also avoided some of the benefits of regulation, such as access to liquidity provided by the Federal Reserve.

OUTCOMES FROM ENRON'S DEMISE

The most significant outcome from Enron's demise is a greater awareness of corporate governance, or lack thereof. Enron's problems followed by alleged frauds associated with Tyco, Global Crossing, ImCone Systems, and WorldCom shocked investors, and stock prices suffered during the summer of 2002 as they wondered which company was the next to be exposed. In the short run, the loss of investor confidence in the stock market cost billions of dollars. In the long run, investor's insistence on better corporate governance and transparency in corporate reporting will have a beneficial effect on the markets.

Auditors

Auditors are coming under increased pressure to be accountable. Arthur Anderson LLP had been in business in the United States for 89 years, and it had non-member firms in 83 countries. It was one of the Big Five auditing/ accounting firms. However, Arthur Anderson is associated with the accounting blowups of Enron, Sunbeam, Waste Management, and the Baptist Foundation of Arizona, and its reputation has been shredded. Because of these associations, long-standing customers including Delta Airlines, FedEx Corp., Freddie Mac, Merck & Co., Sun Trust Banks, and other major clients have dropped Arthur Anderson as their auditor. Delta had used Anderson for 53 years, Freddie Mac for 32 years, and Merck for 30 years.[50] The U.S. General Service Administration suspended Anderson from doing business with the government for 12 months.

In March 2002, the SEC announced that it was planning reviews of the design, implementation, and operating effectiveness of each of the Big Five auditing firms to make sure that they are in compliance with the independence rules.[51] In April 2000, legislation was introduced in the House Financial Services Committee that would empower the SEC to create and supervise an oversight authority for auditors.[52]

Sarbanes-Oxley Act of 2002

The Sarbanes-Oxley Act of 2002 was signed into law in July 2002.[53] This law makes the most significant changes in corporate governance since the Securities Act of 1933 and the Securities Exchange Act of 1934. The purpose of the new law is to protect investors by improving the accuracy and reliability of corporate disclosures. The law created an independent Public Company Accounting Oversight Board to oversee the audit of public companies to protect the interest of investors and further the public interest in providing useful and accurate information. Other sections of the act include but are not limited to Auditor Independence, Corporate Responsibility, and Enhanced Financial Disclosures. The law also deals with corporate and criminal fraud, and it provides criminal penalties for defrauding shareholders of publicly traded companies.

Because the SEC has oversight and enforcement authority over the Public Company Accounting Oversight Board, it is likely that the SEC will have input into auditing and corporate governance issues after the establishment of the board in 2003 and as its policies come into being.

Accounting

Accounting practices will change to become more transparent. Part of the problem is that the U.S. Generally Accepted Accounting Principles (GAAP) rules contribute to the confusion in revenue recognition. Under GAAP rules,

$$Earnings = Revenues - Expenses$$

When earnings are not growing as fast as sales revenues, some companies adjust the amount or timing of the revenues to resolve the problem.[54] The two criteria for reporting revenue are:

1. substantial completion of the earnings process, and
2. a reasonably determined price.

Substantial completion requires that the company has done what is necessary to receive the money for the sale of goods or services. The second criterion requires that there be no remaining uncertainties about the money to be received for the sale. In the retail business, revenue is received when a customer pays for the goods, such as food or gasoline. Finally, neither of the two criteria require that cash be exchanged for the goods or services. Note that cash and revenue recognition are not linked under these rules.

Consider what happened when Quest Communications bought fiber-optic capacity in Asia from Global Crossing and sold fiber-optic capacity in the United States to Global Crossing. It booked $664 million in "swap revenue."[55] Accounting for capacity swap transactions boils down to the "form" of revenue versus the "substance" of the transaction.

Similarly, some companies use "pro forma earnings" to inform or deceive investors.[56] There is no GAAP definition of pro form earnings. It usually refers to regular earnings before taking into account extraordinary items.

Financial reports should provide investors with more information, instead of being designed primarily to help companies hide information from investors. The use of SPEs in Enron is one example of a device used to hide information. Although companies may be responsible for the debts of their SPEs, the (FASB) and regulators did not require that this fact be reported to stockholders.[57] Enron and others have argued that the additional disclosure imposed an administrative burden and had practical implementation problems.

Because of the pressure to be transparent, Dynergy took out an advertisement in the *Wall Street Journal* (3/4/02, A16) with the vice president and assistant controller claiming that the firm ensures an accurate financial picture, uses mark-to-market accounting, and that senior management is involved in the day-to-day operations.

In related activities, the conflicts of interest that arise when the auditors also serve as consultants to the same firm will come under fire. The Monetary Authority of Singapore wants banks that have employed the same auditors for five years or more to change firms by 2006.[58]

Corporate Governance and Executive Compensation

Corporate chief executive officers and directors must assume greater accountability for the actions of their companies. There is increased pressure on boards of directors to monitor and supervise their companies better. This can best be accomplished by having a majority of independent directors and maintaining key committees that are comprised of independent directors.

Financial Executives International (FEI) is a professional association representing about 15,000 individuals who are senior financial executives, accountants, academics, and others. FEI developed a set of 12 recommendations for "Improving Financial Management, Financial Reporting and Corporate Governance."[59] The recommendations are in four sections: strengthening financial management and ethical conduct; rebuilding confidence in financial reporting and auditing; modernizing financial reporting; and improving corporate governance and the effectiveness of audits.

Executive compensation schemes must reflect the realities of the market place. However, they should not be designed to encourage excess risk taking by making the compensation dependent on the stock price. The use of stock options ties executive compensation to the stock market performance and may promote self-interest rather than stockholder interest.

Shareholders suffer when stock prices decline. However, many stock options granted to executives can be repriced if the stock declines in value, or cancelled and then reissued at a later date when the price is low.

Although stock options are a form of compensation, they are not expensed when they are granted. Accounting Principles Board Opinion and (SFAS) No. 123 require that a footnote be provided to estimate the cost of the option if it was expensed. The Black Scholes option pricing model is commonly used to value the options. However, there is no uniform standard as to how to measure the "volatility" component of that model. Therefore, different methods will result in different option values.

Employee Pension Plans

Enron employees could invest up to 6 percent of their base pay in a 401(k) retirement plan that offered a wide range of investment options including mutual funds and Enron stock. Enron matched the employee contributions up to 3 percent in Enron stock. They were required to hold the stock until they reached age 50. Because Enron's stock was soaring, many employees took advantage of the free stock, and they did not diversify their portfolios. That was their mistake.

In general, employee pension plans must be given greater flexibility in their investment activities, and not limited to the employer's stock. Surveys by benefit consultants suggest that only 20 percent of the companies that offer 401(k) retirement plans to their employees require that they hold company shares in their retirement savings account. However, following Enron's debacle, many firms are relaxing rules that limit employee's rights to sell their company's stock.

A bigger issue is that about half of the workers on private payrolls do not have any employer-sponsored retirement plan.[60]

Security Analysts

As a result of Enron and an agreement with the New York state attorney general, Merrill Lynch, the nation's largest securities firm, is developing guidelines for its analysts.[61] First, Merrill Lynch will tell investors more about its investment banking relationships with the firms it recommends. It also will have guidelines that place more emphasis on cash flow and less on pro forma earnings. The analysts are also going to consider off-balance sheet activities.

OpCo Energy Company

In May 2002, Enron proposed to creditors the organization of a new firm to be called OpCo Energy Company. It will operate an electric power and natural gas pipeline company in North America, Central America, and South America.[62] It will have three business segments: transportation services, power distribution, and generation and production. The new company could have about 15,000 miles of pipelines, $10.8 billion in total assets, and projected earnings before interest, income taxes, depreciation and amortization (EBITDA) of $1.3 billion in 2003.

The real issue is whether the arrogant corporate culture, and opaque disclosures in reporting to investors will continue to exist in the new company. Only time will tell.

Civil and Criminal Complaints

In the case of the *United States Securities and Exchange Commission v. Andrew S. Fastow* (October 2, 2002) the summary of the civil complaint states that "The defendant, Andrew S. Fastow, the former Chief Financial Officer of Enron Corp., engaged in a fraudulent scheme to defraud Enron security holders and to enrich himself and others. Fastow's fraudulent conduct involved entering into undisclosed side deals, manufacturing of earnings through sham transactions, inflating the value of Enron's investments, backdating documents, and other illegal acts."

Both Andrew Fastow and Michael Kopper were "control persons" of Enron in the context of federal securities laws. Fastow had signed Enron's confidentiality agreement and certificate of compliance with the firm's code of ethics. It is interesting to note that Section 406 of the Sarbanes-Oxley Act of 2002 requires senior financial officers to sign a code of ethics. The fact that Fastow signed it is evidence that such codes do not stop wrongdoing by those intent on defrauding their companies. The confidentiality agreement that Fastow signed required employees to disclose business activities outside the firm that might be considered conflicts of interest. Similarly, the code of ethics prohibited employees from engaging in activities that could be considered conflicts of interest.

Part of Fastow's and Kopper's problem was that under accounting rules, an SPE could only receive off-balance sheet treatment if independent third-party investors made a substantive equity capital investment (e.g., 3 percent), and the third-party investment was genuinely at risk, among other things. However, Fastow, Kopper, and others controlled the third-party investors, and the third-party investors were not truly at risk. Thus, those SPEs should have been consolidated on Enron's balance sheet. In addition, Fastow, Kopper, and others used their influence over Enron's business operations and SPEs to unlawfully generate millions of dollars to enrich themselves.

In the criminal complaint, Fastow was charged with fraud and deceit in connection with the purchase and sale of securities (15 U.S.C., §§ 78j(b) and 78ff), wire fraud (18 U.S.C. §1343), mail fraud (18 U.S.C. § 1341), laundering of proceeds generated by fraud (18 U.S.C. §§ 1956(h) and 1957), and conspiracy to commit, and aiding and abetting the commission of the foregoing offenses (18 U.S.C., §§ 371 and 372). These charges are listed in his arrest warrant that is shown in Exhibit 1.

Michael Kopper was charged with money laundering (18 U.S.C. §§ 1956(h) and 1957) and conspiracy to commit wire fraud (18 U.S.C., § 371). He pled guilty to both charges.

NOTES

1. U.S. Census Bureau, *Statistical Abstract of the United States, 2000, Table 879;* and U.S. Census Bureau, *Statistical Abstract of the United States, 2001*, Tables 711, 718, 739. Business bankruptcies are filed under Chapter 7, 9, 11, or XII. Chapter 7 is liquidation; Chapter 9 is for municipalities; and Chapter 11 is reorganization. Before Chapter 11, when the Bankruptcy Act of 1978 was enacted, Chapter XII was for companies with large holdings of real property.

2. www.BankruptcyData.com (accessed 3 December 2002).

3. Maynard (February 24, 2002).

4. washingtonpost.com, Timeline of Enron's Collapse (accessed 20 February 2002); Eichenwald (January 13, 2002).

5. SEC Form 8-K (July 15, 1997) stated that because of the merger between Enron and Portland General, Enron Corp. of Delaware merged into Enron Oregon Corp. of Oregon, and the name Enron Oregon Corp. was changed to Enron Corp. Consequently, Enron Corp. is now incorporated in Oregon.

6. Zellner, et al. (December 17, 2001).

7. Witt and Behr (May 22, 2002).

8. "The Enron Debacle," (2001). The Osprey Trust investors included Putnam Investors, Vanguard Group, Travelers and Prudential, and others (Morgenson, January 25, 2002).

9. Behr (January 22, 2002).

10. Eichenwald and Henriques (February 10, 2002); Johnson (March 8, 2002); Smith and Emshwiller (February 4, 2002); Behr (January 12, 2002); Behr (February 4, 2002). Kopper invested $115,000 in Big River Funding and Little River Funding. Little River Funding owned Big River, and Big River was Chewco's limited partner. In December 1997, Kopper transferred his interest to his domestic partner, William D. Dodson, who had invested $10,000. Enron bought out their interests for $10.5 million. Barclays had made a loan to Big River (Eichenwald and Barboza, June 26, 2002), therefore Big River's investment in Chewco did not meet the 3 percent equity investment requirement and its financial statements had to be consolidated into Enron, contributing to Enron's restatement of earnings in November 2001. In August 2002,

Kopper pled guilty to two felony charges in connection with his work at Enron (Weil and Kranhold, August 21, 2002).

11. Eichenwald (February 26, 2002). Two other inside investors are Ben F. Glisan, Jr., former Treasurer of Enron; and Kristina Mordaunt, a lawyer working for Enron; Emshwiller and Smith (January 21, 2002).

12. Ibid.

13. Gleckman, et al., (March 4, 2001).

14. McKinnon and Hitt (February 4, 2002).

15. Simpson (February 7, 2002); Johnson (January 17, 2002).

16. Barboza (April 10, 2002); Chaffin and Fidler (April 8, 2002).

17. See Raghavan, Kranhold, and Barrrionuevo (August 26, 2002) for a discussion of Enron's corporate culture.

18. Schroeder (May 8, 2002).

19. Smith (January 17, 2002).

20. Weil (April 3, 2002); Morgenson (January 17, 2002).

21. Jordan (December 3, 2001); Smith and Kranhold (May 6, 2002).

22. Mandel (May 20, 2002); Benson (May 8, 2002); Kranhold and Smith (May 9, 2002); Sherman (May 7, 2002).

23. Morgan (January 13, 2002).

24. McNulty (February 8, 2002).

25. "Timeline of Enron's Collapse," *washingtonpost.com* (accessed 15 March 2002); Davis (November 29, 2001); Eichenwald and Henriques (February 10, 2002).

26. Spagat (January 21, 2002).

27. Yost (February 25, 2002).

28. Grimaldi (May 6, 2002).

29. Milbank and Sipress (January 25, 2002).

30. Phillips (January 21, 2002).

31. Cummings and Hamburger (January 15, 2002); Also see Milbank and Kessler (January 18, 2002) for additional information about Enron's political ties.

32. Hedges, Zeleny, and James (January 13, 2002).

33. Edsall (January 17, 2002).

34. JEDI stands for Joint Energy Development Investments LP and was a joint venture with the California Public Employees' Retirement System. The Chewco, JEDI, and LJM1 SPEs were not mentioned in the October 16, 2001 Press Release, but they appear in the Form 10Q, filed September 30, 2001. LJM1, LJM2 and other SPEs are mentioned in the "First Interim Report of Neat Batson" (2002).

35. Morgenson (January 17, 2002); Colvin (January 21, 2002); Also see McLean (2001) for a further discussion of Enron's falling returns.

36. Citigroup appears to have hedged its loans, but JP Morgan Chase incurred large losses and sued Enron.

37. According to Enron's Form 10-Q (filed 11/19/01), the "Trigger Events" included the stock price falling below $59.78 in case of the Osprey partnership, and $34.13 in the case of the Marlin partnership. As of November 16, 2001, Enron's stock price was $16 per share. See Eichenwald and Henriques (February 10, 2002) for a discussion of the Chewco, Rapter, and JEDI partnerships.

38. Enron could have filed for bankruptcy in Houston, where its headquarters were located, or Delaware where most of its subsidiaries were incorporated. The Delaware bankruptcy courts were backlogged at that time. ("Enron Scurries to File for Chapter

11," November 30, 2001). For details on the bankruptcy filing, see *eLaw* at http://www.elaw4enron.com/ or Enron's Web site, www.enron.com.

39. Ahrens (April 23, 2001).

40. Schultz and Francis (January 23, 2002); Francis and Schultz (February 7, 2002), A2, A10.

41. Stevenson and Gerth (January 20, 2002).

42. Kranhold (April 23, 2002).

43. Kochan (2001).

44. Smith and Greil (February 1, 2002).

45. Mollenkamp (January 23, 2002).

46. Silverman, (January 15, 2002).

47. "Enron 'to File for Bankruptcy,'" (November 20, 2001).

48. Stevenson (April 12, 2002).

49. For additional discussion of this point, see Silverman (January 17, 2002).

50. Michaels (March 11, 2002).

51. United States Securities and Exchange Commission Press Release 2002–40 (March 2002).

52. See Walker (April 9, 2002) for the General Accounting Office's views concerning oversight of the accounting profession, auditor independence, and corporate governance.

53. Public Law No: 107–204.

54. Todd (2002).

55. Millstead and Smith (March 30, 2002).

56. See D'Avolio, Gildor, and Schleifer (2001) for a discussion of pro forma earnings, stock options and discretionary accruals. See Reason and Leach (2002) for information about pro forma earnings and how the SEC found Trump Hotels & Casino Resorts, Inc., had materially mislead investors.

57. For a discussion of this point, see Simpson (April 10, 2002).

58. Day (2002).

59. For information about FEI and the recommendations, see www.fei.org.

60. Wessel (March 7, 2002).

61. "Merrill Sets Analyst Guides," (March 6, 2002); "What Does the Merrill Agreement Mean?" (April 23, 2002).

62. Enron Corp. Press Release May 3, 2002; For details of the proposed restructuring, see OpCo Energy Company, Business Plan, May 2002.

REFERENCES

Ahrens, Frank, "Enron Expects Asset Write-Off of $14 billion," *washingtonpost.com*, (April 23, 2002), www.washingtonpost.com (accessed 23 April 2002).

Barboza, David, "Enron Offered Management Aid to Companies," *The New York Times on the Web*, April 10, 2002, www.nytimes.com (accessed 10 April 2002).

Behr, Peter, "Hidden Numbers Crushed Enron," *washingtonpost.com*, January 12, 2002, www.washingtonpost.com (accessed 13 January 2002).

——— "Enron Raised Funds in Private Offering," *washingtonpost.com*, January 22, 2002, A01, www.washingtonpost.com (accessed 22 January 2002).

Benson, Michael, "California Calls for Power-Firm Probe," *Wall Street Journal*, May 8, 2002, A9.

Chaffin, Joshua, and Stephen Fidler, "Enron Revealed to be Rotten to the Core," *FT.com*, April 8, 2002, www.ft.com (accessed 9 April 2002).

Colvin, Geoffrey, "One Number That Won't Lie," *Fortune*, January 21, 2002, 42.

Cummings, Jeanne, and Tom Hamburger, "Enron's Premeltdown Clout in Washington Draws Scrutiny," *Wall Street Journal*, January 15, 2002, A18.

D'Avolio, Gene, Efi Gildor, and Andrei Shleifer, "Technology, Information Production, and Market Efficiency," appears in *Economic Policy for The Information Economy*, Federal Reserve Bank of Kansas City, 2001, 125–160.

Davis, Bob, "Enron CEO's Deep Political Connections Run Silent During Crises," *Wall Street Journal*, November 29, 2001, A10.

Day, Phillip, "In Singapore, A Glimpse of the World Post-Enron," *Wall Street Journal*, March 14, 2002, A12.

Eichenwald, Kurt, "Enron Executive Said to Be Aiding in Federal Inquiry," *The New York Times on the Web*, February 26, 2002, www.nytimes.com (accessed 26 February 2002).

Eichenwald, Kurt, and David Barboza, "Enron Criminal Investigation is Said to Expand to Bankers," *The New York Times on the Web*, June 26, 2002, www.nytimes.com (accessed 26 June 2002).

Edsall, Thomas B., "Legislators Rush to Dump Enron Money," *washingtonpost.com*, January 17, 2002, A01, www.washingtonpost.com (accessed 17 January 2002).

Eichenwald, Kurt, "Audacious Climb to Success Ended in a Dizzying Plunge," *The New York Times on the Web*, January 13, 2002, www.nytimes.com (accessed 20 March 2002).

Eichenwald, Kurt, and Diana B. Henriques, "Web of Details Did Enron In as Warnings Went Unheeded," *The New York Times on the Web*, February 10, 2002, www.nytimes.com (accessed 20 March 2002).

Emshwiller, John R., and Rebecca Smith, "Murky Waters: A Primer of Enron Partnerships," *Wall Street Journal*, January 21, 2002, C1, C14.

Enron Corp., SEC Form 8-K (filed 7/15/97).

Enron Corp., SEC Form 8-K (filed 11/8/01).

Enron Corp., SEC Form 10-Q (filed 9/30/01).

Enron Corp., SEC Form 10-Q (filed 11/19/01).

Enron Corp., Press Release, "Restating 3rd quarter earnings," October 16, 2001, www.enron.com (accessed 15 February 2002).

Enron Corp., Press Release, "Enron Presents Process to Creditors' Committee for Separating Power, Pipeline Company from Bankruptcy," May 3, 2002, www.enron.com (accessed 5 May 2002).

"Enron to 'File for Bankruptcy,'" *BBC News*, November 20, 2001, news.bbc.co.uk (accessed 13 January 2002).

"Enron Scurries to File for Chapter 11," *Wall Street Journal*, November 30, 2001, A3, A6.

First Interim Report of Neal Batson, Court Appointed Examiner, United States Bankruptcy Court, Southern District of New York, Re Enron Corp., *et al*, Debtors, Chapter 11: Case No. 01–16034 (AJG), September 21, 2002.

Francis, Theo, and Ellen E. Schultz, "Enron Senior Officers' Pensions are Intact," *Wall Street Journal*, February 7, 2002, A2, A10.

Gleckman, Howard, Dean Foust, Michael Arndt, Kathleen Kerwin, "Tax Dodging: Enron Isn't Alone," *BusinessWeek*, March 4, 2002, 40–41.

Grimaldi, James V., "Enron Pipeline Leaves Scar on South America," *washington-post.com*, May 6, 2002, A 01, www.washingtonpost.com (accessed 6 May 2002).

Hedges, Stephen J., Jeff Zeleny, and Frank James, "Enron 'Players' Worked D.C. Ties," *Chicago Tribune*, January 13, 2002, www.chicagotribune.com (accessed 13 January 2002).

Johnson, Carrie, "After Enron, a New Focus on Boards," *The Washington Post on Line*, March 8, 2002, E01, www.washingtonpost.com (accessed 8 March 2002).

Johnston, David Cay, "Enron Avoided Income Taxes in 4 of 5 Years," *The New York Times on the Web*, January 17, 2002, www.nytimes.com (accessed 17 January 2002).

Jordan, Miriam, "Enron's Brazil Investments Contributed to Collapse," *Wall Street Journal*, December 3, 2001, A8.

Kochan, Nick, "Enron Fallout: Why Insurers Fail Banks," *The Banker*, 2001, www.thebanker.com (accessed 12 March 2002).

Kranhold, Kathryn, "Florida Panel May Sue Alliance Over Pension's Enron Losses," *Wall Street Journal*, April 23, 2002, B2.

Kranhold, Kathryn, and Rebecca Smith, " Two Other Firms In Enron Scheme, Documents Say," *Wall Street Journal*, May 9, 2002, A1.

McKinnon, John D., and Greg Hitt, "How Treasury Lost in Battle to Quash Dubious Security," *Wall Street Journal*, February 4, 2002, A1, A8.

McLean, Bethany, "Why Enron Went Bust," *Fortune*, December 24, 2001, 59–68.

McNulty, Sheila, "Enron: Big Bucks from a Company," *FT.com*, February 8, 2002, www.ft.com (accessed 3 April 2002).

Mandel, Michael J., "And the Enron Award Goes to . . . Enron," *BusinessWeek*, May 20, 2002, 46.

Maynard, Micheline, "Bankruptcy Maneuver Stirs Fight in Airport Car Rental Industry," *Tuscaloosa News*, February 24, 2002, 4D.

"Merrill Sets Analyst Guides," *CNNmoney*, March 6, 2002, money.cnn.com (accessed 6 March 2002).

Michaels, Adrian, "Shredded Reputations," *FT.com*, March 11, 2002, www.ft.com (accessed 12 March 2002).

Milbank, Dana, and Glenn Kessler, "Enron's Influence Reached Deep Into Administration," *washingtonpost.com*, January 18, 2002, A01, www.washingtonpost.com (accessed 18 January 2002).

Milbank, Dana, and Alan Sipress, "NSC Aided Enron's Efforts," *washingtonpost.com*, January 25, 2002, A18, www.washingtonpost.com (accessed 25 January 2002).

Millstead, David, and Jeff Smith, "Quest, SEC at Odds Over Accounting," *Rocky Mountain News*, March 30, 2002, 1C, 12C.

Mollenkamp, Carrick, "Bank of America Posts 49% Jump in Net, Gaining from Debt Unit," *Wall Street Journal*, January 23, 2002, A2.

Morgan, Dan, "Enron Also Courted Democrats," *washingtonpost.com*, January 13, 2002, A01, www.washingtonpost.com (accessed 13 January 2002).

Morgenson, Gretchen, "Enron Letter Suggests $1.3 Billion More Down the Drain," *The New York Times on the Web*, January 17, 2002, www.nytimes.com (accessed 17 January 2002).

Morgenson, Gretchen, "Many May Be Surprised to Enron Investors," *The New York Times on the Web*, January 25, 2002, www.nytimes.com (accessed 25 January 2002).

OpCo Energy Company, Business Plan, May 2002, www.enron.com (accessed 6 May 2002).

Phillips, Michael M., "Enron's Washington Friends Pressed India Over Power-Plant Project at Every Turn," *Wall Street Journal*, January 21, 2002, A8.

Raghavan, Anita, Kathryn Kranhold, and Alexei Barrioneuvo, "How Enron Bosses Created a Culture of Pushing Limits," *Wall Street Journal*, August 26, 2002, A1, A7.

Reason, Tim, and Edward Leach, "Lies, Damn Lies, and Pro Forma," *CFO*, March 2002, 73–75.

Schroeder, Michael, "Enron's Board Was Warned in '99 On Accounting," *Wall Street Journal*, May 8, 2002, A2.

Schultz, Ellen E., and Theo Francis, "Enron Pensions had More Room at the Top," *Wall Street Journal*, January 23, 2002, A4.

Sherman, Mark, "Memo Describes Enron Role in Calif." *washingtonpost.com* (May 7, 2002), www.wasinghintonpost.com (accessed 7 May 2002).

Silverman, Gary, "Northern Trust Earnings Fall on Loan Exposure to Enron," *FT.com*, January 15, 2002, www.ft.com (accessed 15 January 2002).

Silverman, Gary, "JP Morgan Chase and Citigroup Suffer From Enron Role," *FT.com*, January 17, 2002, www.ft.com (Accessed 18 January 2002).

Simpson, Glenn R., "For Enron, Holland was a Good Tax Haven," *Wall Street Journal*, February 7, 2002, A10.

Simpson, Glenn R., "Deals that Took Enron Under Had Many Supporters," *Wall Street Journal*, April 10, 2002, A1, A13.

Smith, Randall, and Anita Greil, "CSFB Expects $1 Billion Loss After Change," February 1, 2002, C1.

Smith, Rebecca, "A Blockbuster Deal Shows How Enron Overplayed its Hand," *Wall Street Journal*, January 17, 2002, A1, A6.

Smith, Rebecca, and John R. Emshwiller, "Enron Internal Probe Finds Wide Abuses," *Wall Street Journal*, February 4, 2002, A3, A8.

Smith, Rebecca, and Kathryn Kranhold, "Enron Knew Foreign Portfolio had Lost Value," *Wall Street Journal*, May 6, 2002, C1, C20.

Spagat, Eliot, "Enron Repercussions Hit Texas Politicians," *Wall Street Journal*, January 21, 2002, A8.

Stevenson, Richard W., "Enron Trading Gave Prices Artificial Lift, Panel is Told," *The New York Times on the Web*, April 12, 2002, www.nytimes.com (accessed 12 April 2002).

Stevenson, Richard W., and Jeff Gerth, "Safeguards Failed as Enron Fell," *Tuscaloosa News*, January 20, 2002, 1A, 6A.

"The Ship that Sank Quietly," *The Economist*, February 16, 2002, 57.

"The Enron Debacle," *BusinessWeek*, November 12, 2001, 107.

"Timeline of Enron's Collapse," *washingtonpost.com* www.washingtonpost.com (accessed 15 February 2002).

Todd, Rebecca, "Revenue Reporting and Accounting Fraud, "The Emperor's New Clothes," The Michel/Shaked Group, Research From Our Experts, Boston, MA, 2002, www.michel-shaked.com (accessed 18 April 2002).

United States Bureau of the Census, *Statistical Abstract of the United States, 2000*, Washington, D.C., 2000.

United States Bureau of the Census, *Statistical Abstract of the United States, 2001*, Washington, D.C., 2001.

United States Securities and Exchange Commission Press Release, "SEC Announces Final Plans for Completing Reviews of Auditor Independence Systems and Controls," 2002–40, March 19, 2002.

United States Securities and Exchange Commission v. Andrew S. Fastow, United States District Court, Southern District of Texas, Houston Division, criminal and civil complaints, Case Number H-02–889-M (October 2, 2002).

Walker, David M., Comptroller General of the United States, Testimony before the Committee on Financial Services, House of Representatives, "Protecting the Public's Interest," GAO-02–601T, April 9, 2002.

Weil, Jonathan, "Enron's Auditors Debated Partnership Losses," *Wall Street Journal*, April 3, 2002, C1, C12.

Weil, Jonathan, and Kathryn Kranhold, "First Guilty Plea In Enron Case Expected Today," *Wall Street Journal*, August 21, 2002, A1, A6.

Wessel, David, "Enron and a Bigger Ill: Americans Don't Save," *Wall Street Journal*, March 7, 2002, A1.

"What Does the Merrill Agreement Mean?" *CNNmoney*, April 23, 2002, cnn.money.com (accessed 23 April 2002).

Witt, April, and Peter Behr, "Enron's Other Strategy: Taxes," *washingtonpost.com*, May 22, 2002, A01, www.washingtonpost.com (accessed 22 May 2002).

www.BankruptcyData.com (accessed 12 March 2003).

Yost, Pete, "Enron Projects Used Government Loans," *washingtonpost.com*, February 25, 2002, www.washingtonpost.com (accessed 25 January 2002).

Zellner, Wendy, Stephanie Anderson Forest, Emily Thornton, Peter Coy, Heather Timmons, Louis Lavelle, and David Henry, "The Fall of Enron," *BusinessWeek*, December 17, 2001, 30–36.

About the Editors and Contributors

MARCELO DABÓS is a Professor of Economics and Finance and the former director of the Department of Economics and the Masters Program in Finance at the Universidad de San Andrés, Buenos Aires, Argentina. Dr. Dabós has his Ph.D. in Economics from the University of Chicago. He has been a visiting scholar and a consultant at the International Monetary Fund; a researcher at the National Opinion Research Center, University of Chicago; a researcher at the Central Bank of the Argentine Republic; and an economist at Duff and Phelps Credit Rating Agency, Buenos Aires.

BENTON E. GUP holds the Robert Hunt Cochrane-Alabama Bankers Association Chair of Banking at the University of Alabama. He also held banking chairs at the University of Tulsa and the University of Virginia. Dr. Gup is the author and/or editor of 22 books and more than 90 articles about banking and financial topics. He has served as a consultant to government and industry. In addition, he teaches a course at the University of Melbourne, Australia.

GEORGE G. KAUFMAN is the John J. Smith Professor of Finance and Economics at Loyola University in Chicago, the co-chair of the Shadow Financial Regulatory Committee, and a consultant to the Federal Reserve Bank of Chicago. He also serves as a consultant to various government agencies and to industry. Dr. Kaufman has an extensive list of textbooks, monographs, and articles dealing with financial economics, institutions, markets, and regulations.

JÚLIA KIRÁLY received her Ph.D. in Economics from the Budapest University of Economics, Hungary, where she is a Fellow Lecturer. In 2002, she was appointed President of Postabank Ltd, in Budapest. Dr. Király has several textbooks published for the International Training Center for Bankers Ltd. (Hungary), and has published extensively in academic professional journals, including those of the World Bank.

CHARLES G. LEATHERS is a Professor of Economics at the University of Alabama. He specializes in financial markets and institutions, public sector economics, and history of thought. Dr. Leathers' articles have appeared in leading economic journals, and he is the co-author, with J. Patrick Raines, of the book *Economists and the Stock Market.*

JOSEPH R. MASON is an Assistant Professor of Finance at Drexel University's LeBow College of Business, Sloan Fellow at the Wharton Financial Institutions Center, and Visiting Scholar at the Federal Reserve Bank of Philadelphia. Dr. Mason's research spans the fields of banking, corporate finance, financial history, and monetary economics, focusing on issues related to both theory and public policy. He is the recipient of research grants or awards from the National Science Foundation, the Federal Reserve Bank of St. Louis, Drexel University, and the University of Illinois and has been consultant to many agencies and firms, including the Conference Board, the G-30, and the World Bank Group.

DAVID NICKERSON is a Professor in the Department of Economics and Finance at Colorado State University. He previously held positions at Duke University, University of British Columbia, American University, the Office of Thrift Supervision, the U.S. Treasury, and the Federal Home Loan Mortgage Corporation. He is widely published in economics, finance, and applied mathematics journals.

JOE PEEK holds the Gratton Endowed Chair in International Banking and Financial Economics at the Gratton College of Business, University of Kentucky. Previously, he held positions as a Professor at Boston College, a Visiting Economist at the Federal Reserve Bank of Boston, and a Visiting Erskine Fellow at the University of Canterbury in Christ Church, New Zealand. His research interests include international banking, bank regulation, monetary policy, and credit availability. He has published extensively in leading academic journals.

RONNIE J. PHILLIPS is the Department Chair and Professor of Economics at Colorado State University. He has been a Visiting Scholar at the FDIC, the Comptroller of the Currency, and at the Jerome Levy Economics Institute of Bard College. He is a past president of the Association for Evolutionary Economics (AFEE). His publications on financial system issues have appeared in books, academic journals, newspapers, magazines, and public policy briefs.

J. PATRICK RAINES holds the F. Carlyle Tiller Chair in Business, is a Professor of Economics, and Chairman of the Economics Department at the University of Richmond, Virginia. His specialty fields are money and banking, comparative economic systems, and history of thought. Raines is the co-author, with Charles Leathers, of the book *Economists and the Stock Market* and his articles have appeared in leading economic journals.

DANIEL A. SCHIFFMAN is an Assistant Professor of Economics at Bar Ilan University, Ramat Gan, Israel. He received his Ph.D. from Columbia University. In 2001, Shiffman was awarded the Allan Nevins Prize for his dissertation that dealt with the fragility of railroad operations during the Great Depression.

STEVEN A. SEELIG is a Financial Sector Advisor at the International Monetary Fund. Previously, he was Deputy Director of Research and Statistics at the Federal Deposit Insurance Corporation (FDIC), as well as editor of *The Banking Review*. He also served as Director of the Division of Liquidation and was Chief Financial Officer for the FDIC. He has taught at George Washington University and Fordham University.

TOSHIYUKI SOUMA is a Lecturer of the Department of Economics at Kyoto Gakuen University in Japan. He is a Ph.D. candidate of Osaka University, received his BA in Economics from the Ritsumeikan University, and MA from Osaka University. His main research areas include Japanese banking and life insurance. His recent work includes "Efficient Lending and a New Aspect of Government Deposit Insurance Agency."

DR. KAZUNORI SUZUKI is Professor of Finance at Chuo University, Graduate School of International Accounting (CGSA) in Japan. He received his BA in Laws from the University of Tokyo, MBA with distinction from INSEAD in France, and Ph.D. in Finance from the University of London (London Business School). He was formally employed by The Fuji Bank, Ltd., where he worked in derivatives and investment banking (M&A) divisions. His main research areas include corporate finance, valuation, and M&A.

CHRIS TERRY is an Associate Professor and Head of the School of Finance and Economics at the University of Technology, Sydney. He was awarded his Doctorate from New York University in 1975, the same year he joined the New South Wales Institute of Technology, which became the University of Technology, Sydney. He was Head of the Economics Department from 1983 to 1986, Head of School of Finance and Economics from 1987 to 1989, and Associate Dean (Postgraduate Programs and Research) in 1994 and 1995.

ROWAN TRAYLER is a Senior Lecturer in the School of Finance and Economics at the University of Technology, Sydney. Prior to joining the faculty at the University of Technology in 1987, he worked for 16 years in the finance industry including 11 years at Barclays Bank Australia Ltd. Since joining the University of Technology, Rowan has been involved in the development of the postgraduate Master of Business in Finance, lecturing at both the postgraduate and undergraduate level in Banking and Finance.

ÉVA VÁRHEGYI is the Chief Researcher at Financial Research Ltd., in Budapest, Hungary. He received his Ph.D. in Economics from Budapest University of Economics, and he has an extensive list of academic publications. Dr. Váhegyi serves on various Boards of Directors, including the National Bank of Hungary, Hungarian Bankers Association, Financial Research Ltd., and the Association for Hungarian Economics. He is a consultant to industry and government.

ADRIAN VAN RIXTEL is a Senior Economist in the Directorate Monetary Policy of the European Central Bank. Previously, he held positions at the Monetary and Economic Policy Department of De Nederlandsche Bank (Netherlands Central Bank) and private financial institutions both in London and Amsterdam. Dr. van Rixtel took his Ph.D. at the Tinbergen Institute, Free University Amsterdam, in the Netherlands. He has extensive experience covering Asian economies, in particular the Japanese economy, and held visiting scholar positions at the Bank of Japan and Ministry of Finance. His research on Japan has been published in various articles and books and discussed in publications such as *The Economist* and *Wall Street Journal*.

JAMES A. WILCOX is the Kruttschnitt Professor of Financial Institutions at the Haas School of Business at the University of California, Berkeley. His articles have been published in the *American Economic Review*, the *Journal of Finance*, the *Journal of Economic Perspectives*, the *Journal of Money, Credit and Banking*, the *Journal of Banking and Finance*, the *Journal of Housing Economics*, the *Review of Economics and Statistics*, and elsewhere. From 1999–2001, Jim was the Chief Economist at the Office of the Comptroller of the Currency. He has also served as the senior economist for monetary policy and macroeconomics for the President's Council of Economic Advisers and as an economist for the Board of Governors of the Federal Reserve System.

ARTHUR E. WILMARTH, JR. is a Professor of Law at George Washington University. Before joining GW's law faculty, he was a partner in a major Washington, D.C. law firm. He has written numerous articles on banking law and regulation, and is the co-author of a book on corporate law. Wilmarth has been an advocate in a number of leading banking cases before the United States Supreme Court and other federal courts, and he has testified before Congress on banking issues.

YUPANA WIWATTANAKANTANG is an Associate Professor at the Center for Economic Institutions, Institute of Economic Research of Hitotsubashi University in Japan. Her research interests are in the area of corporate finance and governance and financial systems in East Asia. Two of her recent works were on the top ten most downloaded list of the SSRN in 2001 and 2002 for the following journals/topics: Governance and Ownership, Corporate Finance: Capital Structure & Payout Policies, IO: Firm Structure, Purpose, Organization and Contracting, and the EFA 2002 Berlin Meetings Presentation Papers.

Index